THE MAGNIFICENT BASTARDS

Also by the Author

Battle for Hue
Into Laos
Death Valley
Into Cambodia
Operation Buffalo

THE MAGNIFICENT BASTARDS

BASTARDS

The Joint Army-Marine Defense of Dong Ha, 1968

KEITH WILLIAM NOLAN

★
PRESIDIO

For Kelly and Erik

Dai Do maps (figures 1–6) reprinted courtesy *Marine Corps Gazette*.
Nhi Ha maps (figures 7–9) by Kelly Williams.

Typography by ProImage
Printed in the United States of America

CONTENTS

PREFACE

It was one of the most prolonged and costly campaigns of the war, but, inexplicably, it never gained the immortality of Hue or Khe Sanh or Con Thien. It should have. It began on the last day of April 1968 when a Marine battalion landing team, reinforced with a company from a regular rifle battalion, locked horns with major elements of a North Vietnamese Army division in the village complex of Dai Do. The enemy infantrymen, entrenched among the hootches and hedgerows, were fully equipped with light and heavy machine guns and rocket-propelled grenades, and were backed up by rocket and artillery batteries across the demilitarized zone (DMZ). The Marines, outnumbered but superbly led and already battle hardened, dug them out spiderhole by spiderhole. The battle lasted three days, and was Tarawa-like in its intensity. Although the Marine battalion was gutted by casualties, the enemy units were practically obliterated, and their smashed entrenchments were filled with their dead as the survivors retreated back to the DMZ.

Presumably, the enemy regiments blocked at Dai Do had been marching toward the 3d Marine Division headquarters at Dong Ha. To secure the various approaches to Dong Ha, a grunt battalion from the U.S. Army's Americal Division was attached to the 3d Marine Division and positioned on the right flank of the Marine battalion landing team engaged in Dai Do. The North Vietnamese had indeed moved fresh units into the area, and on the last day of the Dai Do action, the Army battalion ran into a hornet's nest in the village of Nhi Ha. It took four days to clear Nhi Ha, after which the Army battalion, in its first conventional battle, dug in amid the rubble and repelled several nights' worth of counterattacks from across the DMZ. The enemy also shelled Nhi Ha, but they never took it, and in the end they left heaps of their own dead around that perimeter, too. By then, Nhi Ha looked like Verdun.

In Vietnam, that was victory.

The reconstruction of this campaign began with archival research, but the reality between the dry lines of official prose was fleshed out

by those who survived and were willing to tell their tale. I'm indebted
to all of them. Those who were interviewed (or who reviewed the rough
draft) from the 3d Marine Division, 3d Marine Regiment, and various supporting units include Maj. Gen. Dennis J. Murphy (Ret.); Cols.
William H. Dabney and Bruce M. McLaren (Ret.); Lt. Col. Walter H.
Shauer (Ret.); and ex–BM2 Jerry Anderson, USN.

From Battalion Landing Team 2/4 (3d Marine Division): Maj. Gen.
James E. Livingston; Brig. Gen. William Weise (Ret.); Cols. James
T. Ferland (USMCR), Robert J. Mastrion, J. R. Vargas, and James L.
Williams (Ret.); Lt. Cols. Judson D. Hilton (Ret.), Bayard V. Taylor
(Ret.), and George F. Warren (Ret.); Maj. James L. O'Neill (Ret.); Capt.
Edward S. Dawson (Ret.); ex-Capts. Peter A. Acly, James H. Butler,
and Lorraine L. Forehand; ex–1st Lts. David R. Jones, David K. McAdams,
Frederick H. Morgan, C. William Muter, and Alexander F. Prescott;
ex–Lt. Frederick P. Lillis, MC, USN; CWO2 Donald J. Gregg (USMCR);
WO1 John J. Kachmar (USANG); 1st Sgts. Reymundo Del Rio (Ret.)
and Ronald W. Taylor (Ret.); MGySgt. James W. Rogers (Ret.); GySgts.
Pedro P. Balignasay (Ret.), Percy E. Brandon (Ret.), James Eggleston
(Ret.), and Ernest L. Pace (Ret.); SSgts. Tom Alvarado (Ret.) and Robert
J. Ward (Ret.); ex-SSgts. Dennis F. Harter and Richard J. Tyrell; ex-Sgts.
Dan Bokemeyer, Charles M. Bollinger, Nicolas R. Cardona, Phil Donaghy,
Van A. Hahner, Doug Light, and Peter W. Schlesiona; ex-Cpls. Dale R.
Barnes, Ronald J. Dean, John Hanna, E. Michael Helms, Kenneth G. Johnson,
James R. Lashley, and Jim Parkins; ex-LCpl. Philip L. Cornwell; ex-Pfc.
Marshall J. Serna; and ex-HM2 Roger D. Pittman, USN.

From the 1st Battalion, 3d Marines (3d Marine Division): Majs. Kim
E. Fox (Ret.) and Ralph C. McCormick (Ret.); MSgt. Robert G. Robinson
(Ret.); GySgt. Norman J. Doucette (Ret.); ex-Sgts. Ronald E. Lawrence
and Robert Rohner; ex-Cpls. Michael R. Conroy, Ross E. Osborn, Doug
Urban, and Craig Walden; ex-LCpls. James Dudula and Paul F. Roughan;
and ex-HM2 Carmen J. Maiocco, USN.

From the 3d Battalion, 21st Infantry (Americal Division), and sup-
porting units: Brig. Gen. Dennis H. Leach (Ret.); Cols. Robert E. Corrigan
(Ret.) and William P. Snyder (Ret.); Lt. Cols. Roger D. Hieb (Ret.),
Travis P. Kirkland (Ret.), Richard J. Skrzysowski (USAR, Ret.), and
Paul N. Yurchak (Ret.); Majs. John M. Householder (Ret.), Kenneth
W. Johnson (Ret.), and William A. Stull (USANG); ex-Capts. Hal Bell,
Jan S. Hildebrand, and Laurence V. McNamara; ex-1st Lts. Robert V.

Gibbs, John R. Jaquez, Terry D. Smith, and John D. Spencer; ex-Sfc. William F. Ochs; ex-SSgts. Bill A. Baird, Bernard J. Bulte, Don DeLano, James M. Goad, and James L. Stone; ex-Sgts. Jimmie Lee Coulthard, Terrance Farrand, Larry Haddock, Gregory B. Harp, Thomas E. Hemphill, Michael L. Matalik, Laurance H. See, and Roger W. Starr; ex-Sp5s Neil E. Hannan, William W. Karp, and Wallace H. Nunn; and ex-Sp4s Charles C. Cox, Dan Dinklage, Bill Eakins, John C. Fulcher, Ronald F. Imoe, Bill Kuziara, Tony May, Eugene J. McDonald, Don Miller, and Terry Moore.

Many thanks also to ex-1st Lt. Barry Romo, who lost his nephew, Robert, in Nhi Ha, and Dennis L. Barker, who lost his brother, Paul. Great assistance was also provided by Benis M. Frank, Joyce Bonnett, and Joyce Conyers of the Marine Corps Historical Center (Washington, D.C.); Decorations & Medals Branch, Headquarters, U.S. Marine Corps (Washington, D.C.); James E. Crum and Tony May of the 196th Locate-A-Brother (P.O. Box 531, Phoenix, Oregon 97535); William H. Knight, President, 196th LIB Association; Ron Ward, Vietnam editor of the Americal Division Veterans Association newsletter; John H. Claggett, Military Reference, National Archives (Suitland, Maryland); CWO3 James Garrett, Military Awards Branch, Department of the Army (Alexandria, Virginia); Col. Morris J. Herbert (Ret.), Association of Graduates, U.S. Military Academy (West Point, New York); John J. Slonaker, Chief, Historical Reference Branch, U.S. Army Military History Institute (Carlisle Barracks, Pennsylvania); and Lt. Col. Tip A. Horsley and Dorothy M. Flowers, Information Support Division, U.S. Army Reserve Personnel Center (St. Louis, Missouri).

Keith William Nolan
Maplewood, Missouri

PROLOGUE: WILD BILL WEISE

"Look, I'm telling you guys—they're lined up twelve deep here waiting to get infantry battalions," the 3d Marine Division personnel officer (G1) told the three recently arrived light colonels who stood before the field desk in his tent. It was 12 October 1967, and they were in the division rear at Phu Bai, Republic of Vietnam.

"You're just going to have to wait your turn."

Lieutenant Colonel William Weise, one of the three, was not hearing what he wanted to hear. As he had just told the G1, he had come to Vietnam to do nothing but command an infantry battalion in combat.

The silver oak leaf on Weise's cover was seven days old. His last assignment as a major had been a thirteen-month tour as an adviser to the Republic of Korea Marine Corps. He had waived reassignment to the United States so he could get to Vietnam before the war ended. When he got orders sending him to the 3d Marine Division, Weise wrote ahead to the commanding general, asking to serve as the operations officer of either an infantry battalion or a regiment. Arriving not as a major but as a freshly minted lieutenant colonel, Bill Weise, an intelligent, forceful man, sorely wanted an infantry command. His career demanded it (Weise was very ambitious), as did his sense of duty. He listened, heartsick, as the G1 continued, ". . . there's only three slots open in this outfit: the division special services officer, the division embarkation officer, and the assistant base defense coordinator at Dong Ha Combat Base."

Shit, here I go, Weise thought. Risk my marriage with two overseas tours in a row, and I'm going to wind up as a division office pogue. Weise knew the G1 and implored him, "You can't do this to me!" But the G1's hands were tied; the division commander, Maj. Gen. Bruno A. Hochmuth, personally assigned all field-grade officers. The general would soon welcome these three aboard, but it would be another two days before he would meet with them again to discuss their assignments. Weise and his two hard-charging, like-minded compatriots, Edward LaMontagne and George Meyers, thus had time to talk to officers they knew on the division staff about getting battalions.

Their meeting with General Hochmuth was in his command bunker. The 3d Marine Division was an overtaxed organization, and the general, sitting at his field desk, was too busy to ask them to sit or to offer the customary cup of coffee. There was no small talk: "Well, okay, Meyers, you're going up to Dong Ha to help coordinate the defenses up there."

"Yes, sir."

"LaMontagne, you're going to be my embarkation officer."

"Yes, sir."

God, thought Weise, he's going to make *me* the special services officer. But Hochmuth surprised him: "Weise, I see that you've had a lot of experience in reconnaissance. I'm not happy with the way my recon battalion is being deployed, so I want you to take over. We've got a good young major in there by the name of Bell. He's going to be transferred in three weeks. Meanwhile, I want you to see as much of the AO as you can. See how we're deployed. Go around the area. You'll take over when Bell leaves. Now, does anybody have any questions?"

"No, sir," said LaMontagne.

"No, sir," replied Meyers.

"Sir, I don't have any questions," Weise blurted out, "but I want the general to know personally that I really want an infantry battalion."

Weise had been expressly warned during his two days of politicking that it would be unwise to do anything but click his heels when the general made his decision. Weise, however, had picked up the nickname Wild Bill during his sixteen years in the Marine Corps, and he had sometimes gotten his way by being audacious: ". . . whatever job you give me, I'm going to do, sir—but I don't want to sit back there with a recon battalion and just send those kids out on patrol. I want an infantry battalion."

"Weise," Hochmuth snapped, "you get the hell outta here. When I want your advice on how to run my division, I'll ask for it. Meanwhile, you get out there and do your job."

There was a lot of ground for the disappointed Lieutenant Colonel Weise to cover before he took over the 3d Reconnaissance Battalion. The 3d Marine Division's four infantry regiments (the 3d, 4th, 9th, and 26th Marines) and its artillery (the 12th Marines) were positioned throughout Quang Tri and Thua Thien provinces, the two northern-most provinces of the five that defined the I Corps Tactical Zone. The division main command post at Phu Bai was in the Viet Cong (VC) guerrilla badlands of Thua Thien Province. The division forward command post at Dong Ha, in Quang Tri Province, was just below the DMZ, which divided North and South Vietnam. The war on the Z was with the North Vietnamese Army (NVA). Dong Ha controlled an eighty-kilometer frontage of combat bases that faced the DMZ from the beachhead at Cua Viet, west to the jungled mountains of Khe Sanh. The Ben Hai River and the DMZ, which for political reasons the Marines could not cross, afforded the enemy a sanctuary for their artillery batteries and a staging area for battalion- and regimental-sized assaults.

Lieutenant Colonel Weise visited every battalion in the division. With a few days to spare before he was to take over 3d Recon, he went to visit a good friend of his who was a battalion executive officer with the 7th Marines in the 1st Marine Division, the only other Marine division in Vietnam. They were dug in along the Hai Van Pass above Da Nang, and at approximately 0300 on 26 October 1967, while sleeping near the battalion command post (CP), Weise was awakened and directed to the covered-circuit radio. The division chief of staff was on the other end.

"Hey, Weise, get your ass back up here," said the colonel. "You know Two-Four?" Two-Four is shorthand for the 2d Battalion, 4th Marines, which was under the operational control of the 9th Marines and participating in Operation Kingfisher below the DMZ. Weise answered that he had visited 2/4, and mentioned the battalion commander by name. "He's been hit," the chief of staff said. "You got it. They're in a firefight."

Jesus, Weise thought, expecting to be helicoptered directly into 2/4's night action. Instead, it took him two days to make his way back north by chopper. By then, 2/4 had been pulled back to the Dong Ha Combat Base. What a sorry sight, Weise thought. The battalion he found really looked wanting in terms of numbers and esprit. They were, however, Marines—and he knew how to breathe fire into Marines. Beat up or not, the 2d Battalion, 4th Marines, was *his,* and Bill Weise was exactly where he wanted to be.

PART ONE SCRUB BRUSH AND SAND DUNES

The 2d Battalion, 4th Marines, had been known as the "Magnificent Bastards" since its first major operation in Vietnam, Starlite, in which it helped take apart a VC regiment. That had been more than two years before its keelhauling on Operation Kingfisher, at which time the men in 2/4 no longer felt as their motto proclaimed: Second to None. Upon assuming command of 2/4 on 28 October 1967, Lt. Col. William Weise saw as his primary task resurrecting the spirit of the original Magnificent Bastards. This he stressed to his staff officers and company commanders, along with his two favorite maxims:

Good guys kill Marines. I am not going to be a murderer.

Marines will do exactly what you expect them to do. If you expect them to do nothing, they'll do nothing. If you expect them to do great things, they'll do great things.

Special Landing Forces (SLF) A and B of the 9th Marine Amphibious Brigade (MAB) in Okinawa provided the 3d Marine Division an opportunity to remove two of its battalions from the war zone on a rotating basis and have them return refreshed and reinforced. Not surprisingly, Weise's punched-out battalion was selected for this duty. The newly christened Battalion Landing Team (BLT) 2/4 became the infantry fist of SLF Alpha, 9th MAB, with its rear aboard the USS *Iwo Jima*. As the end of Weise's standard six-month command tour approached, BLT 2/4 was again operating on the DMZ under the operational control of the 3d Marines, 3d Marine Division. But it was a different 2/4; it was a battalion that had been reshaped in Weise's Spartan, aggressive, by-the-book image.

CHAPTER 1 NIGHT OWLS

Saturday, 27 April 1968. Fifteen hundred. The enemy artillery was walking inexorably toward the sandy-soiled, waist-deep crater where Capt. Robert J. Mastrion, commander of Golf Company, BLT 2/4, had sprinted when the kettledrumming to the north began, and where he presently crouched with his company gunnery sergeant. The next round is going to kill us, he thought. We have to move. Gunnery Sergeant Billy R. Armer made his move first, sprinting out of the crater in one direction. He was followed in the next heartbeat by Captain Mastrion, who leapt to the lip of the crater in the opposite direction. Mastrion hit the edge and leaned forward to run. Before he could step off, however, the next round crashed through the soft soil under his feet. He could feel the impact.

The shell exploded inside the crater. Captain Mastrion was enveloped in a roar of sand as the concussion lifted him off his feet. He went spinning like a rag doll, and actually saw the heel of his jungle boot smack his nose. Mastrion crash-landed on his back. The wind had been knocked out of him and he hurt all over, but he couldn't find any wounds. The area's soft soil had saved him, allowing the artillery shell to sink in before detonating, and absorbing most of the deadly metal fragments. As it was, the back of Mastrion's flak jacket looked as though it had been sandblasted, and the knapsack secured to his web belt and hanging over his buttocks was shredded. One of his cargo pockets, those baggy thigh pockets on jungle utilities, was also torn open, and a C-ration can containing turkey loaf had been mangled by a single large chunk of steel.

Gunny Armer had also been lucky, suffering only a welt between his upper lip and nose. Nineteen rounds had thunderclapped in. When no more incoming shrieks filled the air, Mastrion jumped up and shouted to his artillery forward observer, "Lay some smoke in here to cover us, and let's get the hell outta here!"

The forward observer, 2d Lt. Peter A. Acly, was on his first patrol but was wired into its details. In fact, when Golf Company's Marines had saddled up that morning in their semipermanent patrol base at Lam Xuan West, Mastrion had made Acly responsible for land navigation because he had a high-quality artillery compass. Lam Xuan West sat on the western bank of twisting, turning, but generally north-south Jones Creek, about eight kilometers below the DMZ. The hamlet was deserted and bombed out, as were all the villages in the battalion AO, and the terrain was a flat, heat-shimmering expanse of brush-dotted, shell-pocked rice paddies and sand dunes. Hedgerows and tree lines divided the land into squares. The ocean was only seven kilometers to the east. Golf Company's mission that morning had been to patrol about twenty-seven hundred meters northwest from Lam Xuan West so as to reconnoiter the rubbled remnants of Lai An. Weise had informed Mastrion that Golf was to move into Lai An after dark as part of a three-company night operation, and Mastrion had wanted a daylight look at the place to reacquaint himself with its subtleties.

Golf Company had just been approaching the raised, east-west trail at the southern edge of Lai An when the shelling began. The muffled booming of enemy artillery was an everyday event. Since the target was usually someone else, it had not been until the first salvo was actually screaming down for an imminent and very personal impact that humping, sweating, spread-out Golf Company had dropped to its collective gut. Lieutenant Acly thought he had heard an NVA mortar firing from An My, located thirty-five hundred meters to the northeast, across Jones Creek. With the aid of his radioman, Acly organized his first real fire mission on that pos. A 105mm battery firing out of Camp Kistler on the coast to the southeast responded to the call by plastering An My with high-explosive shells, while Acly called for white phosphorus shells on Lai An to form a smoke screen that would allow Golf Company to back up without again drawing the attention of the enemy's artillery spotters.

The company withdrew to Pho Con, which was situated about midway between Lam Xuan West and Lai An. There Golf Company dug in and waited for the cover of darkness, when it would again move north into Lai An in coordination with the battalion's sweep on the other side of Jones Creek. In the meantime, a medevac chopper touched down briefly to take aboard two casualties from the shelling.

Captain Mastrion, who was in increasingly severe pain, was not medevacked. He had not even reported his back injury to battalion. "I was hurting," he later said, "but I wasn't about to start feeling sorry for myself at that point." Mastrion could not bring himself to leave, knowing that a hairy, one-of-a-kind night operation was only a few hours away. "When you're the company commander, you've got to gut it out."

Lieutenant Colonel Weise had outlined the night maneuver the day before at the BLT 2/4 command post in Mai Xa Chanh West. It was code-named Operation Night Owl. The colonel's map board was propped up against one of the inside walls of the bullet-pocked Buddhist temple that they had converted into a headquarters. The roof had been blown off, except for a few beams and shingles. Weise's staff officers and company commanders, flak jackets on and helmets at their feet, sat on scrounged up Vietnamese chairs and benches, which were comparatively low and small. The Marines appeared to be sitting on children's furniture.

Weise and his handpicked operations officer, Maj. George F. "Fritz" Warren, explained that the 3d Marines had provided intelligence indicating that an NVA battalion had assumed bivouac positions above Alpha 1, an Army of the Republic of Vietnam (ARVN) combat outpost situated one kilometer east of Jones Creek and almost seven klicks northwest of Mai Xa Chanh West. Alpha 1, located just three kilometers south of the DMZ, was the most forward allied position in the sector. The poorly led and poorly supported ARVN troops were not, however, known for aggressive operations. According to intel from the 3d Marines, the NVA battalion in question had moved into the deserted hamlet of An My, which was only eighteen hundred meters northwest of Alpha 1. Weise and Warren had secured permission from regiment to slip through the ARVN Tactical Area of Responsibility (TAOR) and initiate a nighttime spoiling attack on the NVA in An My.

Operation Night Owl, to commence the following evening, was part of Operation Napoleon/Saline, the code name for all 3d Marine Regiment activities below the eastern DMZ. The maneuver was to be led by Echo Company, commanded by Capt. James E. Livingston, which was currently headquartered in an old, shot-to-hell concrete schoolhouse in Nhi Ha. This otherwise deserted village was on the east bank of Jones Creek, three kilometers north of the battalion command post at Mai Xa Chanh West, which was on the west bank. Mai Xa Chanh West sat at the corner where Jones Creek, a tributary that averages thirty meters in width, empties into the slow-moving, greenish brown Cua Viet River, which runs generally east-west and empties into the South China Sea just seven kilometers to the northeast. The 3d Marines' CP (Camp Kistler) was situated on the south bank of the Cua Viet, with one side bordering the ocean. This waterway defined BLT 2/4's reason for being where it was. The Cua Viet has a branch, the Bo Dieu River, which originates three kilometers farther inland from Mai Xa Chanh West. Four kilometers upstream, the Bo Dieu flowed past the new 3d Marine Division CP in the Dong Ha Combat Base (DHCB), located on its south bank. The bulk of all division supplies were moved by the Navy's Task Force (TF) Clearwater from Camp Kistler to the DHCB along the Cua Viet and Bo Dieu rivers, so this link with the ocean had to be kept open.

Lieutenant Colonel Weise explained that Livingston's Echo Company was to lead the battalion's northward movement during the hours of darkness. They were to go in blacked-out and stripped-down, with camouflage paint covering exposed skin, and cumbersome helmets and flak jackets left behind. They would move in single file, a standard formation for nighttime tactical moves. The single-file column facilitated control but made massing fires to the front more difficult in case of ambush. Given this risk, they would have to rely on noise and light discipline so as not to become targets themselves. Radio silence was to be maintained among the maneuver elements, while those radiomen who remained at Mai Xa Chanh West were to simulate routine radio traffic on the battalion tactical net. If the NVA managed to find the BLT's frequencies, their eavesdropping would be of no help.

Nor, Weise continued, would BLT 2/4 signal its punch with the customary prep fires. To ensure coordination with the ARVN at Alpha 1, Weise planned to helicopter up that afternoon to brief their U.S. Army advisers. Four tubes from the battalion's 81mm mortar platoon and seven hundred rounds of ammunition were also to be choppered up to Alpha 1, so as to avoid the red tape involved in getting artillery from regiment at Camp Kistler and division at the DHCB. Weise's forward air controller was also to be placed at Alpha 1 in case air support was required. Naval gunfire from destroyers steaming offshore could also be brought to bear. The NVA in An My, however, were to experience none of this fire until after the attack had commenced on their hopefully unsuspecting positions.

Following Echo Company's lead in the night march, Lieutenant Colonel Weise, Major Warren, and the other members of their dozen-man mini-CP would fall in with Foxtrot Company, commanded by Capt. James H. Butler, which was in Mai Xa Chanh East, directly across Jones Creek from the CP. Foxtrot's own CP was in a Catholic church, whose cross-topped steeple still survived intact. The two-company column would silently guide on preselected checkpoints past Alpha 1, until it drew near the southern fringe of An My. At that point, a slim, shallow branch of Jones Creek running northeast would serve as the line of departure. Echo Company was to break east and then north, bypass An My, and assume positions on the far side. The company's assault would then come from the unexpected northern side. Meanwhile, Foxtrot was to establish a base of fire in the scrubby sand dunes east of An My. Foxtrot was not to fire a shot until Echo had launched its assault, and then only at figures moving south of An My.

Those NVA able to escape Echo's assault and Foxtrot's grazing fire would run into Captain Mastrion and Golf Company's blocking positions in Lai An.

The battalion's last rifle company, Hotel, commanded by Capt. James L. Williams, would not participate in Night Owl. Hotel Company occupied a two-platoon patrol base (Objective Delta) in a small, unnamed hamlet twenty-five hundred meters southwest of Mai Xa Chanh West. Hotel also manned a separate platoon patrol base (Objective Charlie), which was another four hundred meters to the southwest, and only a kilometer east of a Bo Dieu tributary that divided BLT 2/4's TAOR from that of the 1st ARVN Infantry Division.

Lieutenant Colonel Weise, who placed a premium on thorough, detailed operations orders (inadequate briefings had been one of the problems in 2/4 when he first got the battalion), finally began to wrap up the chalk talk. In a war where the hours of darkness generally belonged to the enemy, a night attack made sense precisely because it was the response the NVA would least expect. Nevertheless, Major Warren could sense—and he knew that Weise could, too—a certain apprehension among their officers that was too subtle to have been detected by an outsider. The uncertainty was shared to a degree even by Warren. The battalion had never before conducted a full-fledged night attack (given the difficulty involved, few battalions had), and a lot of things could go wrong out there in the dark—to include Marines accidentally shooting other Marines. Warren's doubts were short-lived, however. Weise had gradually prepared them for just such a sophisticated scheme of maneuver, and Warren and the rest knew that Weise would be out there, too, with his own blackened face, and with his jingling rifle sling secured with olive-drab tape. It made a difference.

When Operation Night Owl got rolling after dark on 27 April 1968, 1st Lt. David R. Jones's Echo Company platoon was in the lead, and Jones himself walked point. The column skirted the eastern side of Alpha 1, where the ARVN troops had marked a safe path through their perimeter minefield. Jones looked at Alpha 1 through his starlight scope, which gave the world a fuzzy green cast, and saw ARVN soldiers looking back at him through their own night observation devices. He figured that if the ARVN knew where they were, so did the NVA. He did not expect to find much in An My.

Farther back, Lieutenant Colonel Weise was just another bareheaded, blacked-out silhouette in the column. Along with Major Warren, the mini-CP included Sgt. Maj. John M. "Big John" Malnar, the battalion sergeant major, and Sgt. Charles W. Bollinger, who humped a PRC-25 radio and served as the battalion tactical net radio operator. Weise never went anywhere without Malnar, Bollinger, and his runner, Cpl. Greg R. Kraus.

After Echo Company moved north of An My and Foxtrot slipped to the east, the mini-CP settled in with Echo. At that point, the command group was just one more group of Marines in the dunes. "You lack control," said Warren. "A night operation runs its course and all you can do is sort it out when it's over." It was time to stay close to the ground—until 0400, when Echo was scheduled to launch the attack on An My. The 0400 kickoff time was typical for a night attack. "The dog hours of the early morning," Warren explained, "when the enemy's sure the night's over and nothing's going to take place, and half the sentries are asleep."

Some of the Marines were asleep, too. Captain Butler of Foxtrot came awake with a start in the shell crater where he had set up his command post. He had not known he was asleep. His radioman was asleep, too, and Butler realized why he had awakened: Weise's voice was a whisper on the radio. The battalion commander wanted to make sure that Butler was in position. Weise would chew Butler out the next morning for falling asleep, but Butler was not surprised that he had. His company had spent the previous night on a trial run with the handheld infrared scopes issued for Night Owl.

"There we were, up for the second straight night," Butler recalled later. "As much as we tried to stay awake, as dark as it was out there, you thought your eyes were open but they weren't."

Captain Butler's crater was atop a low sand dune, and he presently sat up at its edge with his infrared scope. Its range was short and he could not actually see An My, which was about a klick to the northwest. Butler knew that Echo was up there somewhere with Weise, ready to drive the NVA into Foxtrot's fires. He also knew that Golf Company was about two klicks to the southwest, setting up their blocking position in Lai An. Suddenly, the muffled report of automatic weapons shattered the silence. It was too early for the assault on An My. Butler turned to see that the night was alive with red and green tracers where the map in his head indicated Lai An was.

This is nuts, thought LCpl. James R. Lashley, a machine-gun team leader in 1st Platoon, G BLT 2/4. Unable to leave helmets and flak jackets behind in their temporary position at Pho Con, the troops, who were already humping a lot of ammo, had to wear them, and Lashley thought they sounded like a herd of water buffalo with tin cans on their backs! Lashley was both angry and scared, but mostly he was exhausted. He had been in the bush for eight months. He was a short, wiry guy, blondish and bespectacled, and a proud, able Marine. He was also a bright young man—and a realist. It seemed to him that the powers that be were not. His platoon had been operating above the Cua Viet for eight weeks and had seen a lot of action. Given the heat, the humidity, their heavy combat load, and the soft, unstable texture of the terrain that made even a short patrol a real ass-kicker, their unrelenting schedule of daylight sweeps and night ambushes, listening posts, and foxhole watch had taken a brutal physical and mental toll.

"At times we were really sharp," Lashley recalled, "but I could see the difference." He had not blacked out his face, neck, hands, or arms before saddling up for the night maneuver, nor had he soundproofed his gear with tape. "We were losing the edge you need to survive in combat. We were becoming ambivalent and disinterested about the most elementary rules of combat discipline. We were just going through the motions."

Moving out from Pho Con, Golf Company closed on Lai An at Captain Mastrion's direction in two separate maneuver elements. Golf Three, led by 1st Lt. James T. Ferland, had the point and the mission of securing the burial mounds that dotted the approach to Lai An, from which the platoon could cover the movement of the rest of the company into their blocking positions. The company's executive officer, 1st Lt. Jack E. Deichman, accompanied Golf Three, as did the 60mm mortar section from the weapons platoon.

Captain Mastrion moved with the lead platoon of the follow-up element, SSgt. Reymundo Del Rio's Golf One, along with a composite machine-gun and rocket section from the weapons platoon. Golf Two, commanded by 2d Lt. Frederick H. "Rick" Morgan, brought up the rear. Their slow, cautious columns moved across the flatlands and through a wet rice paddy that seemed to be an unending, splashing obstacle in the otherwise still and silent darkness. When they finally closed on the east-west trail running along the bottom of Lai An, no one was more relieved than Captain Mastrion. No one had had a harder time on the move. Because of his injured back, it had become painful for Mastrion just to stand, and a numb sensation was creeping into his legs.

When Mastrion's back finally gave out completely after Night Owl and he was medevacked, a rumor spread that he had been relieved of command. More fantastically, there was talk that the captain's injuries had actually been the work of a grunt "doing him a job" with a hand grenade. Untrue on both counts, but widely believed. Mastrion had been with Golf Company for only a month, and there were Marines who had come to some ugly judgments about their new skipper. One thrice-wounded grunt commented:

The troops considered Captain Mastrion to be a gung-ho cow-boy with a foolhardy disregard for the company's safety. We were worn out, but here's this prick who wanted to "get some." Well, we weren't ready to hear that at that point in time. It was that zeal. The sixty mike-mike mortar section had Mastrion's CP at Lam Xuan West bracketed. I was pretty close to some of those guys and they said, "If we get hit, he's going to be the first to go." We were too tired to be angry. Being angry took energy, and we were out of energy. We were just trying to survive, and we were going to take him out. It was real.

Captain Mastrion, a small, dark man with eyeglasses and a black handlebar mustache, was a jocular, straightforward product of Brooklyn, New York, and a Marine of much experience. Twenty-eight years old at the time, he had enlisted at seventeen and was later commissioned from the ranks. He served several short assignments in Vietnam between 1964 and 1967 before joining 2/4 as an assistant operations officer in late 1967. Mastrion had replaced a paternalistic and soft-spoken captain as commander of Golf Company. That, Weise commented, was the root of the problem. "Mastrion was a terrific company commander, but he was a completely different kind of personality from his predecessor, who was the kind of guy people did things for because they wanted to please him. People who worked for Mastrion were a little scared of him. He was a demanding, no-nonsense, you-do-it-this-way auto-crat. He was a fighter, and he suffered no fools."

Weise, who suffered no fools himself, added that Mastrion "handled his company extremely well when the shit hit the fan." In fact, Mastrion earned the Silver Star on only his eighth day with Golf Company—after leading a twelve-hour-long assault on Nhi Ha in which he received two flesh wounds, and had his radio handset shot from his hand at one point.

Captain Mastrion soldiered through Operation Night Owl in stoic fashion despite his wrenched back. As Golf Company began assuming blocking positions south of Lai An's raised trail, the battalion intelligence officer called Mastrion to report that he had an unconfirmed report that "two thousand NVA are coming down the west bank of Jones Creek at twenty-two hundred." Mastrion looked at the luminescent dial on his watch. It was 2206, and Golf Company was precisely where the S2 had said the NVA would be moving. Mastrion was about to make a wiseass comment to their usually reliable S2 when there was a sudden commotion about fifteen meters ahead of him in the dark. Gunny Armer was up there, helping Staff Sergeant Del Rio of Golf One place one squad at a time into position. As best as it could be pieced together afterward, the commotion began when a Marine heard Vietnamese voices in the dark. Wondering if it was one of their scout interpreters, the Marine called out, "Hey, Gunny . . . hey, Gunny. . . ."

Gunny Armer said, "Who's that?" just as an NVA potato-masher grenade came out of nowhere to bounce off his chest and explode at his feet. Someone screamed, "Jesus, gooks!" and in the first crazy, confused seconds, Cpl. Vernal J. Yealock's squad took devastating AK-47 fire at virtually point-blank range. Only Yealock and his grenadier were not hit. The other eight men in the squad were dropped, and one who'd been hit in the head began an incoherent keening. Del Rio ran to his men and flung himself beside Armer, who'd taken a lot of small shell fragments in his face and chest. The gunny kept mumbling, "Son of a bitch, I'm hit . . . son of a bitch, I'm hit . . . !"

Captain Mastrion was still on the radio, talking to the intelligence officer. "You'd better upgrade that report a little because they're here!" he shouted. It seemed that Golf Company's north-moving column had inadvertently intersected a spread-out NVA column moving northeast to southwest in the open paddies. The two lines had formed an irregular X in the dark, which was suddenly exposed as the NVA's green tracers erupted along one leg and the Marines responded with red tracers along the other. There were shouts and shadows and chaos. The weapons section moving with Mastrion instantly went into action. Two 3.5-inch rocket-launcher teams began shooting at nearby NVA muzzle flashes to disrupt that fire, and to give the four M60 crews they were teamed up with time to get into advantageous positions. The machine guns then suppressed the closest enemy positions.

There was a thirty-second crescendo of fire from the NVA soldiers closest to the center of the X, and then it seemed that they had scattered under the heavy return fire. The NVA farthest away were still blazing away. Their AK-47 automatic rifles had a cracking, bone-chilling report. Mastrion tried to count the number of tracers burning over his prone figure, but gave up. There were NVA strung out to the south-west from the point of contact, and still more to the northwest, although he could not get a feel for how many there were in that direction. He estimated that he was up against two companies, and called for reinforcements.

Lieutenant Colonel Weise, in position to attack An My, returned to radio silence after a quick reply: "This is Dixie Diner Six. You're on your own. If I come over there with Foxtrot or Echo we're gonna be Marines fighting Marines."

Having been told by Captain Mastrion to bring in the artillery, Lieutenant Acly lay on his stomach with his radioman, fumbling in the dark to find his map and his red-lensed flashlight. The red lens preserved a man's night vision. The light was not invisible, however, and Acly tried to work up the mission as fast as he could—before the NVA phantoms could spot him. Acly got a fire mission from A/1/12, a 105mm battery at Camp Kistler, as well as 81mm fire from BLT 2/4's prepositioned tubes at Alpha 1. The rounds whistled overhead, flash-booming in the dark as Acly walked them to within two hundred meters. A platoon radioman reported on Mastrion's company net that several NVA had broken from cover. Acly copied the grid coordinates and adjusted the arty. The voice on the radio said that it was right on target.

Golf Company was later credited with eight kills. Meanwhile, Marines were shouting and still shooting, and sporadic, ineffective NVA fire was zipping in from a distance as Golf consolidated in an area of low mounds about fifty meters west of the contact area. The company's senior Navy corpsman approached Mastrion then and told him that the man with a head injury was most likely going to die "if we don't get him out pretty quick and get him to a doctor." Mastrion turned to his forward air controller (FAC), a young lance corporal instead of the lieutenant normally assigned to the job, and said, "Okay, have 'em get an emergency medevac. Call me when he gets here, and I'll try to find out between now and then what the situation is. If we can, we'll get the head injury out; if not, we're going to wave the medevac off."

The FAC placed four unlit strobe lights at the corners of a fifty-by-fifty-meter square to mark the landing zone. The wounded were gathered there with designated litter teams. A night medevac in a potentially hot landing zone (LZ) was risky, and the FAC had argued against it. Mastrion, however, thought they could pull it off. He calculated that Golf Company was about four hundred meters east of an unnamed hamlet they had reconned that afternoon. He figured the NVA to have retreated to that cover, and he instructed Lieutenant Morgan of Golf Two to dispatch a squad-sized patrol to confirm that the NVA were actually at this relatively safe distance.

Lieutenant Acly ordered the arty to cease fire when the medevac and his wingman came into the area at 0130 with their lights off. The helicopters, Korean War–vintage CH-34 Sea Horses, were from Marine Medium Helicopter Squadron 362 (the Ugly Angels), which was colocated with the BLT 2/4 rear aboard the USS *Iwo Jima.* The flight leader came up on the FAC's air net and asked how far the NVA were from the LZ. Mastrion told the FAC, "Tell him I estimate it to be four hundred meters to my west."

Mastrion turned again to his senior corpsman, who said that the man with the head injury was getting worse. That made up Mastrion's mind about the risk, and he told the FAC to "bring 'em in." The lance corporal moved out then to light the four marking strobes. Brave man, Acly thought: The strobes made the FAC a target for the tracers zipping in from the distance. The helicopters planned to come in one at a time. The flight leader approached first and was in a hover above the LZ when he flipped on his landing lights for just a moment to get the lay of the land before setting down between the strobes.

In the flash of the landing lights, Captain Mastrion noticed to his horror a small building directly to the south. He recognized the building from the afternoon recon as one on the outer edge of another small, unnamed hamlet that sat near the village to the west, where the NVA had retreated. According to Mastrion's estimate of his position, that building should not have been to the south. It should have been to the southwest, and Mastrion recognized instantly that he had miscalculated his pos. He was four hundred meters farther west of Jones Creek than he had thought, almost on top of the hamlet the NVA were in. The fire he thought he had been taking from that hamlet had actually been from NVA even farther away.

It was too late to wave off the lead helo—it had already landed. At that moment, contact erupted between Lieutenant Morgan's recon squad to the west and an NVA element out looking for the Marines. The NVA, at the edge of the LZ, began raking the medevac ship with fire. Mastrion later said with remarkable honesty:

> I really miscalculated the distances. I thought I was farther towards the creek, but it was so dark that we must have wandered over. Out in those sand dunes at night you really don't know where the hell you are anyway. It was almost like navigating at sea. There are many decisions I made in the many months I was in combat that you could second-guess, but this is one decision that I never had to second-guess—that was a bad, bad, bad, bad decision. We had been up for a long time. It may have been fatigue, it may have been the pain from the injury, it may have been blatant stupidity, or a combination, but it was a very bad call and it got that medevac shot up.

Though Mastrion may not have called in a medevac had he correctly understood his nose-to-nose position with the NVA, the flight leader, Capt. Ben R. Cascio, an experienced and aggressive pilot, would have attempted such a mission. The Ugly Angels had that reputation when it came to emergency evacuations. Cascio, however, would have handled the mission differently, pausing in the LZ only long enough to take aboard the man with the critical head injury before pulling pitch.

As it was, the misinformed Captain Cascio powered down to settle completely into the LZ and give the Marines rushing to his Sea Horse time to get all the casualties aboard. The crew chief and door gunner were just helping the first wounded man into the cabin when the NVA suddenly opened fire. The Sea Horse was taking hits as Cascio brought his RPMs up so that he could lift out of the LZ. It seemed to take forever. Green tracers were flying everywhere. Sparks shot out of the exhausts. The whirling rotor blades filled the air with sand. A rocket-propelled grenade exploded in front of the Sea Horse, shattering the Plexiglas windshield. A sudden scream came over the air net, then obscenities mixed in with, "We gotta get outta here. . . . We gotta get outta here . . . !"

Captain Cascio's left eye had been blown out and everyone in the crew was wounded. When the RPG exploded, Staff Sergeant Del Rio, who was helping Lieutenant Morgan load the wounded, went prone in the blinding whirlwind. The helicopter blades were right above him. He just knew that the shot-to-pieces helicopter was going to roll over on its side. The blades were going to kill him. He started to scramble away on his hands and knees, but then, to his amazement, the Sea Horse lifted off even as bullets continued to thump into it. Everyone in Golf Company watched anxiously as the helo headed south, making it only about three hundred meters before coming down hard. The copilot somehow got it airborne again and, trailing sparks, made it all the way to the boat ramp at the 3d Marines' CP at the mouth of the Cua Viet River. There the wingman sat down to take aboard the wounded crewmen and infantrymen and fly them to the medical facilities aboard the *Iwo Jima*.

The next morning, when Weise went to Camp Kistler to personally brief the regimental commander on Night Owl, he inspected the damaged helicopter. It had bullet holes through the engine, some of the controls were shot away, and the cockpit was spattered with blood. "How that thing got off the ground, I'll never know," Weise said later. "It was just unbelievable. It was a miracle."

But it was an incomplete miracle. In the confusion, the man with the head wound had not been placed aboard the medevac. He continued to cry out incoherently. "There was this mournful yowl, like a banshee crying," said Lance Corporal Lashley. It sent chills down his spine. Lashley was sitting in a little hole of scooped-out sand, with his extra machine-gun ammo unshouldered and ready for use by his nearby M60 team. They wanted the head-shot Marine put out of his unholy misery. They wanted him to die fast. He was going to die anyway. They wanted the corpsman to take him out with a morphine overdose so he would stop giving away their position.

"That was the thought that night," Lashley remembered. "It may have been me who said it. I know I thought it."

At that point, Lieutenant Colonel Weise instructed Captain Mastrion to pull out of Lai An and move back to Pho Con. Mastrion agreed. Golf Company had a paddy strength of only about 150 men, and he was convinced that they were terribly outnumbered. But Lieutenant Ferland, the company's longest-serving officer, with six months in the boonies, was flabbergasted when Lieutenant Deichman, their exec, passed the word to him. Ferland wanted to hunker down in their freshly dug holes among the burial mounds, call in artillery around them, and ride out the night. He did not like Deichman. "I want to stay here," Ferland said angrily. "When you're in an ambush zone, whenever you move, there's great potential of being hit again. As far as I'm concerned, we're surrounded. If we pull back we're going to run into more shit."

Lieutenant Deichman, who had a pretty strong personality himself, and who respected Mastrion, told Ferland to move out. Ferland then called Mastrion directly to make his case as respectfully as he could with a skipper he did not like. "We're okay here, we have to stay here," he said. Mastrion, thinking of the S2's report of two thousand NVA, which his platoon commanders did not know about, replied, "No, you have to pull back. I understand you're okay there, but the fact is we've been told to withdraw."

Mastrion doesn't have it together, he just isn't rational, thought Lieutenant Morgan, who also believed that the order to move was crazy. Mastrion's compliance with the order to pull back could certainly be second-guessed. The man was not, however, flipping out. Mastrion conferred with Acly. He wanted artillery called in behind them and adjusted at hundred-meter intervals as they withdrew; he also wanted artillery fire worked along their flanks. Acly complied. Mastrion then turned to Del Rio, telling him to get a head count and ensure that no one was left behind. Del Rio was the acting gunny: Armer had accidentally been medevacked when he jumped into the shot-up Sea Horse to help a wounded man aboard.

Golf One, now commanded by its platoon sergeant, Staff Sergeant Wade, moved out behind Lieutenant Ferland's Golf Three, which again had the point. Moving east until they hit Jones Creek, the two platoons then swung south and reached Pho Con without incident. Lieutenant Morgan's Golf Two remained with the company headquarters, which was taking care of the man with the head wound. When Ferland informed Mastrion that they were in position at Pho Con, Mastrion told Morgan to start moving. Morgan's first two squads disappeared into the darkness, but Morgan and his third squad stayed with Mastrion and the senior corpsman. They were not going to move until the wounded Marine died. They didn't want to carry him when he was still alive because every time they tried to lift the poncho in which he lay, he let out a terrible groan.

Mastrion hoped that the NVA would not discover their vulnerability.

The young Marine finally died about five hours after having been shot. When one of the men helping carry the body fell and twisted his ankle, a limping and disabled Captain Mastrion took his place. Lieutenant Morgan sent his last squad ahead to secure the litter team, then positioned himself at the rear of the column with a young grenadier. Morgan had also picked up an M79, and the two of them operated their single-shot, breech-loading weapons as fast as they could, pumping a barrage into the hamlet behind them. The NVA did not return the fire.

Golf Company completed its withdrawal to Pho Con by 0300. Meanwhile, the rest of the op was on schedule, and at about 0400 on Sunday, 28 April, Echo Company crossed the line of departure north of An My and commenced an on-line, firing-as-they-walked assault into the tiny, blacked-out hamlet. There was no response. The NVA had bugged out. All that remained were the still-warm coals of doused cooking fires, indicating that the NVA squatters had only recently vacated the premises. They left behind nothing of value.

"There was a great feeling of disappointment," said Major Warren. There was also suspicion about the ARVN at lonely, vulnerable Alpha 1. The ARVN were only trying to survive, not win, their endless war. One does not live to hide another day by picking fights with a better-led, better-equipped opponent. Weise and Warren were convinced that their allies had forewarned the NVA about Operation Night Owl. The troops had other explanations. "We had to tape everything down to make it silent," commented a regimental sniper attached to Echo Company, "but if you ever heard a Marine company going through the night, especially when they're tired, you'd know we were fooling ourselves."

Come daylight, the companies returned to their patrol bases. Just east of Lai An, the Vietnamese scout with Echo Company talked a wounded NVA out of a bunker in which he'd been discovered. Skirting on past Pho Con, Echo came under a thirty-two-round barrage of 130mm artillery fire from the DMZ while crossing the big, calf-deep rice paddy. It offered no cover, and Echo made a run for it. "Hell, the CP group got in front of the platoons," remembered the company's forward observer (FO). "We were really humping to get out of that goddamn place." The soft paddies absorbed the shells before they exploded. "You'd hear these things come in and you'd dive under water with your mouth open for the concussion," commented the attached sniper. "The thing would blow up, then you'd hear shrap-metal just raking overhead. You'd get up and run again—and then you'd dive underwater, get up, and run again. . . ."

Marine artillery fired counterbattery missions, followed by three air strikes on suspected enemy gun positions. There were seven secondary explosions. Echo Company had one man slightly wounded. Before Echo pushed on for Nhi Ha, a medevac landed for the wounded prisoner they had in tow throughout the barrage. Talk was that the enemy soldier had been hit again by his own artillery. Whatever the specifics of his injuries, he did not survive, as was recorded in the BLT journal: "POW was DOA at DHCB."

Captain Mastrion did not make Golf Company's early afternoon hump back to Lam Xuan West. After bringing in a Sea Horse for the last of the wounded—and their one poncho-covered killed in action (KIA)—Mastrion wanted to get in a quick catnap before they saddled up to depart Pho Con. He woke up in excruciating pain. His back muscles had spasmed, and he could neither feel nor move his legs. Mastrion was finally medevacked.

Lieutenant Deichman, the exec, got Golf Company moving again after taking some twenty rounds of flat-trajectory artillery fire—and after Lieutenant Acly laid in a smoke screen to cover their movement. Golf's hump back to Lam Xuan West and Echo's return to Nhi Ha relieved a squad-sized detachment that had been sent up from battalion to guard the footbridge between the two hamlets during the night. The Marines had set up on the Nhi Ha side with a dangerously thin half-moon of one-man fighting holes.

"Without a doubt, this was the most hair-raising night I spent in Nam," wrote Cpl. Peter W. Schlesiona, late of Golf Company. He had been sent back to battalion with severe jungle rot and ringworm, and was the man in charge of the detail. He and another corporal alternated between radio watch and walking the line to keep people awake. During the night, they heard the sounds of Golf's fight and of the helicopters. "As it was night, we rightly assumed these were medevac choppers," wrote Schlesiona. "This made us particularly bitter the next morning as we helplessly watched Vietnamese civilians looting the personal effects that Golf Company Marines had left at their positions in Lam Xuan West. The most we could do was fire, uselessly, over their heads, as any direct action would have meant deserting our positions."

The battalion's assistant operations officer, Capt. "J. R." Vargas, took command of Golf Company after its return to Lam Xuan West. His was only an interim command—until a full-time replacement could be found for Mastrion—but Golf was glad to have him aboard. More precisely, they were glad to have him *back* aboard: Captain Vargas had previously commanded the company for more than two months and was, in fact, the soft-spoken, paternalistic skipper whom Mastrion had replaced. "When the word circulated that Vargas was coming back, people were ecstatic," Acly said later. At the time, Acly wrote in his pocket notebook, "Everybody loves him, and he seems to be a rather charismatic personality."

On Monday, 29 April 1968, BLT 2/4 became involved in the opening act of a major, across-the-DMZ offensive by the 320th NVA Division that would be met at a number of far-flung locations and be known collectively as the Battle of Dong Ha. The NVA objective was probably the Dong Ha Combat Base, which was a kilometer south of the town of the same name. The DHCB was the major logistics base and headquarters location of the 3d Marine Division. "The establishment of these functions at Dong Ha was logical," wrote one of the division's assistant operations officers, "since it was situated at the junction of the only major north-south (National Route QL 1) and east-west (National Route QL 9) land lines of communications in the area of operations, as well as being accessible to shallow-draft cargo craft from the Gulf of Tonkin via the Cua Viet River and its tributary, the Bo Dieu."

The first contact of the offensive occurred in the afternoon of 29 April when two NVA battalions were engaged on Route 1 as they marched south from the DMZ. The NVA were met only seven klicks above Dong Ha by two battalions of the 2d Regiment, 1st ARVN Infantry Division, whose TAOR extended to both sides of Route 1 and included Dong Ha and the DHCB. The NVA offensive had been anticipated to some degree. Task Force Clearwater, colocated with the 3d Marines at Camp Kistler, had advised division two days earlier that a number of incidents, "each in itself relatively insignificant," led to the conclusion "when taken as a whole that the enemy might be preparing to interdict the waterway." These incidents included knowledge of a VC platoon that had been detailed to diagram the waterway between Camp Kistler and the DHCB, and to collect data on the number of boats plying the rivers. There had also been, noted the report prepared by the assistant ops officer, "a substantial increase during the last week of April in attacks by fire, generally by rockets from the local area and by tube artillery located north of the DMZ, against both the port facilities at the mouth of the Cua Viet and the offloading ramp at Dong Ha."

The first of May was considered a likely candidate for the timing of any spectacular Communist maneuver. The division-level report continued: "Given the intelligence available and the approach of Mayday, the contact of the 2d ARVN on the 29th was not a great surprise."

With the ARVN and NVA engaged above Dong Ha, Maj. Gen. Rathvon M. Tompkins, who had been in command of the 3d Marine Division since November 1967, when Major General Hochmuth was killed in a chopper crash, committed part of the division reserve. Task Force Robbie, as the reserve was designated, was at Cam Lo, ten klicks west of Dong Ha in the 9th Marines' TAOR. A light force consisting of a rifle company from 1/9 and a tank company from the 3d Tank Battalion was organized, and together they moved out posthaste on Route 8B, a provincial road running east from Cam Lo to intersect Route 1 about two klicks north of Dong Ha. It was the most direct route to the battle. It was also the most predictable, and the reaction force, while traveling in column through Thon Cam Vu three kilometers out of Cam Lo, encountered mines and entrenched NVA with rocket-propelled grenades. Although claiming twenty-six NVA killed, the Marines had four tanks damaged and were forced to extricate themselves from the hamlet with four dead and twenty-nine wounded. In addition, seven Marines were reported missing after the fighting withdrawal. Their bodies were subsequently recovered.

In response to the disaster in Thon Cam Vu, Major General Tompkins instructed 3/9 to reduce the NVA positions there. The attack was to commence the next day, with tank support. In the meantime, the unreinforced ARVN battalions were still heavily engaged on Route 1. If uncontained, the NVA could push on to Dong Ha. To prevent this, division alerted the 3d Marines, who were relatively unengaged on the east flank, to release a rifle company to protect the bridge on Route 1 above Dong Ha.

Colonel Milton A. Hull, commander of the 3d Marines, placed Captain Livingston's E BLT 2/4 opcon to division, and Sea Horses lifted the company from Nhi Ha to the north end of the bridge, where it dug in beside a populated hamlet. Propeller-driven Skyraiders were bombing and napalming farther up the highway, and Livingston took a quick jeep ride just as the battle was petering out. The ARVN had held, and they showed Livingston a number of freshly killed NVA who had new uniforms, web gear, and weapons. Livingston was impressed: "It was clear to me we had some fresh troops moving down against us. I knew it was for real."

"With everything else that was going on, Colonel Hull had me 'spread the regiment out along the Cua Viet,'" wrote Maj. Dennis J. Murphy, the regimental S3 at Camp Kistler. "Hull was looking days ahead." Hull had operational control of three battalions. BLT 2/4 was deployed north of the Cua Viet, and his other rifle battalion, 1/3, was to the south. Hull's third element, the 1st Amphibian Tractor Battalion, was tied down in strongpoints along the coastal side of the regimental TAOR. Hull realigned all of these units before nightfall, a move that led Murphy to comment, "I was concerned, as was 2/4, 1/3, and the Amtracs, that we were getting too thin, and we'd have some trouble massing force. When I started to resist the 'spreading,' Hull said, 'The bastards are going to try to take Dong Ha, and we've got to be able to keep them from getting across the river.'"

Major Murphy added that "by the time Colonel Hull was satisfied that we had all the potential routes covered, the Marine units—especially Bill Weise—were calling me the 'fastest grease pencil in the East.'"

Weise was very concerned about regiment's instructions. To the north of the BLT CP in Mai Xa Chanh West, Vargas's G Company had to expand the Lam Xuan West perimeter to include E Company's vacated positions across Jones Creek in Nhi Ha. To the east, Butler's F Company remained in Mai Xa Chanh East as the BLT reserve, but placed a platoon in My Loc, which was also on the northern shore of the Cua Viet but two klicks farther downriver. Weise could not move F or G Companies without regiment's approval. His only remaining maneuver element was Williams's H Company, which was screening the western flank from Objective Charlie and Objective Delta.

From the roof of his farmhouse CP, Captain Williams had a clear view of the tributary that divided BLT 2/4 from the ARVN TAOR. The area was particularly vulnerable, because the two ARVN battalions previously in position there were the ones that had been moved west to meet the NVA coming down Route 1. The 320th NVA Division would, in fact, exploit this weak seam the next morning, and BLT 2/4 would thus be committed.

Captain Mastrion, medevacked two days before the battle, was still an immobile patient aboard the USS *Iwo Jima* when a Marine from the battalion rear addressed the sickbay. The Marine said that the battalion was in trouble, and had taken terrible casualties. He said that any of the wounded who could still function should return to the field. The situation was that bad. Several young Marines on the ward, including some with gauze-packed bullet wounds who had just been medevacked from the same battle, got up to go back ashore. Mastrion joined them. He figured that the very least he could do was stand radio watch, from a prone position, at the command amtrac in Mai Xa Chanh West.

Mastrion had a corpsman tightly wrap his aching back with an elastic bandage so he could stand, then asked the corpsman to find him some crutches so he could get around. The corpsman produced two canes of uneven length. Mastrion had someone go to the ship's armory to draw a .45-caliber pistol for him, while he hobbled down to the below-deck hangar where the medevac choppers were lowered by elevator. The hangar deck was heaped with bloody gear. Mastrion rummaged through the discarded equipment in search of jungle utilities with which to replace his blue hospital pajamas. He also found the jungle boots that had been cut off his feet when he'd arrived. One of his dog tags was still secured to the cut laces of the left boot.

The other walking wounded soon gathered in the hangar, along with shipboard support personnel who had volunteered to serve as riflemen, "and when the birds came in we just got on them and went ashore," said Mastrion. "It wasn't anything dramatic. Nobody was whistling the Marine Corps hymn or anything. We just went. What were you going to do? Your friends are in trouble, so you just got up and did it."

CHAPTER 2 FORGED IN FIRE

When Bill Weise was a thirty-year-old captain, he was greeted by his new battalion commander with the unwelcome news that the colonel planned to use him as his logistics officer. Weise replied that he was more interested in the battalion's vacant rifle company commander billet. "Colonel," he said, "I can out run, fight, fuck, or fart anybody that you have in mind for that job."

Wild Bill Weise got the job. Weise was from a working-class neighborhood in Philadelphia, where his father, who had been a doughboy in France, was a coppersmith at the Navy Yard. Weise attended college on an academic scholarship, and graduated in 1951 with a degree in political science. His plans for law school were put on hold by the Korean War, however. Where Weise came from, service to the nation was expected; it wasn't an issue. His older brother had been in the Navy in World War II, and his younger brother, who later became an Episcopal priest, was an Army infantryman headed for Korea himself.

Weise allowed himself to be drafted. When volunteers for the Marines were sought at the induction center, he made a spur-of-the-moment decision to do his two years with the best. The next stop for Private Weise, in October 1951, was the Marine Corps Recruit Depot at Parris Island, South Carolina, where he was selected for officer training. Weise was commissioned a second lieutenant in 1952, and upon graduation from The Basic School in Quantico, Virginia, in 1953, was assigned to the 3d Marine Division at Camp Pendelton, California. Because he finished in the top 10 percent of his Basic class, he was awarded a regular commission.

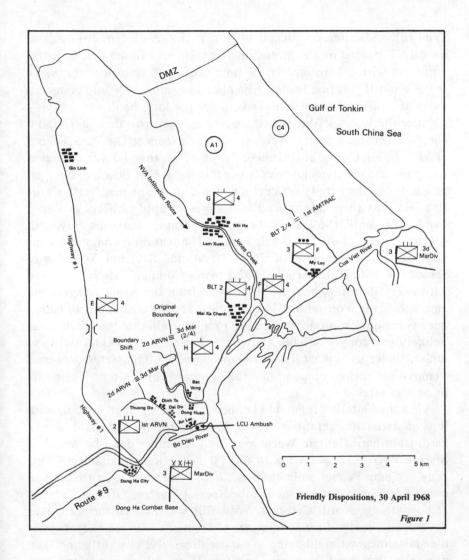

Friendly Dispositions, 30 April 1968

Figure 1

Lieutenant Weise began his twelve-month Korea tour in July 1953 with the weapons platoon of G/3/5, 1st Marine Division. His baptism of fire came during the last three weeks of the war. There were daily shellings on the battalion line, and numerous Chinese attacks against their outposts in which Weise helped direct supporting arms. Weise's

Wild Bill nickname originated in Korea: He loved demolitions, and used TNT instead of an entrenching tool. He also found that he loved being out with the troops. By the time he rotated stateside after serving as a mortar section leader, rifle platoon commander, and company executive officer, he knew he was in for the long haul.

After the Korean War, Weise married and had two daughters and a son, who became a doctor. Weise served three years at The Basic School and Education Center at Quantico, during which time he was promoted to captain and underwent Army Ranger training at Fort Benning, Georgia, and attended the supply officer course at Camp Lejeune, North Carolina. He was then sidetracked into several supply billets at Camp Pendelton—until 1959, when he got out of more logistics duty with his run-fight-fuck-or-fart proclamation. The battalion commander instead gave him command of F/2/1, 1st Marine Division. Weise truly earned the Wild Bill sobriquet with Foxtrot Company. He ran the men hard every morning, and, taking his cue from the Army Rangers, he emphasized night operations, long marches, and the desirability of taking unconventional approaches through rough terrain that the enemy was unlikely to strongly defend. One night, during a regimental field exercise, Weise used what had been considered an impassable deer trail to move his entire company into the opposing force's rear. Their surprise was total.

After the battalion rotated to Okinawa, Weise finished his tour with it as an assistant operations officer. From there, the play-hard, drink-hard, train-hard Captain Weise moved to the super gung-ho world of Marine Recon. He served with the 1st Force Reconnaissance Company at Camp Pendelton in 1960–62, a tour that included airborne and scuba training and attendance at the Special Warfare Officers' School at Fort Bragg, North Carolina. Wild Bill was part of the team that developed a method for submarines to recover recon teams from hostile shorelines without having to expose themselves by surfacing. The procedure involved swimming out five thousand meters from shore at night, signaling the sub with an aquahorn, then using a scuba bottle to run a line down from the periscope to the forward escape drop, which each man would then swim down to lock into the sub. It was exciting and risky stuff, as was Weise's participation in the first night carrier launch of recon parachutists in the Navy's largest twin-engined bomber, and his team's free-fall parachute jump through the bomb-bay doors.

Weise made major during a 1962–65 tour as the Inspector-Instructor, 3d Force Reconnaissance Company, USMC Reserve, in Mobile, Alabama. In 1965–66, he attended the Army Command and General Staff College at Fort Leavenworth, Kansas. He was then assigned as an adviser to the Republic of Korea Marine Corps via the U.S. Naval Advisory Group, Korea.

As earlier described, newly promoted Lieutenant Colonel Weise's Vietnam tour began in October 1967 with his surprise assignment as commander of 2/4 following Operation Kingfisher. The battalion was down to about three hundred effectives, one-third the battalion's normal wartime strength. The NVA had gutted it. Weise knew the wounded lieutenant colonel he replaced to be an intelligent, brave, and conscientious Marine officer. The problem, as Weise saw it, was that the battalion, having fought the VC down south for so long, had been afforded no time to adapt to facing the NVA when it came north. Operation Kingfisher had been the battalion's first campaign on the DMZ, and its tempo had been intense.

Captain James Williams, then the battalion's assistant operations officer, was Weise's touchstone to what had gone before. Williams participated only in the tail end of Operation Kingfisher, but from what he had seen, it had been "an absolute abomination. There was no security. There was poor light discipline. The battalion wasn't doing the simplest things that you learn in school, like flank security, or observation posts, or putting out listening posts at night far enough where they can do something. It was a real mess."

The 2d Battalion, 4th Marines, had joined Operation Kingfisher from Camp Evans on 11 September 1967, and initially served as the 9th Marines' roving battalion outside Con Thien. The battalion was shelled every day from the DMZ. On 21 September 1967, it was ambushed by entrenched NVA and, despite a lot of courage and firepower (the battalion claimed thirty-nine confirmed kills), the Marines were forced to withdraw at dusk with 16 KIA and 118 WIA. Fifteen of those dead Marines had not been recovered. The battalion then defended a bridge on Route 561 in Leatherneck Square. The NVA attacked after midnight on 14 October 1967, probing first against H Company. Repelled there, the NVA used tear gas and rocket-propelled grenades (RPGs) to breach G Company's sector. The fighting was hand to hand, and individual Marine heroism was again stunning, but the NVA killed the company commander, forward observer, and three platoon commanders. Two of those dead lieutenants had joined the unit only that morning. The assistant operations officer, sent to take command of G Company, was killed before he could reach it. The NVA fought to within hand-grenade range of the battalion CP. The battalion medical chief was killed, and the fire support coordinator, headquarters commandant, forward air controller, and battalion sergeant major were wounded before the NVA were pushed out by E and F Companies. The NVA left twenty-four bodies, but the battalion suffered twenty-one KIA and twenty-three WIA in what became known as the Battle of Bastards' Bridge.

The battalion was withdrawn to regimental reserve at the DHCB to recover from the debacle. It was at that point that Captain Williams left 3d Recon at Khe Sanh and joined 2/4 as the new assistant operations officer. Soon thereafter, 2/4 participated in the final phase of Operation Kingfisher, a sweep on the west side of Route 561 with 3/3 in blocking positions at Bastards' Bridge. The battalion commander gave his assembled officers a pep talk the day before the sweep commenced. After telling them that "the S-three shop will brief you on the details," the colonel left the tent, leaving Williams and his boss gaping in astonishment. Neither man had any knowledge whatsoever of the operation, but having been pointed in the general direction, they made up the order of march, et cetera, as they went along. They were not going to embarrass the colonel.

Afterward, though, Williams confronted the S3: "What the hell? We're going on a big operation and we don't know anything more than that? The colonel told the troops that *we* would brief them on the details!"

"Well, that's the way it goes," the S3 replied with a shrug. "We usually just kind of wing it around here. . . ."

There was no contact on the first day of the sweep, 25 October 1967, but, given the nature of the area, the battalion commander asked for an emergency ammunition drop at dusk. He knew that the helicopters would reveal their position, but he took the calculated risk that once resupplied they could move on to their first night's objective before the NVA could respond. Unfortunately, more ammunition was delivered than requested, and the battalion, unable to carry it all, was forced to squat in place. The situation was made worse after dark by battle-rattled Marines who imagined themselves being overrun by every shadow, and who popped flares accordingly. The illumination pinpointed them, and ten artillery rounds crashed in shortly before midnight, wounding the battalion commander and killing his executive officer.

The regimental operations officer took temporary command of the battalion. The next day, following several sharp contacts, 2/4 got into a firefight with 3/3 as it moved into the area to reinforce the embattled Bastards. The battalion battened down for the night, intermixed and uncoordinated with 3/3, while taking casualties from NVA shellings and probes. After the NVA pulled back, Williams suggested to the interim battalion commander that, since their lines were so screwed up, word be passed for everyone to hunker down and anything that moved be considered enemy and shot on sight. No sooner had the directive been issued than one of 2/4's company commanders began acting irrationally. He was scared, really scared, and Williams was directed to relieve the man. Unclear as to the company's exact position, and expecting to be shot by his own side, Williams crawled around, whispering the password like a mantra until he found the fighting hole occupied by the company command group.

In the morning, having lost eight men killed and forty-five wounded in the previous two days (they reported nineteen NVA kills), 2/4 was ordered to move to Charlie 2, and then on to Cam Lo. Williams was still an acting company commander during the withdrawal when they found a dead Marine from 3/3. They brought the man's body out with them in a poncho. It took six Marines to carry the corpse; it was so hot that another team of six had to spell them every few minutes. Along the way, they encountered a company from 3/3 and an indignant captain who snapped, "Hey, that's my Marine! We take care of our own guys—give him to us!" Angered by the officer's brusque, unthanking tone, Williams shot back, "You left him out there. We brought him this far, so we'll carry him the rest of the way. Fuck you!" When the captain responded by taking a swing at him, Williams countered the blow and their first sergeants jumped in to pull the two skippers apart. It was a fitting, self-defeating end to the operation.

We are really fucked up, Williams thought.

The next day, 28 October, the 2d Battalion, 4th Marines, moved back to the DHCB, where Lieutenant Colonel Weise joined them later in the day. He arrived with the new battalion exec, Maj. Charles W. "Chuck"

Knapp, who was new to Weise as well but who would soon prove to be a cornerstone in his rebuilding efforts. Knapp had been an enlisted man in World War II and a junior officer in Korea. According to Weise, Knapp was "very intelligent" and had a "quiet, unassuming manner, but was tough and could raise the roof when necessary. He seemed to have the answers to questions before they were asked, and solved problems before others knew they existed."

After giving the battalion priority on replacements, division headquarters also greatly facilitated Weise's reconstruction plan by moving 2/4 into defensive positions around the Ai Tu airfield north of Quang Tri City. The war there was with the Viet Cong. Officially, 2/4 was participating in Operation Osceola, with the mission of constant patrolling to the depth of enemy rocket range on the airfield complex. Unofficially, the operation was a time-out for Weise to absorb replacements, establish his leadership, and train his battalion in a hostile but low-intensity environment.

At Ai Tu, Weise put Captain Williams in charge of their company-at-a-time training program, in which marksmanship, camouflage, and basic patrolling and security techniques were stressed. They practiced crossing streams with ropes at unlikely, seemingly unfordable spots. They learned to move into villages through the hedgerows in order to avoid the booby traps and ambushes that covered the trails where the going was easier. They conducted live-fire, fire-and-maneuver exercises against mock enemy positions. There was the usual Weise emphasis on night work, and on properly briefing and debriefing each patrol. Weise dictated that machine gunners were no longer to be used as automatic riflemen with the assault squads. A good M60 gunner, he said, could put well-aimed fire on visible targets up to two thousand meters away; furthermore, by squeezing off three-round bursts instead of letting the weapon run away on full automatic, a gunner could keep the barrel from burning out while keeping his fire on target. "When I first took over the battalion, the guys weren't carrying their tripods," Weise commented. "They were shooting John Wayne-style with a bipod or from the hip. We had to kick ass on that one. I threatened to relieve one company commander if he didn't get the tripods back on his machine guns. It was a matter of getting back to the basics in a lot of things, just requiring them to do what most of them already knew how to do."

Lieutenant Colonel Weise was a crew-cut, tough-as-nails cigar chewer who had his initials tattooed on his left forearm. That had been done with a needle and coal dust when he was twelve. He was a big man who came on strong and could get pretty boisterous when angry. Captain Williams, who was given command of H Company a month after Weise's arrival, was skeptical of the new battalion commander:

We were really gunshy of Weise because our impression was that he was a hip-shooter. He would see something wrong and he wouldn't investigate—he'd just take immediate, instantaneous action, and sometimes it was wrong. He made hasty judgments of his commanders. That was because he was under so much pressure to shape us up, and he was pushing real hard to overcome all this inertia that the battalion had built up. What he was doing was gaining a strong, firm control to compensate for the previous total lack of leadership from battalion level. We didn't fight him, but we company commanders looked askance sometimes and we grumbled to each other.

Although their troops needed physical conditioning, Williams was initially unimpressed when Weise ordered the companies to conduct physical training (PT) at Ai Tu:

We company commanders thought the idea of doing PT in a battle zone and running in cadence with company formations was a little much. Admittedly we were in a kind of rear area, but we were certainly within range of artillery and rockets. We thought it was hokey and not very tactical, not very safe, but we came around. We never did take any incoming, and it did get us back to thinking like Marines again. Gradually, Weise got our confidence and we found out he was maybe a little flamboyant and hot-doggy, but he had the substance to go with it.

During the two months the battalion spent at Ai Tu, 2/4 lost six KIA and seventy-eight WIA against seventeen confirmed kills, forty probable kills, and two prisoners. The battalion's command chronology spoke of the decrease in contacts and booby-trap incidents that corresponded with 2/4's familiarization with the terrain and the enemy, and noted that "newly arrived unit leaders and troopers alike received invaluable training and experience from the numerous small-unit operations. A steady improvement in the tactical employment of units was evident."

After the Magnificent Bastards were relieved at Ai Tu, stage two of their rebirth began on 6 January 1968 when the battalion disembarked at Subic Bay in the Philippines for seven days of training, liberty, and refurbishment. The battalion, newly redesignated as BLT 2/4, was brought up to full strength, and old weapons and equipment were rehabilitated or replaced.

It was a shiny battalion that sailed back to I Corps and the 1968 Tet Offensive, and it was on that brutal proving ground that even the most skeptical became Weise converts. "He did the right things," said Williams. It was that simple. The commander of the battalion's Headquarters & Service (H&S) Company, 1st Lt. Edward S. "Ted" Dawson, a Korean War veteran and ex–master sergeant, considered Weise exceptional in his ability to develop initiative in his subordinates by issuing mission-type orders and keeping abreast of progress without over-supervising. According to Dawson:

Bill Weise didn't feel that he had to have the last word on everything. That's true leadership. Never once did Weise approach me and say, "This is the way we're going to do it, and that's the bottom line." He said, "We need to do such-and-such. I want you to come up with a concept and get back to me." After being there awhile, it was, "Take care of it." When you have the reins let loose that far, you do the very best job you can. Weise, as well as Knapp and Warren, were prepared to explain in detail, without criticism, when they disagreed with an idea. In a combat situation, it's easy to say, "No, we're not going to do it that way, we're going to do it this way," and just carry on. But a couple minutes dedicated to recognizing an individual's idea shows that the commander is not a demigod, but one who is interested in what you have to offer. A positive outlook is contagious, and I would have moved heaven and earth to accomplish any task that Bill Weise gave me.

"I thought commanders who flew in helicopters while their troops were in a firefight were assholes," said Weise. "You have to go where the action is to find out what's going on."

Lieutenant Colonel Weise, at thirty-nine, did just that. Wearing helmet and flak jacket, he carried an M16 rifle and six magazines, a compass, and a map case, and had his binocular case taped to the left side of his flak jacket. He also shouldered a small rucksack in which he toted his toothbrush, shaving gear, an extra pair of socks, and his poncho. He did not wear his rank insignia in forward areas, and he ordered all other shiny objects removed. Rings were worn around the neck, and watches carried in pockets or kept covered. As to a commander's fire-drawing circle of radiomen, Weise commented, "It's hard to disguise a PRC-25 radio, but we usually used the short antenna and kept spread out."

Lieutenant Colonel Weise, who was wounded three times in his six months with the Magnificent Bastards, was usually side by side with Big John Malnar, his six-foot-three-inch, shotgun-toting battalion sergeant major. No man in the battalion had more combat experience than Malnar, and no man was closer to the colonel. Like Weise, Malnar came from a hardscrabble background. He grew up in Sawyerville, Illinois, and enlisted in the Marines three weeks after his seventeenth birthday in 1943. He saw action as a tank crewman and infantryman on Saipan, Tinian, and Okinawa, where his older brother was killed.

Malnar barely survived his next war, Korea, where as a sergeant and squad leader in G/3/1 in September 1950 he landed at Inchon. He was awarded a Bronze Star on D day for cutting a path through a barbed-wire obstacle despite enemy fire that killed the man who was with him. Two days later he earned the Silver Star when he climbed atop a tank and, with enemy fire bouncing off the armor around him, put its external .50-caliber machine gun to lethal use on a North Korean machine-gun crew. Just eight days after that, Malnar got another Bronze Star when his patrol took fire while passing under a railroad trestle on the outskirts of Seoul; he used a Browning automatic rifle to cover the recovery of their wounded even though he was shot five times in the leg and had one of his testicles blown away.

Sergeant Major Malnar, who was hit two more times in Vietnam at the age of forty-one, had to wear a two-inch sole on his custom-made, all-leather boot to compensate for the bone he lost in his wounded leg. The mask he wore during their long, hard humps across those paddies and sand dunes could not completely conceal that his leg was hurting, but he never complained.

Sergeant Major Malnar had volunteered for duty in Vietnam. He never married. The Marine Corps was his whole world, and he was the kind of loyal, tough, battle-wise sergeant major a battalion commander had to love. Malnar got things done. He was a strong, forceful taskmaster. He was a sounding board. He was a fatherly counselor. He was a provider of impossible-to-find bennies, thanks to that unique network of senior noncommissioned officers that extended through battalion, regiment, and division, and all the way to the III Marine Amphibious Force (MAF) in Da Nang. Malnar had the reputation of being a gruff sonofabitch. He was not, nor should he have been, a buddy to any of the junior enlisted men, and he viewed lieutenants and captains as part of the necessary rabble. "He tolerated us captains," remembered one officer. "Occasionally, if he remembered, he'd say 'sir.'"

In rebuilding BLT 2/4 Lieutenant Colonel Weise had one other godsend in addition to the service of men such as Big John Malnar: The battalion was always employed just within its growing capabilities. Each operation required more than the last, but with a constant emphasis on lessons learned, it became that much more able. "We were just a really aggressive outfit, and the initiative was ours," said Captain Williams. "Other units were always waiting for the enemy to do something. With us it was exactly the opposite. We were doing it to them. You have to put the credit right at the top. I witnessed this extraordinary evolution of a battalion that was on its ass in proficiency, morale, esprit, and discipline—the four indicators of leadership—as Weise turned it into probably the finest fighting outfit in Vietnam."

Weise's tactical right-hand man was his S3, Major Warren, a positive and personable Marine who was "gung-ho in a clean-cut sort of way." Prematurely graying at thirty-five, Fritz Warren was one of fourteen children from a low-income Catholic family in Jacksonville, Florida. He had come to the Marine Corps via Parris Island at seventeen, after dropping out of high school and forging his parents' names to the enlistment papers in a patriotic flush at the beginning of the Korean War. He never made it to Korea, but he did make sergeant and earn an appointment to the Naval Academy at Annapolis, Maryland.

Warren graduated in the Class of 1957; one of his early assignments was as Wild Bill's exec during the gung-ho F/2/1 days. They impressed each other enough that when they next crossed paths in December 1967, when Warren was assistant S3 of SLF Alpha and assisting 2/4's conversion to BLT status, Weise instantly asked him to come aboard when his six months of shipboard staff duty were up. The S3 Weise had inherited from Operation Kingfisher was too inexperienced. Warren was the only officer Weise asked for by name and was able to get. "Warren was an unusually talented operations officer," Weise wrote. "He could keep a dozen balls in the air and react swiftly to the changing tides of combat. A man of very high morals, he was also very brave."

Because he did not join BLT 2/4 until 19 February 1968, Major Warren missed the battalion's first two landings. Operations Ballistic Armor and Fortress Attack (22–31 January 1968) were fallow affairs, however, with only five friendly injuries and a dozen confirmed or probable kills. During the Tet Offensive in February, BLT 2/4 was opcon to the 4th Marines on Operation Lancaster II north of Camp Carroll. There it started running into NVA platoons, and during the month lost ten dead and ninety-eight wounded against thirty-five confirmed kills.

The tempo picked up again when BLT 2/4 was placed under the operational control of Colonel Hull's 3d Marines during Operation Napoleon/Saline. The battalion replaced BLT 3/1 in Mai Xa Chanh West on 5 March. The NVA response was immediate. That night, a mortar and rocket barrage preceded a ground attack that was repulsed with only two Marines seriously wounded. The enemy left behind thirteen bodies. The battalion followed up with a series of successful assaults to clear and reclear the evacuated hamlets above the Cua Viet River on both sides of Jones Creek.

The number of enemy they killed was impressive, at least until BLT 2/4 hit Lam Xuan East on 12 March. Weise described the engagement as "a fiasco from the start," and wrote that "Foxtrot was sucked into a preplanned meatgrinder when the point squad chased a few NVA, who had deliberately exposed themselves, into a carefully-prepared fortified ambush." The NVA held their fire until the Marines were so close that they could not employ supporting arms. "The forward platoon was chewed up trying to extract the point squad, and soon the entire company was involved," wrote Weise. Eighteen Marines were killed. Golf Company was sent to relieve the pressure, as were elements of Echo and two tanks. The BLT's attached recon platoon recovered the wounded, while Weise made the decision to break contact and regroup. The dead were left in the ville. "I hated to leave those bodies, even temporarily. It went against everything that Marines stood for, but I couldn't see killing more of my Marines to pull back Marines who were already dead."

Following prep fires, Hotel Company provided a feint and then a base of fire from the south, while Echo boarded amtracs to attack from the west across Jones Creek on 13 March. "The amtracs got stuck in the mud," Weise wrote. "Only Captain Livingston and a few Marines were able to make it across into Lam Xuan East. The remainder of Echo couldn't get across. I did not want to send Golf or Hotel into the ville from their positions because they would have been exposed to the same murderous enemy fire that chewed up Foxtrot the day before."

Faced again with tenacious NVA resistance that included mortar, rocket, and artillery fire, and with darkness approaching, Weise again decided to withdraw. Lam Xuan East, thoroughly shattered by air and arty, was not actually secured until 15 March, by which time the enemy had retired with their casualties.

Lieutenant Colonel Weise was tagged by higher command as being unaggressive at Lam Xuan East. "Even though they almost relieved Weise, he did not come down on us company commanders who had made the recommendation to break contact," said Captain Williams. "Weise could see that it was unjust criticism. It's easy to sit back at regiment or division and point your finger, but all they were doing was showing their ignorance. If anything, Weise was a little overly aggressive."

Weise's vindication came during an 18 March assault on Vinh Quan Thuong. This time, the recon platoon discovered the NVA before a rifle company could be sucked in. Given sufficient time to plan, muster supporting arms, and get into assault positions, BLT 2/4 was able to conduct a coordinated attack with the initiative in its hands and the whole day to get the job done. Echo and Hotel overran Vinh Quan Thuong while Golf Company hit the enemy flank. The NVA were killed in their holes; as the mopping up began, Weise turned to Warren and said with satisfaction, "Well, they can't say we weren't aggressive this time."

BLT 2/4 was credited with killing 474 NVA during the March 1968 battles, while losing the lives of 59 Marines and Navy corpsmen, plus 360 wounded. The tragedy was that, tactical excellence and sheer guts aside, those Americans died in vain. What was required was all-out war against Hanoi, plus pacification operations along the densely populated coast of South Vietnam. The first option, however, was denied by the politics of a limited war; the latter was denied by Gen. William C.

Westmoreland's search-and-destroy strategy. Instead, the 3d Marine Division was forced to squat along a defensive, strongpoint-and-barrier system facing the DMZ. This was a battlefield of Hanoi's choosing, for it pulled the Marines away from the defense and development of the South Vietnamese people. Furthermore, their DMZ sanctuary allowed the NVA to generally pick the time and place of battle. Willing to absorb terrible casualties for the political goal of demoralizing the U.S. home front with a seemingly endless stream of American body bags, the NVA played off the Marines' superaggressive, storm-the-beach approach to battle. The NVA tactics had the Marines seizing the same hamlets time and time again. Ho Chi Minh's taunt to the French also applied to the Americans: "You will kill ten of our men and we will kill one of yours, and in the end it will be you who tire of it."

Actually, a ten-to-one kill ratio may have tilted the war of attrition in the 3d Marine Division's favor. But such punishment was never actually inflicted, despite such crippling numbers as the 474 NVA kills reported by BLT 2/4 during the hamlet battles. That figure was false, as it turned so-called guesstimates of the damage delivered by supporting arms into confirmed kills. Major Warren considered such manipulations the most distressing part of his duties, and he would later comment that "Weise succumbed to this body count situation in reporting that kind of stuff." Weise was certainly not alone. As Warren noted in a document prepared two years after his tour and originally classified for internal use only, "the actual operational necessity of survival in a command billet was a suitable body count ratio of enemy to friendly KIAs." There was, Warren added, intense pressure from regiment "to submit estimates early in a battle when virtually no information was actually available . . . the early estimates were expected to be revised upwards as the battle progressed." The result was that regiment "not only allowed but implicitly encouraged their subordinate commanders to become professional liars."

Whatever career-enhancing juggling was done with the reporting of enemy casualties, the NVA thought well enough of BLT 2/4 to shift their infiltration routes west to the ARVN TAOR around Dong Ha. The Bastards made only infrequent contact during April 1968, usually at night with ambush operations Weise had begun implementing to compensate for the sudden paucity of targets. The lull gave BLT 2/4 time to break in the influx of replacements, and to analyze what had been done right and not so right in its first major campaign under Weise. The result was an updated, Ai Tu–style training schedule out in the sticks at Mai Xa Chanh West.

"People thought Weise must be crazy having us train out there," Warren noted, although he did not agree. The battalion was surviving, he thought, precisely because of Weise's exacting standards and unrelenting, train-train-train-to-perfection philosophy. "He believed that his most important responsibility was to make sure not a single life would be lost because the men weren't properly trained. He never let up. He expected great things of people. He demanded the same things of himself."

CHAPTER 3 ROUND ONE

Despite the heat mirages blurring the view through his sniper scope, LCpl. James L. O'Neill could see movement five hundred meters away among the brush and hootches of Dong Huan. The hamlet sat on the far bank of the tributary the Marines were approaching, and O'Neill turned to Lieutenant Boyle, the 1st Platoon commander in H BLT 2/4, to report, "Sir, I think we got a whole bunch of gooks in front of us."

"Take a look again."

Lance Corporal O'Neill, a sniper, brought his scope-mounted, bolt-action rifle back to his shoulder. He was sitting at the edge of a paddy east of the two standing structures of what was marked as Bac Vong on their maps. He looked at the lieutenant again. "Hey, I'm watchin' a lot of movement out there. I don't know if it's ours or theirs. All I see is movement."

"Shoot one of 'em."

"Sir, what if it's one of *ours?*"

"We don't have anybody out there. Just shoot one."

O'Neill had reason to hesitate: The other side of the tributary belonged to the ARVN. Hotel One's patrol had departed the company patrol base, Objective Delta, early that morning, Tuesday, 30 April 1968, with the mission of investigating the NVA positions that had fired on a routine, predawn patrol by river patrol craft of TF Clearwater. From Objective Delta, Hotel Company could hear the NVA automatic weapons and rocket-propelled grenades, and see the red .50-caliber tracers streaming back from the patrol boat. The NVA seemed to have been in the vicinity of Dong Huan, which was on the south bank of a Bo Dieu tributary that sliced east to west before curving north. Lieutenant Boyle's orders had been to move south the thirteen hundred meters between Objective Delta and Bac Vong, which sat on the north side of the tributary five hundred meters above Dong Huan. The thin, head-high tributary between Bac Vong defined the western edge of BLT 2/4's TAOR. However, the ARVN forces responsible for the opposite side had been committed the afternoon before to the Route 1 battle.

Screw it, O'Neill thought as he assumed his prone firing position. If it is the ARVN, I'll just swear up and down somebody else did it. . . .

Lance Corporal O'Neill, twenty, had chambered a 7.62mm match round in his Remington Model 700, and now, helmet off, he focused through the scope on a shirtless soldier who was unknowingly facing the cross hairs as he walked down a trail. There were too many trees for a clean shot. O'Neill waited until the man sat down in a waist-deep spiderhole. He fired. The recoil took his eye off the target, as did the well-oiled maneuver of bringing the bolt back and chambering a new round. O'Neill snapped his focus back to the trail and scanned down it until he found the hole just off to the left of it. The man was leaning back in the hole. It was unclear if he'd been hit, so O'Neill squeezed off a second shot. When he reacquired the target, there was no doubt about his marksmanship: The man was missing half of his head.

It was approximately 0810. Lieutenant Boyle, a capable, ruddy-faced young man who'd had Hotel One for three weeks, called up his squad leaders. He and his platoon sergeant, SSgt. Richard A. Kelleher, explained that they were to lay down a base of fire from their position east of Bac Vong while Cpl. James A. Summey's squad maneuvered to a small footbridge that crossed the blueline into Dong Huan. Summey's squad made it to the creek's edge before surprising five soldiers wearing green fatigues and pith helmets, and carrying AK-47s. They were clearly North Vietnamese regulars. The NVA were on the opposite bank and were rushing for cover, but the squad dropped three of them. The NVA returned fire and Boyle pulled the squad back, then requested that their artillery spotter call for supporting fire as the exchange of automatic weapons fire intensified.

Hotel Company had established an observation post on the roof of a battle-scarred, two-story concrete farmhouse in the deserted hamlet designated Objective Delta. Captain Williams was up top with a pair of binoculars, watching Hotel One's progress. He could also see the routine river traffic to the south on the Bo Dieu River. A pair of Navy utility landing craft (LCUs) proceeded downriver with several patrol boats. The patrol boats, which answered to the call sign Traffic Cop, placed .30- and .50-caliber machine-gun fire into Dong Huan, already shuddering under the barrage of 105mm artillery fire being brought to bear. The patrol boats added their 81mm mortars to the onslaught.

The NVA, who were well entrenched, opened up on Traffic Cop and the passing LCUs. Captain Williams was still watching through his binos when a Soviet-made 57mm recoilless rifle suddenly opened fire from Dong Huan—it was a five-hundred-meter shot to the Bo Dieu River—and one of the LCUs shook as it took two or three broadside hits. As the LCUs U-turned and headed for Dong Ha with casualties aboard, Williams dropped down the ladder from the tarp-shaded observation post (OP) and radioed battalion. The word from Dixie Diner 6 was exactly what Williams expected: Hotel Company was to attack and seize Dong Huan.[1]

It was supposed to be Captain Williams's last operation with Hotel Company. He had only a week remaining on his twelve-and-twenty, the twelve months and twenty days of a Marine's tour in Vietnam. Williams had built a fine reputation. "The skipper was a by-the-book officer of exacting standards," said a lieutenant of this thirty-year-old family man from Winona, Minnesota, "and he was also a gentleman, a sensitive man, a man who was capable of doing what was necessary to accomplish the mission, but not without a good deal of feeling and concern for his troops."

Captain Williams was also incredibly brave. He and Captain Livingston of Echo Company had led the way during the assault on Vinh Quan Thuong and became battalion legends because of it. Bogged down under artillery and rocket fire, Williams jumped up with his entrenching tool still in hand and, along with the grease-gun–toting Livingston, personally led the final, reenergized charge into the enemy ville. They overran an NVA artillery spotter who was dying at his radio. The radio

1. At this point, Capt. G. W. Smith, USN, the TF Clearwater commander, closed the Bo Dieu River to supply traffic until the Marines could clear the banks.

was still squawking. Williams's Vietnamese scout said that the NVA at the other end was asking for a status report. Williams thought back to their recent arrival at Mai Xa Chanh West when Hanoi Hannah had welcomed the battalion and its commander by name, and had mocked the so-called Magnificent Bastards. Williams instructed his scout, "Get on that radio; I've got a message for the other end: 'You have just been overrun by Hotel Company of the Second Battalion, Fourth Marines. Lieutenant Colonel Weise sends his regards.'"

Captain Williams's assault on Dong Huan was going to be rough. An aerial observer was on station above the battlefield, and had already ordered one air strike on the hamlet. It was followed by firing runs from three helicopter gunships, and then another bomb run that claimed to have knocked out two 12.7mm machine guns. The Soviet-built 12.7mm was effective against both ground troops and aircraft, and the presence of such a weapon in Dong Huan was one of the factors that led Weise to later write:

> I felt uneasy. Something big was happening. . . . Small enemy units and individuals often fired at river boats and "disappeared" before we could react. This time I had a feeling the enemy would not run. . . . Everything about the situation favored the enemy defenders. The approaches to Dong Huan offered no cover and very little concealment. Surrounded by open rice paddies, and separated from Bac Vong by an unfordable stream, Dong Huan, itself, was hidden by dense hedgerows.

The enemy had chosen their position well. Given the enemy's talent for engineering situations in which they were dug in and their opponents were in the open—the Marine response to the NVA recoilless rifle fire was obvious—Weise also had to be concerned with nearby Dai Do. The largest ville in the area, it was situated five hundred very open meters west and southwest of Dong Huan. No NVA had been spotted in Dai Do, but if they were there they could bring long-range sniper and machine-gun fire to bear on any assault of Dong Huan.

Lieutenant Colonel Weise explained to Williams over the radio that he had secured permission from regiment to commit Foxtrot Company, the battalion reserve, to cover Dai Do. Foxtrot was to move out immediately aboard amtracs from Mai Xa Chanh East. The battalion's attached tank platoon, which could muster just two M48 tanks, was also on the way. Weise explained that he, too, was going to be battlefield bound shortly (he would arrive about 1005) aboard a Navy LCM-6 Monitor gunboat, which would pick him up at Mai Xa Chanh West and bring him up the Bo Dieu with his command group. Weise later wrote:

> I ordered Capt Williams to assemble Hotel Company in Bac Vong. . . . Using the limited concealment afforded by the stream bank, Hotel Company would move north . . . to a fording point, cross the stream, and turn south to Dong Huan. Foxtrot Company, mounted on amtracs, would then cross the stream, move to the cemetery east of Dai Do, pour fire into Dai Do to silence [suspected] enemy weapons there, create a diversion for Hotel Company as it moved into its assault position, and protect Hotel's right flank and rear during its assault. Foxtrot . . . would also be prepared to assault Dai Do.

From Objective Delta, Williams retraced Hotel One's route to the vicinity of Bac Vong with his headquarters and mortar section, plus Hotel Three under SSgt. Ronald W. Taylor. Hotel Two, led by SSgt. Robert J. Ward, moved down from Objective Charlie to join Williams, as did SSgt. T. Garvin, who commanded the two tanks from A Company, 3d Tank Battalion, which presently arrived from the BLT CP. In addition, 1st Lt. C. W. Muter, commander of the BLT's attached platoon from D Company, 3d Reconnaissance Battalion, also showed up. Muter and four of his recon Marines had been in the area on a relatively routine patrol unrelated to the fray they now joined.

The first order of business was to secure Bac Vong, which afforded a direct, vegetation-covered line of fire into Dong Huan. Since the blueline was a real tank obstacle, Captain Williams planned to deploy Garvin's two tanks in Bac Vong and use their 90mm main guns and .50-caliber machine guns as a base of fire. Muter's recon team would secure the tanks.

They reached Bac Vong, which proved empty, at about 1115. As the tanks and recon team deployed along the brushy bank, Williams instructed Staff Sergeant Ward to move upstream with Hotel Two to find a place to ford the stream. They reconned along seven hundred meters of the tributary before finding a relatively narrow and shallow spot across which a bamboo fishing screen had been rigged. A step in the wrong, muddy place would sink a combat-loaded Marine to his chin, but by leaning against the screen they were able to get across with weapons, ammunition, and radios held high.

Captain Williams fed Hotel Three across the stream behind Hotel Two, with Hotel One bringing up the rear. This channelized, single-file crossing (completed by about 1300) drew only sporadic fire from Dong Huan. The tanks and recon team in Bac Vong, however, were under heavy fire, and they responded in kind. Lieutenant Muter, talking on the radio, caught a flash of movement out of the corner of his eye, and he looked up from his map just as an NVA ran out of Dong Huan to the edge of the creek. The NVA had an RPG over his shoulder and took aim at the tank beside which Muter was kneeling. In the same instant, Muter saw Bergmann, one of his recon troops, carefully aiming his M16 at the NVA. Unlike most grunts, Bergmann avoided the temptation to start shooting from the hip, and instead stood in the classic Marine Corps firing stance with one elbow up and the other tucked under his weapon. Bergmann squeezed off his one, make-it-count shot in the same millisecond that the 90mm cannon on the tank roared its disapproval at the RPG-toting enemy soldier. The NVA disappeared from the face of the earth. Bergmann had been concentrating so hard that he had not heard the tank gun. All he knew was that his target had evaporated with one well-aimed squeeze of the trigger, and he held his M16 in front of him as he exclaimed in awe: "Jee-sus Christ!"

A pair of USMC F-4 Phantoms prepped Dong Huan as Hotel Company crossed the creek, and 1st Lt. Alexander F. "Scotty" Prescott IV, the company exec, helped spot for the aerial observer, who was up in an O-1E Birddog. It was a real aerial show, with the two low-flying pilots putting their bombs and napalm, better known as snake 'n' nape, right into the hamlet. How can anyone be alive in there? Prescott wondered. They're getting plastered with napalm and five hundred pounders, man. They're just getting the shit pounded out of them. Over the roar of the jets' fire, Prescott could hear the sharp popping of AK-47s from within the village. Ballsy, he thought. These aren't rice farmers. These are professional soldiers.

As one of the Phantoms pulled out of a run, a big napalm fireball spread over the ville even as the aerial observer called excitedly on the radio, "You're takin' fire! You're takin' fire!"

The pilot's voice was strained by the g's he was pulling as he sky-rocketed up from his treetop-level bombing run, but he was sporting nonetheless: "Uhhh, uhhhh . . . I think that's only fair. . . ."

Captain Williams left Lieutenant Prescott at the fording site with their gunnery sergeant, mortar section, and reserve platoon, while he moved to their line of departure and set up some four hundred meters north of Dong Huan with Staff Sergeants Ward (Hotel Two) and Taylor (Hotel Three) facing south. Taylor was on the left flank and Ward on the right, where Foxtrot Company was presently approaching. Foxtrot had just crossed over on amtracs, and was to take Dai Do under fire after deploying along its own LD.

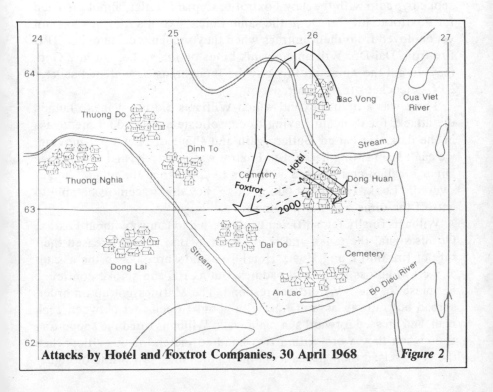

Attacks by Hotel and Foxtrot Companies, 30 April 1968   *Figure 2*

Meanwhile, Williams had his 60mm mortars and M60 machine guns take Dong Huan under fire to keep the NVAs' heads down. Between that barrage and the tree-shaking tank fire from across the creek, the NVA got off only a shot or two in return. In fact, some of the grunts catnapped behind the paddy dikes as the prep fires poured in. With the jets no longer on station, Williams put his artillery spotter, 2d Lt. Carl R. Gibson, from H/3/12, to good use. This was Gibson's baptism of fire, but he did a well-trained job of raining 105mm and 155mm fire on Dong Huan, with a mix of high explosive (HE), white phosphorus, and smoke rounds. In addition, the Traffic Cop patrol boats and the Monitor command boat on the Bo Dieu fired thousands of .30- and .50-caliber machine-gun rounds, and 81mm mortar rounds by the dozen. The Monitor also pumped 20mm cannon fire into the increasingly smoky battlefield.

By 1330, Captain Williams was ready to assault Dong Huan. He spoke by radio with the new Foxtrot 6, Captain Butler, about the need for Foxtrot to hit Dai Do at the same time. Foxtrot's Marines had not yet deployed from their amtracs when they suddenly came under RPG fire from Dai Do. Williams put his binos on the scene. Oh, my God, they've got the range on this guy, he thought, as he watched several RPGs ricochet off the amtracs.

There was a point beyond which Williams did not want to launch the attack, for it meant having to consolidate and conduct medevacs in the dark. He called Butler again and shouted, "Let's get moving, we can't keep sitting here!" But Foxtrot was not ready, and when Dixie Diner 6 called and pressed Williams to commence the attack, he answered, "Look, Foxtrot is taking hits. They don't seem to be able to get off the dime and get moving!"

Williams finally felt sufficiently compelled to launch without Foxtrot. On his signal the tanks and recon team in Bac Vong increased their rate of fire into Dong Huan. Hotel Two and Three began the assault at a crawl across the naked paddies, but as HE and smoke continued to splash in, the NVA did not respond. The Marines got up on order, spread out into an assault line with about fifteen feet between each man, and pressed forward at a rapid walk. Williams lifted the supporting fires when they were within two hundred meters of the ville; when the NVA raised their heads from their holes they saw a line of eighty screaming, firing-from-the-hip Marines rushing at them from out of the smoke.

"When those Marines hit the ville," Williams later wrote, "you couldn't hold them back." The attack "was so smooth that it looked like a rehearsed SDT [Schools Demonstration Troops] assault demo at Quantico." Williams added that:

> in fact, it *had* been rehearsed. During 2/4's earlier operations along the Cua Viet River, our attacks had, on several occasions, lost momentum and gotten unnecessarily bogged down. Our Marines, trained from the first day of boot camp to look out for one another, were allowing their attachment for their buddies to jeopardize all of us. When one youngster would get hit, three more would stop their assault fire and forward movement and run over to assist their fallen buddy. This phenomenon was particularly troublesome in the earlier attacks on Vinh Quan Thuong and Lam Xuan East and Jim Livingston and I, along with some encouragement from [Weise], resolved to do something about it. During the lull in the action that occurred in April, we cordoned off an area in front of our perimeter at Mai Xa Chanh [West] and drilled our squads and platoons in live-fire assaults. We stressed the fact that in the attack, continued momentum is essential and once committed to the assault, nothing must stop them.

Williams added that when several Marines rushed to help a wounded buddy "part of that was just an excuse to get out of the fire, and it was killing us—literally—because once you lose fire superiority they gain it and you're pinned down. I told them, 'I don't care if it's your *mother* that goes down, you leave her lying there and you keep going.'"

That's exactly what Hotel Company did at Dong Huan. Kills were made at eyeball-to-eyeball range. Lance Corporal Phil Donaghy of Hotel Two, under fire for the first time, was only four quick steps from that first hedgerow when an NVA suddenly rose halfway from his spiderhole in the vegetation. The man looked terrified. He was screaming. It sounded as though he was shouting the surrender call of *chieu hoi,* but he was still clutching his AK-47, and before Donaghy could think, he fired his M16 into the man. The entire squad seemed to zero in on him at that same instant, and the NVA was lifted backward out of his hole.

Captain Williams's forward observer, Lieutenant Gibson, called in one fire mission too many just as Hotel Two and Three hit Dong Huan. Williams heard the artillery battery report "shot out" over Gibson's radio, and he shouted at Gibson to adjust the next salvo farther into the ville. Williams grabbed his own radio then to urgently instruct Hotel Two and Three to slow down. When he got no response, he double-timed forward, yelling like a crazy man, "Slow down, slow down, there's rounds on the way!"

If the lead elements had been about ten seconds deeper into the ville when the salvo landed, they would have been caught in the splash. As it was, the timing had been perfect: The last rounds impacted as the first Marines went through the hedgerow.

Captain Williams caught up with Staff Sergeant Taylor, who was standing on a dike in front of the hedge, and shouted, "We still got artillery comin' in! Stop your troops!"

"We can't, we're already started!" Taylor said.

Williams turned to Gibson. "You can't let any more artillery come in because we can't stop!" he shouted.

Williams had noticed an NVA in a spiderhole about fifteen meters to his left as he'd rushed up. He saw the NVA only out of the corner of his eye and, considering everything else, it really didn't register—until a Chicom grenade suddenly exploded behind him. The blast was like a hard kick in the ass, and it sent him sprawling. By the time Williams regained his senses and thought to unholster his .45, the NVA had reappeared. He was holding up the overhead cover to his spiderhole in one hand and looking right at Williams. He had recognized this shouting, gesticulating Marine as a leader, and he pulled the string on another grenade. The NVA flicked the Chicom at Williams, then disappeared back into his covered hole.

The top-heavy, stick-handled grenade bounced toward Williams as if in slow motion. It was taking so long that he knew it would explode just as it rolled to within lethal range. The grenade stopped. It was a dud. By then Williams was in a two-handed prone position with his .45 pistol aimed at the spiderhole. When the NVA popped back up, presumably with a third grenade, the captain began squeezing off rounds. The enemy soldier dropped, apparently hit. Williams couldn't tell for sure, but at least there were no more Chicoms.

Williams realized then that he'd been hit by the first grenade—a single, deep fragment wound in his left buttock. It was bleeding badly and the pain was starting, but he knew he had lucked out. An American grenade would have blown off my whole leg, he thought.[2]

Others had also been hit by the grenade, including Staff Sergeant Taylor. His flak jacket was torn up badly, his helmet cover was nicked, and he had several fragments in his left thigh. Taylor was a tall, soft-spoken, twenty-nine-year-old country boy who had been a Marine since dropping out of high school at seventeen. His people were coal miners from Madisonville, Kentucky. He was on his second infantry tour in Vietnam and operated with a calm expertise.

Lieutenant Prescott, the exec, took command and led the well-trained Hotel Company Marines past their flattened leaders to press the attack. Williams was feeling quite alone and very helpless as he lay near Taylor, when to his horror he saw a bypassed NVA who had emerged from a spiderhole. The man was about twenty-five meters away, jogging purposefully through the dissipating smoke screen. He looked right at Williams and Taylor. It would have been easy for him to swing his AK-47 around and blow them away without a thought. Williams tensed. He knew that this was it. But the NVA never fired; he just kept moving. Williams turned to the Navy corpsman who had been bandaging them and told him to find an M16 and organize some security.

They were joined shortly by LCpl. Dale R. Barnes, who had moved up from the exec's former position at the fording site. Barnes had carried Captain Williams's radio for five and a half months, and he ran full tilt across the paddies with several Marines from the reserve platoon as soon as he heard his skipper was down. They had not been ordered forward, but knew they would be needed. Barnes knelt beside Williams,

2. Captain Williams was awarded a second Silver Star and the Purple Heart for his actions and wound at Dong Huan. His first Silver Star had been for Vinh Quan Thuong. He later received the Bronze Star Medal with Combat V (BSMv) as an end-of-tour award.

who told him that they had wounded in the hedgerow. Barnes drew his .45 and started forward on all fours. A single shot cracked over his head from the hedge—stray or targeted, friendly or enemy, he did not know—and he hit the deck and crawled on in as fast as he could. The first Marine he found was also lying prone. The man had been wounded in the arm and was terrified that if he moved he would be hit again.

"Everything is clear," Barnes shouted. He didn't really believe it, but he wanted to get the man up and out of there. He braced the man against him with his arm around his shoulder, and hustled back to the captain. Barnes went back in, hoisted an unconscious, wounded Marine on his back, and had just about cleared the hedgerow when he collapsed from heat exhaustion.

Meanwhile, Captain Williams instructed the corpsman to find their gunny and bring him forward. The corpsman ran back alone, and reported simply that the gunny was still at the fording site with the mortar section. Williams was perplexed: "Is he hurt?"

"No, sir."

"Well, what's he doing?"

"He's hiding in a hole, sir."

Son of a bitch, Williams thought. It seemed that every time the fighting started, the gunny would disappear, then reappear afterward. The gunny was on his second tour in Vietnam and was most unhappy to be back. Fawning and obsequious to officers, he was forever finding reasons to go back to the ship.

"You go back there and you get that gunny up here," Williams shouted to the corpsman. "And you tell him that's an order; I want him up here *now!* Get him up here even if you have to do it at gunpoint!"

The gunny finally appeared, ashen faced and trembling. Williams told him to make sure that the NVA he'd shot at was really dead. The gunny's pistol didn't work, so he borrowed Taylor's, fired a few rounds at the spiderhole, and handed back the pistol. There was no response from the spiderhole. Williams told one of the radiomen to go check it out, and to bring back the dead NVA's gold-starred belt buckle if he could. He wanted it as a souvenir.

As the radioman approached the spiderhole, an NVA suddenly jumped up. Perhaps Williams had only wounded the man, or perhaps it was a different enemy soldier. Either way, the man took off in a panicked run as the radioman hastily opened up with his M16. He missed, and Williams bellowed, "Gunny, get that damn gook—*you* let him get away!"

"I'm not running after him!" the gunny shouted back.

"Goddamnit, I told you to get that gook, and you're going to get him!" But the gunny still didn't budge. Williams finally told him, "You get out there and provide some security for us or you're a dead man!" The gunny reluctantly got back up, which was lucky for him. "I'd have shot him. There's no question in my mind," Williams said later. "The adrenaline was pumping; it was a life-or-death situation for all of us, and I wasn't in any frame of mind to fool around."

While things bogged down temporarily on Hotel Three's side, Staff Sergeant Ward kept things moving fast on Hotel Two's flank. That was not surprising, for the profane, loud, and forceful Ward was an absolute madman in combat. He was a tough guy from New York who had dropped out of high school at sixteen to join up. He used forged permission papers and ID to fool the recruiters. Ward went on to fight in Korea, and was on his second tour in Vietnam.

The wiry, tattooed, abrasive redhead sported a crew cut and always wore a red bandanna around his neck. He carried a shotgun, pistol, eight grenades, a hatchet, several knives, and an entrenching tool. His troops called him Sergeant Knife. He was thirty-four, and a real character. He was also a hard old pro. Ward had left his platoon sergeant back with the mortar section because the man was due to rotate in two days. As Hotel Two charged into Dong Huan, the squad leader on the left flank, Sgt. Robert J. Enedy, went down with a blood-pumping belly wound. Enedy was a popular, respected Marine, and when he went down his men began diving for cover. Ward pivoted his other two squads to bear down on the NVA to their left, and had just gotten his people moving again when a Chicom potato-masher landed right in front of him. He tried to kick it away, but missed. The explosion peppered his face and jaw with metal fragments, knocking him down.

"Sergeant Ward's hit!" someone screamed.

Realizing that morale was flagging all around him, Ward jumped back up, pissed off and in pain, shouting, "Fuckin' let's go!"

Staff Sergeant Ward ran to the NVA position that was holding them up. There were dead NVA in it—and a couple of live ones. Fucking pricks! he thought as he emptied his shotgun into the slit trench. He put the twelve-gauge down and threw hand grenades at the next trench full of NVA. He suddenly glimpsed an NVA out of the corner of his eye. The man was leaning around the corner of a shattered concrete house. Ward turned and saw another Chicom coming at him. He reached for his shotgun before rolling out of the way, but the grenade went off, blowing the weapon out of his hands, and his diver's watch with the jungle band and compass off his wrist. It also stung Ward's left hand with shell fragments and slammed him down so hard that his head was spinning and his eyes wouldn't focus.

Ward tried to stand, but couldn't. After the platoon corpsman bandaged his hand, Ward said, "Slap me in the face!" That seemed to set his equilibrium right. Ward stood and unholstered his .45, but he couldn't chamber a round one-handed. He gave the pistol to his radioman and told him to pull the slide back. The Marine did so and handed the weapon back as Ward, moving forward again, bellowed amid the din: "Fuckin' let's go, Second Platoon. . . ."[3]

The north-to-south plunge through the approximately three hundred meters of Dong Huan's hedges, tree lines, houses, and drainage ditches was a madhouse of some fifteen minutes' duration. Lieutenant Prescott brought up the reserve platoon, Hotel One, to support Hotel Three. In short order, the platoon commander, Lieutenant Boyle, picked up shell splinters in the arm, and Staff Sergeant Kelleher was hit badly enough to qualify for a medevac. One of their men, LCpl. Robert A. McPherson, was killed. Hotel Company's charge-Charge-CHARGE maneuver had bypassed entrenched NVA pockets, which had to be methodically reduced by light antitank weapons (LAWs) and M79s as Lieutenant Prescott turned the show around to consolidate what they had. This took a good hour or so. The Marines killed every NVA who did not run or hide well. They took no prisoners. The company was credited with thirty confirmed kills. It also captured the recoilless rifle that had started the donnybrook.

---

3. Staff Sergeant Ward was awarded the Silver Star and Purple Heart for Dong Huan. He picked up his second Purple Heart during the subsequent battle for Nhi Ha (25 May 1968), and finished his tour on Okinawa, where, true to his crazy, alcohol-fueled ways he was court-martialed for fistfighting. His name was removed from the gunnery sergeant list, and he was never promoted.

Sergeant Joe N. Jones, a huge black man and second-tour professional, was the platoon sergeant of Hotel Three. Jones took command
when Taylor was wounded; he described the action as follows when
interviewed three weeks later by the division historical section:

> We were in high spirits and seeing dead gooks all over the area.
> I guess that helped the Marines to continue on through the as-
> sault. Of course we had a lot of people pushing. I myself and all
> my squad leaders and team leaders and everybody else was pushing
> as hard as they could. We assaulted through the ville, and we got
> snipers firing, and we had to go back in and, goddamn, there was
> dead gooks all over the place. Wounded Marines was all over the
> place. Everybody was all mixed up then; different squads from
> different platoons was all over the damn ville.

"It was so fucking confusing" was how Staff Sergeant Ward put it.
So much so that just before Lieutenant Prescott gave the word to
U-turn and mop up, he and Lieutenant Gibson, the FO, actually got
ahead of their assault line. At that point, an NVA wearing a bush hat
and light green fatigues popped up about twenty feet away. He disappeared back into the ville's overgrown vegetation when Prescott started
firing his .45 at him. He was the only live NVA that Prescott saw.

The village gave way to open paddies leading south to An Lac and
west to Dai Do, where Foxtrot was engaged in a furious firefight of
its own. When Prescott reached the edge of the ville, not knowing what
was waiting for them out there, he told his group to back up.

Lieutenant Gibson, who was only three feet behind Prescott, suddenly dropped as they turned back. He had been shot in the forehead,
presumably by an NVA sniper who saw his radioman beside him and
figured he was an officer. Gibson had been in Vietnam just ten days.

Lieutenant Prescott radioed Williams that they had secured the re-
coilless rifle, then requested permission to pull back and consolidate.
Hotel Company set up a tight 180 against the tributary running past
Dong Huan where the footbridge connected them with Bac Vong.
"Lieutenant Prescott really had a head on his shoulders in putting the
unit back together, and calming everybody down," recalled radioman
Barnes of his new company commander. At the creekside medevac point,
Prescott was surrounded by bedlam. On one side of him was a crying,

nearly hysterical corpsman who couldn't believe that his best friend, Bucky McPherson, was dead. On the other side another corpsman screamed that Sergeant Enedy was gray faced from loss of blood and that he was holding in his intestines as they slipped through his gut wound.

"We gotta get him outta here, Lieutenant!" the corpsman shouted. "We gotta get him out—he's dying, he's dying!"

"Put him on the ground," Prescott answered. "Hold him. We're doing what we can, we're trying to get medevacs in."

No helicopters could land. The NVA had begun lobbing sporadic artillery fire into the area, and there was a near-constant rain of USMC artillery in support of Foxtrot Company in Dai Do. Prescott had to rely instead on the battalion's fourteen-foot fire-team assault boats, better known as skimmers, which were made of fiberglass and had thirty-five-horsepower outboard motors. At about 1530, several of them came upriver from the BLT CP to shuttle back Hotel's thirty or so wounded, and to bring forward wooden, rope-handled boxes of ammunition and grenades.

Meanwhile, amid this hurry-hurry-hurry, life-and-death scene at the medevac point, Lieutenant Prescott was stunned to see Colonel Hull, the 3d Marines CO, approaching with his operations officer, sergeant major, and radioman. Fire Raider 6, as Hull was known on the radio, was a real Old Corps warrior. He had taken a skimmer of his own straight from Camp Kistler to Dong Huan. The colonel walked up to Prescott and began questioning him about the fight. Prescott was too busy to answer. "Excuse me, but I don't have time for this, sir," he told the colonel. "I got other things to do."

Lieutenant Prescott, always an irreverent sort, operated under the philosophy of What are they going to do? Shave my head and send me to Vietnam? Major Murphy, the regimental S3, didn't appreciate Prescott's offhand dismissal, and glared at him. "Lieutenant, do you know who you're talking to?" Murphy asked.

"Major, I don't care *who* I'm talking to right now. I got a company to run here—you'll have to excuse me."

Colonel Hull, who was squat, gray haired, and bulldog faced, stepped between them. "That's all right, son," he said, "you just go ahead and do your job. Where can we help?"

"You can help me get these wounded out," Prescott replied. With that, Hull and Murphy picked up a wounded Marine by his arms and legs and hustled him down to a skimmer.

Captain Williams was loaded into a skimmer, too. Williams, crammed in with five or six other wounded Marines for the top-speed, fifteen-minute ride to Mai Xa Chanh West, later wrote, "the bottom of the boat was completely covered with blood to the depth of several inches in some places. I remember it sloshing around in the boat as we sped across the water. I remember a discarded canteen actually floating in blood."

The flat-bottomed skimmers brought the casualties to the beach at Mai Xa Chanh West. There, the BLT's two Navy surgeons and several corpsmen determined their priority for evacuation—routine, priority, or emergency—by the Sea Horses of HMM-362, which were making round-robin flights between the beach and the USS *Iwo Jima*. The helicopters were lowered one at a time by elevator to the below-deck hangar, where they were met by corpsmen who conducted a second triage, then carried the casualties' litters to the ship's below-deck surgery. Each chopper was announced over the ship's public address system with a chilling monotone: "Medevacs inbound. . . . Medevacs inbound. . . ."

Second Lieutenant Bayard V. "Vic" Taylor, the exec of H BLT 2/4, was filled with helpless rage as he began recognizing the faces of men from his company among the casualties. Taylor had recently given up Hotel One to replace Prescott, who was supposed to move to the S3 shop in a couple of days. Taylor had made an admin run to the *Iwo Jima* that morning to pick up the company payroll. He was a real field Marine and he thought he should have been out there, but all he could do at the moment was walk over to where the KIAs had been unloaded. They were laid out of the way to one side of the hangar, and Taylor and their tough little company first sergeant, 1st Sgt. Clifford Martin, knelt beside each poncho-wrapped body to formally identify them. There were three from Dong Huan.

Second Lieutenant Gibson, the twenty-two-year-old FO from Radford, Virginia, had been a short, stocky, muscular, and very bright young man with a dark mustache. He had been polite, quiet, and unassuming—like most second lieutenants joining a battle-seasoned outfit. He had gotten married about a month before shipping out for Vietnam.

Sergeant Enedy, also twenty-two, of San Diego, California, had been alive when they put him in the skimmer, but he died en route to the ship. He'd been a short, dumpy, humorous little guy, perpetually unshaven, with dark blond hair and a mustache. He'd also been a tough field Marine, and the squad he'd honchoed through countless patrols and firefights took his death hard.

Lance Corporal McPherson, a nineteen-year-old native of Cannonsburg, Pennsylvania, had been a lean, handsome, talkative kid from a single-parent home. He'd been the 3.5-inch rocket squad leader in Lieutenant Taylor's old platoon, and the cord was pulling tight in Taylor's gut as he folded back Bucky McPherson's poncho shroud. Only four days earlier McPherson had told him that he kind of liked this Marine Corps and that after he got out, he wanted to go to college and come back as an officer. McPherson had been shot up badly and the sun had started to turn him black. The only way Taylor could positively identify him was by his USMC bulldog tattoo.

"Medevacs inbound. . . . Medevacs inbound. . . ."

Lieutenant Taylor saw Captain Williams in the next load. The skipper, lying on a stretcher and waiting his turn on the hangar deck, was arguing with the corpsman kneeling beside him. Per standard operating procedure (SOP), the sailor wanted to put Williams's weapon, ammo, and gear on the growing pile off to one side of the hangar bay. The problem was that although the field corpsmen were trustworthy, their shipboard, noncombat counterparts had a reputation for looting gear and personal items from the anonymous piles of casualty discards.

So, his adrenaline still pumping, Williams shouted, "You're not taking my forty-five!"

"Sir, I've *got* to take your forty-five."

"Like hell! I'll turn my forty-five over to a *Marine*—I'm not going to give it to any fucking Navy man in the rear!"

First Sergeant Martin waved the corpsman away and took the pistol from Williams. The captain, still energized, shouted to Taylor and Martin from his stretcher about how the company had attacked across four hundred meters of open ground and annihilated the enemy dug in before them. "Boy, you should have been there, you should have been there! They weren't going to let anything stand in their way!"

PART TWO PIECEMEALED

By late afternoon on 30 April 1968, the assault by H BLT 2/4 on
Dong Huan was over, but F BLT 2/4 was heavily engaged in Dai
Do. At the same time, a company placed opcon to the battalion,
B/1/3, came under heavy fire in An Lac. The battlefield resembled
an open-topped, bluelined horseshoe some two kilometers in depth
and a klick wide. Framed by one unnamed tributary to the east and
another to the west, and with the Bo Dieu River as the southern
edge, it contained five evacuated hamlets. Dong Huan was situated
at the eastern edge and An Lac at the southern, with Dai Do snug
against the western tributary. Dinh To and Thuong Do sat along the
same creek north of Dai Do. This horseshoe had been an ARVN
TAOR. With the ARVN redeployed to the Dong Ha area, BLT 2/4
had been given the mission of clearing the horseshoe. Lieutenant
Colonel Weise requested via regiment that the 3d Marine Division
approve a boundary change to annex the battle area to the BLT 2/4
TAOR. Weise was adamant ("We wanted to be able to fire and
maneuver with a free hand"), and he commented about the several
hours of delay before the shift was finally ordered: "It shouldn't
have taken that long, but that's the way it was when you were
dealing with the ARVN. On previous joint operations we had tried
to get artillery fire missions and air strikes cleared through ARVN
fire support coordination centers, and you may as well be assuming
a twelve-hour delay for something that should take half an hour.
They were very slow with coordination, and I knew damn well that
I wasn't going to commit any of my troops in their area unless I
had operational control of it."

CHAPTER 4 A TOEHOLD IN DAI DO

Well, looking back, every time we've had a new second lieutenant we've really had a good initiation for him," the seasoned lieutenant had told the new one with matter-of-fact humor when asked about the outfit and the area. The seasoned lieutenant had gone on to say that "some of those guys didn't survive their baptism of fire."

The new lieutenant, 2d Lt. David K. McAdams, thought of that observation as he got his platoon, Foxtrot One, onto the amtracs that had arrived late in the morning of 30 April 1968 to move F BLT 2/4 from Mai Xa Chanh East to Dai Do. McAdams had been in Vietnam for six days and in command of this platoon, his first, for two. His mouth was dry. His adrenaline was pumping. He was not alone. A young Marine from the other platoon boarding the amtracs claimed that his jungle rot was so bad he ought to be medevacked back to the ship. McAdams watched as the seasoned officer who had spoken with him, 1st Lt. James Wainwright, the company exec, told the balking Marine to get his ass in gear. Wainwright was the most experienced officer in the company. He had been a correctional officer in civilian life, and was older than the average lieutenant. His black hair was flecked with gray, and he was a tough, gruff, chunky little man with heavy jowls, a black mustache, and perpetual five o'clock shadow.

Lieutenant Wainwright finally had to use some assertive leadership in the form of the butt end of his M16 and some good, solid thumps to convince the malingerer to get saddled up.

The new Foxtrot 6, Capt. James Butler, a soft-spoken, twenty-five-year-old career officer from Texas, had left Wainwright to get the company mounted up while he took a skimmer over to the BLT CP to get the word on Hotel's developing fight and Foxtrot's planned role. Weise was already moving out aboard the Monitor, so Major Warren briefed Butler. The skipper had relied heavily on Wainwright during his previous three weeks of no-contact command, but he elected to leave him behind this time. Unable to secure permission from regiment for Foxtrot Two to rejoin the company from My Loc, and with the rest of Foxtrot moving out, Butler wanted his seasoned exec with that lone platoon. Butler also sent the scout observer and radioman from his artillery team, his 81mm FO team, and his 60mm mortar section to My Loc. The platoon at My Loc was commanded by a staff sergeant. "Butler felt the staff sergeant was the more experienced and capable platoon commander, and wanted to keep a close eye on us second lieutenants," McAdams recalled.

Captain Butler was a member of the Naval Academy Class of 1965. His father, also an academy graduate, was a retired Marine major general. Butler rejoined his company as it moved past Mai Xa Chanh West atop the BLT's attached amtrac platoon from B/1st Amphibian Tractor Battalion. He had McAdams's Foxtrot One and 2d Lt. Robert Lanham's Foxtrot Three riding atop rather than inside the platoon's four armored, sandbag-topped LVTP5 amtracs because the vehicles' highly volatile gasoline fuel tanks were located directly beneath the troop compartments. Two of the amtracs had a 106mm recoilless rifle mounted on top.

At the BLT CP, Major Warren had described for Butler the plan to have Foxtrot ford the tributary between Bac Vong and Dong Huan, then move on Hotel's west flank and assault southward into Dai Do when the latter hit Dong Huan. Warren noted that they still had no indication of enemy forces in Dai Do.

Foxtrot's amtracs rolled past the two tanks firing into Dong Huan, then easily carried the two platoons across the blueline north of Hotel's fording site. Hotel had been given priority on artillery fires dedicated to BLT 2/4, and Foxtrot was unable to get a smoke screen. This had been a concern of Butler's from the beginning. The map showed nothing but open ground between the stream and the objective. Butler didn't care if any NVA had been spotted in Dai Do or not; he wanted as much smoke as he could get when they crossed the line of departure. His FO, 2d Lt. J. M. Basel, made an initial request for a smoke mission as they pulled out of Mai Xa Chanh West. Before crossing the creek,

Basel tried again, but for "reasons I never fully understood, the artillery was not ready to fire the mission or had more pressing missions. Captain Butler eventually gave the order to commence the attack without smoke cover."

Feeling naked, Foxtrot Company closed on Dai Do from the northeast with its four amtracs spread out in the dry, thigh-high grass. The hedgerows at the edge of the hamlet were in view when, at approximately 1350, the first RPG came out of nowhere toward them. It hit the right rear of the amtrac on which Captain Butler rode with Foxtrot Three. The RPG exploded where the side of the advancing amtrac crowned onto the flat deck. In the sudden flash, Butler saw the radioman from the naval gunfire team spill off the deck, wounded and screaming. There had been five radio operators on the captain's vehicle, and their flock of antennas must have looked like a red flag to the enemy.

Lance Corporal Donald J. Gregg, a nineteen-year-old squad leader, was wounded in his right wrist and leg by fragments from the same RPG. He jumped down into the grass. Other Marines fell off in confusion, and Gregg got them behind the cover of the halted amtrac. Most of the men in his squad had been wounded or otherwise shook up, including one who'd taken some bad hits in his shoulder and upper chest, and their M79 man, whose face was peppered with metal shards and whose glasses had been blown off.

More RPGs exploded around Foxtrot Three's other amtrac. As the Marines dismounted, Pfc. Norman I. Phipps, twenty, of Haysi, Virginia, was killed instantly by shell fragments—the first Foxtrot Marine to die that day.

The NVA also opened fire from Dai Do with automatic weapons. Captain Butler grabbed his radio handset to respond to Hotel 6, who was calling for him to assault Dai Do. Butler was not ready. Although there was a lull in the NVA fire, that first volley of ten to fifteen rocket-propelled grenades had damaged two amtracs and produced multiple casualties. It was a bad start.

Butler was finally able to get some arty going on Dai Do, and the two 106mm recoilless rifles on their amtracs also began pumping HE downrange. Under this cover, the two Foxtrot platoons started forward behind a rolling shock wave of from-the-hip, on-the-move firing. The field was dry and hard—and terribly long and open. The NVA let the

Marines get within a hundred meters of the first hedgerow, then opened up again. The roar of their AK-47s was sudden and shattering. The wall of fire dropped the Marines on the left and right of the already wounded Lance Corporal Gregg. He could hear the crack of bullets all around him as he crawled to the casualty on his right. The Marine had been shot in the leg. It was a traumatic, bone-breaking wound, and Gregg and another Marine held the man to calm him down, then dragged him far enough back toward the amtracs for others to move forward to assist him.

Gregg then crawled back to help the Marine who had fallen on his left. It was LCpl. Kenneth C. Baxter, nineteen, of Council Bluffs, Iowa. He was dead. Baxter, tall and blond, had been a replacement in Gregg's squad and was quiet and hardworking, like most new guys. He had been shot in the head. Gregg managed to pull Baxter off the paddy dike he'd fallen across as another dirt-kicking burst of AK-47 fire hit all around him. Gregg tried to move back with the body but couldn't. He was too exhausted to crawl, and there was too much enemy fire to allow him to get up and drag the man. Gregg finally rolled away and began shooting into the hedgerow. He couldn't see the enemy.

Private First Class John J. Kachmar of Foxtrot Three glimpsed two or three NVA in the hedgerow in the brief instant before they opened fire. It looked as though they were rushing from one position to another. Kachmar, already firing from the waist, swung his M16 to his shoulder, and had just squeezed off a couple of semiaimed rounds when the NVA opened fire in unison. In the sudden roar, Kachmar saw the new guy in his fire team, Frenchy LaRiviera, bounce backward and scream as he was hit. Kachmar crawled to him in the tall, concealing grass. LaRiviera's right arm was smashed below the shoulder, but his system wasn't registering the pain yet. Kachmar applied a battle dressing. It was soaked with blood in moments, so he used an extra belt–suspender strap that he kept in his medical pouch for use as a tourniquet. When he pulled it tight, LaRiviera passed out from the sudden jolt of pain.

Kachmar raised up to drag his buddy back—and was instantly a target. He returned the fire as best he could from the prone. His guess was that the NVA who had shot at him was in a tree at the hamlet's edge. Kachmar couldn't get higher than the two-foot rice stalks hiding them, so after discarding LaRiviera's weapon, ammo, and web gear, he got a grip on the man's flak jacket, got his legs around his body, and shoved off on his back. He pushed along with an upside-down frog kick. LaRiviera shoved weakly with his feet, too. They were making it inch by laborious inch when an AK-47 round ripped into one of the ammo magazines in a bandolier across Kachmar's chest, sending a metal fragment into his nose. It was a minor wound, but it hurt like hell, and Kachmar, exasperated, unslung the M16 he'd been dragging in the dirt around his neck and fired another ineffectual burst into the treetop.

Behind them, Corporal V——heard movement and called for identification. Kachmar shouted back, "It's me, Kachmar! I'm over here with Frenchy! He's hit! I need help!"

Corporal V——hollered back that he would get help. Kachmar lay in the grass under sporadic fire for five minutes before he realized that no one was coming. Feeling exposed and alone, Kachmar pulled LaRiviera toward an M60 firing to their rear. Exhausted and sweat-soaked, he drained most of his last canteen, then poured the rest over LaRiviera's face. The young Marine was going into shock and carrying on nonsense conversations.

They finally made it back to the dike and mound from which the M60 was firing. Several other Marines were there, including their platoon sergeant, Staff Sergeant Chateau, whom Kachmar was wildly relieved to see. Chateau had a corpsman tend to LaRiviera, then told Kachmar, "You're dead."

"What are you talkin' about?"

"V——said you and Frenchy were dead," replied the noncom. He sounded disgusted.

Maybe Corporal V——really thought Kachmar had been killed. Maybe not. Maybe the idea of leading a team back for Kachmar and LaRiviera had completely unnerved him. It didn't matter to Kachmar, who was boiling. "I'm going to kill the motherfucker," he shouted.

"Nah, nah, nah," Chateau replied. "V——'s been hit, he's in one of the amtracs."

Kachmar was still at a fever pitch. He saw an M79 grenade launcher lying unattended nearby and asked who it belonged to. Chateau asked why, and Kachmar answered, "Because I'm going to fire up that gook who was trying to kill me and Frenchy! That cocksucker wanted to kill me!" They were still taking fire from Dai Do. Kachmar didn't care.

He went up on the mound to get a clear view, and fired his first M79 round at the tree at the edge of the hamlet. It was a long shot, and the round fell short. Kachmar lobbed his next round at nearly maximum elevation from a kneeling position. Bingo. He fired two more rounds before Chateau got ahold of the back of his web belt and hauled him off the mound. "Stop it," the platoon sergeant yelled, "you're going to get killed! Enough!"

While Foxtrot Three's assault on the left flank stalled, Lieutenant McAdams and Foxtrot One on the right flank were clear of the cross fire and able to conduct a fire-and-maneuver assault all the way to the edge of Dai Do.

It was Lieutenant McAdams's baptism of fire. The assault was a matter of jumping up and running, then falling down and doing it again. Sweat-slick and worn out, McAdams, a large, pithy, slow-talking farm boy from Gaston, Oregon, was basically going it alone: Both his platoon sergeant and right guide were on light duty because of jungle rot, and had been left at Mai Xa Chanh East. As a result, McAdams had difficulty maintaining contact with and controlling his platoon during the long maneuver. Nevertheless, he later wrote that the attack "was a classic frontal assault out of The Basic School. We maneuvered by fire team rushes until the artillery got hot. We then crawled in to get closer. Then, when the artillery was lifted, we went in shooting. Fortunately, we were not receiving heavy fire."

At about 1505, Lieutenant McAdams went through the first hedgerow and over the first slit trench, where several NVA with weapons were huddled, apparently dead. The Marines ensured that they were by firing into the bodies as they rushed past, not stopping until they reached the next trench line some twenty meters into the hamlet. McAdams jumped into it at the urging of his veteran radioman, Cpl. Richard J. "Mongoose" Tyrell, who was very impressed by his gutsy new lieutenant. Tyrell wanted McAdams to understand, though, that his role was to be to the rear of his platoon, controlling all the elements, rather than leading the charge. McAdams and Tyrell could count only a dozen Marines still with them, including four who'd gotten mixed in from the other platoon. McAdams discovered then that two of his men had been hit in the legs. Their trench was bordered by vegetation and seemed to be one side of a complete square with a burial mound in the middle of it. They were in the hamlet's cemetery.

Lieutenant McAdams and Tyrell could see two NVA standing in the chest-deep trench across from them. They were about thirty meters away, and seemed to be looking around for the Marines who had made it into their lines. When McAdams called up his M79 man, the NVA took notice and disappeared. The grenadier's subsequent shot landed reasonably close to where McAdams pointed, but they figured the NVA had gotten away. Butler and Basel had meanwhile organized some arty to protect McAdams's little position. The salvos were so close that McAdams, afraid he was going to get hit by friendly fire, made adjustments from the bottom of his trench.

The barrage did its job; no NVA closed with the Marines.

Captain Butler, who was terribly frustrated at not having a reserve platoon to exploit McAdams's toehold in northeastern Dai Do, and the rest of Foxtrot Company were being plastered with 130mm NVA artillery fire in the open fields where they lay pinned down. Muffled kettledrumming signaled each five-gun cannonade from the foothills on the North Vietnamese side of the DMZ. The salvos were terrifying in their accuracy. They weren't doing much physical damage, however, because the NVA did not use variable time fuses capable of causing airbursts. Lieutenant Basel later wrote that "we were picking fragments from our flak jackets," but what "saved us was they appeared to adjust with time fuses and fire for effect with quick fuses. If they had hit us with time or VT fuses, I doubt that many of us would have seen another day. As it was, the quick fuses buried in the sand and much of the lethal effect was lost."

"Foxtrot was hanging by the skin of its teeth," Lieutenant Colonel Weise later wrote, "and we were pounding enemy positions with artillery, naval gunfire, and organic weapons. . . . Foxtrot Company needed assistance. I ordered it to hold on, hoping to reinforce with Golf Company." Weise's view of the flat, smoky battlefield was from the Navy Monitor steaming back and forth on the Bo Dieu River in an effort to avoid enemy fire. Lieutenant Kelley and his half-dozen crewmen, all wearing helmets and flak jackets, returned the fire with .30- and .50-caliber machine guns and a pair of 20mm cannons. Weise and Big John Malnar manned the deck-mounted 81mm mortar in support of the ground attacks. They also lobbed rounds at targets of opportunity, namely NVA soldiers who appeared as olive-drab dots in the distance as they moved across an open area. It was impossible to tell if the NVA were retreating or reinforcing, but Weise could see that his rounds were landing where intended. It was impossible to tell what damage they inflicted.

Weise was sure of at least one direct hit by the Monitor. When the NVA artillery cranked up, he brought his binoculars up for another look at two Vietnamese sampans about two hundred meters upriver. The people on board wore fisherman's garb, and the southern shore of the Bo Dieu was, in fact, populated. But Weise did not think they were villagers. Presumably, civilians would have headed for shore when the first round hit the water. Weise suspected that they were NVA artillery spotters with a radio aboard one of the sampans. Taking no chances, he instructed the gunboat commander to swing his 20mm cannons around. The rapidly firing guns blew the sampans apart.

It was at about that time (1530) that Colonel Hull boarded the Monitor. Weise wrote that although "the enemy had been firing at everything that moved on the water," the regimental commander "seemed unimpressed by his own daring dash up the river or by the artillery and mortar rounds exploding around us. He had already been ashore to visit Hotel Company."[1]

Colonel Hull and Lieutenant Colonel Weise discussed the situation. Hotel Company had just pushed a large number of NVA out of Dong Huan, and Foxtrot was pinned down by another large force in Dai Do. There were also an undetermined number of NVA in An Lac. Though Hull had given Weise permission to reinforce with Golf Company, helicopters had not yet been made available to move it from Lam Xuan West. Echo Company was opcon to division at the Dong Ha bridge, a situation Weise hoped Hull could remedy. "I don't have any more troops," he told the regimental commander. "I want to get Echo Company."

"I'm working on Echo Company," replied Hull. "Division said they would probably release them, but they weren't sure about it."

1. Hull was a three-war Marine. He earned the Silver Star as a first lieutenant in 1944 with the Chinese Communists, wreaking clandestine havoc on Japanese garrisons in occupied China. Hull got the Navy Cross and Purple Heart in 1950 as the skipper of D/2/7, during a savage take-the-hill battle at the Chosin Reservoir. Hull fought his regiment with the same conventional, hit-'em-hard style. One of his staff officers said, "Hull gave the impression of being a gruff-type commander, but he was really a person who listened as well as growled."

Weise then made his first personal request for what Major Warren had been raising cain about via radio: "You know, we could *really* use some tanks and Ontos. We could also use a hell of a lot more close air support."

Hull said he would work on it. In the meantime, the pressure was on to reopen the river. He told Weise that he was giving him opcon of B/1/3, commanded by 1st Lt. George C. Norris, which was currently in the battalion base camp at Giao Liem on the populated southern side of the Cua Viet River. Giao Liem was three klicks due south of Mai Xa Chanh West, along a Cua Viet tributary. Like BLT 2/4, 1/3 was resupplied by Mike boats from Camp Kistler. A platoon of amtracs was to be made available to carry B/1/3 up the Bo Dieu to the western edge of An Lac, which was on the north shore about seven hundred meters southeast of Dai Do. That would put B/1/3 in a position to assault Dai Do from the south after clearing An Lac, thus taking the pressure off Foxtrot's pinned-down attack on the northern side.

Lieutenant Norris, marching to a point outside Giao Liem to meet the amtracs, came up on the BLT 2/4 net at about 1550. Weise had worked with Norris during Operation Task Force Kilo (29 March– 2 April 1968), a multibattalion push to the DMZ, and had been "very much impressed with the way he handled himself. He was a good combat leader and he ran a damn good company." Weise briefed Norris via radio, and by 1625 the Monitor had pulled several hundred meters downriver from An Lac so it could support the landing by fire. Weise described the scene as follows:

Covered by a heavy bombardment of artillery and naval gunfire, Bravo Company, atop the amtracs, crossed the river in a classic amphibious assault wave. As the assault wave neared the northern bank, the enemy opened up. . . . The scene reminded me of films of the Iwo Jima assault in World War II. The direct-fire weapons of the River Assault Group boats gave excellent support as Bravo Company dismounted and fought its way over the river banks.

Bravo 1/3 was pinned down in An Lac and reporting heavy casualties when Hull got back in his skimmer to return to his Camp Kistler CP. Weise thought the appearance of yet another NVA unit had made a believer out of Hull, and he stressed once more to him, "We're in a

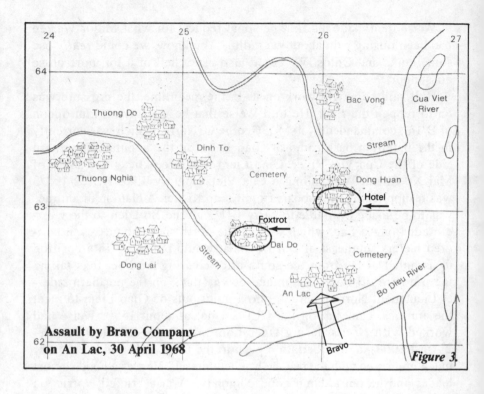

Assault by Bravo Company on An Lac, 30 April 1968

Figure 3.

world of hurt here. There's a whole lot of bad guys and not many of us good guys."

The regimental commander, however, did not release the Foxtrot platoon at My Loc, nor did he commit additional elements from 1/3 at Giao Liem. The latter option would have been judicious considering the shot-up condition of 1/3's orphan company, Bravo, and the fact that things were quiet in the Giao Liem TAOR. That Hull did not commit these elements indicated his wait-and-see frame of mind. Hull could not be sure that Weise was not simply up against three NVA platoons or companies in the three fortified hamlets. With only two infantry battalions, 1/3 and BLT 2/4, currently opcon to his regiment, Hull had reason to be prudent with his resources. BLT 2/4's action in the horseshoe was already drawing resources away from the Jones Creek approach to the Cua Viet River, and Hull was not willing to invest the bulk of 1/3 in a battle he was not yet convinced would be the major one.

Weise had a real three-ring circus on his hands in Dong Huan, An Lac, and Dai Do, and every combat instinct he had told him to pile on with everything available. He was correct, but so was Colonel Hull. The NVA would shortly exploit the growing holes along Jones Creek, just as he feared. Hull would be forced to divide his resources between two simultaneous, large-scale enemy actions.

It was galling to the Marines to be on the defensive and literally outnumbered. Major Warren, interviewed three weeks after the event by the division historical section, put it this way:

> One of the things that hampered the BLT commander was the lack of enough people at the right time. . . . He only had one and two-thirds companies to play with at the very beginning. . . . Committing the organization piecemeal has always been a very bad tactic. It is one that the BLT commander did not desire in this case, and repeatedly made requests to commit all of his unit at one time, or at least in sufficient strength to continue pressing the attack forward once he gained some initial success.

There were other problems. The BLT's attached tank platoon fielded only two tanks, and requests for additional tanks went unanswered by division. The BLT's attached antitank platoon—which had five tracked Ontos vehicles, each equipped with six 106mm recoilless rifles—had previously been chopped to another command, and division failed to act on requests to return it. "Too bad," Weise wrote, "because the Cua Viet area was ideal country for tracked vehicles and we sorely missed the firepower of the thirty 106mm recoilless rifles of those light, highly mobile vehicles." The BLT's attached 105mm artillery battery at the DHCB had likewise been chopped to the division's artillery regiment. The battery was thus firing missions for other units within range of the DHCB, and the result, Warren would angrily report, was an "inefficiency of general support artillery in situations where continuous dedicated fire support is crucial to success on the battlefield."

BLT 2/4 was not totally stripped of support, however. Weise could count on naval gunfire from the five-inch guns on the destroyers offshore, and from the eight-inchers of a cruiser. Weise wrote that "the ships loved to shoot," and that their fire was "accurate, reliable, and, best of all, available when needed."

Weise could also count on his attached 4.2-inch mortar battery, W/3/12, commanded by Capt. F. X. Conlon, which was located with the BLT CP at Mai Xa Chanh West. The four-deuce mortar was a highly lethal and accurate weapon, and Whiskey Battery did a superb job. The battery exec, 1st Lt. W. A. Sadler, was aboard ship when the battle began because his tour was actually over, but as he later wrote, he "scrounged some gear and hopped on an inbound helicopter. We flew just above the surface of the river. When I reached the CP, I ran straight to the battery position." The four-deuces had been in action from the beginning, "firing three or four missions at the same time," Sadler wrote. "It sounded like one continuous roar. We fired everything we had and were resupplied by helo in the middle of our position. Our Marines fired their mortars until the base plates had sunk out of sight. The guns were out of action for a very few minutes, just long enough to pull the base plates out and reset them."

What was needed most was close air support, which was not provided in anywhere near the quantity necessary. "Somebody screwed up," Weise said later. "They should have assigned us priority. I was very, very unhappy then, and I'm still very unhappy about it."

The big picture offered a partial explanation. Major General Tompkins, whose division had few reserves to spare, was being forced to feel two pulses at once: Simultaneous with BLT 2/4's engagement was the ongoing Battle of Thon Cam Vu (29 April–1 May 1968) in the 9th Marines' TAOR. Thon Cam Vu was only six kilometers west of Dai Do. The battle there involved the tanks of Task Force Robbie, the division reserve, and the infantrymen of 3/9. The latter lost 29 KIA and 115 WIA while reducing an NVA battalion. A body count of 66 was claimed by 3/9, but every jet and artillery round committed to Thon Cam Vu was one less for BLT 2/4. The 3d Marine Division was stretched to the point where its commanding general had to rob Peter to pay Paul. In effect, no echelon from battalion to regiment to division was fighting the way it wanted to. The situation produced a lot of hard feelings among the commanders involved.

The Marines of B/1/3, pinned down on the beach at An Lac, had most recently been engaged in a spectacular melee at Charlie 4, located where the DMZ met the South China Sea. It had been an intramural event. Charlie 4 was a seemingly impregnable strongpoint, and since Bravo Company was not required to stand watch during its first night there after weeks in the field, attitudes became relaxed. Lieutenant Norris ended up in a boozy game of blackjack in his bunker. When their big first sergeant turned into a nasty drunk and would not listen to the gunnery sergeant's gentle suggestions to retire, the wiry little gunny jumped up and sucker-punched the topkick, knocking him cold. Norris was tight with the gunny but thought it only fair to jump him in response, and the fist-swinging brawl piled outside. It was then that a radioman with the company headquarters jumped atop the bunker with a grenade. He looked crazy—as though he was going to kill someone. It wasn't funny anymore.

Lieutenant Norris succeeded in talking the man down before he pulled the pin. Norris and his quick-fisted gunny, GySgt. Norman J. Doucette, realized then that the radioman was stoned. They were shocked. The use of marijuana by Marines was, in fact, a relatively new phenomenon; although generally smoked only in base camps, strongpoints, or village defensive positions, its presence explained to Doucette why he'd been finding glassy-eyed grunts on night watch during the past few months. If he had understood then what he later learned, he would have administered more than a mere kick in the rear and a harsh word or two.

Norris and Doucette gathered Bravo Company's hung-over Marines the next morning to read them the riot act. Norris barked at the formation, "If any of you guys want to take me out with a grenade—*do it now.*"

Lieutenant Norris, a twenty-six year old from Des Moines, Iowa, was a big man and, sporting a black mustache and a red bandanna around his neck, he was nothing if not colorful. His call sign was King George. Norris had been on line with Bravo Company for eleven months as a platoon commander, executive officer, and company commander. He was not a career man, but he had a lot of pride in the Marine Corps, and he had resisted reassignment to battalion. He had signed on to see the war, not sit it out in the rear.

"We had a great company commander, and we were elite compared to other units," recalled LCpl. Doug Urban, who spent eighteen months in Bravo Company. "We were strictly business—very, very professional— and the guys were incredibly tight."

Nevertheless, Lieutenant Norris's landing with B/1/3 in An Lac was a complete disaster. A particularly confusing fog of war dominated the event. When the amtracs churned across the Bo Dieu River toward An Lac, the Bravo Company Marines sitting on top were completely shocked by the wall of NVA fire that greeted them. It was the first indication that the NVA occupied An Lac in strength. Although Weise later wrote that the "primary concern at the time was to clear An Lac and open the river," and that Bravo was to continue its attack to relieve Foxtrot "only after An Lac was cleared," the Bravo Marines had not understood their mission that way. They had been under the impression that An Lac was relatively secure, that it was only a jumping-off point for the urgent business of reinforcing Foxtrot.

Bravo Company's landing was an unanticipated, stumbled-into meat grinder, not the "classic amphibious assault" of Weise's description. Bravo Company would also take exception to the statement that it had been covered "by a heavy bombardment of artillery and naval gunfire." According to Gunny Doucette, "There was nothing—*nothing*." No smoke rounds were fired to obscure Bravo's approach, so the NVA in An Lac had a shooting-gallery view of the landing. Their fire geysered the water around the low-riding amtracs as they trundled in with .30-caliber machine guns blazing. As soon as the amtracs hit sand again, the Marines dismounted and sought cover behind burial mounds on the western fringe of An Lac. There they returned the fire of the invisible, entrenched enemy to the east.

The casualties piled up quickly. Lieutenant Norris was hit a few steps onto the beach, then hit again as several Marines tried to move him back in a poncho. King George was dead.

Second Lieutenant John M. Odell, a platoon commander, was KIA.

Sergeant Harold J. Vierheller, a platoon sergeant, was KIA.

Altogether, seven Bravo Company Marines were killed and fourteen were seriously wounded in perhaps the first five minutes of chaos on the fire-swept beach. Two of the amtracs were hit by RPGs and began exploding. "It was total chaos," recalled Lance Corporal Urban. Bravo Company, caught off guard and decapitated before anyone had gotten anything organized, bogged down in the enemy's killing zone. "Everybody just freaked," said Urban. "We weren't a company anymore. We were just a bunch of people lying on the ground trying to get a handle on this thing. Anything above two feet was dead."

Because Gunny Doucette did not know that King George was dead, he did not understand the breakdown on the beach. We're getting the living shit kicked out of us, he thought, and my goddamn Marines are hiding behind all these goddamn graves. What the hell's going on here?

Gunny Doucette, who was never without a short stubby cigar, had fought in Korea and had been with B/1/3 in Vietnam for nearly a year. He may have been an idiosyncratic, hardassed lifer, but he was also a tough, dedicated Marine who led by example. He ranged the beachhead at An Lac with utter abandon, waving his favorite walking stick—a golf putter—above his head as he tried to get the company organized. He reached the position of a redheaded sergeant who had made it with a squad or two around the northern fringe of An Lac and was firing south into the thicketed hamlet. Doucette wanted them to rush the NVA from that flank. "We got to get in the tree line—we gotta secure that fuckin' tree line!" he shouted.

The redheaded sergeant had plenty of reason to balk, and he did. He said that by assaulting from the north, they would charge right into the Marine fire coming from the burial mounds to the west.

"I don't give a shit!" screamed Doucette. "We'll maybe lose a couple of men—but we got to take the fuckin' tree line 'cause that's where the fire's comin' from!"

Not one Marine moved. Gunny Doucette cursed the redheaded sergeant in the heat of the moment as a goddamned yellow bastard. A Marine ran to him then to report that Lieutenant Norris had been killed. Doucette could not believe it, and he started back down the line to find the skipper, convinced that he might still be alive. King George was bulletproof.

Gunny Doucette never made it to Norris. He stooped over a prostrate, seemingly wounded man who was lying in the open. The gunny's left shoulder was to the enemy tree line. He stopped for only a moment to check the casualty, who turned out to be a dead young Marine, but in that instant he became a stationary target. Before Doucette could push on, an NVA marksman dropped him with a head shot. There was a sudden white flash in his face and the simultaneous sensation of what felt like a baseball bat connecting with his left cheekbone. The round exited through his right cheek, taking most of his tongue with it and shattering most of his teeth as it knocked him down. It was an excruciating, blood-pumping wound. Doucette rolled onto his left shoulder so his back was to the enemy soldier who had nailed him, and he froze in instant recognition of his foe's marksmanship. If I move again, I've had it, he thought.

Gunny Doucette lay there helplessly, looking at his grunts behind the burial mounds. They looked back at him, but not one of his fellow Marines came to his aid. Finally, one gutsy kid, a Filipino-American Navy corpsman, crawled out and secured a battle dressing to each of his shot-open cheeks. That son of a whore, Doucette thought with great affection as the corpsman bounded off to aid their other wounded. Doucette's wound kept bleeding, though. His utilities clung wetly to him. The sand around him was red. Doucette, convinced he was bleeding to death, prayed like he had never prayed before. It was all he could do. No one else was going to get him out of there. Amid the shouting and gunfire, nothing really seemed to be happening. Not a goddamn thing, Doucette thought, and he cursed the bastards who had gotten them into this, and the other bastards who didn't pick up the ball and attack and take the initiative. Somebody went and left us lying right here to just get slaughtered, he thought.

CHAPTER 5 NO FREE RIDES

When some close air support became available, Captain Butler of Foxtrot Company, pinned down outside Dai Do, used it to support Lieutenant McAdams, who had a toehold in the hamlet itself. McAdams brought the napalm to within forty meters of his slit trench, then said, "Goddamn, it's hot here—don't get it any closer!"

Captain Butler was working with both USMC and USAF Phantoms, and this—his first experience with the Air Force—proved that the pilots were all brave in the face of the NVA fire but that doctrine made the Marine aviators more effective. The Marines ran their strikes down the length of the NVA entrenchments and thus parallel to the opposite Marine lines, which placed them at maximum exposure to ground fire but gave them the broadest opportunity to hit their targets. The Air Force pilots came in from behind to flash for a moment over friendly lines and then for a moment over the enemy. This minimized their exposure to ground fire but allowed them to hit only a small segment of the enemy line—and increased the risk of friendly casualties. Butler complained about this to Weise, and later commented that "the Air Force put twenty-millimeter casings right down our shirts. It was new to us and a little bit disconcerting—we didn't know who they were shooting at."

Captain Butler's command group was under enough fire as it was. Lieutenant Basel, the FO, two weeks in-country and in his first action, was shot in the back of the arm. Basel refused medevac until the next morning. Once the bullet was removed by the battalion surgeon, he rushed to rejoin the still-embattled company.

Staff Sergeant Pedro P. Balignasay, the acting gunny, was another tough nut. Butler told him to move back to the amtracs and bring one forward to evacuate their wounded. When Butler later turned at the sound of an approaching amtrac, he spotted Balignasay walking in front to guide it in. The amtrac was a big target, but the gunny acted as if he were invincible.

Four hours into the assault, Lieutenant Colonel Weise called Butler to get a sitrep on how many people he had left. Butler reported that he was down to twenty-six effectives. Without a reserve platoon to renew the attack, Butler recommended that Foxtrot disengage because "with our casualties, even if we get in there, they'll counterattack and they'll kick our butts out of there. If I get in there, I can't hold it."

Weise agreed. He ordered Foxtrot to withdraw east to Dong Huan and establish a joint perimeter with Hotel Company. "If you encounter a lot of resistance," Butler later explained, "there's no sense in throwing good lives away just to take that position. That's what supporting arms are for."

It took two hours to break contact. Captain Butler used the .30-caliber machine guns on his four amtracs to cover McAdams's pickup squad in Dai Do, then he had the Phantoms go in hot while that little group pulled back. "It was so close we could feel the air drawn from us by the napalm, but it was effective and got us out of there," recalled Tyrell, the platoon radioman. To keep the NVA down, the Phantoms also conducted dummy passes that were even closer to the Marines. Butler brought in the artillery as his platoon commanders, Lieutenants McAdams and Lanham, got their troops backpedaling across the open paddies. The men were exhausted and a little demoralized, and events began to unravel as darkness approached. "It was disorganized. There had been a melee out there," Butler conceded. "The NVA had a good opportunity to really clean our clocks, but they didn't seize upon it."

Foxtrot straggled into Dong Huan, where Hotel Company had been too busy skimmer-boating its own casualties out to thoroughly clear the whole hamlet. Foxtrot was securing the section that would become its night position, when Corporal Tyrell noticed a sandaled foot under some hay in the deserted animal pen beside a hootch. He could see a human form under the hay, and imagined that a wounded NVA had crawled under there to die. Before bending down to search the body for anything of intel value, Tyrell gave the foot a good kick to ensure that the man was really dead. Before his eyes the NVA sat up amidst the hay, his right hand on the stock of his AK-47 and his left grasping the pistol grip and trigger. Tyrell shot first—one instinctive, unthinking squeeze of the trigger—and then his M16 jammed. He grabbed a .45 from a corpsman behind him, and wheeled back to empty the pistol at point-blank range.

Private First Class Kachmar saw one of the new guys urinating into the open mouth of a dead NVA. Kachmar shoved the man away from the corpse and shouted, "You fucking asshole, what're ya doin' that for?" The new guy just looked at him blankly.

Continuing on, Kachmar and the two Marines left in his fire team were passing an NVA entrenchment when Kachmar suddenly saw something white move inside it. The white was the bandage on a wounded enemy soldier who was going for his weapon, and in that millisecond of recognition Kachmar, with his M16 still at his waist, fired two or three rounds into the man from ten feet away. Kachmar and his two stunned buddies pulled away the overhead cover of sandbags and grass and discovered both an AK-47 and a Czech first-aid kit beside the body. "I don't think he could have actually even fired the weapon," Kachmar reflected, "but I didn't know that at the time. I just shot. I just fired. It was pure combat instinct. I probably wouldn't have done it if I had thought about it, but to think about it would have been foolish."

Bravo Company finally secured the embattled beachhead at An Lac, despite the loss of their company commander, thanks to a handful of Marines such as SSgt. Robert G. Robinson, a deep-voiced black platoon sergeant who was subsequently awarded the Silver Star for his actions there. When his radioman took an AK-47 round in his PRC-25, Robinson cut the shoulder straps and took the radio himself as he told the Marine to find cover. Robinson pulled down the telltale antenna and was calling for fire support when an AK-47 round hit his left shoulder and lodged in his flak jacket. He scooped up a handful of mud to cover the bloody rip. With sand-encrusted M16s jamming up, he collected what clean weapons and ammo he could find among their casualties, then distributed what he had gathered. By that time he could see puffs of smoke from where RPGs were being launched about two hundred meters away, and he could discern that most of the

AK-47 fire on his platoon was coming from entrenchments beneath a small archway and gate in the hamlet. The fire support he was able to bring to bear silenced those positions.

Bravo Company also managed to seize part of An Lac about an hour before dark. At this point, Weise later wrote that he "ordered the company (now confused, disorganized, and with only one officer left) to halt, reorganize, form a defensive perimeter in the western half of the hamlet, evacuate casualties, and carry out resupply."

The only remaining officer was 2d Lt. Thomas R. Keppen, who was brand-new and floundering. Weise, trying to get the young lieutenant calmed down over the radio, sent Muter's eighteen-man reconnaissance platoon down to reinforce Bravo Company.

Lieutenant Muter organized the evacuation of the wounded, and face-shot, tooth-shattered Gunny Doucette, weak from loss of blood but thanking the Lord, was finally loaded in an amtrac leaving the beachhead. When the ramp went down at Mai Xa Chanh West, Doucette, who didn't know where he was, was helped onto a Sea Horse. Medevacked to the DHCB, he ended up lying on a stretcher in a hallway at the base aid station. His turn for medical attention did not come; there were too many emergencies ahead of him. So his litter was carried to the airfield for a helo ride farther down the medevac chain to Da Nang. He was by then an unmoving form on his stretcher, with a haphazardly bandaged, ripped-open face. He overheard one of the crewmen remark that he must be dead. Doucette looked up bitterly at the man and gave him the finger.

Lieutenant Colonel Weise was furious. He had ordered Foxtrot to break contact in Dai Do based on Captain Butler's report that his two-platoon company had taken heavy casualties and was down to twenty-six effectives. At least that was what Butler believed after radio conversations with his two pinned-down platoon commanders. After getting reorganized and counting heads in Dong Huan, Butler had to call Weise to report that his casualties were less than reported. He actually had fifty-five effectives. It was a big difference, and Weise later said, "It was then that I realized Butler had lost control of his troops. He was fairly calm, but I got the impression he was kind of lost. He just didn't have a handle on things, just didn't know what he was supposed to be doing."

Weise was also upset because a dead Marine had been left behind in the confusion of Foxtrot's withdrawal. He wondered if the best option would be to relieve Butler in the morning. "Foxtrot didn't withdraw in a good tactical group," Weise observed. "There was a lack of control and organization, and Butler's troops pulled back individually. We found some of them straggling along the river bank during the night. In fact, the Navy thought they were enemy and asked for permission to fire. I wanted to be sure they were NVA. I looked through the starlight scope and saw that they were clearly Marines. Some Marines actually forded that little stream and walked all the way back to Mai Xa Chanh West."

In the end, Weise decided to give Butler another chance. It was, after all, his first engagement as a company commander after two months of staff duty with the battalion. Weise instead chewed Butler out over the radio for reporting too many casualties. He told him to get his act together and know where his troops were, and to make sure they were resupplied with ammo and ready to go. "We need you tomorrow," Weise told Butler. "I want you to be ready to fight. I don't want you straggling around."

Captain Butler's performance during the remainder of the Battle of Dai Do continued to be unsatisfactory, in Weise's opinion. Afterward, he zeroed out the young academy graduate's career with a negative fitness report. Most of Butler's peers in BLT 2/4 considered that best for all concerned. "Butler was in way over his head," remarked a fellow captain. "He wasn't stupid, but to lead Marines in combat you better have the balls of a pissed-off gorilla. He was too nice a guy. There's a time to pat somebody on the back and a time to kick some butt. I don't think he ever figured out when was the time to do which. You have leaders, followers, and managers, and Butler was a manager."

Another company commander said that Captain Butler was "just a nice, decent, mild-mannered Clark Kent who never turned into Superman. Even at the point of life or death, he never had that particular spark."

Nevertheless, Foxtrot Company's Marines generally thought well of their urbane and amiable skipper. An acting platoon sergeant on his second tour called Butler a "helluva guy and one of the best officers I ever had." The Marine who served as the captain's radioman after Dai Do spoke of Butler's "intelligence, courage, and quiet confidence." Considering that Foxtrot was required to attack Dai Do with no reserve platoon, no mortar section, and no prep fires ("It was clear that we couldn't generate the combat power to get into the village," wrote the company's artillery FO), one officer commented that Weise's rebuke of the inexperienced Butler at the end of day one revealed "a lack of empathy, a failure to realize what he really asked that company to do when he threw it into the heart of the enemy position early in the fight."

With the sun hanging on the horizon, Foxtrot and Hotel Companies registered artillery and mortar concentrations around their freshly dug fighting positions in Dong Huan, as did B/1/3 and Muter's recon platoon in half-secured An Lac. Lieutenant Colonel Weise, still coordinating from the Monitor on the Bo Dieu, did not anticipate that taking the rest of An Lac would be a problem. The NVA had broken contact entirely with Bravo Company, and would presumably use the cover of darkness to get out of the hamlet. Dai Do was now the main concern. To secure the position, Weise planned to use the only uncommitted company available to him, Vargas's Golf, which was presently in its patrol base at Lam Xuan West. Helicopters were being organized to lift the company to the BLT CP at Mai Xa Chanh West. Weise wrote that from there he "hoped to move Golf Company to An Lac by Navy LCM-8 landing craft during darkness, to land at night behind Bravo Company, and launch a predawn attack on Dai Do."

Captain Vargas was a combat leader in whom Weise placed absolute confidence. Vargas had originally commanded Golf Company through the Tet Offensive and the beginning of the Cua Viet campaign. He had been automatically reassigned to battalion after his second wound at Vinh Quan Thuong, but had bent the rules as soon as he'd learned about his replacement's medevac two days earlier:

Colonel Weise was listening to the radio also. He didn't even have a chance to say, "You want your company back?" I was already packing my gear and moving out. Weise knew where I was going. He said, "Go on, go back," and I left the CP in about five minutes in one of those recon speed boats. It was a quick run up Jones Creek to Lam Xuan West. When the boat engine went off, hell, I already had a bunch of young troopers coming over to greet me, saying, "We're glad to have you back."

At 1737, Major Warren radioed Captain Vargas to prepare to helilift back to Mai Xa Chanh West. Within two hours, twin-bladed CH-46 Sea Knights, which could carry a platoon apiece, were approaching Lam Xuan West. A clearing in the rubbled hamlet served as the landing zone, and Lieutenant Morgan of Golf Two, along with his radioman and one squad, went up the lowered back ramp of the first Sea Knight that landed. Before anyone else could board, the helicopter abruptly began to lift off. Morgan could hear nothing over the engines, but he was stunned to see enemy tracers passing by the porthole windows of the ascending helicopter.

The NVA also began shelling the landing zone. Captain Vargas aborted the mission, then turned to Staff Sergeant Del Rio, his acting gunny, to say, "No free ride today. We have to walk back." Following the contours of Jones Creek, it was a three-kilometer hump from Lam Xuan West to Mai Xa Chanh West. Golf Company ran out of daylight very quickly. With the artillery and mortar fire continuing to crash in, the hot night air was heavy with smoke and the smell of gunpowder as the Marines began moving out. Although the men had discarded everything but their fighting gear, Del Rio had not gone far when he suddenly doubled back to the LZ—where he had left the waterproof olive-drab bag in which he kept his personal gear. He removed from it a small, framed photograph of his wife and three children, then started back up the column to rejoin the captain. He would keep that photograph forever.

The enemy had strategically placed their forward observers. The NVA artillery, having already fired more than a hundred rounds into Lam Xuan West, presently shifted onto Lieutenant Ferland and Golf Three as the platoon led the company down the western bank of Jones Creek. Between the shouting, commotion, and explosions, the Marines could no longer hear the boom of the guns in North Vietnam. They could not anticipate the next volley. Staff Sergeant Del Rio, along with Sgt. Robert J. Colasanti, the platoon sergeant, had to haul more than one flattened, shook-up Marine back to his feet and shout at him to keep moving, keep moving, keep moving. The artillery fire, accurate and nerve-shaking though it was, was not lethal because the shells burrowed several feet into the soft, wet earth along the creek before exploding.

"The troops were on the verge of panic," said Lieutenant Ferland, "but Captain Vargas kept good control of the situation."

Vargas and Del Rio spent most of their time with Golf Three on point, and Golf Two, which came next in the column. Lieutenant Deichman, the exec, had positioned himself at the tail end with Golf One to ensure that no one was left behind. Their artillery spotter, Lieutenant Acly, had been overlooked, however, and apparently was the last Marine to straggle out of Lam Xuan West. Acly had rolled behind an earthen berm near the LZ when the patrol base first came under fire. In the confusion, he missed the order to move out. All he knew was that when he looked back over his shoulder to check up on his FO team, it was gone. Everyone was gone. There was a moment of hard-breathing, sweat-soaked panic before Acly got his senses back, then he crawled south through the smoke-shrouded brush, under mortar fire the whole time. No one answered his shouts. Finally, after two hundred meters or so, he heard whispers and saw four equally lost Marines crouched in the dark. Acly called out to identify himself. He took a long drink from his canteen, then the five of them moved out to rejoin the column. Running and diving and shoving off again in the loose, sandy soil, they crossed hundreds of lonely meters before finally catching up with the bunched-up tail of the column.

"People seemed to be operating on their own," Acly said later. "Nothing seemed to be very organized." Massive amounts of illumination went up at intervals over the Dai Do battlefield some six klicks to the southwest. Not understanding the circumstances over there, the Golf Company Marines were infuriated that their own artillery was making them a better target. "It was like broad daylight," said Acly. "It freaked everybody out because we were totally illuminated."

Captain Vargas had an artillery shell explode ten feet from him. It was another subsurface, lifesaving explosion, but the concussion knocked Vargas into the shallows of Jones Creek. Several young Marines helped him up. Although he saw that his right trouser leg was torn—he had shell fragments in his knee and calf—he felt no pain through the adrenaline rush. Likewise, Staff Sergeant Del Rio, who had been knocked down, splattered with mud, and otherwise scared to death by several near misses, didn't realize he'd taken a piece of metal in his right leg until after they reached Mai Xa Chanh West. Lieutenant Ferland had several fragment wounds in his right arm and lower right leg, and his platoon sergeant, Colasanti, was also stung but unfazed. More than twenty Marines had

Lt. Col. William Weise, commander of BLT 2/4 during the Battle of Dai Do. *Courtesy W. Weise.*

Maj. G. F. "Fritz" Warren, BLT 2/4 S3, conducts a briefing in the unit's Mai Xa Chanh West command post. *Courtesy W. Weise.*

Lt. Col. Weise (left) and Maj. Warren celebrate Weise's thirty-ninth birthday at Mai Xa Chanh West on 10 March 1968. *Courtesy W. Weise.*

Sgt. Maj. John M. "Big John" Malnar, the BLT 2/4 sergeant major, during a moment of casual reflection at Mai Xa Chanh West. *Courtesy W. Weise.*

1st Lt. Judson D. Hilton (without hat), BLT 2/4's forward air controller at Dai Do, poses with his tactical air control party at Subic Bay, Philippines, in January 1968. *Courtesy J. D. Hilton.*

Capt. James L. Williams led H BLT 2/4 during the initial assault on Dong Huan on 30 April 1968. He was seriously wounded by an enemy grenade. *Courtesy J. L. O'Neill.*

LCpl. James L. O'Neill, a sniper attached to H BLT 2/4, got one kill at Dong Huan on 30 April 1968, then two dozen more in Dinh To on 2 May. *Courtesy J. L. O'Neill.*

2d Lt. Bayard V. "Vic" Taylor (center), a former enlisted man, wound up as skipper of H BLT 2/4 in Dai Do. *Courtesy B. V. Taylor.*

Capt. James H. Butler
(holding canteen cup) was
the CO of F BLT 2/4 dur-
ing the Battle of Dai Do.
Courtesy W. Weise.

A trio of BLT 2/4 Marines check out a 12.7mm machine gun captured during the Battle of Dai Do. *Courtesy W. Weise.*

1st Lt. George C. Norris (center) was killed, and GySgt. Norman J. Doucette (right) was badly wounded when their company, B/1/3, was attached to BLT 2/4 on 30 April 1968. *Courtesy N. J. Doucette.*

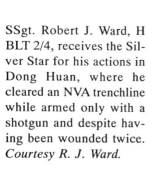

SSgt. Robert J. Ward, H BLT 2/4, receives the Silver Star for his actions in Dong Huan, where he cleared an NVA trenchline while armed only with a shotgun and despite having been wounded twice. *Courtesy R. J. Ward.*

Cpl. Richard J. "Mongoose" Tyrell, F BLT 2/4. *Courtesy R. J. Tyrell.*

Capt. J. R. Vargas was awarded the Medal of Honor for his actions while commanding G BLT 2/4 in Dai Do. *Courtesy J. R. Vargas.*

SSgt. Reymundo Del Rio (center) gunny of G BLT 2/4 during the Battle of Dai Do, is presented the Bronze Star with his skipper, Capt. Vargas, at his side. *Courtesy R. Del Rio.*

1st Lt. Hilton (right) stands in front of an M48 tank, the type used by Marine tankers during the Battle of Dai Do. *Courtesy J. D. Hilton.*

such superficial wounds, and another six had been hit badly enough to require medical evacuation after they finally secured inside the battalion perimeter. The worst of these was a black Marine whose right arm was blown off below the shoulder. The man was probably in shock, because he made no sound as a corpsman applied a tourniquet to the stump. Two Marines helped him walk back between them.

Golf Company took about three hundred rounds in the first kilometer of its march. The fire petered out then, and the Marines continued the last two klicks to Mai Xa Chanh West, where they arrived "exhausted and literally dropping in our tracks," as one grunt put it. It had been a three-hour march.

Captain Vargas climbed aboard a Mechanical Mule for the drive to Warren's command amtrac beside the Buddhist temple. The driver was Corporal Schlesiona, one of Golf's light-duty personnel at the BLT CP, who later recounted:

One thing that stands out in my mind is driving around in a rather permanent state of panic. The weather had, for some time, been dry, hot, and sunny, baking the dirt "streets" of Mai Xa Chanh West. In daylight, you couldn't drive around without goggles and something over your nose and mouth. It was a blinding, choking struggle. That night, with all the activity in the compound, it was like a duststorm and, with no headlights, it was white knuckles on the steering wheel just to stay on the path and still find your way to some specific place.

Before hopping aboard the Mechanical Mule for this death-defying ride, Captain Vargas had one of his corpsmen pluck the fragments out of his leg and bandage the wound. Vargas traded his tatterdemalion trousers for a fresh, wound-concealing pair and swore the young corpsman to secrecy: "Boy, don't say a damn thing to anybody, 'cause this means I have to go!"

At the CP, Major Warren briefed Vargas from his map board in the light and shadows of a kerosene lantern. He explained that two Navy LCM-8 landing craft, better known as Mike boats, would arrive shortly to transport Golf Company upriver to B/1/3's pos in An Lac by about 0300. They would be accompanied on the Mike boats by the battalion's two tanks, which had previously bogged down at Bac Vong and returned to the CP. The assault on Dai Do was to be launched at about 0400 so as to utilize the cover of the predawn darkness. Warren outlined the plan, then told Vargas, "You'll get your five-paragraph order from Colonel Weise, who's on a gunboat in the middle of this river. You will have to brief your troops as to what to do while you are afloat."

But the plan was never executed. Major Murphy, the regimental S3, radioed Warren and informed him that the two Mike boats were not en route. The TF Clearwater commander would not release the craft from Camp Kistler because he considered a nighttime run too risky. Warren was incredulous. There had been no enemy activity on the Cua Viet River between Camp Kistler and the BLT CP, and the NVA positions in Dong Huan and An Lac that had fired on river traffic during the day had since been silenced. Warren later said that "knowing my nature, I'm sure I must have expressed concern and disappointment in the fact that the battalion commander, who wanted to use the cover of darkness in order to protect the lives of his people when he got his operation started, could not do so."

Warren told Vargas that he would have until daylight to get fitted up for the attack, then radioed Weise with the bad news. Dixie Diner 6 (who was getting his sleep in five- and ten-minute snatches aboard the Monitor) was angry; but as Warren put it, "Once he realized that there was nothing he could do, he had so many other things going on in his area that he didn't worry about it."

Golf Company's Marines crashed where they could amid the demolished hootches around the BLT CP. Most found a piece of bare earth on which to unroll their ponchos and that was it. It was, however, better than what Captain Vargas got. "I remember closing my eyes for maybe thirty minutes," he said later. Vargas briefed his platoon commanders at one in the morning, then woke his gunny up at about three to help him make sure everything had been lashed down. "I went around to check that everybody had plenty of ammo and to ensure that everybody was carrying two mortar rounds in their packs, including myself. I wanted to double-check the weapons, I wanted to double-check that everybody understood how and when and where we were going, and what we were going to be faced with—and before I knew it the sun was coming up."

*   *   *

Inside Dong Huan, cutoff NVA who had lain low until dark tried to slip through Hotel Three's side of the line. The Marines opened fire on the shadows, and at dawn they found two extra enemy bodies in front of their positions among the hedgerows.

Meanwhile, in An Lac, Lieutenant Keppen, the new, green commander of B/1/3, was getting shook up again. One of the problems was that the NVA had begun jamming his radio net with a high-pitched electronic tone that effectively shut down his communications with Lieutenant Colonel Weise on the Monitor. The jamming wasn't perfect, but Weise couldn't make Keppen understand through the constant buzz that he should switch to the BLT's alternate frequency. Weise finally felt compelled to put ashore aboard a skimmer with his sergeant major and radiomen.

Weise spoke with Lieutenant Keppen, who was very relieved to see the colonel, and made sure they were straightened out on a new frequency; then Weise and his little group worked down Bravo Company's line in the predawn darkness. Weise wanted to ensure that the troops had enough ammunition and that there was a leader assigned to each group, and to let the Marines in the shot-up company know that someone up the chain knew they were there and was concerned about them.

The grunts were keyed up. "We had to be very careful that the Marines didn't shoot us," Weise remembered. But by and large, "they were in pretty good shape considering that they had taken heavy casualties. They had gotten all of their wounded out. They had even gotten their dead out. We adjusted the lines somewhat, but they were in reasonably good positions. Had they been hit real hard, I think that new lieutenant would have been able to handle himself."

Lieutenant Colonel Weise and Big John Malnar were still working their way through Bravo's position when there was an explosion about ten meters in front of their command group. It was probably an enemy mortar round. Weise was wounded superficially in his right thigh. He had the wound bandaged but did not report it. He had been wounded before—taking shell fragments in his left thigh and shoulder during Operation Task Force Kilo—and that injury had likewise not been reported outside battalion channels. Weise knew that battalion commanders with two Purple Hearts had to give up their commands, so he reckoned that what division didn't know wouldn't hurt them.

Weise spent the rest of the night with Bravo Company. An hour before sunrise, he instructed Keppen to send a patrol into the eastern side of half-secured An Lac. The patrol reported that the NVA had withdrawn. Bravo Company reoccupied the remainder of the hamlet at first light, amid enemy artillery and recoilless rifle fire that killed one Marine and wounded four. Bravo Company got its payback two and a half hours later when thirty to forty NVA, including many wearing Soviet-style helmets, were caught in the open fields between An Lac and Dong Huan. Hotel Company in Dong Huan, the first to spot them and take them under fire, thought the NVA had slipped out of Dai Do in order to hit An Lac. Weise suspected that the NVA were what remained of the force that had held An Lac and had retired into the fields on order. It was unclear whether they planned to continue their retreat or await reinforcements and then double back and assault.

Whatever the case, the Marines excitedly tried to line up the small, bobbing figures in their rifle sights. "Look at all them fuckin' gooks," shouted one Bravo Company Marine. "Let's kill 'em!" The NVA pulled back toward Dai Do, hounded by mortar and artillery fire. It was a real turkey shoot. "We caught them in the open before they could get their act together," said Weise later. "Some of them were moving and some of them were just standing or sitting there like they were waiting to do something before we opened up. We put a lot of fire on them. Some of them began running, some of them hit the ground—and, of course, you could see some of them drop."

CHAPTER 6 HIGH DIDDLE DIDDLE, RIGHT UP THE MIDDLE

L ieutenant Colonel Weise briefed Captain Vargas, the CO of G BLT 2/4, on the situation in Dai Do at about 0945 on Wednesday, 1 May 1968. They spoke aboard Vargas's Mike boat, the leader of the two that had pushed up onto the beach at Mai Xa Chanh West some thirty minutes earlier to take aboard Golf Company and its two attached tanks. Vargas, who thought his company was going to be in reserve during the attack on Dai Do, was in for a surprise.

"The minute you hit, you're going for broke," Weise told him. "You're going to have to go right into the attack. The other companies in there have been torn apart."

Naval gunfire and artillery were already pounding the objective. Weise estimated that the NVA held Dai Do with a reinforced company. His plan to seize the square, hedgerow-encased hamlet called for Golf Company to put ashore east of An Lac and then to pass around the right flank of B/1/3. Golf would then attack northwest across the seven hundred meters of rice paddies between eastern An Lac and the southeastern underbelly of Dai Do. Hotel Company, to the east in Dong Huan, was to provide a base of fire that would shift north as Golf progressed in the assault. Foxtrot Company, also located in Dong Huan, was to move out to where it faced the northeastern edge of Dai Do and provide a second base of fire, while B/1/3 remained in reserve in An Lac.

Dai Do, with roughly three hundred meters to each of its four sides, was surrounded by paddies except along its southwestern edge, which was snug against the bank of the unnamed tributary that ran northwest from the Bo Dieu. Separated from Dai Do by a hundred open meters, the long, narrow hamlet of Dinh To was situated to the northwest along this blueline, where it merged with the equally thin village of Thuong Do. Viewed together, the three hamlets looked like a tilted "L," with Dinh To and Thuong Do forming the lean vertical leg along the blueline, and Dai Do the fat horizontal leg jutting into the paddies. Given the enemy's capacity to reinforce from the DMZ, it was a good guess that additional NVA units stood ready in Dinh To and Thuong Do. At the very least, these hamlets offered the NVA in Dai Do a covered escape route.

Dai Do was being napalmed and bombed by a pair of A-4 Skyhawks when the ramps of Golf Company's Mike boats went down on the shoreline immediately east of An Lac. Nearby, a Navy Monitor sent a stream of 20mm automatic-cannon fire into the swirl of dust and smoke partially obscuring the objective. Lieutenant Colonel Weise disembarked with Vargas, who immediately placed his exec, Lieutenant Deichman, in the first wood line off the beach along with the company mortars. Vargas wanted Deichman to remain at the splash point to coordinate their supporting arms. The 60mm mortar section began shelling Dai Do as Vargas moved on to the forward edge of An Lac, where he deployed his Marines in a defensive perimeter with their backs to the river. The two attached tanks moved up with them, their main guns booming downrange.

Captain Vargas, a twenty-nine-year-old Mexican American from Winslow, Arizona, held a platoon commanders' meeting to finalize the assault plan. They would launch with Lieutenant Ferland's Golf Three on the left flank, and Lieutenant Morgan's Golf Two on the right. Vargas counted Jay Ferland, a sandy-haired working man's son from Manchester, New Hampshire, as his best platoon commander. Rick Morgan, the son of a bank president in Charleston, West Virginia, was a similarly confident, forceful, and aggressive officer, but Vargas saw him as a greenhorn who questioned too many orders. Both lieutenants had gotten married less than a month before shipping out for Vietnam.

The two tanks would move between and slightly to the rear of the assault platoons. Captain Vargas and his gunny, Staff Sergeant Del Rio, would follow the tanks with the company headquarters. Stocky, dark Ray Del Rio was a thirty-year-old Mexican American from Texas. He had been with Golf Company for only two weeks. He was, however, a strong, up-front professional, and veteran of a tour with D/1/9—the company made infamous by Morley Safer and CBS News when its Marines put their Zippo lighters to Cam Ne in 1965.

Staff Sergeant Wade, another pro, had the reserve platoon, Golf One, which since the Night Owl disaster had only two squads. Vargas also spoke with Lieutenant Acly, his forward observer, a twenty-two-year-old Yale graduate from upper-crust Stockbridge, Massachusetts. Vargas wanted Acly to plaster Dai Do with a barrage of white phosphorus and delay-fused high-explosive shells. He wanted to roll his company across those murderously open paddies while the barrage kept the NVA pinned to the bottom of their spiderholes. And he wanted an artillery-delivered smoke screen to cover them during the final few strides of their assault into the enemy entrenchments. Vargas basically wanted the same fire support that Hotel Company had enjoyed the day before during its successful assault, but he did not get what he needed. Acly explained why in a tape-recorded interview with the division historical team:

> Part of Captain Vargas's plan for the initial assault on Dai Do was to utilize a three-zero minute artillery preparation of the ville. Now there was air support in the area—Skyhawks are flying in, dropping napalm and rocketing and using their cannons on the ville—so when I planned the artillery prep, initially [division headquarters imposed] a check-fire on the area due to the prevalence of aircraft. Not exactly sure why, but this check-fire was not lifted, with the result that we started our initial assault without having one round of artillery on the ville. Some system should be worked out so that check-fires on artillery are held to a minimum 'cause I'm sure it would have saved us a lot of grief if we had had our artillery functioning the way it's supposed to function.

The Skyhawk pilots flew low and slow to place their high-drag bombs and tumbling, fire-blossoming napalm canisters right into the teeth of the enemy entrenchments along the southeastern edge of Dai Do. They did a superb job and were not the source of the problem. The red tape that muzzled the artillery came from division-level fire support coordinators at the DHCB who were overly concerned about the one-in-a-million chance of an artillery round meeting an aircraft in midair. Air and arty were supposed to be able to work in unison. The proper application of doctrine would have had the arty check-fired only when the Skyhawks were actually conducting their firing runs. The total cessation of artillery fires in this case was completely unjustified, according to the infantry officers waiting to attack. From the time Golf Company landed at An Lac (1040) until it launched its assault on Dai Do at 1253, the Skyhawks came on station only infrequently. Weise later wrote that although BLT 2/4 had finally been given priority for close air support (CAS), the battalion still "didn't get all the CAS we requested, nor as quickly as we needed it. . . . We learned to operate without relying on CAS, the king of Marine Corps supporting arms."

Dixie Diner 6 added a bitter addendum: ". . . lives were lost because of inadequate or unresponsive support in critical situations."

The NVA were, at intervals, shelling Dong Huan and An Lac. Since Lieutenant Acly did not know how long the company would remain in the open area off the beach before moving out, he and his out-of-work FO team started to dig in. They were not successful. The day was getting hotter and the ground was brick hard. After a few rebuffed swings of their entrenching tools, they said the hell with it and settled for the relative cover of a paddy dike. Acly was crouched behind the dike when a Skyhawk dropped another bomb on Dai Do. He heard a quick, hissing sound—*zzzppppt*—just as a metal shard ripped his left sleeve from shoulder to elbow and smacked into the dirt beside him. He hadn't even been scratched. Burning his fingers on the red-hot, two-inch fragment, he stowed it in his pack to take home as a souvenir. Acly was impressed. So were the NVA in Dai Do. The napalm especially got them stirred up. Lieutenant Prescott, the new Hotel skipper, said in his own interview with the division historical section that after the napalm hit, there were "gooks running through the ville, hopping out of various trench lines, and [we] were taking them under fire from our position. Foxtrot Company was working the back end of the village with a one-oh-six recoilless rifle mounted on an amtrac. . . ."

Lance Corporal Lashley, the machine-gun team leader with Golf One, was seriously wounded only a few steps into the assault on Dai Do. Lashley, with eight months in the bush, was down to seventeen days before he was to leave the field and begin outprocessing at the end of his two-year enlistment. He had written home the night before with the good news ("I don't have to go out on anymore squad sized patrols or ambushes since I have so little time to do"), but he had, without objection, boarded the Mike boats with everyone else. Lashley did not think his dedication made him a standout. "All the grunts I served with were incredibly brave," he later wrote. "To saddle up and move out when you were inadequately supplied, undermanned, and outgunned is an inherently brave act."

Lance Corporal Lashley, who'd previously suffered two flesh wounds, was, nonetheless, totally unimpressed with their across-the-paddies scheme to assault Dai Do. It's crazy, he thought. He had some real doubts about his ability to survive, so while the Skyhawks worked out he turned to his gunner and good friend, Mike Zywicke, who was also a Kingfisher vet, and said, "We're gettin' too short for this shit. Man, I just don't *know* about this one."

When Golf Company started off, Lashley, to the rear with the reserve platoon, stood atop a burial mound to orient himself on the area. "I was just standing on the mound, checking out the scene like a goddamn tourist. . . ." A single round from the first heavy burst of gunfire directed at Golf caught Lashley high up on the left arm, shattering the humerus. He was left-handed, and his arm, which had been raised, dropped straight down like a piece of dead meat. Still on his feet but in terrible pain, Lashley stared in shock at the blood pumping out. I've been shot! he thought. He couldn't believe it.

Lashley stumbled off the mound and collapsed, but Mike Zywicke quickly pulled him to cover and bellowed for a corpsman. Zywicke and the other members of the machine-gun team had to move out then with the rest of the platoon while the corpsman wrestled Lashley's flak jacket off, administered a morphine syrette, and hooked up a serum albumin IV. The corpsman also secured a battle dressing around the wound, which was still bleeding badly. When the pain wouldn't go away, the sympathetic corpsman cheated and administered a second shot of morphine. It didn't help. Lashley could only lie there, twisting in the grass as the battle was joined up ahead.

"Wow, man, these guys are crazy," LCpl. James Parkins of Golf Two muttered to himself on the way in, cursing the lifers. "They're so gungy, they're gonna get us all killed." Parkins, embittered by their earlier hamlet-to-hamlet battles above the Cua Viet, wondered if his own chain of command was as much the enemy as the NVA waiting for them in Dai Do. Both seemed pretty good at killing Marines. "Once again, we were real thankful to our leaders for taking us right into the open without too much fire support," Parkins said later. "There was a lot of animosity, but you couldn't say, 'This is stupid, I'm not going to do it,' 'cause if you weren't there and your buddy got shot, you'd think, Oh man. . . . You kept those thoughts to yourself, just kind of mumbling as you went forward."

The M16 rifle was prone to misfire. Its reputation was such that many a Marine advanced toward Dai Do with his three-piece cleaning rod already screwed together and taped ready-to-go along the rifle's stock. The cleaning rod was used to pound jammed rounds out of the chamber. Golf Two and Three crossed about two hundred of the seven hundred meters between An Lac and Dai Do before the NVA began sniping at them, especially from one-man spiderholes that dotted the open field. Fire also came from the entrenchments hidden among the trees and hedgerows at the edge of Dai Do itself. The dry brown grass was about thigh high, and the grunts, returning fire, moved through it in a low crouch. No one in the lead platoons was hit.

About fifteen minutes into the assault—at which point Golf Two and Three, still unscathed, had advanced to within three hundred meters of Dai Do—there was a sudden, decibel-doubling increase in the enemy fire.

Lieutenant Ferland and Golf Three took the brunt of it. The NVA were firing not only from the front, but from both sides of the tributary that ran past the western edge of the paddies from the direction of Dai Do. The NVA on the near bank were entrenched in hedgerows, and Ferland's squad on that flank was immediately pinned down. Ferland detached another squad to suppress the NVA fire, while pushing on with his one remaining squad, anxious to keep up with Golf Two. In short order, though, Ferland and his men became bogged down in the face of heavier and heavier automatic weapons and rocket-propelled grenade fire from the front.

Several Marines were wounded. The NVA had opened up with several 12.7mm machine guns—a heavy, much-feared weapon—and Captain Vargas instructed Golf Two to halt until he could get Golf Three moving again. Vargas ran back to his reserve platoon and found the grunts lying prone to avoid the rounds snapping overhead. Vargas ordered them into the attack, but by the time they were advancing in fire-team rushes, enemy mortars were pumping out rounds. Enemy artillery also opened fire, and the fields the Marines were advancing across had never looked so naked as they geysered with incoming rounds. Golf One's grunts had no choice but to keep leapfrogging forward, unable to even return fire for fear of hitting other Marines hidden in the tall grass ahead of them.

Lieutenant Ferland, meanwhile, received a call from his 1st Squad leader, whom he had put in charge of the two-squad action on the left flank. The corporal reported that he had two dead and six wounded. At the same time, Golf's backup company, B/1/3, which had a wide-open view of events from An Lac, reported that a hundred NVA were visible on either side of the blueline on Golf Three's flank. In response, Golf's 60mm mortar section in An Lac commenced firing. While Ferland adjusted the mortars onto the noisy but, to him, basically unseen targets on the far side of the creek (expending most of the mortar section's ammunition in the process), Vargas directed one of the supporting tanks to swing left and blast the NVA in the hedgerows. Immediately before the tank arrived, a pair of ammo-laden Marines made it up to Ferland's position in response to his call for more machine-gun ammunition. One of the men was Cpl. Richard R. Britton, an S2 scout with BLT 2/4 who had been attached to Golf that morning after eight months out in the bush with other companies. Britton described his dash up to Ferland:

> I slung my M14 on my shoulder, placed a couple of M60 ammo belts around my neck, and picked up two more M60 ammo cans. Another Marine quickly picked up more M60 ammo. The Marines laid down heavy fire, especially the M79 man and a machine gunner, and the other Marine and I raced towards the pinned-down squad with the ammo. Enemy fire hit all around us and RPG rounds screamed past us as we zigzagged our way forward. We dove face down into the ground several times because of the intense enemy fire, but finally reached the forward squad of Marines.

Then the tank arrived. Lieutenant Ferland wanted a fire team to guide it into position on the left. Britton said he'd go. Ferland asked for two more Marines to accompany him, and, as Britton wrote:

> Two men quickly moved toward the lieutenant and me, shouting to us they were ready to go. These Marines and I got into posi-

tion and the lieutenant and his men laid down cover fire. I ran as fast as I could toward the tank. Heavy automatic fire erupted around me and I quickly dove behind a dike. I returned cover fire for the rest of my fire team as best I could, but they got only a short distance before being hit and pinned down. I was way out in the open and I realized if I stayed where I was any longer I would be killed. I burst from my position and ran toward the tank. A bullet struck the heel of my right boot and sent me spinning into the rice paddy. By then I had only a few yards to go to get to the tank. The enemy rifle fire directed at me finally let up. I think the NVA thought they had killed me. I took advantage of the pause and ran to the rear of the tank and took cover.

Corporal Britton climbed onto the tank and shouted instructions to the tank commander. Marines from Golf Three's 1st and 2d Squads also pointed out targets as the tank fired its 90mm cannon into the enemy entrenchments. Some NVA literally disintegrated in the roar, but others popped up with RPGs over their shoulders. Britton noted that twice as he directed fire he was "knocked off the tank by exploding enemy rockets, but I climbed back on. I was sure the tank would be knocked out of action if it stayed any longer."

The tank commander felt the same way. The tank had been damaged so that it could move only backward, and backward it went in a noisy, dusty beeline for An Lac. Captain Vargas ran to the retreating vehicle and grabbed the external phone mounted on the rear of the tank. Vargas threatened to court-martial the tank commander if he did not stop, but the excited tanker told him to go to hell and kept on trucking. The tank did, however, make one stop before disappearing into the trees. It stopped to take aboard wounded. One of them was Lance Corporal Lashley with his shattered arm. After he was helped onto the tank's back deck, he was shocked to see his good buddy, Mike Zywicke, lying there beside the turret. He had no idea that Mike had been hit. Mike was hurt too badly to talk, so Lashley held his hands as the tank started rolling back, bullets ricocheting off its armor.

The tank still on line between Golf Two and Three exhausted its basic load of sixty-seven 90mm HE rounds. This tank also started to retreat, and Captain Vargas, again feeling insanely exposed as he used the external phone at the rear of the tank, chewed out the tank commander. "You can't leave me out here! Just keep driving for the village!"

"I'm outta ammo! I don't have any need—"

"There *is* a need," Vargas interrupted, "because the psychological effect of a piece of armor coming across the rice paddy, whether it has any ammo or not, is a tremendous weapon!"

The tanker was unconvinced. "I'm getting the hell out of here!" he shouted. Suicide was not part of his game plan.

"No way," Vargas barked. "You're going in there with us, or I am personally going to shoot a three-five in your tail!"

Lieutenant Colonel Weise, who was monitoring the radio in An Lac and intended to get more ammo up to the tank, finally got the tanker turned around with a no-nonsense affirmation of his company commander's threat. "I don't know what the enemy's going to do to you, but if you come back here I'm going to blow you away. I'm back here where I can see you, so turn that goddamn tank around!"

In the thick of the fight was, of all people, 1st Lt. Judson D. Hilton, the battalion's forward air controller. Hilton should have been back in An Lac with Weise, but had mistakenly thought the colonel intended to accompany the assault and had thus tagged along. Hilton shouldered his M14 and sprayed those treetops where he thought snipers were located. Nearby, Staff Sergeant Del Rio caught a glimpse of several NVA who had stood up in the brush to fire on the Marines. They were about sixty meters away, with their backs to Del Rio, and he assumed a sitting-kneeling firing position as he squared his M16 sights on the first of the fully exposed enemy soldiers. Del Rio, previously a competitive shooter, squeezed off a single shot. The NVA pitched face first into the brush. He never knew what hit him, and his overly excited comrades, firing on their own targets, never realized that a Marine marksman was shooting at them from the rear. Del Rio did not fire on automatic. Fire superiority was great, he thought, but he doubted that all the wild, ammo-burning fire of his young Marines really ever hit anything. Del Rio instead fired single shots down the line, dropping the enemy soldiers one at a time as though they were bull's-eyes on the shooting range.

From the positions their platoons had assumed in the thigh-high grass east and northeast of Dai Do, Lieutenant McAdams of Foxtrot One and Lieutenant Lanham of Foxtrot Three delivered fire into the hamlet to support Golf's assault. Neither friend nor foe was visible, but Golf marked its progress at intervals with smoke grenades, and Captain Butler made sure that his men fired to the right of the smoke. At one point, though, Butler saw .30-caliber fire from one of the amtracs impacting on Golf's side of the smoke. Unable to get the amtrac commander on the radio, Butler realized that the young, hard-charging lieutenant was blazing away with a machine gun. Butler shouted at him, "I need you to be a *commander,* not a gunner! You have somebody else who can do that! I need you on the radio so you can control your troops!"

Enemy soldiers became visible in the distance as they moved back and forth between Dai Do and Dinh To in small groups, and the 106mm recoilless rifles on the amtracs fired at them. In the smoke and dust of the explosions, the effect was not clear, but the recoilless rifles barked until they were almost out of ammunition.

By that time, the missing body of the Foxtrot Marine killed the day before had been recovered, and Lieutenant Colonel Weise instructed Butler to return to the cover of Dong Huan. Shortly thereafter, at 1445, as Foxtrot was just starting to move, the NVA artillery batteries in the DMZ that had been placing intermittent fire on Golf shifted the fire of two of their tubes onto Foxtrot. The enemy did not need to make a single adjustment in their accurate, twenty-round barrage, which—delivered two rounds at a time—whipped shell fragments over the heads of the helpless grunts while showering them with dirt clods and debris.

Eight men were wounded, including Lieutenant Lanham and Staff Sergeant Balignasay, the acting gunny. Balignasay, at forty, was a crewcut, pineapple-shaped Filipino who had fought the Japanese in World War II as a teenage member of the Hukbalahap guerrillas. He was also a Korean War veteran, and was on his second tour in Vietnam. Balignasay was hit when he and seven other Marines sought shelter behind a big boulder, only to have an NVA artillery round land ten feet from them. Balignasay caught a large shell fragment in his upper left thigh. It was a bad, blood-gushing wound. It also happened in a moment of mass confusion, and Balignasay and the men wounded with him were left where they lay. Most of the Marines were already lying prone. Others jumped up between salvos to put some distance between themselves and the amtracs, which the NVA seemed to be using as registration points, or to lead the retreat into Dong Huan. It was nearly an hour before anyone returned to where Balignasay had been left to bandage himself. Balignasay, on the verge of bleeding to death, was finally loaded into an amtrac.[1]

The artillery fire also killed three Foxtrot Marines. Private First Class Kachmar ended up evacuating one of the dead grunts, whose head had been blown off, leaving behind just a flap of bloody, hairy scalp. Kachmar first tried to carry the body out, but could not. He was too hot and tired. He finally began dragging the dead Marine behind him, holding the feet under his armpits. When he stopped to catch his breath, he looked at the dog tag laced into the dead man's jungle boot. It was common practice to wear one dog tag around your neck and one on your boot, the premise being that whatever killed you probably wouldn't remove both your head and your legs. Kachmar realized that he knew the headless Marine. He saw the man's face in his mind. He had been a funny little guy, blue eyed and sandy haired, who always seemed to be in trouble with the powers that be. Kachmar couldn't drag him anymore. Tired as he was, he hoisted the body over his shoulders in a fireman's carry. Ignoring the blood and body fluids that gushed nauseatingly onto his face and down the front of his flak jacket, he started marching.

Lieutenant Morgan and Golf Two had been ordered to halt when they were 150 meters from Dai Do. The platoon was hunkered down and blindly returning fire against the entrenched enemy when a black Marine was suddenly shot through the throat. The wound was mortal. Next, Lance Corporal Parkins, who was firing his M14 from behind a burial mound, saw his good buddy, Mitch, who was about eight feet to his right behind another mound, get shot in the head. Mitch's head dropped against the M16's sights, and blood pumped out onto the plastic stock.

1. After recuperating from his wound, Balignasay rejoined the battalion and was promoted to gunnery sergeant. Balignasay was awarded the Silver Star for his actions during a highly successful sapper attack on Firebase Russell in February 1969; despite grenade fragments in his face and a bullet wound through his arm, the gunny used his twelve-inch bolo knife from his days as a Huk to dispatch five sappers in hand-to-hand combat.

Parkins and Mitch had been trading bursts of automatic fire with a pair of NVA who were somewhere in the hedgerow to their front. The fire that had dropped Mitch gave Parkins a feel for where those two were specifically. Parkins turned his M14 on its side so that the recoil wouldn't send the barrel up, but would instead allow him to scan side to side with his burst, then began firing into that spot. One of the NVA, wearing a pith helmet, suddenly jumped up to run away. Parkins couldn't tell if he'd hit the man. Maybe the NVA made it to safety. Probably not: The whole platoon seemed to be shooting at this one and only visible target.

The second NVA who had had Parkins and Mitch in his sights ceased firing, too—the Marines later found him dead in his hole—and Parkins rolled over to his grievously wounded buddy. The side of Mitch's face was a bloody mess. It looked as though he'd been shot in or along one eye socket, and there was an exit wound behind his ear. Mitch wasn't screaming. He was in shock, and he asked Parkins if he remembered the words to the song that he'd been trying to teach him before they'd started across the paddies: "I'm on a little vacation in South Vietnam—an expense paid trip for one—I've got my own little rifle . . ."

"Don't worry about it, Mitch, I got 'em," Parkins assured his delirious friend. "Everything looks good. It's no problem."

"Am I bleeding?"

"Just a little bit. I think you got grazed on the side of the head."

Mitch's voice was small and tentative, as though he was a little scared and not sure what was happening. He kept saying that he was cold and thirsty. The blood was pouring out. Parkins, a nonsmoker, removed the cellophane wrapper from Mitch's cigarets and used it as a protective cover over one of the wounds before unsnapping Mitch's first-aid kit and securing a bandage around his head. He did not believe that what he was doing would make a difference.

Golf Company was bogged down for two hours before Captain Vargas was able to position his reserve platoon between his two battered assault platoons and suppress enough of the enemy fire to allow a renewed assault. This time the Marines were able to leapfrog right into Dai Do. Captain Vargas, who carried an M16 plus a .45 pistol in a shoulder holster, caught shell fragments in his right arm while maneuvering toward an NVA machine gun firing from inside a bunker that resembled a burial mound. The bunker was located about a hundred feet in front of the hamlet's hedgerow edge, and had been bypassed by the first Marines to get into Dai Do. The NVA gunner inside had opened fire on the Marines following them in. Vargas and one of his radiomen got behind the bunker, and the captain flipped the brush-camouflaged top off of it. There were three enemy soldiers inside. Before they could react, Vargas swung his M16 on them, shooting them all at point-blank range. The radioman tossed a grenade in for good measure.

Lieutenant Ferland of Golf Three crawled past a freshly killed NVA on the way in and, because he hated the guaranteed-to-jam M16, took his dead foe's AK-47. Ferland also pulled the extra ammo magazines off the body and stuffed them in his cargo pocket. Moving to the berm at the hamlet's edge, he spotted a bare-chested NVA with black shorts and an SKS carbine turning to crawl away from the trenchlike depression that ran down the enemy's side of the berm. The NVA was about twenty meters away and had his back to both Ferland and a black sergeant who had moved up on the lieutenant's right. Ferland quickly shouldered his AK-47, sighted in, and squeezed off a single shot at the same time that the black noncom let fly with a burst from his M16. The back of the NVA's head popped open from what appeared to be a single hit, and Ferland and the NCO jumped over the berm, continuing the assault with the hard-chargers who were up with them, shouting and firing and throwing grenades.

Other young Marines hung back in the tall grass.

Staff Sergeant Wade, the commander of Golf One, reached a ditch beside a trail in the ville. He stopped there with several of his Marines to get reorganized. From a culvert under the ditch an NVA, who must have been hiding inside, suddenly jumped up and began running away from the Marines. Wade cut him down with his M16.

There was little return fire as the Marines worked in teams to clear each entrenchment they encountered in the vegetation. The NVA were in retreat, and could be seen bobbing between hedgerows as they ran. The grunts blasted away at them as Golf Company began sweeping through the right flank of the village. The vegetation was thin enough in spots to see all the way to the paddies on the other side. There were still enough hootches, trees, and hedgerows left that Lieutenant Morgan and Golf Two, anchoring the right flank, had worked forward only about fifty meters when they lost touch with the platoon on their left. The NVA chose that moment to begin lobbing in 82mm mortar rounds on Morgan and his men. One Marine was killed. The other eleven bunched-up Marines in the dead man's squad were seriously wounded by the first round of what became a five-minute barrage. The attack stalled out. The senior corpsman moved up to help treat the casualties, who were then carried back and loaded aboard the lone tank that was still with them. One man required a tracheotomy. When he was hoisted onto the tank in a poncho, the Marine had a plastic tube sticking from the hollow of his throat and his eyes were crossed. The casualty-stacked tank, never resupplied with ammo, headed back for An Lac.

Captain Vargas, juggling radios, became aware that the 1st and 2d Squads of Golf Three, on the far left flank, had been pinned down again fifty meters short of Dai Do by NVA holding their ground in the hamlet's southern corner. Vargas got Golf Company moving again. The Marines completed their sweep across the hamlet, then swung around in as even a line as the vegetation allowed to push through to the two pinned-down squads. The forward elements had gone only thirty meters when they came under heavy fire.

The NVA were counterattacking. They could be seen by an aerial observer as they crossed the open space between Dai Do and Dinh To. The aerial observer also reported that he had NVA in the open and likewise moving south from the vicinity of Truc Kinh, which was about two klicks to the northwest. Artillery and naval gunfire worked them over, as did helicopter gunships with rockets and machine guns. Jets also flashed in to drop bombs and napalm. Enemy in the open in broad daylight was a rare sight, and the pilots were excited as they coordinated with each other on the air net. "Hey, there's a whole bunch of 'em down there, over there by that tree on the north end of the village. I'm going in!"

"Let me get in there, let me get in there!"

"No, wait your turn!"

"There's thirty of them over here in this graveyard. I see some and they got weapons on their shoulders . . . !"

The situation was not nearly so clear to thinned-down and ammo-light Golf Company. Captain Vargas had his men pop green smoke to mark their positions for the pilots. The Marines thought the air support had allowed their two pinned-down squads to break through, because figures soon became visible running toward them through the brush. A grunt shouted, "Hey, Gunny, more Marines coming on our left!" Del Rio also thought they were Marines—until they got closer. They were NVA, lots of them.

It was 1625. On Captain Vargas's order, Golf Company began pulling back, but Staff Sergeant Del Rio, only a few steps into the retreat, was sent reeling by an explosion. He came to lying on his back in a shallow trench. He felt as though he'd been knocked out for only a few seconds. It was hard to tell. He realized that his helmet was gone and that he had blood running down his face from a wound on his forehead. He was also bleeding from his left knee. His M16 was gone. Del Rio unholstered his .45 pistol, chambered a round, and was lying there trying to get his brain unscrambled when two NVA suddenly jumped over him. They kept on running. They had looked right at him, but with one bloody leg stretched out in front of him and the other bent underneath, and with blood smeared on his face, the NVA had probably assumed he was dead, despite his open eyes. Del Rio got to his knees and shot one of them in the back. The other NVA darted around a hedgerow and disappeared.

Shit, I'm going to die here! thought Del Rio. In pain and confused about where to go, he joined two wounded and equally disoriented Marines. They helped each other stay on their feet as they moved out. They hoped they were going in the right direction. Another NVA sprang into view to one side of them, running in the same direction but paying them no attention. Del Rio knocked him down with a few shots from his pistol.

Meanwhile, Captain Vargas was standing up to direct his Marines past his command group and rearward some fifty meters more to a drainage ditch that would make a good defensive position. When no more Marines could be seen coming, the rear guard began pulling back. The NVA were right on top of them. Lieutenant Hilton, the misplaced air officer, threw his heavy, reliable M14 rifle to his shoulder and started banging away at those enemy troops he could see as they darted from one spot of cover to the next. The young sergeant walking backward beside Hilton had an M16 in each hand and was firing the weapons simultaneously on full automatic. Vargas was squeezing off his own M16 bursts. Although the NVA exposed themselves for only a few seconds at a time, some of them were going down in the cross fire. Vargas noticed that some of the enemy soldiers didn't even have weapons in their hands. They were apparently hapless survivors of the original defenders of Dai Do who had been swept up in the counterattack.

Staff Sergeant Del Rio had made it to the edge of the brushy-banked drainage ditch when several NVA, in full, reckless pursuit, came through the bushes where he and a number of Marines were starting to set up. The Marines and NVA collided. Del Rio saw a Marine swing an empty or jammed M16 like a baseball bat. He saw another Marine jump atop an enemy soldier, smashing the man's head again and again with an entrenching tool. The other NVA ran right through them, as a shocked Del Rio turned to fire his pistol at them.

CHAPTER 7 SURROUNDED

T he north-south drainage ditch that became Golf Company's rallying point, and from behind which the Marines rose to fire, had bushes growing thickly along both banks. They had to shoot blindly through the vegetation, and lob their hand grenades and M79 fire at the unseen foe. The volume of their barrage compensated for what it lacked in accuracy, and the NVA were forced to seek cover. The enemy counterattack lost its momentum.

Captain Vargas had forty-five men with him along the ditch. He had a dozen or so other men, the survivors of the two squads on the left flank, pinned down in their own little last-stand position. Golf Company had started toward Dai Do with more than 150 Marines.

The NVA, having regrouped, tried to outflank the Marines at a point where Lieutenant Morgan and Golf Two had formed a line facing north above the drainage ditch. When fifteen to twenty NVA moved down a trench flinging Chicom grenades ahead of them, what was left of Golf Two began pulling back. They had no choice. They had expended almost all their ammunition repelling the first counterattack, and many a grunt's M16 had failed so often that he had broken the weapon down, thrown away the bolt, and picked up an AK-47 instead.

Fortunately, the check-fire on artillery support had finally been lifted, so Lieutenant Acly quickly worked up a fire mission to put HE on the NVA trying to outflank them—an act for which he later got a Bronze Star. It took five minutes to go through the fire support bureaucracy, then two 105mm howitzers began firing from Camp Kistler. Golf was on the gun-target line, so each round roared in over their heads. Acly, who was behind a burial mound with his radioman and could not actually see the enemy, started the barrage long and then worked it back to within fifty meters of their position. The two tubes fired one round every thirty seconds, maintaining that pace—one shell crashing right after the other, for fifteen minutes until the enemy fire petered out.

"I was really worried about Golf Company," Lieutenant Colonel Weise later wrote. At the same time the NVA launched their ground assault on G BLT 2/4, they also shelled Weise's CP and B/1/3 in An Lac, and F and H BLT 2/4 in Dong Huan. When the NVA initiated their flanking maneuver some thirty-five minutes later, at about 1700 on 1 May, Weise had Golf's perimeter boxed in with naval gunfire, artillery, and 81mm and 4.2-inch mortar fire. "But something more was needed to take the pressure off Vargas and give the enemy something else to worry about," wrote Weise. That something was B/1/3, and Weise's account noted that, "from its location in An Lac, Bravo Company, mounted on amtracs, would move quickly north (about 500 meters) into the southern edge of Dai Do, dismount, and fight its way to link up with Golf."

As Bravo moved out of An Lac, Captain Livingston's Echo Company began moving in. Livingston, who was super gung-ho, had monitored the battalion tac net since the battle began the previous morning, and had chafed at his role as guardian of the Dong Ha bridge under the opcon of the 3d Marine Division. Weise had sorely missed the presence of Captain Jim, as he called his longest-serving company commander, and had made repeated requests through regiment for Echo Company's return. When Golf ran into serious resistance in the opening moves of its assault on Dai Do, Weise's requests became more desperate.

Division headquarters, which had its own concerns about an NVA drive down Route 1, finally relented, and Weise wrote, "My morale went up several notches when I learned that Echo Company had been released by 3d Marine Division and was en route to my position in An Lac."[1]

---

1. The commencement of E BLT 2/4's move was inopportune in one regard: The troops, when ordered to saddle up, had just been clambering aboard several supply trucks that had arrived at their bridge position from the DHCB. The trucks were stacked not with C rations but with real food. The Marines had time only to stuff some oranges in their cargo pockets. They had to leave the steaks, soda, and ice cream untouched.

It was a two-kilometer hump from E Company's bridge position northeast to the stream it would have to cross to reach An Lac. Captain Livingston put his best officer, Lieutenant Jones, on point with Echo Three, and they started down a footpath that sliced through deserted hamlets and fallow farmland. The trail took them to the brushy bank of the creek, where it ran past Dai Do. Here, the point squad, led by Sgt. James W. Rogers, spotted an NVA squad on the other side. The enemy wore pith helmets and fatigues, and they were swinging AK-47s as they moved at a fast trot through the high grass in the hamlet. In seconds they would be gone. Jones couldn't afford to wait to get permission from the captain to engage them, so he told Rogers to open fire. There were about a dozen ammo-heavy Marines in the point squad. They all cut loose, creating a terrific roar with their automatic weapons and grenade launchers.

The NVA disappeared into the brush without returning a single shot. Lieutenant Jones wanted to pursue, but Livingston pulled in the reins. "No way!" he shouted over the radio. "Our job is to get across the creek and hook up with battalion."

Captain Livingston, following behind with 2d Lt. Michael L. Cecil's Echo One and 1st Lt. James Sims's Echo Two, began taking fire from Dong Lai, which was due north of them. A hundred open meters lay between the hamlet and the grassy burial mounds behind which Echo One and Two dropped to begin lobbing M79 rounds and firing M60s in return. There were only a handful of NVA in Dong Lai, and the Marines could not see any of them through the cover of hedgerows and banana trees in the village.

The NVA could see them, though. Sergeant Elbert E. Cox, Jr., a machine-gun section leader, was shot in the back of the head. Cox was a big man, age twenty-five, from Chesapeake, Virginia. He was a veteran of Operation Kingfisher, but though a competent and experienced NCO, his men considered him abrasive and he was immensely unpopular. Sergeant Cox lay in the grass now, gasping for air and crying out, "Oh, mom, I'm hit!" The cry sent chills down the backs of the grunts who had run up to wrap useless bandages around Cox's shattered head, and console this man they disliked. "Don't worry, Sarge, you'll be all right. . . . *Corpsman, up!*"

Sergeant Cox died. Lance Corporal Anthony Taylor, a rifleman in Echo Two, was also hit by a sniper from Dong Lai. He died, too. Taylor had been an easygoing, twenty-one-year-old black from Newark, New Jersey.

Hey, this ain't my war, right? thought LCpl. Van A. Hahner. The enemy fire had gotten heavy, and Hahner, who'd only recently been attached to Echo Company with a two-man regimental sniper team, had his head down and a cigaret lit. Hahner had been in-country nine months. He didn't see any use in shooting at what he couldn't see. This was a job for arty. The team sniper, for whom Hahner acted as cover man, was similarly uninvolved. An angry lieutenant shouted at them, "Throw some sniper fire back!" The sniper went first. He rose up from behind their mound with his Remington Model 700, but before he could focus the scope he had to drop back down to avoid the rounds suddenly cracking past his head. It was Hahner's turn. He shouldered his heavy, hard-kicking M14 as he came up and fired into the hamlet about six feet over the heads of the Marines pinned down in front of him. Having killed a bush or two, he dropped back behind the mound. There, he thought. I've done my duty.

"Hey, you're shootin' right by us!"

"He's not hitting you, so don't worry about it!" the lieutenant shouted at the Marines caught in the middle. He then turned his attention back to the sniper team. "I thought I told you to return fire!" he shouted.

Hahner got off several more quick shots before two bullets from the other side smacked into the headstone atop his burial mound. The rounds hit with dusty blasts about an inch below his eyes, and he went down quickly. Man, I've had enough of this, Hahner thought. The lieutenant kept bugging him, so he decided he was going to be cool. He wasn't going to go over the top again. But as soon as Hahner put his left knee out, before he could even fire from around the side of the mound in a crouched position, the NVA marksman shot him. The round went through his leg in a straight line from shin to thigh, and zipped on out to graze his rib cage. Hahner let out a scream as he was knocked down. Two Marines, under fire themselves, quickly pulled him back behind the mound. The pain was immediate, but so was Hahner's relief that he had not been shot in the stomach. It was his first thought. He knew he would live.

Hahner had the presence of mind to hand the shoulder rig for his .357 Colt Python to his partner and ask him to get the pistol back to one of the men in their sniper section. It was a commercial handgun, and Hahner had not finished paying the man for it. A corpsman tore open the bloody trouser leg and gave him an encouraging grin. "Hey, you got a million-dollar wound, baby—you're goin' home. You're okay. . . ."

The sniper made one more go of it with his long-barreled, bolt-action rifle, but was dropped by a round that went through his arm. Unable to get artillery support, Captain Livingston had his 60mm mortar section pump a barrage of white phosphorus (WP) and HE on Dong Lai. While the NVAs' heads were down, Echo One and Two pushed past the fortified hamlet and joined Echo Three along the creek, which ran southeast another five hundred meters to the Bo Dieu River. Echo Company followed it down, using the four-foot bank as cover. When the Marines were opposite An Lac, Sergeant Rogers's point squad forded the sluggish, muddy, hundred-foot-wide obstacle. Lieutenant Jones dropped his helmet and unshouldered his flak jacket and pack in the hasty perimeter that Jones established, then waded back into the water. Livingston followed him and, joined by a half-dozen other tall Marines planted at intervals across the neck-deep tributary, helped the rest of the company across. Everyone felt terribly exposed out there. The line moved fast.

"I don't think we were really keeping anything too dry," recalled Lieutenant Jones. "We were just moving 'em across shoving 'em across—and keeping 'em from going under." The NVA fired an occasional sniper round at them without effect. At one point Jones, who was facing north in midstream, saw a slow-moving RPG coming right down the creek at them. He ducked under the water. "I think I counted to a thousand."

At 1745, when B/1/3 was still three hundred meters short of its linkup with Golf Company, the amtracs atop which the Marines rode became the targets of AK-47 and RPG fire from NVA entrenched in Dai Do's southern corner. The effect was immediate. The Marines dismounted and sought shelter behind the burial mounds in the high grass of the open field. Bravo Company's new commander, 1st Lt. T. A. Brown, who had transferred from D/1/3 only that morning, tried to organize an assault on the hamlet. When he realized that no one but his radioman was following him, he started back—only to have a rocket-propelled grenade explode behind him. Brown was seriously wounded in the shoulder.

Lieutenant Keppen, the greenhorn platoon commander, was again the only officer left in Bravo Company. He was losing people very quickly to the devastating NVA fire, and he screamed hysterically on the radio, "You gotta help me! We're surrounded out here! They're all over the place! They're going to kill us all!"

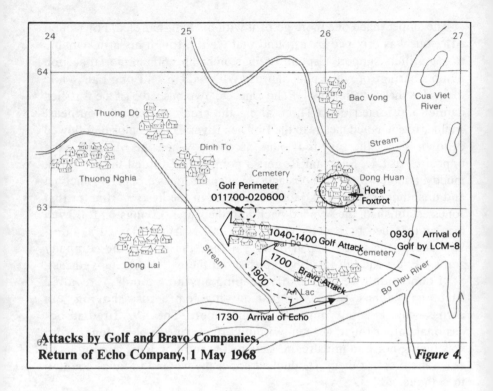

Attacks by Golf and Bravo Companies, Return of Echo Company, 1 May 1968   *Figure 4*

Captain Vargas came up on the net. "Now listen to me, Bravo, take it easy. I'm right over here. You're okay. Just pull your line in and talk to your people and stop yelling. Stop yelling and calm down and you'll be all right. . . ." Vargas explained to Keppen that if he pulled Bravo Company back to An Lac, as he was shouting that he was going to do, outnumbered Golf might be overrun. Keppen came around as Vargas kept talking. He was confused and inexperienced, but he was no coward. Given some direction, he did the best he could in a desperate situation. Vargas could offer Keppen no more than moral support at the time, though, because as noted in the battalion journal, "The CO of Company G reported that NVA troops had moved between Company B and his position, making it difficult for either Company B or Company G to take the enemy under fire without endangering friendly troops."

*   *   *

One of the Bravo Company corpsmen was screaming for help. Crawling as low as a snake, Pfc. Paul F. "Birdshit" Roughan, ammo bearer for a machine-gun team—and a tough, rough-edged eighteen year old from Worcester, Massachusetts—worked his way up to the corpsman's burial mound from the cover of his own. Roughan was not with his team because their M60 had been disabled by a direct hit. He left his own weapon and ammo with his team so he could get closer to the earth. There was a paddy dike to the left of the corpsman's mound, and the corpsman—barely able to get his head up for all the fire—pointed out the casualties he had spotted on the other side, the side facing the invisible enemy in the hedgerows. Roughan could see both casualties. One of them, a black Marine, was obviously dead. The other, a white Marine named Blakesley, was sprawled across the dead grunt. Blakesley had multiple wounds and was moaning deliriously, "Corpsman . . . corpsman . . ."

What an eerie, ungodly call, Roughan thought. He and the corpsman spent several minutes behind the mound, trying to figure out how to get to Blakesley. The corpsman, completely unnerved, handed his medical bag to Roughan. "It's impossible, we can't get to him! Don't even try it, it's crazy!"

The corpsman bounded rearward. You skinny little shit! Roughan thought, enraged. The sonofabitch asks for a volunteer, and then *didi maus* when the shit gets too hot! Blakesley was still moaning for a corpsman. Oh shit, how am I going to do this? Roughan figured the only way to get Blakesley was in an unburdened fireman's carry. He kept his helmet on, but shrugged out of his hot and heavy flak jacket. He also left the corpsman's bag as he shoved off on his belly toward the dike that separated him from the wounded man. He had covered about fifty feet when something exploded a few meters to his left. When he came back to reality, he felt no pain. He was just numb, except for the warm sensation of blood running down his neck. He'd been hit on the left side of the back of the neck, and he felt along the painless edge of the pockmark, trying to determine the extent of his injuries. He did not discover the exit wound on the other side.

Roughan bellowed for a corpsman. He could still hear Blakesley's delirious groaning. When he realized that no one was coming for them, he crawled back to the mound. Too tired to keep pushing along on his belly, he continued rearward in a stumbling crouch with his head tilted to the right, cradled in his right hand, to staunch the flow of blood. His team leader's helmeted head popped up from behind another mound. "Hey, Birdie, whataya doin' comin' back here? I thought you volunteered to help the doc?"

"I've been hit, I've been hit!" Roughan shouted.

After pulling Roughan behind the mound, the gunner secured a battle dressing around his ammo bearer's neck. The last thing Roughan said to the four-man M60 team with which he had spent the four best and worst months of his life seemed very important at the time: "Any more pogey bait packages I might get while I'm doing time in the hospital, just open 'em up and share 'em."

Crawling again until that became too tiring, Roughan completed his under-fire maneuver to An Lac in an exhausted, zigzagging stagger. He was placed aboard a skimmer—the driver had one hand on the throttle, and a .45 in the other—and taken downriver to Mai Xa Chanh West. The beach there was crowded with casualties. Roughan, numb and spent, lay on his back and called to a corpsman, "Can I have some water?"

"Sure you can," came the reply.

"Can I have a smoke?"

"Sure, no problem."

Oh shit, he thought. This is not a good sign. Roughan had been taught that casualties should not even ask for these things because they could adversely affect them. He was afraid that he was so far gone that the corpsmen weren't even observing the usual precautions. Mustering his best John Wayne drawl for the corpsman, Roughan said, "Well, Doc, whaddya think my chances are?"

"Hey, where there's life, there's hope."

A Sea Horse landed and two Marines lifted Roughan's litter. He did not know that other Marines had pulled Blakesley to safety. All he knew was that he had failed. He thought he had left the man to die. He felt guilty and angry—and sad, too. He knew that the camaraderie of Bravo Company was something he would miss forever. As they lifted his stretcher into the chopper, he realized he was crying.

By the afternoon of the second day of the Battle of Dai Do, the beachfront hamlet of An Lac had become a going concern. Lieutenant Colonel Weise had established the antenna farm of his Alpha Command Group in the village, and he had brought forward his hard-charging

S2, Capt. Richard J. Murphy (call sign Dixie Deuce), to take charge of the various elements gathered there. These included the 60mm mortar sections from B/1/3 and Golf Company, as well as BLT 2/4's 81mm mortar platoon, the amtrac platoon, the reconnaissance platoon, and various medical and communications personnel. The BLT's forward supply point had also been established in An Lac. Newly arrived Echo Company assumed security positions around the hamlet as B/1/3 struggled under fire to reach Dai Do.

An Lac was the first step in the medevac chain. Navy corpsmen performed initial triage there before the wounded were evacuated by skimmer to Mai Xa Chanh West. Further emergency treatment was rendered by the Navy surgeons and corpsmen at the battalion aid station on the beach. Sea Horses from HMM-362 then flew the casualties to either the USS *Iwo Jima* or the hospital ship *Repose*.

This extended medevac chain was the result of lessons learned. During BLT 2/4's initial operations above the Cua Viet, company commanders requested emergency medevacs whenever a man was seriously wounded. Although Marine pilots would brave enemy fire, the overly protective rules under which they operated did not allow them to fly through the artillery and naval gunfire being employed by the ground unit in need. A request for an emergency medevac thus resulted in a check-fire. Major Warren commented in his postbattle dialogue with the division historical section:

> Invariably, we may save the life of one Marine and lose the life of three or four more because of not having the fire. It took us a while to learn this lesson, but once we did learn it, then we always established a forward triage station to which we would bring the wounded people regardless of the severity of the wound, knowing full well that we might lose some in the evacuation process. From the forward triage station, we would take immediate first-aid, life saving action and then move them back to the Charlie Papa, which could be as much as two or three miles from the forward triage station.

Helicopters could land at the CP at Mai Xa Chanh West without a check-fire being imposed on the engaged units in Dai Do. Warren added that because the medevac system allowed continual artillery fires it became "one of the things that allowed us to even exist in this particular battle where the enemy were so numerically superior."

Colonel Hull, meanwhile, was not satisfied with the support provided by Marine chopper units. The issue was not courage but rather institutions. Hull had seen U.S. Army helicopters in action in the 3d Marine Division TAOR and had been much impressed. The emphasis of the Army aviation units had been on providing maximum support to the ground unit in need, and their flexible, mission-oriented doctrine allowed their dust-off pilots to make the most of their guts, initiative, and flying skills. The Army pilots flew in bad weather and landed in hot LZs that Marine pilots were usually not permitted near. The Army pilots did not require artillery check-fires when conducting medevac missions, and could thus perform the lifesaving function without disrupting the conduct of ground operations.

"These people do more with helicopters than we do," Colonel Hull stated during his end-of-tour debriefing in July 1968. He added that Marine aviation units were overly interested in husbanding their assets. During the Battle of Dai Do, Capt. L. L. Forehand, BLT 2/4's S4, used his Helicopter Support Team (HST) to establish an LZ opposite An Lac on the south shore of the Bo Dieu. This LZ was, Forehand wrote later,

> in close proximity to the rear fringe of the battle area but not under either direct or indirect enemy fire. This was done on my order to shorten the distance for transporting casualties [but] at no time would any USMC helicopter touch down near the battle area. One aircraft did eventually land, refused casualties, and departed. When questioned via radio by both myself and the HST Team Leader, the pilot replied he was afraid of drawing fire. At that point he did, and I missed.

Captain Forehand recounted later that he delivered the friendly fire with an M16, and that he "put a magazine after the sonofabitch."

It is unknown how many seriously wounded Marines died on the Dai Do battlefield because of the lack of helicopter medevacs. Major Warren stated that of the 287 casualties who were medevacked from

Mai Xa Chanh West, "there were only four [who] died of wounds in the process of the evacuation or the treatment back aboard the ship."

Those numbers were so low because of the tremendous care the wounded received on the beach at Mai Xa Chanh West from the first doctors they saw, Lieutenants Frederick P. Lillis and Runas Powers of the Navy Medical Corps. "Our battalion surgeons and their team worked wonders by saving numerous lives, limbs, and organs," said Warren, who was a witness to their work on boatload after boatload of maimed young Marines. "You splint it, clean it, patch it, put an IV in, and the helicopters are right there to take 'em back to the ship," explained Lillis. Everyone did their tireless part. "Somebody on the ship even sent us X-ray film and developer. Well, of course, we were ten miles from any electrical plug—but someone was trying to help."

When the Battle of Dai Do was over, Dr. Powers was recommended for a Bronze Star Medal with Combat V. Dr. Lillis was not. Both were draftees who had no intention of serving beyond their two-year obligations. Neither had volunteered to serve with a grunt battalion. Lillis made no bones about his desire to be reassigned to shipboard hospital duty. Powers, a thin, soft-spoken, and self-deprecating black doctor, adapted to the situation and earned the admiration of all who knew him. Lillis, on the other hand, had no interest in the staff responsibilities of a battalion surgeon, and conducted himself in a casual, irreverent manner that rubbed Weise and others the wrong way. There were those who liked Lillis, however, including one of his corpsmen, Roger Pittman, who described the doctor as "tall, gangly, and friendly. He was a free-thinker and a neat guy. He was not military, and his nonmilitary personal conduct did not lend itself well to the hardcore. He liked to mix in with the troops."

"I didn't answer the colonel as briskly and as professionally as the rest of his officers did," Lillis reflected. "I probably should have." It was not that the longer-haired, laid-back Lillis was antimilitary. It was more that he was amilitary. "The military was unnatural for me, and since I was Navy and since I was medical, I felt I didn't have to put up with all that regimentation stuff." Captain Butler, who also liked Lillis, was in the CP when an F Company corpsman called with a medical question. "I remember somebody explaining to Lillis how to use the radio, to say, 'Fox Six, this is Dixie Diner Med,' et cetera," said Butler.

"They went through a real long explanation, and then Lillis picks up the handset and says, 'Hello?' It just had everybody in stitches, but that's the way he was."

Another real character who played a support role in the Battle of Dai Do was Lang Forehand, the battalion logistics officer. Although irreverent, his otherwise forceful, rough-and-ready persona was one that Weise approved of enthusiastically. He was a crazy bastard and a fighter, and he was smart. During the engagement, Forehand constantly shuttled by skimmer between Mai Xa Chanh West and his forward supply point at An Lac. Weise later wrote that this up-front and exceptionally well-organized logistics officer "performed miracles with his Otter drivers and supply personnel. . . . These unsung heroes kept our assault units resupplied and evacuated the wounded, often exposing themselves to direct enemy fire."

Captain Forehand had been the S4 of 2/4 since October 1967, and he loved Bill Weise. He was a graduate of North Georgia College, a military school, and had been a Marine for thirteen years. He was the product of a distinguished and fairly wealthy Southern family whose roots in Jesup, Georgia, predated the Revolutionary War, and whose male members were mostly doctors, lawyers, and military officers. His uncle was a general, and his father an admiral. Lang Forehand, however, was a black sheep. He had been married and divorced once before going to Vietnam, and passed over twice for promotion. He did things his way, and he stepped on toes. He never did make major. "Although he had a Southern accent, he looked more like a tough guy from the streets of Brooklyn," said Weise. "He was a former boxer, and he was known to punch a few guys out in bars. Anybody pushed him hard enough, you had a fight on your hands."

Whatever Captain Forehand's sins were, they were not related to the battlefield. He had served a brief orientation tour with the ARVN in 1964, and had landed in Santo Domingo as the commander of an antitank company during the Dominican Republic expedition of 1965. Since his assignment to 2/4, he had done nothing but impress Weise:

Lang Forehand was one hundred percent Marine, and nothing would stop him: he would get the job done. He was very effective as a leader, and he could think along with you. When he was listening to what my tactical plan was, Lang was already thinking in terms of "how many boxes of machine-gun ammo, how many eighty-one rounds, how much resupply in water and rations and so forth will be required? If they're moving around this way, I figure I'll resupply 'em right here and they ought to be here by this time. . . ." He had his logisitics plan worked out by the time you were done briefing your company commanders, and he listened to what their plans were and could tell exactly where to resupply them.

Captain Forehand, who was thirty-seven years old at the time of Dai Do, very much wanted to command a rifle company in combat. He never did get a company, but his seven-month tour as S4 got him Bronze Star and Navy Commendation Medals with Combat V. His BSMv was for the battalion's assault on Vinh Quan Thuong, and the citation read in part: "When the triage area came under a heavy volume of small-arms fire, Captain Forehand unhesitatingly manned the .50-caliber machine gun mounted on his vehicle, and as it advanced toward an enemy position, he killed three soldiers and caused several others to flee."

Captain Forehand's role at Dai Do was pivotal, although essentially routine. The systems that worked were already in place, to include using skimmers to transport supplies from the BLT CP to the scene of combat, and to evacuate casualties. It was a nonstop round-robin, and no trip was made, either way, with an empty boat. The Otter crews also earned their pay in the resupply effort. Forehand wrote that even though the M76 Otter "was always broke," the boxy, open-topped, tracked vehicle "did more than it was ever designed to do." The Otter was able to negotiate water obstacles by floating. "The vehicle was totally devoid of armor," Forehand continued, "had a high profile on land, and was mounted with a .50-cal MG that invited RPGs. It was slow and ungainly in water, but could and did perform in places that would not support an LVT. These craft were invaluable and those who manned them were completely without fear."

Incredibly, BLT 2/4's Logistical Support Group suffered only one casualty during the Dai Do debacle. This was Forehand's own radioman, who was shot in the arm while he and the captain were up one of the tributaries in their skimmer. The casualties would have been worse except that on the second day of the battle, Weise assigned Lieutenant Muter's recon platoon to the logistical lifeline. Forehand used it to secure the forward triage station at An Lac, as well as to control the skimmer evacuations. Come nightfall, Forehand and Muter would personally accompany a small recon detachment to place strobe lights at certain points along the river to guide the skimmers and Otters in the round-the-clock resupply effort.

"Charlie was doing what he was paid to do, which was more than I can say for Division and Regimental staff," wrote Captain Forehand. Their lack of support capstoned his bitter opinion that the Weise breed of warrior was the exception to senior officers who were generally unable "to force themselves to leave their underground bunkers long enough to see that there was a shooting war in progress."

With no help coming from higher headquarters, BLT 2/4 survived the Dai Do engagement, logistically speaking, thanks to the five-day supply level that Forehand maintained at the CP at all times. Major Warren noted that he'd "never been in a battalion that had as much in the way of ammunition and supplies," and this prestocked surplus, unreplenished by the powers that be, was just enough to carry the battalion through the battle. BLT 2/4 had those supplies going into the fight because Forehand had a behind-the-scenes network of logistical personnel in place at strategic points along the Da Nang-to-Dong Ha supply chain. "Best thieves I ever had," Forehand remarked. Forehand also worked behind the lines. He found the junior officers in charge of supporting activities at the DHCB eager to help, unlike their superiors. When several overused 4.2-inch mortars malfunctioned during the battle, Forehand went directly to the captain who controlled the ordnance technicians at the DHCB. He traded the captain several captured AK-47s for the immediate, no-red-tape use of one of his teams. The technicians accompanied Forehand back to the BLT CP aboard his skimmer, and in short order the mortars were firing again.

There were repercussions. Immediately after the battle, the division G4, a colonel with whom Forehand had had some well-chosen words over the long haul, had both Forehand and the ordnance captain standing tall before his field desk at the DHCB. The colonel was a heavyset, cannonball-shaped man whom Forehand referred to as Dong Ha Fats. The colonel was furious with them for going behind his back. He accused Forehand of insubordination and grand theft. "That really bothers me, Colonel, that gets me right under my cigarets," answered the hot-tempered Forehand, who was within days of rotation and who had already decided to resign his commission. "Look, Colonel, as big as you are, I couldn't miss you at this range if I tried."

"Major Warren had been doing a tremendous job running things at our Command Post at Mai Xa Chanh, especially hounding Regiment and Division for more air and artillery support," wrote Weise of his radio-juggling operations officer. Warren himself wrote that much of the planning for day two at Dai Do had "involved trying to convince higher headquarters that BLT 2/4 was in fact engaging an enemy force of substantial size." Warren did not consider himself successful in his efforts to bring down upon the NVA in Dai Do the amount of fire-power that their numbers deserved. Division seemed singularly focused on the stretch of Route 1 above Dong Ha (during the day, 3/9 and the ARVN made significant contacts in that area), and regiment appeared overly concerned with possible enemy exploitation of the thinning line along Jones Creek. Except for ill-fated B/1/3, the BLT received no reinforcements. Warren wrote of the "slowness of various echelons of command to realize just how serious the Dai Do threat was," and he later commented that, in his frustration, his radio conversations with regiment "were bordering on the irrational because I knew that Bill Weise was in a shit sandwich, and I was so emotional about the need to get reinforcements there immediately."

During Golf Company's grueling assault on Dai Do, Major Warren had spoken in harsh tones with his regimental counterpart, Major Murphy, about the need to at least get Echo Company and Foxtrot's detached platoon back in the game. Murphy responded by invoking the regimental commander's name: "The order from Colonel Hull is that Weise should belly up."

The sight of the smoke over Dai Do, visible from the CP, caused Warren to explode at this hint that Weise was bellyaching and dragging his feet. "He's so *goddamn* close that his belly's getting split open! *We need some help!*"

Warren was convinced that regiment never fully appreciated the intensity of the Dai Do action. He knew, however, that the tall, imposing, and intense Major Murphy was an intelligent, hands-on combat Marine. He also knew that Murphy and Hull were beholden to division, and it was division headquarters, in fact, that appeared most disconnected from reality. Warren reflected that Murphy's own frustrations with the powers that be must also have been substantial. Warren was correct. Major Murphy was particularly disenchanted with Major General Tompkins. Neither Tompkins nor any member of the 3d Marine Division staff visited BLT 2/4 during the entire Dai Do debacle, and Murphy later wrote that he and Hull believed that the general "had gotten very tired and aged a lot during the first months of 1968. During Dai Do he was more concerned about Khe Sanh, and one night after a long day on the river in the boat, Colonel Hull told him so in rather heated words. They were both physically beat so we calmed the situation with some coffee."

Major General Tompkins had been a Marine for thirty-two years. He was a wiry, peppery, hawk-nosed man who earned his Navy Cross as a battalion commander on Saipan in World War II. Tompkins had performed superbly during the Tet Offensive and the siege of Khe Sanh. His frequent helicopter trips into Khe Sanh had been made at great personal risk, flown as they were through the rocket and artillery fire that pounded the airstrip at the surrounded combat base. The division that Tompkins commanded was itself overextended and undersupported. There was a lot going on and not enough help to go around. Dai Do was not an event that Tompkins completely overlooked. Captain William H. Dabney, an assistant division operations officer (and a former Khe Sanh company commander), noted that as the sun set on G BLT 2/4's precarious, cutoff position on day two at Dai Do, Major General Tompkins walked into the division CP in the DHCB "and directed, without preamble, that all 3d MarDiv tubes that could range on Dai Do shift trails immediately and be prepared to fire at max Ammunition Supply Rate all night!"

With the NVA fully occupied with B/1/3, which was caught in the open, Captain Vargas moved Golf Company a hundred meters back from the drainage ditch to an area with better cover in the eastern corner of Dai Do. An emergency ammo resupply mission was made by several Otters that came up from An Lac through the cemetery at Dai Do's eastern tip, an approach that shielded the vehicles from the majority of enemy fire. After his men finished loading up, Vargas moved Golf another hundred meters into the cover of those burial mounds. His forward observer, Lieutenant Acly, organized several simultaneous artillery missions on Dai Do and on NVA reinforcements reported to be east of Thuong Do and Dinh To. The roar of artillery was nearly continuous. The only breaks came when a check-fire was called to let in the occasional air strike.

It was getting dark, and the fire on Golf was reduced to sporadic sniping. During the lull, Vargas called up his platoon commanders. They decided to dig in where they were and ride out the night with continuous illumination above and a ring of artillery fire around their tight perimeter. Golf would have been too exposed had it tried to cross the open paddies east to Dong Huan or back south to An Lac.

Meanwhile, B/1/3, pinned down in the open, fire-swept paddies three hundred meters from Dai Do's southern corner, was too shot up to effect its assigned linkup with Golf Company. Bravo Company was too shot up to even evacuate its casualties. Lieutenant Colonel Weise instructed Lieutenant Muter to use his recon platoon and the cover of the gathering darkness to begin moving Bravo's casualties back the two hundred meters to An Lac. Muter personally led the back-and-forth, under-fire expeditions into the paddy to drag the wounded rearward. Weise would have expected no less from the cocky, fearless, twenty-five-year-old Muter, who was a married man and a doctor's son from Macon, Georgia. Weise wrote that Muter "seemed to be everywhere, always informed, and ready to do whatever was required without fanfare. Having Lieutenant Muter and his platoon was like having an extra rifle company." Forehand added that "Muter was typical recon: 'I cannot be killed. . . . I am iron. . . .'"[2]

The NVA were already pumping 60mm and 82mm mortar fire on Bravo Company, and a 12.7mm machine gun was burning tracers over the Marines' pinned-down heads when enemy artillery began to hit Bravo's mixed-up, spread-out positions. Enemy shells also fell on Dong Huan. Weise, in contact with inexperienced Lieutenant Keppen, gave Bravo Company permission to pull back to An Lac if he could account for all his casualties. The dead were to be left where they had fallen. Otters assisted with the evacuation of the last of the wounded, then the company straggled rearward under the light of flares and assumed defensive positions.

Captain Livingston spoke with Bravo Company's few surviving NCOs, who looked shell-shocked, and with Lieutenant Keppen. "The lieutenant had had about all he could handle, but he was fairly responsive. I sort of took the fatherly approach. I spent a lot of time trying to get him

---

2. During Lieutenant Muter's Vietnam tour (August 1967–September 1968), he was awarded the Silver Star, two BSMv, four NCMv, and two Purple Hearts.

calmed down, get him organized, and remind him that he was a leader and he had to take responsibility for his actions and the actions of his outfit."[3]

Captain Livingston then helped reorganize Keppen's lines, as well as the two isolated Golf Company squads previously pinned down on the left flank, which had been able to fall back with Bravo Company. "Those kids were all in a state of near shock," Livingston said. "They'd really had the shit beat out of them, but I told them they had to get their stuff together because they might be back in this thing and we might have to depend on them." During the night, Bravo Company heard something to the front; Captain Murphy, in command of the An Lac perimeter, described how "one or two men on the lines opened up with AK-47s. The rest of the men on the line, being acclimatized to the very familiar and peculiar sound of an AK-47, thought they were under attack—and we had an entire company just firing wildly at no particular enemy at all."

Captain Vargas and the other forty-five Golf Company Marines cut off in Dai Do were hunkered down behind burial mounds or in holes they had hastily scooped out with their entrenching tools. It was a tight, virtually back-to-back perimeter. The NVA attacked under the cover of darkness. Acly, the forward observer, adjusted fire missions to within fifty meters. The NVA were most active on Golf Three's side of the line, and they came at the grunts there as shadows that leapfrogged forward in the moments of darkness between illumination rounds—darting, dropping down, then popping up to fire AK-47s. Their tracers were bright green. Their RPGs thumped in with white flashes. Hilton, the misplaced air officer, had recovered an M79 from a medevacked grunt, and although he had never handled a grenade launcher before, he quickly became an expert. The artillery fired a salvo of variable time rounds, which delivered devastating airbursts and turned night into day above the open fields—catching a group of enemy soldiers in startling, freeze-framed clarity as they walked through the tall grass

3. Keppen, who got better with experience like most new lieutenants, continued serving with B/1/3 until killed in a mortar attack on Mutter Ridge on 7 July 1968.

in a fast crouch, helmets on, automatic weapons held in both hands at the waist.

Hilton started lobbing M79 rounds. Nearby, an M60 gunner laced the field with a stream of red tracers. Marines who hadn't seen a thing liberally expended ammo where the machine-gun fire was impacting.

Golf Three later counted ten dead NVA to its front. Golf One didn't get any clear shots. Golf Two spotted an NVA soldier carrying a light machine gun as he walked out of Dai Do. The man did not fire, and he made no attempt to conceal himself. He was apparently unaware that he could be seen. The Marines dropped him.

Weise had made an emergency request for a flareship, and at 2030 one came on station to orbit Dai Do and provide nonstop, parachute-borne illumination. The flareship turned the battlefield into a brightly lit stage, and the NVA probes petered out. One NVA, however, attempted his own personal banzai charge. "He looked like he was delivering the L.A. *Times*," recalled Captain Vargas. "His arms were full of grenades, and he was just throwing them and walking around." Marines fired on the NVA and he went down—but then he got back to his feet. Incredulous, Vargas shouldered his M16 and put two rounds into the man's chest. The NVA was unfazed, and kept throwing grenades. He finally collapsed after multiple hits. "He must have been on drugs," Vargas said later. "There's nothing else that can psyche anybody up that way to take that much punishment and just keep bouncing back up."

Captain Vargas requested an emergency ammunition resupply during the relative lull in the enemy action. The Marines, although they had liberally expended ammo on every half-seen bump in the night, still had a fair amount left—just not enough to repel a major attack. An Otter made a daring run up from An Lac, but someone had been under the impression that Golf still had tanks in support: The Otter carried only 90mm rounds. Vargas gripped his radio handset and shouted, "Hey, Dixie Diner Six, we got a bunch of tank ammo out here! What the hell am I going to do with that?"

"Oh, *shit*. We'll get you some ammo—"

"What the hell am I going to do with these ninety-millimeter rounds? Hit them with a hammer? I can't shove them in a goddamn M16, sir. For Christ's sake! I need some ammo."

"Don't worry, don't worry, I'll get it to you. Hang in there—we'll get you ammo." Weise then turned to Captain Forehand, who was even angrier than the colonel when informed of the mix-up. "Well, I'll be a goddamned sonofabitch!" Forehand cursed in the night. "What asshole did that?" Weise told Forehand to hustle some small-arms ammunition up to Golf Company ASAP. He did not expect Forehand to do it himself, but Forehand swung aboard an Otter after making sure that it was loaded with the right stuff, and roared off across the wide-open, flare-lit paddies. "We got fat on grenades, and we got fat on M16 rounds," said Vargas. "Then they drove off into the darkness. How the hell they ever got through there without getting shot, I'll never know."

"Thanks for the ammunition!" Vargas told Weise. He was laughing like hell. "You can't imagine who just came here!"

"Yeah, it was the Four."

"How'd you know?"

"Well, he heard about what happened, and he went out and unscrewed it."

Lieutenant Acly, who had called in ninety minutes of continuous artillery to break the back of the ground attack, kept the NVA off balance during the lull by shelling Dai Do in thirty-minute intervals for the rest of the night. The shellings were configured as a TOT, or time on target. A TOT involved several artillery batteries firing on the same target, but at different times based on their different distances from the target, so that their rounds were coordinated to all impact in the same second. Each battery computed the time of flight to the target, and when a countdown was given each knew at what point to commence firing. The result was a devastating, twenty-in-one explosion that smothered a target and gave the enemy no time to react. It did, however, give the exhausted grunts time to get some sleep.

PART THREE FIXED BAYONETS

Captain Livingston, CO, E BLT 2/4: "At five o'clock in the morning, I said on the radio, 'We're fixin' to go. Fix bayonets.' That was really something to hear—all those young fellas, a hundred-fifty-something of 'em, clicking bayonets. All down the line you could hear these clicks. They were for real."

During the night of 1–2 May 1968, Battalion Landing Team 2/4 was deployed as follows: G Company (Vargas) was cut off in the eastern tip of Dai Do; F Company (Butler) and H Company (Prescott) were in Dong Huan; and E Company (Livingston) was in An Lac with B/1/3 (Keppen). At 0023 on 2 May, Lieutenant Colonel Weise, who was also in An Lac with his Alpha Command Group, issued his frag order for the next attack on Dai Do. The concept called for E Company to launch a predawn assault into the hamlet with H Company following behind. Once linkup had been achieved with isolated G Company, the three-company attack was to continue through Dai Do and into Dinh To. F Company was to be the BLT reserve. B/1/3 was not to participate. As noted in an after-action report, B/1/3 was "no longer an effective fighting force due to casualties," so the company was to remain in An Lac to "aid in resupply, medevacs, and provide security for the 81mm mortar section."

Captain Livingston, CO, E BLT 2/4: "Bravo Company had a lot of bodies still left on the battlefield, which we passed as we began the attack on Dai Do. It's a sad situation where you're firing and maneuvering past the bodies of your fellow dead Marines."

CHAPTER 8 THE PALACE GUARD

There were voices in the dark about fifty meters ahead of the burial mounds where Sergeant Rogers's squad from Echo Three had established its ambush/listening post. There were also the muffled sounds of equipment and weapons. Someone was walking toward them, and Rogers, who did not have a starlight scope, was very concerned that Marines had entered his kill zone. Rogers whispered into his radio handset as he described the situation to the company headquarters, which was two hundred meters to the rear in An Lac. Captain Livingston personally came up on the net to verify that there were no friendly patrols in the area. At the same time, one of Rogers's men whispered to him, "They're speakin' Vietnamese out there."

It was shortly before dawn on Thursday, 2 May. Captain Livingston thought the NVA might be approaching An Lac to surrender, and he put his Vietnamese interpreter on the radio to tell Rogers what to say to find out. Rogers gave away his position when he called out, *"Chieu hoi, chieu hoi—"*

The reply was an AK-47 burst. The Marines responded with everything they had, including an attached machine-gun team, until there was no more enemy fire. Livingston instructed them to withdraw, and they walked back to the company perimeter as quietly, cautiously, and quickly as they could. Shortly thereafter, when the sun came up and Echo Company was moving in the assault across those same paddies, Rogers's squad passed the scene of its two-minute contact. The Marines found three dead NVA behind a burial mound, along with the 12.7mm machine gun that they had never had the chance to set up.

*   *   *

"We fought the palace guard at Dai Do," said Captain Livingston. "They were big guys with new uniforms, brand-new weapons, and close-cropped haircuts. They were quality troops." The NVA were not guerrillas. The NVA stood and fought, nose to nose, and that was the kind of enemy that Echo 6 wanted. "I was impressed at his anxiousness for combat," wrote Lieutenant Deichman of Golf Company. Deichman had been at An Lac when Livingston had arrived the previous afternoon from the Dong Ha bridge, and he noted that at the time Livingston "sort of had a smile on his face like the combat he had been waiting for had at long last arrived, and he wasn't going to miss it for the world. He was itching for a fight, and he got one."

"Captain Livingston was hardcore as hell, well-respected, and some-times feared," commented a rifleman about his spartan, cigar-chewing skipper. "Even his voice was gung-ho sounding."

Captain Livingston, age twenty-eight, was a Georgia farmer's son. He was a tall man with features that were handsome in a rawboned way. He shaved his head and carried himself with a certain hands-on-hips confidence. He referred to his troops as his youngsters. Livingston's tour had begun with his assumption of command of E/2/4 on 31 October 1967. The company had just come off Operation Kingfisher, where it had taken serious casualties. Morale was not all it could have been. The company was filled with replacements, including four new lieu-tenants. Livingston came on hard from the word go. He was, of course, seriously resented by the old salts in the company, especially after he ordered every Marine in the outfit, regardless of time in service, to get a skinhead, boot camp–style haircut. Mustaches were outlawed, and daily shaving was enforced. There was little time to bitch about this new spit 'n' polish skipper, nor was there time to be idle or bored. When Echo Company was not out on combat operations, Livingston was PTing the hell out of them, and when he wasn't PTing the hell out of them he was holding class or another weapons inspection. Livingston was especially tough on his young, inexperienced lieutenants. At Ai Tu, he'd locked their heels and told them that if they did not get squared away soon they would be relieved of command. He did not have to relieve them, however, because "after I had my platoon commanders clean a platoon's worth of weapons, they understood what I meant about keeping weapons clean—and about making sure that the troops were shaving, and had clean socks, and those kinds of issues that cause Marines not to be combat ready."

Captain Livingston hated what Vietnam was doing to the Marine Corps. "I was uncompromising. A lot of people were beginning to make accommodations. They had lowered their expectations for their Marines. I kept my Marines looking like Marines. I was death on keeping weapons cleaned, and we were famous for conducting office hours in foxholes." "Office hours" involved a monetary fine and a black mark in a Marine's record book, which Livingston and his grand old first sergeant would administer whenever and wherever needed. No-slack Echo Company was also famous for conducting PT on the front lines, even after the battalion had moved from Ai Tu to the sticks around Mai Xa Chanh West. When the tactical situation allowed, Livingston jogged his men around the perimeter in flak jackets, and he had them dig fighting holes large enough in which to do sit-ups, push-ups, and bends-and-thrusts. "We were getting up at oh-five-thirty, before all the other companies, and running around the area doing our morning exercises," remarked Lieutenant Jones. "That was kind of a local joke within the battalion. We hated it, but we always felt that we were the most ready."[1]

On most of Echo Company's hot and sweaty days in the sand dunes and rice paddies, most of its hot and sweaty young Marines hated Captain Livingston. Ultimately, though, they would agree that his hard, unyielding standards kept them alive. Private First Class Michael Helms, who was grievously wounded at Lam Xuan East, wrote that "we blamed the skipper for our woes because it seemed he was always volunteering us. A lot of us figured he would win the Medal of Honor, or die trying. We used to gripe and bitch among ourselves that he would probably kill us all getting it, but he definitely had our respect and, secretly, our admiration. I can think of no other officer I would rather have around when the shit hit the fan."

---

1. Although they had different styles, Captains Livingston, Vargas, and Williams had a lot of faith in each other. They were the mainstays of BLT 2/4 in terms of company leadership during the high-casualty, fast-turnover campaigns along the Cua Viet. As Vargas put it, "The three of us knew that if anything went wrong, the other guy was going to come hell for broke."

*   *   *

It was not quite light and Echo Company was just saddling up to attack Dai Do when a lone NVA was spotted inside the perimeter. The running soldier appeared as only a half-glimpsed shadow to LCpl. Philip L. Cornwell, a machine-gun team leader in Echo Two. Cornwell fired his M60 at the same time that several other Marines opened up with M16s, and the NVA went down immediately. Cornwell tossed a grenade, then ran to the area with his Colt .45 in hand. The NVA was lying facedown, and when he started to get up Cornwell shot him in the back of the head. It was his first confirmed kill. A machine gunner nicknamed El Toro rushed up to congratulate Cornwell—and to hand him a bayonet. "Here, here, he's yours!" said El Toro, grinning broadly.

"El Toro was always happy-go-lucky, but that boy was sick," Cornwell recalled. "He would really smile when he got the chance to cut bodies up."

This time Cornwell used the bayonet. He cut the ears off his kill.

Cornwell had seen El Toro in action two months earlier in an embattled hamlet that was thick with smoke from burning hootches as the Marines grenaded the enemy bunkers beneath each. The men in Echo Two were in a black mood because one of their most popular comrades had been killed by a defective grenade. When Cornwell tossed a grenade of his own into a bunker, an ancient-looking Vietnamese woman emerged. She stood small and gray and wrinkled on the trail, hands clasped against her chest. No civilians were supposed to be in the area. "The sergeant called to ask what to do with her. Word came back to waste her. I wanted to kill her. She was mine. I threw the grenade in that bunker." Cornwell put down his machine gun. He wanted to kill her execution-style with his .45-caliber pistol. He started to unholster the weapon. "El Toro beat me to it. He whipped his machine gun up and just put a burst right through her. I always wondered if it would have bothered me if I'd gotten the chance to kill her. When you're eighteen and in that position day after day, you know you're going to die. There's no doubt whatsoever that you're going to die. The fear, the total fear, cannot be understood. You do things you're not really proud of."

As Echo Company's attack on Dai Do got rolling, two more NVA, previously undetected, were discovered squatting in holes in the tall grass. They immediately raised their hands in surrender. They had apparently deserted their positions in Dai Do and had waited all night to give up. They were quiet and scared, and Lieutenant Jones quickly organized a detail to escort them back to the battalion CP. There they joined two other khaki-clad prisoners, deserters who had approached Hotel Company in Dong Huan during the night with their brand-new, folding-stock AK-47s held over their heads.

Sergeant Ernest L. Pace from the division G2's Interrogator-Translator Team spoke with the prisoners, then reported directly to Weise. Pace said that one prisoner told him twelve NVA companies were in Dai Do alone, and that they had identified themselves as belonging to the 52d Regiment, 320th NVA Division. The prisoners claimed that the only thing they feared were the air strikes. Weise looked at them before they were loaded into a skimmer for the trip downriver. They were sitting under guard with their hands tied behind their backs. They occasionally looked around with great curiosity, but mostly they had downcast eyes. Weise said later, "I'm sure they were wondering whether they were going to be killed. I was very concerned for their safety. We made it a point to impress the intelligence value of prisoners on our troops all the time, but the men were really upset and you had to be careful."

"We fixed bayonets and went for it," Captain Livingston said of Echo Company's assault on Dai Do. Echo Company did not advance from An Lac behind a smoke screen, nor did it enjoy a rolling barrage to keep NVA heads down. Once again, there were problems with the artillery. Echo's new FO, GySgt. James Eggleston, who was serving his second of four combat tours, noted that "all I was able to get out of Dong Ha before the assault was just a half-assed prep, maybe thirty rounds for effect from a one-oh-five battery. Hell, that was it." During the fight itself, Eggleston spotted NVA on the west side of the tributary about a thousand meters away. "I got one round of Willie Peter on them, then a fire support coordinator, a lieutenant in Dong Ha, cease-fired the goddamn mission because he said they were ARVN up there. Those weren't ARVN, I'll guarantee you that. Me and that lieutenant had some hard words over the phone."

Coordination with the ARVN, which did have units on the other side of the creek, was always difficult. Captain Anthony C. Conlon, commander of H/3/12, a 105mm battery at the DHCB, wrote of another problem: "The magnitude of the artillery support [was such that] Hotel Battery expended all ammunition on several occasions during the battle. Needless to say, when calls for fire from BLT 2/4 were coming in and we could not fire due to the paucity of ammunition, I cannot express how helpless we felt."

Nothing could replace the value of constant, coordinated artillery to an infantry assault, but there was some compensation in this instance: BLT 2/4 had finally been given priority for CAS. The Phantoms and Skyhawks had practically been stacked above Dai Do before this fourth frontal assault commenced on the fortified hamlet. "We were piling in on there," wrote Livingston, "and, meanwhile, we were using weapons organic to the company, i.e., the M79s, LAWs, rocket launchers, mortars—the whole bag. We were using anything we could find that would shoot, and then it was high-diddle-diddle-right-up-the-middle right across that same paddy again."

When the NVA in Dai Do opened fire at 0715 on 2 May, Captain Livingston and the company gunny, GySgt. Roscoe Chandler, dropped behind one of the burial mounds dotting the five hundred open meters between An Lac and Dai Do. The lead elements of Echo Company were within two hundred meters of Dai Do. The NVA entrenched in the hedgerows at the hamlet's edge had waited until the Marines were that close before commencing fire. The first volley included RPGs aimed at the numerous radio antennas in the company command group. Livingston and Chandler kept their heads down momentarily as one explosion after another, about eighteen altogether, virtually disintegrated the burial mound they were hunkered behind.

Captain Livingston had Lieutenant Sims's Echo Two forward on the left flank, and Lieutenant Jones's Echo Three on the right. Lieutenant Cecil and Echo One were in reserve. The Marines in the assault platoons could hear bullets thumping into the burial mounds behind which they dove for cover as they ran, crawled, and ducked their way toward Dai Do. Everything was happening in a blur of confusion. At one point, an Echo Two Marine who had gotten ahead of the line was accidentally shot in the back. His flak jacket saved him, but the bullet tore open a magazine in a bandolier slung over his shoulder. The rounds inside began to cook off, and the Marine dropped his M16 as he frantically ripped off his bandoliers and extra machine-gun ammo, knocking off his helmet in the process.

Corporal Nicolas R. Cardona, the wounded man's incredulous squad leader, screamed at the Marine who had shot him to cease fire. The Marine could not hear him over the din, so Cardona finally ran over, took a hard swing with his helmet, and hit the man on top of his own steel pot.

"Stop firing!" Cardona screamed.

Meanwhile, the wounded Marine stood for a second and gave a visible sigh of relief after ripping away his last bandolier. The NVA shot him in the stomach in that unguarded instant. It was only a flesh wound, but the Marine, understandably shook up, raced rearward, scared out of his mind.

Lance Corporal Cornwell's machine-gun team was advancing with Cardona's squad. Cornwell and his best friend, Danny Wilson—a Boston Irishman with an eagle, globe, and anchor tattoo—were both humping M60s and were both loaded down with ammo. They had just jumped up to run to the next piece of cover when Wilson let out a scream. Cornwell spun back and threw himself prone beside him. Wilson had a serious stomach wound, and Cornwell got a battle dressing over the bullet hole as he told his buddy to hang on.

Danny Wilson was taking it well; as soon as a corpsman got to them, Cornwell bounded forward again with his other gunner and the team's ammo bearer. The trio dropped behind cover that was a fraction of an inch higher than their prone bodies, and started blasting the hedgerow with machine-gun fire. They heaved grenades over the bushes between bursts. Chicoms came back at them, and Cornwell was grazed by a fragment across his right hand as he blazed away. The NVA were right on top of them but impossible to see. In an act of desperate, inexperienced bravery, Cornwell's gunner jumped up without warning and charged. He fired as he ran, sweeping the hedgerow, but as soon as he crashed through it the enemy dropped him with three rounds in the leg. The gunner started screaming in pain.

When Echo Company began to bog down on the southeastern side of Dai Do, Captain Vargas's Golf Company attempted to relieve the pressure by sweeping into the hamlet from its previously cutoff position in the eastern corner. Golf Company, whose forty-six members

had come through the long night unscathed, went into the assault high
in spirits but low in supplies. Lieutenant Acly, for example, had dug
in the previous night with a few smokes, no food, and a canteen of
muddy water he'd gotten from the bottom of his foxhole after hitting
the water table. The Otters that had delivered ammunition had also
brought rations, which were distributed to the lowest-ranking men first.
There were not enough meals for the officers and noncoms. Acly's
preattack breakfast consisted of a handful of crackers that one of his
radiomen shared with him. One grunt later wrote that he was "so thirsty
that I was licking the dew off the leaves."

Staff Sergeant Del Rio, wounded twice in two days and weak from
loss of blood, had spent a semisleepless night leaning against some
ammo crates with his pistol in hand. He was sick and exhausted, and
his whole body ached. When two Otters pulled up, Vargas directed
him to get aboard with the other wounded men who had ridden out
the night with them.

"Well, Skipper, I'm not that bad."

"Go on, get on the Otter," said Vargas.

"Okay." Deep down, Del Rio didn't want to argue with the captain.
"I was scared, I wanted out," he said later.[2]

Captain Vargas no longer had a gunny, but he still had Lieutenant
Hilton, the battalion air liaison officer, who had accidentally been swept
up in Golf's initial assault on Dai Do. Hilton had started the morning
with a call from Vargas that Dixie Diner 6 was on the battalion net
and wanted to talk to him. Weise told Hilton he'd thought he was dead
and was glad he was not, then added, "What the hell are you doing
with Vargas?"

"Well, sir, I—"

An angry Weise cut him off. "We'll talk about it later."

Lieutenant Hilton may have been lost, but it didn't bother Vargas,
who used him as a platoon commander. Hilton had an AK-47 slung
over his shoulder and an M79 grenade launcher in hand. As Golf
Company's attack stepped off with a roar of fire, Hilton shouted to

2. Del Rio was awarded a BSMv and his second Purple Heart for Dai Do.
His first Purple Heart was the result of a booby trap encountered during his
first tour.

the Marines he'd been given temporary command of, "Everybody ready? Okay—fire! Let's go!"

Hilton started toward the trees his men had just unloaded into. He'd gone maybe a hundred feet before it registered that they were hollering at him, "Lieutenant, Lieutenant—stop! *Stop!*"

Hilton looked back. No one was with him. They were still at the start line. "Stop, Lieutenant, stop—we gotta reload!"

Hilton hit the deck and called back over his shoulder, "Okay, everybody reload then, goddamnit!"

Things got very serious very quickly. Although the advancing Marines blasted everything ahead of them, they began receiving sporadic return fire about the same time that Echo Company reached the fringes of Dai Do. Lieutenant Ferland of Golf Three sent one fire team after

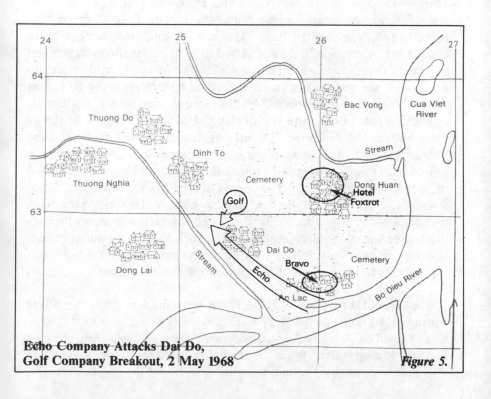

Echo Company Attacks Dai Do, Golf Company Breakout, 2 May 1968

Figure 5.

an enemy soldier detected while firing on Echo Company from a camouflaged spiderhole. The fire team discovered more NVA in a deep trench, which was expertly constructed and camouflaged; the Marines could hear a 60mm mortar pumping out rounds from inside it. Ferland later told the division historical section that when his fire-team leader went after the mortar tube with a hand grenade, "he was shot at several times from an enemy who was no more than about five feet in front of him—yet my fire-team leader could not see him. This is how well they were concealed and dug in. We were unable to secure this mortar tube as far as we know. We did fire M79 rounds and throw hand grenades into that area, not knowing the effect as we were not able to get close enough."

At one point, Lieutenant Ferland and his radioman, LCpl. Jerry Hester, dropped into an NVA communications trench. Hester had his M16 up as they slowly slid along the trench wall toward a sharp, L-shaped turn. They were about five feet from the turn when an NVA with an AK-47 suddenly sprang from around the corner, fired three or four rounds, and then jumped back. The enemy soldier had taken them completely by surprise, and Ferland had to keep his terrified and enraged radioman from charging recklessly after the man. He told Hester to get against the wall and not move. Ferland himself, moving so fast as to fumble, unholstered his .45-caliber pistol, unwrapped it from its protective plastic bag, and frantically pulled the slide back to chamber a round. He was pressed firmly against the trench wall, and the NVA missed when he jumped out to fire another burst. When the man pulled back, Ferland reached around the corner and blindly squeezed off a few shots of his own. The enemy soldier lunged out again, fired, missed, and disappeared. Ferland played 'possum. He wanted the NVA to think he'd gotten him. Ferland readied himself, and when the soldier made his next move around the corner, the lieutenant shot him squarely in the chest, killing him instantly. Ferland, who'd been acting on adrenaline and instinct, began to shake like a leaf.

Lieutenant David Jones of Echo Three was a hard-charger from Silver Spring, Maryland, who led by example. "If you made a mistake, he wasn't down on your case," noted Sergeant Rogers. "He was there showing you how to do it better." When the squad in the center of Jones's formation was pinned down by 12.7mm machine-gun fire at the edge of Dai Do,

Jones shouted over the din to Rogers, who had the squad on the right flank. Jones wanted Rogers to send two men to help suppress the fire on the center squad.

Sergeant Rogers, a twenty-three-year-old career Marine, told his assistant squad leader to take over, then he moved out with Lance Corporal Frank. Bullets kicked up around the pair as they found a good firing position. When they opened up they saw an NVA jump up to run farther back into the thick vegetation. There was a lull in the enemy fire, but as Lieutenant Jones started pushing everyone forward again Frank suddenly went down, clutching his side in agony. Rogers had to get back to his squad, which was moving into the first hedgerow, but he also needed to get Frank to where a corpsman could assist him.

"Can you walk?" asked Rogers.

"Yeah."

"Can you run?"

"Yeah."

Sergeant Rogers covered Frank's withdrawal with his M16 in his right hand and the wounded man's rifle in his left. When Rogers caught up with his squad, he found his assistant squad leader, Cpl. Joseph C. Pickett, twenty-two, of Chicago, dead with a bullet in his neck. Pickett, a black Marine, had not been the senior corporal in the squad. Rogers had selected him as assistant squad leader, though, by dint of his cheerful, fearless enthusiasm. Private Jerry Fields, a nineteen-year-old black from Lexington, Kentucky, was also dead. He'd been shot in the head.

The squad's senior corporal was nowhere to be found, however. The word Rogers got was that the noncom, who'd always been a self-centered whiner, had latched onto a wounded man as an excuse to head back across the paddies. He never came back. In fact, Rogers never saw the man again—even after the battle.

Corporal Cardona, a squad leader in Echo Two, finally made it up to the first hedgerow with his radioman. A dilapidated barbed-wire fence, less than two feet high, ran through the overgrown vegetation on the opposite side. A Marine flung himself prone on Cardona's right, and another made it up to his left.

From the right, a wounded corporal from another squad hollered at Cardona, "There's somebody in that bush!" Cardona bobbed up to his knees and flipped grenades over the bushes as he tried to see where the enemy was. He could hear the NVA firing but saw nothing. The wounded corporal could see the concussion of the automatic weapon as it shook the leaves, though. "I'm going to fire some cover for you! Come over the fence!" he shouted.

Captain Livingston suddenly appeared beside Cardona to help them get organized. The skipper fired his grease gun into the brush as Cardona shouted at a machine gunner to move up on the left and provide more fire. The Marine started forward with his M60 and, to Cardona's horror, was immediately wounded. It was now or never. The wounded corporal on the right was still firing to help them over the hump. Cardona shouted at one of his men, Lance Corporal Mitchell, to get over the fence. Mitchell stared at Cardona as though he was crazy. "Mitchell, we gotta go!" Cardona screamed. When Mitchell started to get up, Cardona shoved him over the fence, then hurdled the shrubs himself and went prone. Mitchell was already firing. Cardona squeezed off a few more rounds, then threw a grenade. Other grunts were doing the same, and the enemy soldier in the bushes was finally silenced.

There were dead NVA in camouflaged spiderholes at the edge of Dai Do, and live ones dug in amid the gutted hootches, hedgerows, and bamboo thickets. Echo Company pressed forward behind a shock wave of M16 and M60 fire. The Marines also used LAWs and M79s against identified enemy positions, then pitched in fragmentation and white phosphorus grenades.

The NVA did not retreat.

One Marine took a direct hit from an RPG—and his blown-off leg went cartwheeling through the air.

Lance Corporal Cornwell was behind another Marine when he saw spiderhole trapdoors abruptly open to either side of the advancing grunt. The Marine hesitated. Before he could decide whom to swing his M16 at first, the NVA shot him in the head. When the situation allowed Cornwell to move forward again, he noticed that the dead Marine had fallen at such an angle that the blood had all rushed to his head. The dead man was purple from the neck up.

Gunnery Sergeant Eggleston, the artillery spotter, crouched over a young Marine who had been hit in the side of the head. The man's brain was exposed, but he was still coherent. He told Eggleston that he knew he was going to die. As Eggleston wrapped a battle dressing around the wound, he told the man he'd be all right—that he was going to get him back. The gunny hefted the wounded Marine over his shoulders in a fireman's carry and humped back toward an Otter that had driven up to within a hundred meters of the hamlet.

Gunnery Sergeant Eggleston was a big man, but when he saw several Marines huddled behind one of the burial mounds with an M60 he called to them for help. The Marines did not move. "We're takin' fire here!" they shouted back. Eggleston moved on to the Otter without assistance, and got the wounded man propped up on the deck inside the open back door. At that instant, he glimpsed the flash of an RPG being fired from behind the first hedgerow. He turned to see the slow-moving projectile arcing toward the vehicle. Eggleston pushed the wounded man inside with an instinctive shove that was so hard and fast he was afraid he had killed him. Then he dove for cover, losing his helmet in the process. The RPG exploded about twenty meters away, just as Eggleston was hitting the deck. He was grazed across the top of his head, and blood ran down his face. The Otter took off at top speed as soon as the RPG impacted, and he could see the wounded man's legs bouncing as they hung out the back. Eggleston secured a battle dressing over his own head, tied it under his chin, and put his helmet back on over the thick bandage before starting back into Dai Do in a crouching walk.

Assigned as a machine gunner, Pfc. Marshall J. Serna of Echo Company had also played corpsman and grenadier on the way to Dai Do. He put a lot of rounds through his M60, but he couldn't see a single NVA; he finally ceased fire and moved to assist the casualties nearest him. Serna grabbed an M79 from one of the wounded men and slung a bag of 40mm shells around his neck. After lobbing several into the first hedgerow, he leapfrogged his way to the next wounded Marine, carrying his M60 in one hand and the M79 in another. By then he was close enough to make some sense of where the NVA had dug in. He fired the M79 at those positions, pausing repeatedly to bandage the wounded man lying beside him. He finally called for a corpsman and charged on through the hedgerow into the hamlet itself.

Someone was shouting, "Machine gun up!"

Serna put down the M79 and clambered into the cleared-out NVA trench from which the call had come. There were about ten Marines in it. The trench was only about forty meters from one that was full of NVA who kept exposing themselves as they rose to fire. There was a bunker in the clearing between the two, and several wounded Marines huddled behind the earthen mound for cover.

"Why hasn't anybody got those guys?" Serna screamed, furious at the other Marines' inaction.

He decided to go after the wounded himself.

The irony was that Serna, who had been raised fatherless and on welfare in Pittsburg, California, had previously been a discipline problem in Echo Company. He had a real problem taking orders. Furthermore, Serna was a pothead who got stoned almost every day he was in Vietnam. He got stoned because he was scared.

Serna had never touched marijuana prior to shipping out to Vietnam in November 1967. During his first day in the transient area in Da Nang, however, a fellow grunt had taken pity on the nervous new guy and fired up a nerve-mellowing joint as he rapped with him about the 'Nam. From then on, Serna smoked grass whenever and wherever he could get away with it, even on patrol. Although no one in the platoon lit up as enthusiastically as he, there were usually takers when he passed a joint. "We just talked and cracked up," Serna recalled. "Hey, a lot of things were ugly but after smoking weed, you didn't give a damn." The marijuana was never smoked openly, and Serna himself told no one that his nerves had become so jangled that he had graduated to morphine. The only person who knew was the corpsman who supplied Serna with morphine syrettes from his medical bag. It started the first time Serna saw the doc thump a syrette into a badly wounded grunt. Serna approached the corpsman afterward and asked, "What the hell did you hit him with? First he's screamin', now he's *laughin'*? Doc, do you think, you know. . . ." After that, Serna would shoot up in his fighting hole when no one was looking.

Oh God, Serna thought as he went over the top with his machine gun and dashed to the bunker behind which the wounded Marines were pinned down. He received the Silver Star for what he did next. Serna dropped to his gut atop the bunker and fired his M60 into the enemy trench in front of them. Return fire cracked past his head as several NVA clambered out to charge his machine gun. Everything was happening fast but with a clarity that was almost like slow motion. Serna could see the pith helmets and the banana-shaped magazines in the

AK-47s of the NVA charging him. He could see his bursts hitting them, but one NVA would not go down. Serna kept firing. He knew he had hit the man in the chest. It terrified him. He figured the man must be on opium. The guy was going to kill him. Serna flashed back to childhood arguments about Superman, whom he hated, and he remembered how stupid it had seemed when the villains shot the superhero in the chest. He had always said he would have shot Superman in his big fat head. Thinking of that, Serna raised his sights and shot the NVA superman in the head. The enemy soldier finally fell.

Serna threw grenades into the NVA trench, then left his M60 atop the bunker as he grabbed one of the wounded. Hunched over, he dragged the man like a sack back to the Marines' trench. Then he ran back to his machine gun. No one followed him. These guys are watching me like they're watching goddamn TV! he thought. Why isn't anybody helping me? Serna resumed firing, hammering out long bursts that burned out the barrel of his M60. Another machine gun lay nearby in the debris, and he kept firing with that weapon until he turned and grabbed another of the wounded. Serna made it back with the man, and then went back for another, screaming at the other grunts for not assisting him.

"What the hell is wrong with you guys?" Serna clambered back out of the trench, shouting, "The hell with you, man—I'm going to kill these sonsofbitches, man!"

Serna picked up the machine gun and started toward the enemy trench in a killing fury. He hadn't gone two steps when an enemy soldier, apparently the last one still alive in the position, flung a grenade at him. He saw it tumbling end over end and spun around to jump back onto the mound. The grenade exploded. When he rose back up to try to kill the NVA, Serna saw that his right leg was pumping blood from a wound below the knee. Oh, goddamn, I'm hit! he thought. He couldn't feel anything, but his leg buckled under him. He lay where he had fallen and bellowed that he was out of ammunition. He was so scared that it took him a moment to remember the ammo bracelet he wore around his wrist. He snapped the half-dozen rounds into the M60 and got behind the weapon to sight in on where the NVA had appeared. Serna waited for the soldier to come up again with another grenade. When the man did, Serna fired a burst into his head and chest. Then Serna passed out.

Awakened during his evacuation by amtrac, Serna was on a stretcher at Mai Xa Chanh West when he saw a newsman lining him up for a photograph. "I don't need this kind of shit, man, to be showin' at home," Serna screamed at the photographer, thinking of his nervous mother.

Bitter and shell-shocked, Serna was in the recovery ward aboard the *Iwo Jima* when he made a decision. "I knew I had reached my limit," he recalled. "I'd seen men snap out there and they got people killed. Rather than going back out there and being a worthless piece of shit, I said no, I better end it now." Serna had been wounded before, but it took three Purple Hearts for an enlisted man to be reassigned off the line, not two, as was the policy for officers. Serna knew one of the corpsmen working the ward, and he talked the man into altering his medical records so that an injury he'd received when burned by a hot machine-gun barrel would show up as enemy related and thus become his ticket out of 'Nam. The trick worked, "but to this day it still bothers me because I'm supposed to be a big war hero."

Lieutenant Ferland of Golf Three slid into an abandoned enemy trench at the forward edge of Dai Do. As the NVA retreated into Dinh To, the next hamlet along the creek, Ferland established radio contact with an aerial observer above the battlefield and called for an air strike.

Lieutenant Ferland's radioman, Hester, was to his right in the trench. Hester was an easygoing, redheaded country boy whom Ferland thought the world of. Because Hester was strong as an ox and because Ferland wanted to be able to move quickly and freely, Hester humped not only the radio and his gear but most of Ferland's stuff as well. Ferland appreciated those long handset cords because Hester could not always keep pace, loaded down as he was.

Private First Class Bill McDade, the platoon's number one grenadier, was to Ferland's left in the trench. McDade was a tough guy from New York City—the type you'd love to know in combat and hate to know in civilian life, according to Ferland. McDade was impressive with the single-shot M79; he could put three rounds in the air before the first one landed.

As Lieutenant Ferland talked to the aerial observer, an RPG exploded in front of their trench, wounding all three men before they could get the air strike in. Ferland caught a metal fragment in his right eye. He thought that both eyes had been hit because his left one clouded in unison with his right. He grabbed his face and slid down to the trench's bottom as he exclaimed, "Oh, shit!" Ferland wasn't in pain, but he couldn't see anything. His right eye felt very heavy, and he thought it was gone. The pressure was not as severe in his left eye. His first thought was that he'd be able to take up skeet shooting again with that eye. Then reality hit: How the hell are we going to get out of here? he wondered.

Although Ferland had been rejoined by his two squads that had fallen back to An Lac the previous evening (they had come up with Echo Company), his shot-up platoon could not spare anybody to escort the wounded trio rearward. The only assistance they got was from a corpsman who wrapped a bandage around Ferland's eyes, treated Hester's wounded arm, and then tended to McDade, who was semidelirious with a head wound. The idea was to have McDade lead them back through the partially cleared hamlet, with Ferland hanging onto McDade's web gear with one hand and keeping a grip on his AK-47 with the other. Hester, who was too badly injured to hold a rifle, would bring up the rear. If they ran into anything, Ferland was to blast them at Hester's direction.

After making it back to An Lac without incident, the three became separated along the medevac chain. Lieutenant Ferland was finally helped aboard a Sea Horse that flew him to the USS *Repose*. He had refused to let go of his folding-stock AK-47 the whole way back, and he still had it in the triage area when a gurney carrying a wounded NVA prisoner was wheeled up beside him. Ferland, who had become delirious and was mumbling to himself, began screaming, "Get this bastard away from me or he's going to get it!" A Navy chaplain came over to calm Ferland as the prisoner was moved away. The chaplain told Ferland he could keep the AK's clip as a souvenir, and Ferland agreed to give up the weapon only if he could toss it overboard. He didn't want it to wind up as some Navy brass hat's undeserved trophy. The chaplain helped Ferland off the gurney, led him to the side of the ship, and together they threw the rifle over the railing.[3]

---

3. The metal shard that had lodged behind Lieutenant Ferland's eyeball was too small and had done too little damage to warrant surgery. The doctors left it where it was, and within four days his eyesight began to return. He went back to BLT 2/4 and became an assistant S3. He later received an end-of-tour NCMv in addition to the BSMv and Purple Heart he got for Dai Do.

*   *   *

Lieutenant Morgan of Golf Two never heard the descent of the 82mm mortar rounds that the NVA fired from Dinh To twenty minutes after his platoon reached the far side of Dai Do. No one could hear the mortars being fired over the general din. The Marines were in and around the hedgerow-covered slit trenches that the NVA had vacated, and they were checking their ammunition supply and refilling magazines when explosions began erupting around them. The enemy fire was right on target, and before Morgan knew it he had fifteen more wounded Marines on his hands.

Meanwhile, Captain Livingston, who had caught fragments from two grenades in his right leg, coordinated the evacuation of Echo Company's approximately ten dead and sixty wounded aboard Otters. The severely wounded included one of the captain's radio operators. As a corpsman worked on the prostrate radioman, Corporal Cardona's squad happened to be passing by on its way forward. Livingston called to Cardona that he needed his radioman. This randomly picked replacement would prove to be a good one: He would very shortly help save the captain's life. Dai Do had been secured, but the battle was not over.

CHAPTER 9 A VILLAGE TOO FAR

At 0914 on 2 May, Echo and Golf Companies reported that Dai Do had been secured and that they were tied in and consolidating along the northwestern edge of the hamlet. One minute later, the NVA in Dinh To began mortaring Dai Do to cover their retreat. The sporadic shelling lasted for fifteen minutes, during which time Colonel Hull arrived by skimmer. Fire Raider 6 joined Lieutenant Colonel Weise and the BLT 2/4 Alpha Command Group in the forward edge of An Lac. While Hull and Weise were talking, the battalion sergeant major, Big John Malnar, raised his binoculars to investigate a lone figure he'd spotted in the paddies between An Lac and Dai Do. "Look, there's someone running right across the front there—shit, it's a fucking gook!" he shouted.

The NVA was in the open about a hundred meters away. The soldier, who wore green fatigues and carried an RPD light machine gun, seemed utterly confused and lost. He was trying to get away from Dai Do, but his escape route made him a shooting-gallery target for the Marines in An Lac. Sergeant Bollinger, the battalion commander's radioman, asked, "Can I get him, Sergeant Major?" When Malnar told him to go ahead, Bollinger shouldered his M14. His first shot led the NVA too much, and his second was behind the running figure. The third caught the man in the head, and he dropped like a stone. As another Marine rushed out to check the body for intel material, Sergeant Major Malnar looked down at his radioman-turned-rifleman and said with mock disgust, "Shit, Bollinger, took ya three fuckin' shots to get 'im."

Colonel Hull had meanwhile informed Weise that he wanted BLT 2/4 to maintain its "momentum" with an assault on Dinh To within an hour. Weise, who later said that he didn't think his superiors "really knew what the hell was going on," listened incredulously to the plan. While BLT 2/4 hit Dinh To, an ARVN unit was to hit Dong Lai, which sat on the opposite side of the narrow tributary on Dinh To's western flank. With or without ARVN support, BLT 2/4 was in no condition to launch another assault into prepared enemy positions, and Weise was aggravated more than ever by Major General Tompkins's failure to visit the battlefield. Weise wondered if regiment was providing division with accurate reports about the magnitude of NVA activity in the Dai Do complex, and he told Hull as bluntly as he could that his battalion had just about run out of steam. "We don't have anything left. We're worn out. We've been fighting here—continuous fighting—and every one of my companies is pretty well shot up."

Hull was adamant. "I *have* to keep the pressure on," the colonel said. "I want you to go."

"Well, we'll do the best we can," said Weise resignedly. "You know, if you really want to catch these guys, land some battalions north of here and drive 'em into us. We can occupy Dai Do and dig in. Drive 'em into Dai Do and we can clean 'em out."

Weise and Major Warren had discussed this hammer-and-anvil plan the day before, and Warren had suggested it then to the regimental operations officer. Specifically, Weise and Warren proposed that the regiment's two remaining battalions, 1/3 and the 1st Amtracs, be placed on either side of BLT 2/4. This would be the anvil against which the battalions inserted north of Dai Do would hammer the NVA as they swept south. Hull, however, could not move 1/3 or the Amtracs without permission from division, and it was doubtful that Major General Tompkins, whose units were stretched thinly along the DMZ, could have come up with the forces needed to make a meaningful hammer. Weise later wrote that whether his recommendation "ever reached the commanding general, I do not know. I do know that no aggressive plan to destroy the enemy was carried out and that we lost a rare, golden opportunity to annihilate the crack 320th NVA Division."

Lieutenant Colonel Weise, who would soon salute the flagpole and dutifully launch into Dinh To with the out-of-steam BLT 2/4, saw folly in the method of attack. He did not see folly in the rationale behind it. Weise was a conventional warrior, and he viewed the 320th NVA Division's offensive within conventional parameters. The confluence of the Cua Viet and Bo Dieu rivers near Dai Do lent strategic value to this otherwise worthless terrain. If the NVA controlled the juncture of the rivers, they could cut resupply down the Bo Dieu to the 3d Marine Division at the DHCB, and down the Cua Viet to the provincial capital, Quang Tri City. The NVA had accomplished this first step, and Weise was of two minds as to what he suspected their next move would be. An attack against the division headquarters was one option:

> Dong Ha was a sprawling combat support and combat service support base. Once a strong enemy got in close, penetration of the thin defensive perimeter, manned by and large by support troops, would have been relatively easy. Enemy assault units might take heavy casualties, particularly after the friendly maneuver battalions near Dong Ha reacted. Heavy casualties would have been a small price to pay for Dong Ha. . . . What could be a greater propaganda victory than destroying and temporarily occupying the largest Marine base in northern I Corps?

Another possibility was an NVA attack through the ARVN defenses at Quang Tri City. The capture of a provincial capital would also have resounding propaganda value. "Such a bold stroke would have been possible if the 320th NVA Division had not been stopped on the north bank of the Bo Dieu," wrote Weise. In stopping the NVA, BLT 2/4 had been forced to go nose to nose with them—taking heavy casualties in the process. Weise thought those Marine losses were justified. "Just think of the casualties suffered in World War II assaults on Tarawa, Peleliu, Iwo Jima, and Sugar Loaf Hill on Okinawa," he wrote. He further reflected that "if the 320th NVA Division *had* planned to attack Dong Ha or Quang Tri, then BLT 2/4 had conducted a successful, albeit unintended spoiling attack. . . . I have fought the Battle of Dai Do many times in my mind and always return to the same conclusion: We accomplished our mission against great odds. Whatever the enemy intended to do, he didn't."[1]

---

1. Captain Forehand, the BLT 2/4 S4, wrote that, in retrospect, had the NVA overrun the division headquarters, "it might have been in the best interest of our side if some of the clowns there had been 'smoked,' but not all of them."

There was another perspective to the Battle of Dai Do, however. This view held that the NVA had, in fact, accomplished exactly what they intended. They had wanted to kill a lot of Marines, and this they did. The NVA never actually attempted to cross the Bo Dieu River to reach Dong Ha or Quang Tri. It was the Navy's TF Clearwater, not the NVA, that shut down logistical traffic on the river. The NVA had simply fired a number of recoilless rifle rounds at river traffic, and then readied themselves for the Marine response. The NVA in their camouflaged, sandbagged, and mutually supporting entrenchments had forced their opponents to fight on ground of their choosing. By plunging full speed ahead into the fortified NVA hamlets, the aggressive Marines aided and abetted NVA tactics. It was really the NVA who were playing the body count game.

"I saw what was happening as wasteful of American lives," wrote Lt. Gen. Victor H. "Brute" Krulak, commanding general of the Fleet Marine Force, Pacific. Krulak was headquartered in Hawaii, and although a frequent visitor to the war zone, he did not have operational control of the Marines in Vietnam. Operational control rested with General Westmoreland in Saigon. Westmoreland saw battles such as Dai Do as victories. Krulak did not. Since June 1966, when Westmoreland formally announced his search-and-destroy strategy—which sought battles such as Dai Do—Krulak had been trying to change the direction of Westmoreland's war horse. The search-and-destroy strategy was aimed at bringing the NVA to battle anytime, anywhere, until overwhelming U.S. firepower had inflicted such heavy casualties on Hanoi's army that it could no longer field a meaningful force. Westmoreland intended to pound the NVA into submission. Krulak understood the folly of this. Search and destroy was a war of attrition, and it was a game that Hanoi was destined to win. Hanoi had time, and it had men to expend by the hundreds of thousands. Washington did not. The North Vietnamese embraced the DMZ battles as a chance to bleed the Americans in empty, meaningless terrain that favored their dug-in forces. Krulak understood, as did his counterparts in Hanoi, that victory did not hinge on the big battles, but on which side could provide security to the villages of South Vietnam's densely populated coast. Westmoreland's strategy pulled U.S. units away from pacification efforts in these areas, and Lieutenant General Krulak, unable to focus U.S. efforts back where he thought they belonged, would write bitterly that "we were pitting

American bodies against North Vietnamese bodies in a backcountry war of attrition, while the enemy was free to make political speeches in the hamlets and villages. . . . However valiant, however skillful were the Army and Marine operations against the large formations . . . in terms of doing what we came to Vietnam to do, the costly, blood-sapping, grinding battles were blows in the air."

"We knew the odds. After being there so many months we were all very realistic. We knew a certain number were going in, and a certain number were coming out," said 2d Lt. Vic Taylor of Hotel Company. "We were going to prevail—that was not a question—but it was a matter of going up and doing it."

Hotel Company had been issued orders for the attack on Dinh To, and Lieutenant Taylor, the acting commander of Hotel Three, walked his line in Dong Huan to make sure that his Marines had their gear and were ready to go. Taylor, a reader of history and a romantic, had grown up watching such movies as *Battle Cry* and *The Sands of Iwo Jima,* and there was a certain dramatic and familiar ring to the things he saw and heard as they saddled up. He thought of the Marine "Devil Dogs" advancing through the wheat at Belleau Wood, and of the next generation of Leathernecks wading through the bloody lagoon at Tarawa. Of his own Marines about to go into battle across the rice paddies, Taylor later wrote:

Some were standing watch, some readied equipment, many slept or lounged, but all were quiet. No nervous jabbering, no false bravado, no whining, no melodramatics—they were professionals. Most were teenagers, many with far less than a year away from home, but they were seasoned by months of fighting with a determined enemy. Despite their youth, despite their short time in the Corps, they were as willing and serious—as professional—as anyone who ever wore a uniform. I was proud to be among them.

Lieutenant Taylor had rejoined Hotel Company only the previous evening from his XO billet aboard the USS *Iwo Jima.* At twenty-eight, Taylor had more experience and confident, soft-spoken maturity than the average second lieutenant. Originally from Chester County, Pennsylvania, he had done three years as an enlisted Marine following high school.

After college he soon became bored with the life of a junior business executive, so when Vietnam cranked up he went back in as an officer. It was in Vietnam that he decided to make the Marine Corps his career.

"Taylor was a real handsome, studly kind of guy, and a great, heroic-looking Marine," said Captain Williams, the former Hotel Company skipper.

Hotel began moving out of Dong Huan at 0955 to cross the five hundred meters of exposed ground between their position and Dai Do. The Marines in the column were well spaced so there would be no mass target on which an NVA artillery spotter could adjust fire. Lieutenant Taylor wrote:

> We plodded forward in our attack formation—H Company, all seventy-five of us. The day was still, the heat intense. We had guzzled all the water we could hold and had refilled canteens in Dong Huan, not knowing when there would be more. Now the sweat poured out, and uniforms were soaked. Little puffs of dust rose from the dry rice paddy at each step. The metal of weapons was almost too hot to touch. Up ahead, I could see the hedgerows and thickets of Dai Do, burning and smoking from earlier attacks. The firing had ceased. Maybe this would be easier than I expected.

Hotel Company's grunts moved through the southeastern side of Dai Do, past the few Marines they could see among the many from Echo and Golf who were safely tucked behind cover. Reaching the muddy, sluggish stream that defined the western edge of the battlefield, Hotel turned northwest along it. The battalion command group had moved into Dai Do, and Lieutenant Prescott, Hotel's new skipper, gave Weise a cigar. "We'll be back shortly," he said.

Lieutenant Prescott assaulted Dinh To with Lieutenant Taylor's Hotel Three hugging the blueline on the left flank, and Lieutenant Boyle's Hotel One moving abreast on the right. Hotel Two was in reserve under the command of Sgt. Bruce Woodruff, who until that morning had been a squad leader in Hotel One. The assault platoons were moving forward aggressively and methodically in team and individual rushes, using trenches, hedgerows, and tumble-down hootches for cover, when they began taking fire from the front. It sounded as if it was coming from two enemy soldiers with AK-47s in separate, camouflaged positions.

More NVA, none of whom the Marines could see, opened up as Hotel Company pushed on. Taylor suspected that the enemy had deployed observation posts ahead of their main line of resistance, and that it was these small teams of NVA who were doing the shooting. Their fire was accurate. Several Marines had already been hit when Taylor and his radioman knelt behind some bushes. Prescott was on the radio. When the radioman extended the handset to Taylor, the young Marine was hit in the elbow by one of the to-whom-it-may-concern bullets snapping blindly through the vegetation.

Hotel Company leapfrogged deeper into Dinh To, returning the increasingly heavy fire but not suppressing it. As Taylor passed seriously wounded men he would thump the nearest Marine and tell him to help get the casualty to the rear. Their corpsmen already had their hands full, so Taylor had no choice but to use able-bodied riflemen. Nevertheless, he did so reluctantly. Their firepower was needed up front. Taylor knew that some of his Marines would rush forward again as soon as they carried a wounded man back, but he had others he knew would drag their feet, hoping, for example, that the gunny might scoop them up to move water cans or ammo in the company rear. As more Marines were hit and others fell out to help them, it became impossible for Hotel to maintain its momentum.

A lot of prep fire had hit Dinh To, but there was still plenty of greenery. There were trees and leafy bamboo thickets, as well as the hedgerows that had once demarcated property lines. There were also thatch-roofed homes with stucco-covered brick walls. Some were demolished, some were not. Some of the fences and empty animal pens were also still standing. Taylor thought it was like going from yard to yard in suburbia. He finally bogged down with the squad on his platoon's right flank. They were hung up against a hedgerow that ran across their front. The entrenched NVA on the other side had every opening through the thick bushes zeroed in, and the enemy on the flanks covered the trenches that ran the length of the hedgerow, one in front and one behind the shrubs.

Meanwhile, Taylor's platoon sergeant, Sgt. Joe Jones, was pinned down with the squad on the left flank. They were under heavy fire along the creek, and had several wounded men. Jones had two machine-gun teams with his squad, but one of the gunners had fallen out with heat exhaustion. The man was in agony, and his comrades bellowed for a corpsman. The squad's M79 man took over the machine gun, but it jammed on him just as the corpsman made it up to help the gunner. The other M60 was still firing, and the grenadier's M79 also still worked. Every M16 in the squad was jammed, however. All the riflemen could do was throw grenades. Infuriated, Jones grabbed the inoperable machine gun. As he was trying to clear the weapon, he spotted one of the NVA who had pinned them down. He told the grenadier to fire on that position. Then, with the M60 back in working order, Jones rushed to their corpsman to provide the covering fire needed to start getting their casualties back. Jones, who was subsequently awarded the Silver Star, later told the division historical team:

> That was the first time we'd ever seen snipers in trees [and] the wounded we had, we couldn't get 'em out because people just didn't seem like they wanted to get out of their covered positions. You almost had to move up to the individual Marine and beat 'em over the head with the weapon that you had to get 'em up to help the wounded out. I don't know. Maybe people was scared or maybe they was just plain tired. I don't know what the story was behind it, but they wouldn't even help carry the wounded out.

North Vietnamese soldiers were firing from the hootches and bushes on the far side of the creek. Sergeant Jones said that once he'd forced some litter teams into action, NVA snipers were able to slip down the near side of the streambed to pour point-blank fire into Hotel Three's flank because his scared grunts had begun "to pull in from the flanks and cluster up in the middle."

Lieutenant Boyle and Hotel One were also in sorry shape. They had bogged down in the face of heavy AK-47 and RPG fire. As understrength as it already was before taking more casualties, the platoon could not properly cover the right flank, where the vegetation gave way to open paddies. There were NVA in that vegetation, as well as behind the burial mounds in the paddies themselves. Hotel Two, brought up from reserve, was also subjected to this fire from three sides and was unable to restore the momentum of the assault.

There was a lot of confusion. Many Marines simply kept their heads down, but there were a number of others who did more, such as LCpl.

Ralph T. Anderson, an eighteen year old from St. Petersburg, Florida. According to his Silver Star citation:

> Observing two Marines pinned down by sniper fire as they attempted to move a companion to safety, Lance Corporal Anderson obtained a pistol and several hand grenades, unhesitatingly left his covered position and began crawling toward the sniper. Advancing beyond friendly lines, he silenced the enemy position, enabling his comrades to move the Marine to safety. Before he could return to his position, however, he was killed by enemy fire.

Almost every M16 in Hotel Company was inoperable due to overuse and a lack of cleaning gear. When Sgt. Donald F. Devoe's carboned-up rifle jammed, he opened a C-ration can of beans and franks and used the grease it contained to lubricate the weapon. Devoe resumed firing.

Lance Corporal Donaghy of Hotel Two, crouched behind an earthen mound, was just rising up to fire his M16 when the Marine doing the same thing beside him was shot in the head. The round went through the man's helmet, which stayed on his head, and he wordlessly turned to look at Donaghy as a fountain of blood spurted from the wound. Slumped over but still conscious, the Marine did not make a sound as the corpsman worked on him. He didn't look as though he was going to survive.

"We were in a nasty, narrow spot and we had a lot of people jammed in that narrow front," Lieutenant Prescott said later. He had moved his command group into a partially demolished hootch maybe fifteen meters up from the stream and was trying to get a handle on the situation.

"Scotty Prescott was a real good leader, and the troops liked him," said Captain Williams, the man Prescott had replaced. "He had a lot of spirit and he had the wiseguy in him." Prescott, a twenty-four-year-old Texan, could also be serious when necessary. From September 1967 to March 1968, when he'd had Hotel Three, he'd been considered by some to be the best platoon commander in the battalion. His follow-me brand of leadership had gotten him shot in the leg during the assault on Vinh Quan Thuong, where he'd also been an on-the-spot grenadier, machine gunner, and LAW rocketman. He'd been bumped up to the exec slot after recuperating. Prescott had no career intentions. He was a citizen-soldier. "Most of the officers were USMC. I was USMCR," he noted. "I never wanted the R dropped off. I was always United States Marine Corps Reserve and proud of it, knowing that at the end of three years I was gone."

Lieutenant Prescott, watching from behind cement cover, saw Cpl. Tyrone W. Austin, a black machine gunner, get shot in the head after setting up right outside the lieutenant's hootch. The round took away half of his head. The corpsman inside the hootch with Prescott went into shock at the sight. He had to be shaken back to reality.

The NVA had moved in too closely for Prescott to call in air or arty— or even his own 60mm mortars, which the gunny had set up at the edge of Dai Do. At about 1200, Prescott radioed Lieutenant Colonel Weise to report that Hotel Company would probably be overrun if not reinforced. Shortly thereafter, Prescott's radioman got off the horn and said excitedly, "Captain Livingston is coming!"

Lieutenant Prescott, who knew then that they would be okay, hollered to Taylor, who was about seventy feet from the hootch, "Echo is coming up!"

"Echo is coming!"

"Echo is coming!"

The word was repeated down the line, and it electrified Hotel Company. Marines who'd had all they could take of eating dirt got up to scream and wave, "C'mon, let's go on. Let's go!"

Lieutenant Prescott came out of his hootch, bellowing for everyone to stay where they were. He had taken only a few steps from cover when he was suddenly spun three-quarters of the way around and dropped on the spot. He had been hit in the small of the back. Prescott was vaguely aware of the sound of an AK-47 squeezing off a shot from across the creek at the same moment he stepped out of the hootch, and he was terribly aware that he could not feel his legs. He figured that his spine had been damaged, and as he lay on the ground he imagined that he would have to spend the rest of his life in a wheelchair. A corpsman and several Marines dragged Prescott back into the beat-up hootch. A thousand thoughts rushed through his mind. He had been shot before, and this did not feel like a gunshot wound. His back was sore. He could feel something wet, but he didn't seem to be bleeding badly. But why don't my legs work? he wondered frantically.

Lieutenant Taylor ran over to the hootch. Prescott passed command to him with three words—"You got it!"—then the corpsman got two Marines to start back with Prescott on the trail to Dai Do. Prescott had an arm over the shoulder of each and, with his feet dragging, he grimaced in pain and mumbled groggily about his useless legs.[2]

After being taken by skimmer to the BLT CP, Lieutenant Prescott was lying facedown on the beach among some other Hotel Company casualties when, perhaps thirty minutes after being medevacked, his feet suddenly began to tingle. He removed his jungle boots and massaged his feet. Feeling returned to his legs. Prescott was unsteady when he stood up, but he felt 100 percent better. There was a half-dollar–sized bruise at the base of his spine, but no blood, and his torn-up gear explained why. The bullet had hit the full canteen on his left hip, mushroomed, and ricocheted against a stud on his cartridge belt. The stud was driven into the small of his back, and the blow had temporarily knocked out the feeling in his legs. The bullet had then zipped through the canteen on his right hip. The first canteen had a small entrance hole and a big exit hole, and the second canteen was completely ripped apart. The luckiest hit of the war, Prescott thought as he showed the canteens to the bloody, bandaged Marines around him.

Lieutenant Colonel Weise had not planned to send Echo Company into Hotel Company's meatgrinder. He thought that Echo Company, which numbered about seventy-five men after its dawn assault into Dai Do, was thoroughly winded. Golf Company, also on hand in Dai Do, was even more beat up. Weise's original idea was to form a composite platoon from the support personnel in An Lac and hustle them into Dinh To aboard amtracs. His next step would then have been to bring Foxtrot Company over from Dong Huan to follow the composite platoon in. Weise contemplated taking command of Foxtrot himself because he did not trust Butler's drive. Captain Livingston, however, made these plans moot. He had been monitoring the situation by radio. He neither waited for nor asked for orders but simply got on

2. Lieutenant Prescott had a BSMv from Operation Kingfisher, and the Silver Star and Purple Heart from Vinh Quan Thuong. He got his second Silver Star and Purple Heart for Dong Huan/Dinh To.

the battalion tac net. "Dixie Diner Six, this is Echo Six. I'm going to help Hotel. They are really fixin' to get into trouble. I'll go get 'em."

Captain Livingston called up his platoon commanders before leaving Dai Do, but just as Lieutenant Jones of Echo Three started to move he heard the thump of an outgoing mortar round. The sound seemed to have come from just ahead of his covered position. Jones was sure that Echo's mortars hadn't been brought forward yet, but he couldn't imagine an enemy mortar being that close to their lines. After waiting for what seemed a long time and hearing nothing, Jones reckoned that it had been an outgoing friendly shell. He came out of his ditch then, just as what was in fact an enemy shell landed right behind him. The round had been fired from such close range that its arc was almost straight up and down, and its time of flight relatively long. The explosion lifted Jones off his feet and sent him crashing into another ditch. He figured out that he was still alive, but beyond that he really didn't know what had happened to him. He could feel a lot of burning sensations cutting through his overall numbness.

Well, this must be what it's like to get hit, he thought. This hurts bad enough that I might be outta here.

Lieutenant Jones's radioman ran up to him from the ditch and said, "Your legs are messed up—you need to get out of here." The back of Jones's flak jacket was shredded, but it had done its job and protected his upper body. Except for small bits of metal in the backs of his arms, the fragments had mostly gouged him in his buttocks and the backs of his legs. He had seventeen serious wounds. Jones radioed Captain Livingston, who told him to hang in there and make sure that someone took care of him—and to find somebody to pass command to. Jones told his radioman to find Sergeant Rogers, the squad leader who was next in the chain of command in the absence of a wounded platoon commander, platoon sergeant, and right guide. That done, the as-yet-unbandaged Jones started rearward with six or seven other walking wounded.

"I wondered how in the hell we were going to assist anyone without ammo," recalled Lance Corporal Cornwell of Echo Two. He was angry and scared as he retrieved his M60 and started forward with the rest of the platoon. The assault pouch on his machine gun, which normally held a hundred-round belt, was only partially filled. That was all he had. "We were almost completely out of ammo, and we were out of water. In that heat, water was as important as ammo. We were hardened. You know what you can do, and you know what you can't do. In our condition, what we were doing was crazy."

There were NVA in bypassed and camouflaged spiderholes to Hotel Company's rear; Echo Company, moving rapidly into Dinh To, rolled right over the top of them. Sergeant Rogers, the new Echo Three commander, suddenly saw an NVA soldier come out of nowhere to run past him on his left. The NVA was going in the same direction as the Marines. Rogers, who could have almost reached out and grabbed the terrified man, hadn't even had a chance to swing his M16 around before an M60 gunner chopped the soldier down. Rogers saw five or six more NVA, panicked by the machine-gun fire, pop from their spiderholes and start running away. The machine gunner turned them into rag dolls before his eyes with one long burst.

It was about 1040. Lieutenant Taylor, who had moved to a bomb crater, turned to see Captain Livingston coming forward at the head of a group of what looked like twenty to thirty Marines. Taylor noticed that Livingston did not flinch despite shots that literally kicked up dirt around his feet. As Livingston directed his Marines into positions to flesh out the gaps in Hotel's lines, Taylor rose up a bit from his cover to greet him. Livingston clambered into the crater with an enthusiastic, "How ya doin', Tiger? C'mon—let's go!"

Echo and Hotel Companies started forward again with their men jumbled together and bayonets fixed. They advanced in leaps and bounds between spots of cover. One of Lieutenant Taylor's radiomen had his loudspeaker tuned to the battalion tac net, and at one point this background noise included their crusty regimental commander, Colonel Hull, coming up on the net to ask Weise, "What's your situation up there?"

"We have two companies in the attack," replied Weise.

"Now, exploit your advantage, exploit your advantage. Don't hold back—exploit your success!"

Weise had a gravelly Philadelphia voice, and he barked back with some anger, "Well, you don't have to tell me that, Six, because what we're going to do is get up there and kill as many of these little yellow bastards as we can."

Sounds like the "Send More Japs" message from Wake Island, thought Taylor. It was pure Weise and it breathed fire into them. The Marines needed that; it was about all they had. Most of their M16s were fouled from constant firing, and they were low on ammo of every type. Some men picked up NVA weapons. Others, out of ammunition, attacked with empty weapons. Taylor saw one Marine go by with no weapon at all. When Taylor called to him, the man explained that his M16 was jammed and that he had used an M79 until he'd run out of shells. He said he was looking for another weapon. Taylor, who had two .45-caliber pistols because past experience had taught him that there wasn't always time to reload, gave the unarmed man one of them, along with a couple of magazines, and off the Marine went.

Lance Corporal Cornwell was in a ditch with maybe twenty other Marines, and when the shout went up to charge the NVA who had them pinned, he reflexively went over the top. Within a few steps he'd fired the last of his ammo, and he dropped to the prone even as he realized that the Marines running with him were being hit. He looked around. One of them was dead; two others were seriously wounded. There was no one else there. Shocked, Cornwell looked back. In the confusion, the other Marines had never left the ditch. They were holding their M16s above their heads and firing blindly. Cornwell screamed at them to stop firing so he could crawl back. He had no idea if the three men with him had been shot by the NVA or by the Marines behind them. Cornwell left his empty M60 behind as he took hold of one of the seriously wounded men and started back in an exhausted, ground-hugging crawl. He made it.

On the right flank, LCpl. James L. Barela of Hotel Two was behind cover and working on his jammed M60 when a Chicom grenade exploded in his position. He and the three grunts with him were all wounded, but then a crazy little Marine from Echo Company got up to throw grenade after grenade; Barela, not wanting to let the man down, moved up with his cleared machine gun. He started firing where they thought the NVA were, then he moved on in the confusion to a trench full of Marines whose weapons were mostly jammed. There was a hootch about twenty-five meters to their front with a trail to the right of it. Two or three enemy soldiers in the hootch provided covering fire for other NVA who were moving into position by crossing the trail. One Marine fired several LAWs into the cement hootch, and another ran to the right to move in on its flank. The NVA cut him down. Barela left his rejammed M60 in the trench and worked his way toward the man with several Marines from Hotel Three. One of them was hit in the arm, so they dragged him back along with the man they'd gone out to rescue. The NVA, meanwhile, were still crossing the trail despite the M79 rounds being lobbed in by a grenadier. Soon they had worked in close enough to fling Chicoms at the trench. Barela still couldn't get his M60 to work.

It was 1340 and the NVA were counterattacking. Lieutenant Taylor had just moved to the cover provided by the banana trees in the courtyard of a shot-up cement hootch with a partially collapsed thatch roof. There was a sudden and definite increase in the amount of NVA fire, and it riddled the banana trees and the masonry wall of the hootch. As banana leaves folded down around them, Taylor looked up to see that the bushes fifty meters to his front were alive with heavily camouflaged enemy soldiers. The closest NVA were already within twenty-five meters. Their pith helmets, fatigues, and web gear were covered with fresh leaves. They looked like moving bushes with little faces, and Taylor flashed back to a ghostly, black-and-white documentary he had seen of identical-looking Viet Minh in an attack on Dien Bien Phu.

Fuck it, he thought. Come on, you assholes! Lieutenant Taylor, firing his .45 when not talking on the radio, was at a fever pitch, as was the Marine nearest him. The grunt was armed only with a pistol and a sandbag full of grenades, and he pitched the frags as fast as he could pull the pins.

Nearby, Pfc. Vincent A. Scafidi of Hotel Three, a lean, tough kid from New York City, earned the Silver Star as he stood with his M60 braced against his hip, killing the enemy soldiers as they came through the brush.

Corporal Britton of the battalion scouts was preparing to grenade an enemy bunker when the counterattack began. Four NVA rushed him, and he pointed his pistol at the closest one. "I fired at least three shots into him and watched him fall at my feet," Britton later wrote. "I suddenly found myself out of ammo in my .45, with no time to put in another magazine." Britton unslung his M16, which he carried with fixed bayonet, and killed the next NVA with a slash to the throat. He shot the third one in the stomach. "As he died, he lunged into me, and his bayonet sliced my left leg just inside the thigh. At this exact moment, the fourth NVA crashed into my right side, knocking my M16 to the ground. I immediately grabbed his rifle with my left hand, pulled my K-Bar knife from its sheath on my belt, and slammed it into his stomach. He slumped against me."

A Chicom grenade landed beside them, and the explosion blew apart Corporal Britton and the last NVA, with the enemy soldier taking most of the blast. Britton's face was bursting with pain, and he put his hands to it. Blood was everywhere. He passed out.

Britton was startled back to reality by a long burst from an M60 as the machine gunner ran up to him. After rolling Britton over, the grunt shouted back that Britton was still alive and needed a doc. The corpsman bandaged Britton's face, and two exhausted Marines half-carried, half-dragged him to where other casualties were waiting to be loaded onto skimmers. Britton passed out again, and did not regain consciousness until he'd been medevacked to the ship and the doctors were working on him. They removed a piece of metal from his right foot, another from his right forearm, and three from his face. The explosion had also broken his nose, both cheekbones, and partially dislocated his jaw. A corpsman visited Britton after surgery, and Britton wrote that the doc "gave me a bullet that he'd removed from the upper chest area of my flak jacket after taking it and the rest of my gear when I arrived on board ship. Sometime during the two days of fighting it was shot at me and lodged in my flak jacket. I really do not know when."

"Captain Livingston and I were in visual contact most of the fight, and I never once saw him take cover or a backward step," Lieutenant Taylor later testified. "Instead, he moved among his troops encouraging, threatening, comforting, urging, pushing, and pulling them to virtually superhuman feats."

Livingston's famous grease gun had jammed up on him, and he had thrown the ammo magazine in one direction and the defective weapon in another. He unholstered his .45 then, but one of his young Marines suggested he become a rifleman and threw an M14 to him, along with a bag full of magazines. Livingston maintained one M14 per squad for use as a sniper weapon, and he put the heavy, reliable weapon to accurate use. "It was survival of the fittest at that point," Livingston recalled. "There were multiple targets—it was a matter of who you wanted to get involved with. I was banging away at a few of 'em. I don't know how many I dinged. I was shooting and people were dropping. There were plenty of them to go around."

Sergeant Rogers of Echo Three was suddenly knocked to the ground, and when he moved his hand to his hip he felt blood. Don't look at the wound, he thought. You'll go into shock! Staying close to the ground, he hollered for a corpsman. One made it up to him and asked, "Where you been hit?"

"I've been shot in the hip!"

The corpsman gave him a quick inspection, then exclaimed, "You dumb ass—you've been shot in the canteen!"

Rogers, thinking he'd been hit, had expected pain, so there was pain. It disappeared when the corpsman shouted at him. Regretting only that he'd just lost his last precious canteen of water, Rogers moved on to assume a prone firing position behind some cover. Everything was happening fast. He could see the enemy coming at them. Everyone was firing. Rogers settled his sights on one NVA, and then another, and another as more popped up in the place of each who went down.

CHAPTER 10 BRING THE WOUNDED, LEAVE THE DEAD

During the buildup to the NVA counterattack, Corporal Cardona of Echo Two had been blasting away at movement in the brush farther up the trail along which his platoon was bogged down. Cardona was on the left side. His squad members lay prone on either side of the footpath, along with other Marines from Echo and Hotel Companies. The Marines were almost stacked on top of each other. They couldn't see anything for all the vegetation. There were wounded everywhere, and corpsmen were making an effort to drag them back.

Cardona's M16 suddenly jammed as he fired down the trail.

At the same time, the machine gunner beside him experienced a jam, too. The gunner looked up then and exclaimed, "Hey, look!"

The NVA were coming down the trail at them.

Corporal Cardona, an experienced, squared-away Marine, shouted at another grunt beside him to grab a grenade, as he himself jerked the pin from one. The two of them let fly and the NVA, firing as they moved, swerved off the relatively open trail and into the thick brush to the right of it.

Cardona sprinted across the trail and ran into Lieutenant Sims, his platoon commander. Cardona explained that their machine gun was jammed and angrily held up his own useless rifle. Sims, armed only with a .45-caliber pistol, handed it to him. "Here, take it!"

Lieutenant Sims was a short, stocky man from Atlanta, Georgia. According to his troops, he didn't have loads of common sense, but he was an educated and concerned young officer who was willing to listen to his seasoned grunts—and took the platoon's casualties hard. Cardona grabbed the pistol that Sims offered, then ran back to where the M60 gunner was trying to clear his weapon. Within minutes, the shout went up that the lieutenant had been hit. Cardona hustled back to where he had last seen Sims, then to a small hootch to the rear of the firing line where dead and wounded Marines were being moved. Sims was inside. He'd been shot in the stomach. Blood was coming out of his mouth. He told Cardona that he couldn't move. Cardona, satisfied that the lieutenant was being taken care of, told Sims to hold on, that they would get him out as soon as possible, then he moved out to rejoin his squad.

Someone hollered that the hootch was on fire. Cardona ran back to find the thatch roof ablaze and caving in. He went inside with several other Marines. "Get me out of here!" Sims screamed. Cardona and another grunt got the lieutenant to his feet. They rushed him outside, then dropped down to avoid the fire snapping through the area. Cardona saw two Marines half-crawling and half-running under the heavy fire as they dragged a mortally wounded black Marine by his arms. The back of the man's head kept banging against the ground, and Cardona screamed, "Pick him up, pick him up! Don't drag him like that—get his head above the ground!"

"They were all superb," Lieutenant Taylor said later of his Marines. "They never gave the counterattack an inch." The NVA outnumbered and outgunned Echo and Hotel, however, and while some enemy elements closed from the front, others used the creek bank as cover to slip into position on the left flank. Those NVA employed AK-47s and RPGs, while the enemy troops in the paddies on the right flank poured 12.7mm machine-gun fire into the ville. On the radio with Weise, Taylor explained that casualties were high, ammo was almost gone, and that "we've got 'em on three sides. I don't think we can hold here. They're wearing us down to the point that they're just going to gobble us up."

Captain Livingston came up on the net to affirm Taylor's picture. "We can't stay here and get all these kids killed," he told Weise.

Neither Livingston nor Taylor wanted to retreat. They wanted reinforcements, but none were available. "Well, I'm going to help you, but you've got to help yourselves, too," Weise told them. "I'll try to get up there with you. I'll send everybody I can spare, but in the meantime you'll need to hold off the counterattack. Pull back to the best position you can and hold."

"Get the wounded and as many dead as we can carry, and let's get the fuck out of here," Lieutenant Taylor bellowed at his Marines. "I'll show you where to stop!" With that, a slight-statured Hotel Company Marine moved past Taylor carrying over his shoulder a wounded man who must have weighed 230 pounds. Another Marine moved rearward with his own weapon, two machine guns, and two radios. They soon discovered that there were still NVA to their rear, so they had to shoot their way out of Dinh To. Sergeant Devoe of Hotel One covered his squad with his M16 as the men started back along the creek. The grunts carried their wounded with them. When Devoe's M16 jammed again, he threw it down and picked up an M79 grenade launcher. He fired its last three rounds, then relieved a wounded Marine of the shotgun he was carrying. He pumped its two remaining shells into the brush. Devoe was finally reduced to covering his Marines with a .45-caliber pistol.

"It was so perfect. It was just a turkey shoot," recalled LCpl. Jim O'Neill, a regimental sniper attached to Hotel Company. During the fighting withdrawal, O'Neill had a clear view of the NVA machine guns and reinforcements in the open fields east of Dinh To. He went to work with his scope-mounted, bolt-action hunting rifle, and killed twenty-four soldiers and wounded approximately ten more, earning himself a BSMv. O'Neill fired from elevated, brushy cover near a pagoda at the forward edge of Dai Do. The range was about seven hundred meters. O'Neill had been led to the area by a corpsman. Before the corpsman got him, a lance corporal from Hotel's helicopter support team had moved past with the comment, "Hey, boy, there's some machine guns out there—you can get some real good shootin' in!"

Hearing that, O'Neill had looked at the Marine next to him, and said, "Let's go get 'em!"

"No way, man. You want to get us killed?"

"But it's a great opportunity—we're gonna take it and get some real decent sniping in!"

"Don't get killed," said the man.

"Hey, if I'm movin' out, you're movin' out with me!"

The Marine shook his head. "Not this time."

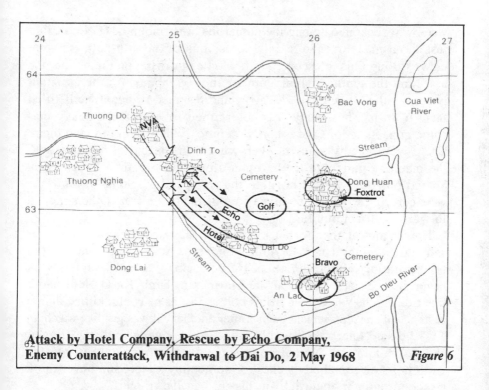

Attack by Hotel Company, Rescue by Echo Company, Enemy Counterattack, Withdrawal to Dai Do, 2 May 1968   *Figure 6*

When the corpsman ran back to them, he gave them no choice but to get cracking. He was very concerned about the wounded who had been moved to the cover of a pagoda at Dai Do's edge. They were within range of those 12.7mm machine guns, and the corpsman jumped on the inactive sniper team. "Hey, there's gooks up front, and there's lots of clear area that would be perfect for you! You gotta get them! They're choppin' everybody up!"

"Hey, we're going," O'Neill said firmly to the other Marine, and then moved out with the corpsman. When O'Neill looked back, the other Marine was following him, ready to fight.

When they reached the pagoda, Lance Corporal O'Neill removed the towel that protected his Remington Model 700 from moisture and dust. The corpsman pointed the enemy positions out. There were three 12.7mm machine guns, each dug into the top of a burial mound. They were well separated among the numerous other mounds. O'Neill could just about make out the facial expressions of the pith-helmeted gun crews through his telescopic sight. He began firing on them, and one at a time the gunners slumped over their weapons. As the assistant gunners pulled their comrades away and resumed firing, O'Neill killed them in turn. The enemy was determined to keep those heavy machine guns in action, and other NVA quickly moved out to man them. There were enemy soldiers everywhere, in the burial mounds with the machine guns and in the open along a footpath between Dinh To and positions farther north in the rice paddies. Some of the NVA were carrying wounded comrades out of the battle area. Others moved forward with ammunition.

How many of them can I kill before they swing those guns over and start aiming at me? O'Neill wondered. At one point, he saw an NVA pointing in their direction. Nerve-racking as that was, the NVA never shifted their fire from the Marines in Dinh To. O'Neill had a free ride and he worked his rifle's bolt as fast as he could, killing ammo bearers and one replacement gunner after another. "It was just like watching TV," he said later. "You would sight in on a gook, pull the trigger, and watch him fall. No noise, no screams, no cries. You just put the cross hairs on somebody's chest or somebody's face, and never think a second thought about it. You just pulled the trigger."

O'Neill spotted a trio of NVA and dropped them one after the other. But the third enemy soldier, after some flopping around, got back to his feet. O'Neill shot him again. The NVA flopped around some more before getting back up.

"I'll fix you!" O'Neill shouted. He chambered his next round with a vengeance. The NVA's head exploded when he squeezed the trigger. "Flop now, you sonofabitch!" he exclaimed.

After firing about 120 shots in the ten to fifteen minutes he was in position near the pagoda, O'Neill, who didn't have earplugs, was half-deaf. He finally had to take several breaks to let the barrel of his rifle cool down. The heat coming off it was distorting his view. He also stopped firing on the two occasions that an aerial observer flew over the burial mounds. Each time the aircraft approached, the NVA manning the heavy machine guns would grab the brush-covered mats beside the open-topped gun bunkers and pull them over them. The camouflage was so effective that even O'Neill lost track of which three mounds he'd been firing at.

When the plane departed, bingo, the NVA would suddenly pop up out of nowhere and resume firing on Dinh To. O'Neill would also resume firing—until an RPG finally flashed in from the village. The fun was over. The NVA hammered the point home by walking mortar fire toward the pagoda. The corpsman had already gotten his wounded moved back, so O'Neill's group pulled back under fire into the cover of Dai Do. The three machine guns were still firing on Echo and Hotel. O'Neill wanted to lay an air strike on them. With that in mind, he moved through Golf's lines and on to where the battalion command group was kneeling around a map on the ground beside a hootch.

Being a lance corporal, O'Neill didn't know anyone there. He just grabbed the closest officer—it was Lieutenant Hilton, the BLT 2/4 FAC—and said, "Excuse me, sir, but we've got machine guns over there and we need something right now to take 'em out. They're chopping everybody up!"

"We're working on it," said Hilton, looking preoccupied. "We got air coming in on them."

"Air *has* been coming in!" said O'Neill, exasperated. He tried to explain how the machine guns were camouflaged. He offered to lead Hilton up to the pagoda to show him exactly where they were. Hilton turned back to the group around the map. "No, no, no, they already have them spotted—"

"Wait a minute! I just got through firing on those things!"

O'Neill was still pumped up from his turkey shoot. He had a hot temper anyway, and it always angered him when the officers never had that extra thirty seconds to explain things to the "enlisted pukes." There really was no time to draw pictures, though, and Lieutenant Colonel Weise cut O'Neill off by saying, "Go over there and sit down till we're done."

The positions of the cleverly camouflaged machine guns had, in fact, been previously described to Lieutenant Hilton, and the air strike he'd requested placed its ordnance squarely on the burial mounds. With Echo and Hotel putting some distance between themselves and the NVA in Dinh To, supporting arms were finally being employed, to include artillery fire within a hundred meters of the retreat's tail end. There were

also air strikes on the fields to the right and Huey gunship runs up
the tributary on the left flank. O'Neill cooled down a bit and turned
to the Marine with him. "Let's go back to our guys and see what we
can do," he said. "We're not doing anything around here."

"Captain Livingston seemed to be everywhere at once. His cool-
ness and calmness were what kept a lot of us from panicking," wrote
Sergeant Rogers of Echo Company's fire-and-maneuver withdrawal
from Dinh To. "Things did not look good at all, but he kept our spirits up and kept us determined that we were going to beat them."

The NVA leapfrogged forward as the Marines retreated. Captain
Livingston saw a 12.7mm machine gun that had been brought forward
and set up behind a berm about seventy-five meters back the way they
had come. Livingston was standing and firing his M14 at the weapon's
crew when one of the machine-gun rounds hit him squarely in the right
thigh. Livingston went down hard and fast, with the bone cracked a
bit and a lot of muscle blown away where the bullet exited. His whole
leg went numb. He couldn't stand on it, and blood was pumping out
of the wound.

It was approximately 1430, and Lieutenant Cecil was the only able-
bodied officer left in Echo Company. He was, however, a new lieutenant in a hell of a firefight, and Livingston instructed his combat-
tested radiomen to find Cecil "and help him run the company." The
radiomen moved out as ordered and Livingston rolled onto his stomach to resume firing. He intended to cover his Marines' withdrawal,
and then somehow get out himself. It never crossed his mind that he
was going to die. He probably would have, though, if not for the fact
that one of his radiomen, the black Marine he had borrowed from Echo
Two, ran back to his position. The radioman moved with a bowlegged
stride because of fragment wounds in his buttocks. He was accompanied by another black Marine who'd been wounded in the arm, and
they called to Livingston, "We're takin' you out!"

"Get the hell out of here!" Livingston shouted back.

"We're not leavin' you!"

Captain Livingston finally hobbled out of harm's way with his weight
on his good foot, and a wounded black Marine under each arm holding him up.

Panic set in when the skipper went down. Sergeant Rogers saw one young Marine jump up and bolt rearward while screaming, "The captain's been hit! Oh my God, let's get out of here!" When Rogers made it back to Dai Do, he saw the grunt's body among those that had been dragged back. The word in Dai Do was that the skipper was still out there, and Rogers headed back into Dinh To with three other Marines.

Livingston was coming their way between his radiomen.

Someone produced a poncho. "Hey, get everybody else out of here first!" Livingston protested as they lifted him onto the makeshift litter. Two of the litter bearers started hassling about something, and Rogers snapped, "Goddamnit, quit fucking around—let's get the hell outta here!"

Captain Livingston looked up at him with fatherly calm. "Sergeant, just take it easy. We'll get out of here, we'll get out of here. . . ."[1]

"I was really scared because I didn't see anyone else behind me," recalled Lance Corporal Cornwell of Echo Two, who had found an M16 to replace his empty M60. He fired the last of its magazine to cover his retreat as he dragged a wounded Marine out of the ditch where they'd been pinned down. "I firmly believe that it was the killer-survival instinct hammered into me by Marine Corps training that helped me to survive." When Cornwell reached an area where he didn't seem to be taking any more fire, he looked at the wounded man he had been dragging along. He was stunned to see that the guy was a high school classmate, Art Tharp, who had been among the eleven of them who had enlisted right out of school and gone through Parris Island together. Cornwell had not seen Art since. He covered the bullet hole in Tharp's chest with the cellophane wrapper from his cigarets, then wrapped the small, clean wound with a battle dressing. Cornwell helped Art onto his back piggyback style, then moved out again. He stooped down to pick up an abandoned weapon, and, firing one-handed while he held onto Art with the other, emptied the magazine. Art was pleading for water, and Cornwell veered over to the stream on the left flank and scooped up a helmetful of muddy water for him. Cornwell knew that he was not supposed to give water to a badly wounded man, but it didn't matter. Art's wound looked

1. Sergeant Rogers was awarded the BSMv for Dai Do/Dinh To, and picked up two Purple Hearts in later engagements at Nhi Ha and Khe Sanh.

mortal, and he figured he was going to die, too. Cornwell got moving again and proved himself wrong. They both made it.

During the withdrawal, Sergeant Jones, the acting commander of Hotel Three, realized that some of the young grunts in his platoon were too scared to remember they were Marines. Jones, a career man, was so angry that he "hated the Corps," as he told the division historical team. Jones, who was providing covering fire with an M60 machine gun, had managed to get two able-bodied men to carry each of their seriously wounded. The litter bearers were exhausted and needed all the help they could get. They didn't get it. "Other guys were standing around with a little wound and they wouldn't even try to help you out. When we did get to relative safety back in the rear, then everybody wanted to pitch in and help us. When help was really needed we couldn't get it."

Half of the exploits that later got Lieutenant Jones, late of Echo Three, the Silver Star were performed after he'd been wounded, relieved of his weapon and gear, and directed to an evacuation point along the creek. Jones could no longer walk with his fragment-peppered legs and buttocks, and neither could any of the other half-dozen Marines who were also waiting for an Otter or a skimmer. None of the casualties had been bandaged. They were unarmed except for a box of grenades, which had apparently been thrown on the creek bank from an Otter and had yet to be carried forward. Lieutenant Jones spotted the NVA as they came around a bend in the stream. They hugged the bank, using the brush to conceal them as they tried to outflank the new line that Echo and Hotel were forming in Dai Do. The NVA were about fifty meters away. Jones rolled toward cover and began heaving hand grenades at the surprised enemy soldiers. The other wounded Marines also threw grenades. The NVA fired back, then disappeared the way they had come. Jones was wildly relieved. The NVA could have killed them all. He could only figure that the enemy, unable to see them, had mistaken the motley collection of wounded Marines for a real squad deployed along the creek.

Lieutenant Taylor stood up and turned his head to say something to one of his Marines when a bullet clipped him across the mouth.

The impact knocked his head back and laid open his lower lip but did not slow him down. With Lieutenant Boyle, the only other officer left in Hotel Company, he made a final, cover-to-cover run through their deserted positions. They shouted to see if any Marines had not yet gotten out, and they checked bodies to ensure that no unconscious Marines had accidentally been left behind. On the way out of Dinh To, Taylor and Boyle bumped into machine gunner Barela of Hotel Two. Barela was heading back in by himself. Taylor called to him to ask where he was going, and Barela answered, "I saw this M60, Lieutenant. I'm going to get it."

Taylor, Boyle, and Barela, too pumped up to consider what they were doing, turned around to go back into Dinh To. Just as they reached the abandoned machine gun, a dozen NVA burst into view through the bushes. Taylor later wrote that "caution prevailed. We let them have the gun."[2]

Lieutenant Taylor caught up with his radiomen, who had been waiting for him a bit to the rear, and the group ran back along the streambed, which made for easier going. They could also make out their surroundings better from the relatively open creek. They popped up over the bank at the edge of Dai Do, where they saw ten to fifteen Marines and could hear others nearby in the vegetation. The Marines were scattered around the well, where Hotel's 60mm mortar section was set up. The first Marine whom Taylor recognized was Sergeant Jones, who was cautiously leaning around the side of a mound to fire his M60 back into Dinh To. Taylor ran up beside him. He thought he could see movement in the brush that the sergeant was blasting.

"My guys really did a bang-up job in getting up those creeks," said Lieutenant Muter of the reconnaissance platoon, who controlled the skimmer operations from An Lac. "The NVA were all over the place, and our little boats all had bullet holes in them." Additional skimmer support was provided by Captain Forehand's boat platoon. This was

2. Lieutenant Taylor got the Silver Star and his second Purple Heart for Dinh To. He was awarded a BSMv for Vinh Quan Thuong and another BSMv and his first Purple Heart for Operation Task Force Kilo; he later received an end-of-tour NCMv.

an ad hoc organization that used Marines who were assigned to light duty because of various infirmities. On the third day of the Battle of Dai Do, its newest member was Corporal Schlesiona of Golf Company. Schlesiona had remained at the BLT CP instead of departing with the rest of Golf the day before because of severe ringworm and jungle rot that had spread over his stomach, groin, thighs, and buttocks. Schlesiona, feeling guilty, had asked to be returned to duty. "The company corpsmen said I'd have to get released by the BLT chief corpsman. The chief was against it and said I'd be of more help down on the beach, loading supplies and helping with the wounded. I could easily have put on my pack and headed out with the company, and my own corpsmen wouldn't have stopped me. But I didn't and it's not been an easy decision to live with."

Actually, Schlesiona could barely walk.

The next morning, as the casualties piled up, Schlesiona learned that the Marine who had taken over his fire team in Golf Three, a man whose name he never knew, had been blown away. Two of the three riflemen in the team, Ralph Peralta and Ed Smith, had also been killed. They were men whom Schlesiona had spent months with. He felt absolutely useless.

Corporal Schlesiona got his weapon and gear then and limped aboard the first empty skimmer he saw. The driver, however, said that since Schlesiona had no real destination there was no point in taking him. Things were so chaotic, he explained, that the boats often had to make several passes up and down the streams before they found Marines to deliver their supplies to. Schlesiona, anxious to get into the fight, asked the driver to let him ride shotgun if nothing else. The driver, who had the smallest type of skimmer, was concerned about Schlesiona taking up extra space, but he finally relented.

After they dropped off their supplies, six combat-loaded Marines got aboard despite the driver's warning that they should wait for a larger boat. The Marines had been instructed to cross the river and establish an outpost to prevent the NVA from setting up mortar tubes to their rear. About three-quarters of the way across, the engine stalled out. Without forward momentum to help keep it afloat, the small, overloaded craft began to sink. When the Marines jumped into the water, the boat came back up. As the driver climbed back aboard to get the engine going again, everyone else dumped their gear to stay afloat;

one Marine lost his rifle as he tried to get out of his pack. With two men hanging onto the sides and the rest back aboard, the driver returned them to their starting point. Schlesiona gave his M16 to the Marine who had lost his, figuring that he could replace the weapon back at the Charlie Papa.

When they got back to the BLT CP, the driver told Schlesiona that his extra weight was a problem and that he was going to go it alone again. Schlesiona then teamed up with another skimmer driver, who before the battle had been assigned to the company office aboard ship. They lightened their load by removing their helmets and jungle boots and stripping down to undershirt, flak jacket, and bush hat. Because of the heat, they cut their trousers into shorts. Schlesiona was unable to get another M16 because the wounded either came back without one, or had traded theirs before leaving for one that was unserviceable. The new driver, however, had an M16 and a .45, and they made dozens of trips between the CP and An Lac, stopping only for gas. They pushed as far as they dared up the inlets to Dong Huan and Dai Do to take aboard casualties who had not yet been transported to An Lac. Three or four times enemy fire struck the water beside their boat. On two occasions they saw NVA in the brush on shore. They returned fire once, but Schlesiona wrote that during the other sighting "we were too far out in the river to be effective with the M16. Frankly, we had misgivings about firing at all since we didn't know where our people were."

Because of the overwhelming number of casualties, the skimmer crews had to put ashore and move inland to help carry the wounded back to the boats. Running around barefoot in that terrain was no fun. The wounded were stripped of excess gear to conserve weight and allow the maximum number to be lifted into each boat. Schlesiona later wrote that although they tried to make the wounded as comfortable as possible, "there wasn't much we could do. We left it up to the less seriously wounded to care for those with severe wounds until we could get them back. We traveled as fast as we could, but this was never fast enough. At high speeds we couldn't see floating debris until almost too late. Plus we had to watch for the swells of the other boats. These people were in no condition to take a lot of bouncing or jolting."

Corporal Cardona was the only NCO left in Echo Two. He was the only unwounded survivor of his squad. The other two squads in the platoon could muster only nine Marines between them. Lieutenant Cecil was the only uninjured officer left, and the company was down to about forty men. Captain Livingston, wounded three times and unable to walk, refused to be carried out. Echo Company needed him, and the normally icy Echo 6 was somewhat upset as he spoke briefly with Weise. "I'll be all right, I'll be all right. Let me stay!"

Lieutenant Colonel Weise, who was also a very reserved man, put his hand on Livingston's shoulder. "Take care of yourself, Jim. We'll take care of it here. You did a good job."[3]

Lance Corporal Cornwell had thought highly of Captain Livingston until that day, but no more. "They destroyed us. There were so few of us left it was unreal," he said later. "The guys were angry, and the word was out that the captain was shot by one of our troops because he led us into a slaughter. I'm glad he got capped—by our men or the gooks it doesn't matter. At least we were getting some payback for him almost getting everyone killed."

Marines such as Sergeant Rogers and Corporal Cardona would never have signed on to such an assessment, but there was no doubt that Echo Company was demoralized. It was evident to Major Warren, the S3, who after two frustrating days of juggling radios at the CP had finally been ordered forward. Warren's skimmer landed him at An Lac about the same time that Livingston was being loaded into another boat. When Livingston's skimmer motored off, Warren realized that the captain's litter team and a good number of Echo Company stragglers were ready to jump onto skimmers themselves. "Livingston's troops actually wanted to leave the battlefield with him," said Warren. "The challenge was to convince those guys that had seen all this terrific combat that Golf Company was still up in that ville, and if they left it was possible Golf would get wiped out. My job was to challenge their loyalty to those other people. The only thing I knew that would motivate them was this guilt trip that I wanted to give them. I wanted

3. Captain Livingston received the Medal of Honor and Purple Heart. He was also awarded the BSMv for Lam Xuan East and the Silver Star for Vinh Quan Thuong. He later served as S3, 4th Marines, during Operation Frequent Wind, the evacuation of Saigon in April 1975.

to reenergize them to their responsibilities as Marines. I grabbed people who I thought were capable of listening and would respond. I appealed to them and got them moving, and they got other guys going."

Major Warren, with stragglers in tow, joined Lieutenant Colonel Weise in Dai Do as Echo and Hotel Companies regrouped and tied in with Golf Company under sporadic fire from Dinh To. The Marines returned fire with everything they could still muster. About every fourth weapon on line was a captured AK-47 or RPD light machine gun. Ammunition and water, both invaluable, were resupplied and distributed. Enemy fire came in from the vicinity of Dong Lai, which was across the tributary on the left flank. The ARVN were supposed to have secured that area but had not. Marines at that end of the line called for Lieutenant Taylor, shouting that they had "gooks in the open." Taylor could see what looked to be a platoon's worth of NVA moving along the stream. He could just make out the silhouettes of their helmets and weapons through the spaces where the leaves had been ripped away from the trees that grew along both banks. He was not absolutely sure that they weren't ARVN, but he was taking no chances. He directed his mortar section to shell them.

Captain Livingston was using a walking stick to hop around the beach at Mai Xa Chanh West when Gunny Thomas of H&S Company brought him a cigar and a big steak sandwich. Thomas had been Livingston's gunny in Echo Company before being wounded and reassigned. Livingston was glad to see him, especially since they had a problem on the medevac beach that needed to be squared away. A television camera crew was filming the dead Marines lined up there on stretchers, and Livingston said that they were "taking off the ponchos from the heads of some of the kids, exposing their faces and taking photographs. That really jerked my jaws. I've never been so jacked in my entire life!"

Captain Livingston and Gunny Thomas angrily ordered the camera crew from the beach.

The number of wounded and dead Marines lined up on the beach was appalling. To fill the gaps up front, untested men were being shuttled to the battlefield. Weise wrote that before Major Warren had come forward, he had "stripped headquarters units of personnel to replace casualties in the rifle companies. A number of these Marines came from the elements at Mai Xa Chanh. Others had come from aboard ship. . . . They were truck drivers, cooks, clerks, supply people, and others. They fit right in and did an admirable job."

Lieutenant Colonel Weise needed every rifle he could get. Colonel Hull had issued an order for BLT 2/4, in coordination with the ARVN on the left flank, to immediately launch another assault on Dinh To.

PART FOUR THE SECOND WAVE

At 1613 on 1 May 1968, the 3d Battalion, 21st Infantry, 196th Light Infantry Brigade (LIB), Americal Division, began airlifting into Mai Xa Chanh East and West.

When the NVA offensive began, BLT 2/4 had companies in Nhi Ha, Lam Xuan West, and Mai Xa Chanh East monitoring the infiltration routes along Jones Creek and screening the BLT CP at Mai Xa Chanh West. On 30 April, after the last of these elements had been committed at Dai Do, Lieutenant Colonel Weise expressed concern to Colonel Hull about the sudden vulnerability of his support elements at the BLT CP. Regiment forwarded a request through 3d Marine Division to III MAF asking that a battalion from the III MAF reserve be placed opcon to Hull to defend Jones Creek. The III MAF reserve was an opcon Army unit, the 196th LIB, and brigade selected one of its battalions, the 3-21st Infantry, for deployment to the 3d Marines. The 3-21st Infantry had only recently moved 150 kilometers north from Fire Support Base (FSB) Center to Camp Evans. The battalion was in the process of building Fire Support Base Belcher near Camp Evans when III MAF airlifted it another fifty kilometers northwest to the Mai Xa Chanhs. This last move placed the far-from-home Army battalion within nine klicks of the DMZ.

By 1250 on 2 May 1968, the 3d Battalion, 21st Infantry, 196th Light Infantry Brigade, Americal Division, was heavily engaged in Nhi Ha and Lam Xuan West.

CHAPTER 11 OUT OF THE FRYING PAN, INTO THE FIRE

The column was four days out from FSB Belcher and eye-deep in elephant grass when a poisonous green viper nailed the point man of 2d Lt. Terry D. Smith's platoon in A Company, 3-21st Infantry.

Overhead, the sky was overcast with the low, leaden clouds of the approaching monsoon, and the patrol was soaked from the cold, nearly constant drizzle. "It was an absolutely miserable area," recalled Lieutenant Smith. The place had previously been defoliated. The trees were dead and without leaves, whereas the underbrush, exposed to direct sunlight through the withered canopy, had grown wildly. The dense, razor-edged elephant grass was ten feet high, so the Alpha Company GIs, moving in single-file columns, had to hack and chop the whole way. Their machetes were loud and progress was slow. It was dank and muggy in the elephant grass, and impossible to see what was ahead. The insects in the underbrush, to include red ants, were huge and vicious, and the mosquitoes were thick. There were leeches, too.

Alpha Company had found nothing of value, not even a hootch. "The hacking through the elephant grass just wore people out," said Lieutenant Smith. "It was just a useless waste of time. There was absolutely nothing there."

The only casualty was the point man, who was bitten twice on his left hand by the green viper, between thumb and index finger. "He was really calm, but I thought he was going to die on me," said Lieutenant Smith. The platoon medic had to keep moving the tourniquet up the point man's arm as it quickly swelled to three times its normal size. The snake had been killed. Its head was chopped off, placed in a plastic bag used to carry radio batteries, and tied to the point man's fatigue shirt so the medical personnel in the rear could identify the species.

Lieutenant Smith immediately requested a helicopter medevac, and in the twenty-five minutes it took a Huey to make the flight from Camp Evans, every grunt in the platoon who had a machete was swinging it to clear a landing zone. They hacked at the thick vegetation, stomped on it, and took running jumps to mash it down with their weight. It was tight quarters nonetheless for the helicopter, and the pilot complained about a tree that the platoon had not had the ordnance to knock down. The Huey came to a hover over the semiflattened vegetation, and grunts lifted the point man up to the skid, where the door gunner hauled him aboard. Thanks to rapid medical assistance, the point man was back with the platoon within a week—by which time the platoon was in heavy combat on the DMZ.

Lieutenant Colonel William P. Snyder was the commander of the 3-21st Infantry, 196th LIB. The chain of events that moved his battalion to FSB Belcher, and then on to the DMZ, began when the 1st Cavalry Division, headquartered at Camp Evans, launched an unrelated attack against the NVA logistical complexes in the A Shau Valley. In the absence of the Cav, the entire 196th LIB was tasked to disengage from its operations in Quang Tin Province and redeploy to Camp Evans, which was to the north in Thua Thien Province.

The realignment required Snyder's 3-21st Infantry (better known as the Gimlets) to airlift lock, stock, and barrel from their mountaintop fire support base, FSB Center, to the brigade headquarters at FSB Baldy for further transportation by C-123 cargo planes to Camp Evans. The move began on 20 April with E/3-21 and the lead elements of D/3-21 arriving at FSB Baldy. When the remainder of Delta caught up the next day, the company moved on to Camp Evans and immediately started up Route 1 on foot to secure the slight rise on which its new firebase would be built. The company ran out of daylight before reaching the hillock, but the next morning, 22 April, Delta continued on to its objective. The GIs spent the rest of the day unloading the ammunition and supplies that followed them up in trucks. The developing perimeter was half a kilometer west of Route 1, where the coastal lowlands began

Marines of BLT 2/4 assault Dai Do. *Courtesy W. Weise.*

A 60mm mortar team in action with B/1/3. *Courtesy N. J. Doucette.*

1st Lt. David R. Jones, E BLT 2/4 (right). *Courtesy D. R. Jones.*

Cpl. Nicolas R. Cardona, E BLT 2/4, was the only man in his squad to emerge unscathed from Echo's assault on Dai Do on 2 May 1968. *Courtesy N. R. Cardona.*

Capt. James E. Livingston, skipper of E BLT 2/4, got the Medal of Honor for his actions while covering his company's retreat from Dinh To on 2 May 1968. *Courtesy J. E. Livingston.*

LCpl. Philip L. Cornwell, E BLT 2/4, checks out a LAW rocket launcher. *Courtesy P. L. Cornwell.*

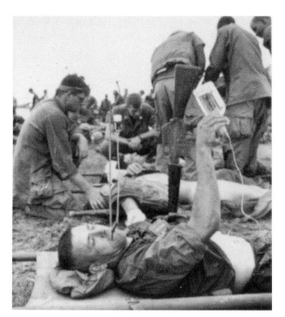

Lt. Col. Weise awaits medical evacuation at the BLT 2/4 casualty collection point in Mai Xa Chanh West. Weise was shot in the lower back when the NVA assaulted Dinh To on 2 May 1968. *Courtesy W. Weise.*

BLT 2/4's command group for the Battle of Dai Do (from left): Maj. Warren, Maj. Knapp, Capt. Murphy, 1st Lt. Smith, Lt. Col. Weise, Sgt. Maj. Malnar, and Capt. Forehand. *Courtesy G. F. Warren.*

HM2 Roger D. Pittman, a corpsman with F BLT 2/4. *Courtesy R. D. Pittman.*

Marines bag the bodies of their dead and collect abandoned gear on 3 May 1968, the day after the bloody debacle at Dai Do. *Courtesy F. H. Morgan.*

BLT 2/4 Marines sweep through Dai Do and Dinh To on 3 May 1968. *Photos courtesy F. H. Morgan.*

Among the C/3-21 grunts ambushed at Nhi Ha on 2 May 1968 were SSgt. James M. Goad (with bush hat in front), Sgt. Jimmie L. Coulthard (seated with hands clasped), Sp4 Derryl D. Odom (standing with fist on hip), and Pfc. Wayne Crist (with glasses). *Courtesy J. L. Coulthard.*

Sgt. Roger W. Starr, a C/ 3-21 machine gunner. *Courtesy R. W. Starr.*

SSgt. Goad of C/3-21 shows off the helmet he was wearing when he was hit in the head with two bullets during an earlier action. He didn't get a scratch. He wasn't as lucky at Nhi Ha in early May 1968. *Courtesy J. M. Goad.*

Capt. Jan S. Hildebrand, the 3-21st Infantry battalion surgeon, in his aid station at Mai Xa Chanh West. *Courtesy J. S. Hildebrand.*

undulating into the foothills that became one side of the Annamite Mountains, which shielded the A Shau Valley.[1]

Also on 22 April, elements of the American Division's 198th LIB relieved the Gimlets on FSB Center, and HHC, A, B, and C/3-21 were shuttled by Chinook helicopter to FSB Baldy. The 3-21st Infantry was accompanied by its supporting artillery battery, D/3-82d Field Artillery (105mm), whose field guns were slingloaded underneath the twin-bladed Chinooks. At FSB Baldy, each soldier was issued clean fatigues, extra ammunition, and another case of rations, as well as mail and a cold beer or soda. After the fixed-wing airlift to Camp Evans, B/3-21 was moved on by Chinook to reinforce Delta Company in the as yet unbuilt FSB Belcher. The rest of the battalion roadmarched up Route 1 the next morning, 23 April, despite sniper fire and a booby-trapped grenade that wounded two Charlie Company GIs. The casualties were medevacked on the spot. After the linkup, Bravo was detailed to build bunkers, fill sandbags, and lay concertina wire at FSB Belcher while waiting for the bulldozers that would be brought in to push up an earthen berm and clear fields of fire.

The rest of the battalion moved out to secure the area. On 28 April, Capt. James F. Humphries, the Delta Company commander, was swinging back out of the foothills toward Route 1 when the point element triggered what was probably a booby-trapped 82mm mortar shell. The first three grunts in the column, all of whom were wounded badly in the legs, were blown down the side of the ridge along whose crest the company was moving.

Lieutenant Colonel Snyder was already airborne in the area, and he medevacked the casualties aboard his Huey. Captain Humphries then instructed 2d Lt. Richard J. Skrzysowski, whose platoon had hit the booby trap, to continue to march and to clear a path down to a narrow stream that Delta would cross in the morning. The stream was the last natural obstacle between the foothills and the safer ground along Route 1. On the way down, several more booby traps were found rusting

---

1. The new position was christened FSB Belcher in honor of Capt. Roland Belcher, the previous commander of D/3-21. Belcher was killed on 8 January 1968 during a savage ambush in Hiep Duc Valley, northwest of FSB Center.

away in the defoliated underbrush. The platoon sergeant blew them in place with plastic explosives.

The platoon sergeant was Sfc. Buford Mathis, a powerfully built career soldier. "Mathis didn't want anybody else fooling with the booby traps," Lieutenant Skrzysowski said later. "He knew what he was doing, so we let him do it."

The explosions marked the platoon's progress. As directed by Captain Humphries, who was still in the foothills with the other two platoons, Skrzysowski and Mathis halted their platoon and dug in just short of the stream. The next morning, 29 April, Captain Humphries told 2d Lt. John T. Dunlap III, another platoon leader, to retrace Skrzysowski's semicleared route down to his overnight position and to continue from there to clear a path to the stream. The rest of Delta Company would follow, and they would then all cross the blueline. Dunlap wanted to cover the ground personally before walking his whole platoon through the booby-trapped terrain. He selected five men to accompany him. Skrzysowski was sitting with Mathis and cleaning his M16 when Dunlap showed up behind the first two grunts of his patrol. A trail ran down to the stream through a bamboo thicket. Skrzysowski suggested to Dunlap that although both trail and bamboo were unchecked, Dunlap should take the trail, "where you can at least *see* this stuff."

Lieutenant Dunlap disagreed. The bamboo might be booby trapped, but the trail almost certainly was. Just before starting into the bamboo, Dunlap looked at Skrzysowski and said, "No sweat, Ski."

Moments later, there was a huge explosion. Lieutenant Dunlap was blown away, and the five grunts with him were grievously wounded. "I just found out that my platoon leader was killed in that last blast I heard," Sgt. Laurance H. See, a squad leader, wrote in a letter to his fiancée as he sat in the company laager, listening to the hysterical screaming below the hill. "It was a 155 Howitzer round. Pieces of it landed all around, so I put my steel pot on. Damn it. Baby I'm pretty shook right now. He was a good lieutenant. We got along pretty well. Now he's dead. It makes me feel weak and empty."

Exercising great caution so no one else would get hurt by other booby traps, a handful of grunts pulled their wounded buddies out of the smoking, splintered bamboo. It was a demoralizing moment. "Without warning, somebody's gone—and there was no enemy to fight," Lieutenant

Skrzysowski said later. "That really hurt. That had an impact that people had problems dealing with."

Captain Humphries ordered every medic in the company to the scene, and a Huey landed in Delta Company's position within fifteen minutes of the explosion to medevac the first three men removed from the shredded bamboo. Another Huey came in within a half hour to medevac the rest. Afterward, Lieutenant Skrzysowski gripped his radio handset with white-knuckled anger as he spoke with Humphries, who he greatly respected, blowing off steam: "We got to get the hell out of here! Losing people in a firefight is one thing, but walking around in an area loaded with booby traps just doesn't make any sense!"

At 1413 on 1 May 1968, Col. Louis Gelling, the 196th LIB commander, ordered Lieutenant Colonel Snyder to execute the 3-21st Infantry's contingency plan to deploy to the DMZ. Other brigade elements would assume control of FSB Belcher. "It was a confusing move," recalled Lieutenant Skrzysowski, whose company was to lead the way into Mai Xa Chanh East. Delta Company was conducting platoon-sized ambushes and road security operations along Route 1. Skrzysowski, whose platoon was dug in near an old French fort, was instructed to secure a pickup zone along the west side of the highway and to assemble his men for helicopter extraction. That was all the information he received. "I wasn't told where we were going, what lift units were going to pick us up, what the mission was, what the threat in the landing zone was— none of the normal things."

Since airlifting to Camp Evans, the 196th LIB had been on standby to respond to an expected NVA offensive. Higher command knew something was coming, but not where, and the 3-21st Infantry was ready to move to the DMZ or Khe Sanh or Da Nang or Quang Tri or Hue, which was the largest city near the A Shau.

Lieutenant Skrzysowski was most concerned about organizing his platoon into helo teams, but no information was forthcoming as to the number or type of helicopters involved. The result was that each helo team was hastily formed with as many combat-loaded soldiers as each pilot determined he could carry as the choppers came in one or two at a time. In short order, Skrzysowski was alone in the pickup zone with his radioman and three grunts. "Everybody was gone, and I had no idea where they were going!" Army Hueys had lifted the platoon out, but then a Marine Sea Knight settled into the pickup zone and a gunnery sergeant waved the tail-end group up the back ramp. "I'm looking out the window, trying to find out where the hell we're going to land. I ask the gunny. Christ, he doesn't know. . . ." Skrzysowski had been issued three maps at the time of their original deployment north, one apiece for Hue, Khe Sanh, and the eastern DMZ, and he broke them out aboard the Sea Knight. He had thought that Hue, the scene of house-to-house fighting during the Tet Offensive, would be the hot spot of this new NVA offensive. Instead of Hue, the Sea Knight unloaded Skrzysowski and his group among the burial mounds in a flat, sandy-soiled cemetery near the bend in a river that would not be identified to him as the Cua Viet until an hour later. He could hear firing off in the distance. "I wondered what the hell was going on," he said. "I was trying to assemble my people, and find my company commander—I had no idea where he was."

Lieutenant Skrzysowski and his RTO were alongside a burial mound when they were joined by a Marine with a major's leaf on his helmet, a cane in one hand, and one foot in a cast. "Who's in charge of this route-step outfit?" the major snapped.

Lieutenant Skrzysowski, who wore no rank insignia, identified himself, then asked, "Where are we? I'm looking for the rest of my people."

The major explained that "all your companies are getting briefed. We got a lot of activity just north of here and it's going to be your job to help us clean it out." The major explained that they were in the middle of an expanding campaign that involved several NVA regiments coming down from the DMZ in an effort to cross the Cua Viet River. He said that the NVA knew the terrain, and added that "most of them are in reinforced bunkers. You're not going to really see these guys until you're right on top of 'em. The bunkers are located within hedgerows, and what ya gotta do is get those M60 machine guns right down low to the ground and start firing into those hedgerows to cover your assault."

"*What?* No artillery, no air?" Skrzysowski said incredulously.

The major explained that there were often simultaneous contacts at several locations—and not always enough supporting arms to go around. Skrzysowski finally asked the major what had happened to his leg. The major joked that he'd had "a meeting engagement with an RPG."

*   *   *

Upon receipt of the redeployment order, Lieutenant Colonel Snyder had Capt. John M. Householder, the 3-21st's S2, helicopter up to Camp Kistler at the mouth of the Cua Viet to establish liaison with the 3d Marines. Snyder flew up to join him shortly. In Snyder's absence, Maj. Paul N. Yurchak, the S3, organized the truck convoy that would soon head north with supplies, while the company commanders conducted impromptu airlifts from their positions in and around FSB Belcher. The Marines provided most of the helicopters; the fifty-kilometer flight to the BLT 2/4 AO placed the Gimlets closer to the DMZ than any other U.S. Army battalion in Vietnam.

The airlift began at 1613. The first battalion element to move north was Captain Humphries's D/3-21 (call sign Black Death), which landed in Mai Xa Chanh East.

Captain Robert E. Corrigan's B/3-21 (Barracuda) was inserted next, landing above Mai Xa Chanh West in accordance with the battalion's mission to secure both sides of Jones Creek.

Because its captain was temporarily absent, 1st Lt. Gerald R. Kohl, the company exec, took C/3-21 (Charlie Tiger) into Mai Xa Chanh East. Next came Capt. Stephen F. Russell's HHC/3-21 and 1st Lt. Jerry D. Perkins's E/3-21 (Eliminator), which were, respectively, the battalion's headquarters and combat support companies. Eliminator controlled two reconnaissance platoons (Assassin and Spectre) and a mortar platoon (Fastballs). The battalion headquarters began establishing hasty positions behind the two grunt companies in Mai Xa Chanh East.

The last line company, Capt. Cecil H. Osborn's[2] A/3-21 (Alpha Annihilator), landed in Mai Xa Chanh East between 1740 and 1900, at which point operational control of the Gimlets passed to the 3d Marine Regiment.

Wait a minute, back up a minute, thought 2d Lt. John R. Jaquez, the Charlie Tiger FO. This is sounding more like World War II, instead of chasing VC through the jungle and worrying about booby traps! A Marine officer had his map spread out on the dirt for the Army officers

2. This officer was later relieved of command. His real name is not used here.

huddled around him, and Jaquez listened incredulously as the Marine casually ran through the suspected locations of the NVA companies, battalions, and regiments in the area. The Marine emphasized that these were NVA regulars, well equipped with AK-47s, RPGs, 12.7mm heavy machine guns, and 60mm and 82mm mortars. Jaquez, already well aware of their proximity to the pinkline—the DMZ—listened carefully as the Marine made it abundantly clear that the enemy had artillery positions that were in range and protected against air strikes by antiaircraft batteries. There's a whole different animal here, thought Jaquez. These aren't dinks. These are real soldiers. It's like real war now.

The Gimlets' supporting artillery, D/3-82 FA, had not caught up with them yet, so 2d Lt. William A. Stull, the Alpha Company FO, had a face-to-face conference with a Marine officer about fire support for that night. Marine artillery was heavily engaged against targets in the Dai Do complex, and the Marine fire support coordinator said, "Okay, now you've got eighty rounds tonight—"

"What the hell do you mean 'eighty rounds'?" asked Stull.

"We've allocated eighty rounds for your company, but don't use 'em unless you need 'em."

"Shit, I shoot more than eighty rounds just getting our targets set up for the night," answered Stull.

The Marine was adamant. "No, those eighty rounds are for if you get into a big battle."

Lieutenant Stull shook his head. We're jumping through hoops, trying to find out who's going to be our support and what the frequencies are, he thought—and then they come up with this eighty rounds crap! He complained to Capt. Charles Heitzman, the artillery liaison officer with the 3-21st Infantry. Heitzman laughed. He said he would work the problem through channels. The answer came back that the 3-82d Field Artillery would slingload ammunition up to the Marines to replace round for round whatever they had to fire for the Army.

The Gimlets were quickly learning just how rich in material they were in comparison to the Marines. The GIs, who had begun digging in almost as soon as they got off the helicopters, were accustomed to trip flares, claymore mines, and concertina wire in abundance, as well as to bunkers built with timber, steel runway matting, and multiple layers of sandbags. The Marine bunkers didn't compare. "The village we occupied was a mess with nothing significant done in the way of defending it by the Marines," wrote Sp4 Don Miller of the 106mm recoilless rifle section in HHC/3-21. "The Marines were using NVA trenches (too small for us), and even *punji* stakes within the perimeter hadn't been removed. One of our guys flopped down in the grass and a stake went through his rucksack. The esprit de corps of the Marines is not in question, but their tactics and leadership always seemed suspect—and I *know* they were poorly supplied. They begged us for the most basic kind of stuff, like rifle cleaning equipment, oil, brushes, bore rods, etc. They seemed so raggedy."

Lieutenant Colonel Snyder was immediately impressed with Colonel Hull, who struck him as an experienced old infantryman with a no-nonsense, to-the-point manner. Hull wanted Snyder to seize and hold Nhi Ha and Lam Xuan West. They spoke in front of the operations map in Hull's CP bunker, and Hull outlined the circumstances that had left these positions uncovered. Whether or not the NVA had already moved back in was an open question. Hull cautioned Snyder that twice before when the Marines had relinquished control of the two hamlets because of other operational commitments they had had to launch attacks to regain the area. Nhi Ha and Lam Xuan West, which straddled Jones Creek and were linked by a footbridge, were important to the NVA because they were situated along the primary infiltration route from southeastern North Vietnam to the enemy base area in the Hai Lang forest south of Quang Tri City. Nhi Ha had served as a way station and rest area for NVA troops on their first day's march south from the DMZ. Both hamlets provided an ideal location from which to launch operations against the Marines' logistical lifeline, the Cua Viet River.

Hull and Snyder spoke until after dark about enemy tactics and capabilities in the area. Hull said to anticipate that Nhi Ha and Lam Xuan West had been occupied by the NVA in at least company strength. "Don't be surprised if the NVA are back in there. Expect them to be in there. We can support you with artillery and mortar fire. Let me know what you need—and go do it."

Lieutenant Colonel Snyder and Captain Householder, along with the colonel's radiotelephone operator (RTO), departed Camp Kistler at 2130 to join the battalion at Mai Xa Chanh East. They did not travel by helicopter as they expected, but on a skimmer moving at top speed through the dark on the Cua Viet River. Since the young Marine driving the skimmer was nonchalant, Snyder and Householder, figuring that he must know the score, masked their own concerns. Nevertheless, it was an exceptionally hairy experience for the newcomers.

As soon as Lieutenant Colonel Snyder put ashore and was led into rubbled Mai Xa Chanh East, Capt. Jan S. Hildebrand, the battalion surgeon, was at his elbow. The doctor was concerned about medical supplies. Captain Hildebrand and two of his battalion medics arrived on one of the first helicopters. Each had worn a helmet and flak jacket, and carried a pistol and M16 for the flight. They'd added whatever medical supplies they could carry on their backs. Hildebrand had wanted to be on the scene in case of heavy contact near the landing zone. When there was none, Hildebrand had concerned himself with getting a fully stocked battalion aid station established. He told Snyder that he didn't have enough medical supplies on hand to sustain the unit in the event of battle. "I *have* to get my supplies in!" he implored the battalion commander.

Army Chinooks were shuttling materials in from FSB Belcher, and Snyder replied, "Don't worry, Jan. I won't let that last helicopter come in without your stuff." The very last Chinook of the night did, in fact, bring in a mermite can for Hildebrand, which he immediately opened—only to discover that it was full of beer! "The top sergeant back at Belcher thought we needed beer more than anything," explained Hildebrand. "I closed that thing so damn fast and hid it from Snyder. Fortunately, nothing happened that night. The next morning, everything came in."

At 2300, Lieutenant Colonel Snyder called his company commanders to the small, roofless building in which he had established his command post. They stood outside in the glow of the illumination rounds going up to the southwest over Dai Do, and northwest over Alpha 1, where an NVA probe was being repelled with massed artillery. Snyder pointed out across the flare-lit paddies, and explained to his company commanders what their objectives were and who was to do what when their attack kicked off in the morning. The terrain ahead of them was bleak and foreboding, like a photo of Verdun.

Lieutenant Colonel Snyder, who was not a harsh man, also expressed concern about their night defensive positions. He told his company commanders to get tied in better so they wouldn't be in too bad a shape during the night. "It was really screwed up. My S3 wasn't on the scene yet himself, so until I got back those guys didn't have a clue as to what they were supposed to do, or who they might be on the lookout for," Snyder later commented. A perimeter had been established in his absence, and while the individual companies were reasonably well deployed, "they didn't have any good sense of how they were located in relation to one another. It's hard to form a night defensive position when you've never been there before, don't know where to go, don't know what you're going to be expected to do, and it was a troublesome scene because it was dark, people were tired, and they didn't know where they were. I mean we were vulnerable. If we'd been hit that night we'd have been in some trouble."

CHAPTER 12 SEARCH AND DESTROY

Lieutenant Colonel Snyder assumed command of the Gimlets on 1 February 1968. They were based at the time on FSB Center and operating in the Hiep Duc and Song Chang valleys of Quang Tin Province. It was Snyder's first infantry assignment in twelve years, and he decided to visit each of his companies in the bush. The first time that Capt. Dennis A. Leach, CO of C/3-21 (and recognized as the best company commander in the battalion), saw Snyder, the new colonel stumbled as he jumped from his Huey. Leach concealed a grimace. He knew that Snyder was a West Pointer with a Ph.D. from Princeton, but he also knew that the new battalion commander had no combat credentials. Leach saw Snyder as another of the Army's fair-haired boys sent to get a minimum of six months of battalion command time and the basic load of hero medals as he got his ticket punched on the way to full colonel.

Captain Leach, who was on his second tour, knew that Lieutenant Colonel Snyder was going to be a disaster. Snyder had chosen to visit Charlie Tiger at that time because Leach had reported a body count. When alerted that the new colonel was on his way, Leach had grinned and said, "Well, guys, dress 'em up a little bit. Lay 'em on the rice paddy dike and gun 'em a couple more times so we'll have a nice little picture here for the colonel."

Lieutenant Colonel Snyder looked at the thoroughly blasted Viet Cong as Leach had the squad leader involved describe how they'd originally bagged them. Snyder was a thin, medium-sized family man with eyeglasses and a soft-spoken manner; as he walked back to his helicopter with Leach he remarked, "You know, those are the first dead people I've ever seen."

Jesus Christ, thought Captain Leach. Here we go again.

Leach could not have been more wrong, however, as he himself soon recognized. "Colonel Snyder turned out to be just a prince of a guy and a good commander," Leach said later. "He didn't come in with a big ego, and he learned fast." Thoughtful, intelligent Bill Snyder, age thirty-nine, may have been in combat for the first time, but he'd been around the Army since he was an eighteen-year-old private. The son of a railroad man, he'd grown up poor on a farm outside Xenia, Ohio, and had enlisted primarily to qualify for the GI Bill so he could go to college after his two years in uniform. Snyder began basic training at Fort McClellan, Alabama, in September 1946, and was assigned as an orderly room clerk with Headquarters, Atlantic Section, at Fort Davis, Panama. A year and a half later he had three stripes and was selected to attend the U.S. Military Academy prep school.

Snyder graduated in the top 15 percent of the USMA Class of 1952 and wound up as a platoon leader in I Company, 504th Parachute Infantry Regiment, 82d Airborne Division, at Fort Bragg. A year later, he joined the 5th Regimental Combat Team in postwar Korea for a 1953–54 tour as a platoon leader and battalion adjutant. He redeployed with the regiment to Fort Lewis, Washington, where he spent a year as a company commander and another as a platoon leader with the regimental tank company. From 1956 to 1958, Snyder was aide to the commandant of cadets at West Point, and he spent the next year at the Infantry Officers' Advanced Course at Fort Benning. After being promoted to captain, Snyder was a semicivilian from 1959 to 1962 as he pursued his doctorate in political science at Princeton University. He finished his dissertation in 1963, and it was published as a book, *The Politics of British Defense Policy, 1945–1962,* by the Ohio State University Press. He started his next book, *Case Studies in Military Systems Analysis,* during a 1962–66 tour as an economics and political science instructor at West Point. By then he was a major, and he finished that book while at the Command and General Staff College (CGSC) at Fort Leavenworth in 1966–67. The book was published by the Industrial College of the Armed Forces, as was a chapter-length contribution he made to another book, *Issues of National Security in the 1970s,* during his year in Vietnam.

Upon graduation from CGSC, the freshly minted Lieutenant Colonel Snyder began his Vietnam tour in July 1967 with the G3 section at Headquarters, U.S. Army Vietnam (USARV). Snyder spent six months with USARV in Bien Hoa near Saigon, then six months with the Gimlets. That was his last assignment with a maneuver unit. After Vietnam, he went to the Pentagon, then graduated from the War College, where he remained as an instructor. He rounded out his career heading the ROTC unit at Princeton. Snyder had sandwiched in those six months with the infantry in Vietnam during this mostly academic career because "if you're a Regular Army officer and you don't command something, you're out of luck. This was my chance. This was something I had to do and wanted to do. I was green in the sense that there were a lot of new weapons and radios I didn't know anything about, but everybody pitched in. If you told people you didn't know, they were glad to explain it to you."

Most considered the 196th LIB, known as the "Chargers," to be head and shoulders above the other two brigades, the 11th and 198th, with which the 196th had been melded to form the Americal Division. The Gimlets saw themselves as the best battalion in the best brigade, so when Snyder showed up from USARV with his transparent career intentions, no one had been much impressed at first glance—to include Major Yurchak, the S3, who served an incredible five tours in the war zone. "The guy he took over from was a rompin', stompin' mean-ass, and here comes smiling Bill Snyder—and the guy was fantastic," said Yurchak. "He was sort of a nice guy, and he smiled a lot and laughed a lot, but he was a wonderful, strong-willed combat commander. He knew what the hell was going on, and he never, never lost his cool."

Lieutenant Colonel Snyder came to be regarded as a breath of fresh air. His predecessor had been known by the call sign Steel Gimlet, and though Yurchak had considered him a "very strict, very good battalion commander," he added that "it was almost impossible to deal with the guy because he was always angry."

Steel Gimlet's command style had been dictatorial and verbally demeaning. He had also been relentless in his career-building determination to bring home the bodies, especially after the 3-21st Infantry moved out of Chu Lai (where the pickings had been slim) and up to FSB Center. Center was situated atop a ridgeline northwest of Tam

Ky that overlooked NVA infiltration routes and populated valleys known for guerrilla activity.[1] Contact, however, was infrequent. To catch up with this enemy that seemed to be everywhere but nowhere, Steel Gimlet, who was under pressure himself from brigade and division, began taking enormous chances. Captain Leach had just moved Charlie Company into a night laager, and was in the process of establishing his listening posts and night ambushes, when the battalion commander called him. Steel Gimlet had a "hot intel report" indicating that an enemy unit would be moving into a certain location at dawn. That location was ten klicks from Leach's current position, and Steel Gimlet wanted Charlie Tiger to conduct a night march so as to be in place by 0500 to ambush the enemy. Such a schedule did not allow for proper planning or a cautious, cross-country approach, but demanded that Charlie Tiger make use of the trails that the enemy often booby trapped or ambushed. Leach later commented:

> I used to beat up on the platoon leaders not to use trails, and I told the battalion commander, "Hey, I can't get there by oh-five-hundred unless I sacrifice security." There was only one trail, I'm talking about two feet wide, that went down into this area. "*Goddamn you!*" Steel Gimlet said. "You're going to do what I say!" "Roger, I want to talk to the TOC duty officer." I had been in command of my company about a month. I was starting to feel good, I was getting my feet on the ground, so I got the TOC duty officer and said, "I want it put in the record that I'm sacrificing the principle of security to go on this wild goose chase." I was so goddamn angry I got on point and we moved down that trail. We got there, put out our security element, set up our fire support element, and attacked the location with our assault team. Nobody had been there in ten years.

1. The 196th LIB operated in III Corps from its arrival in Vietnam in August 1966 until airlifted to I Corps in April 1967. Tasked with securing the Chu Lai airfield, the 3-21st Infantry established a firebase astride Route 1 immediately south of Chu Lai. In late November 1967, the 196th was relieved by the newly arrived 198th, and the 3-21st Infantry was airlifted to FSB Center while other 196th elements moved into FSB East and West on the same commanding ridgeline.

Steel Gimlet rewarded GIs who got a confirmed kill with a three-day pass to the division rear in Chu Lai, where the beach was beautiful. When positive reinforcement did not work, however, he applied the stick. First Lieutenant Roger D. Hieb, whom Leach rated as his best platoon leader, described how Steel Gimlet refused to promote him to first lieutenant with the battalion's other second lieutenants who shared the same date of rank "because my platoon didn't have a high enough body count. I will never forget because then lo and behold—and it was not something we went out looking for—but we had contact and we killed some VC, and he flew out and promoted me and it was disgusting. It was really disgusting."

Such pressures had their consequences. "We didn't cut no slack on any of 'em. There were no civilians," explained one Charlie Tiger NCO. "If there was any doubt—shoot, fire it up. If they didn't run, we didn't fire 'em up. If they ran, they was going to get fired up. I'm sure more than one innocent person died." While moving down a well-vegetated hill, Charlie Company's point element spotted movement in the brush and fired. One Vietnamese male of military age was killed outright, and three men in their twenties were captured. They had neither weapons nor military equipment. They could have been farmers. The officer in charge decided they were probably local guerrillas, and an M60 machine gunner and a squad of grunts formed up in front of the three prisoners, who were in a squatting position. The grunts opened fire on order. The body count was thus four instead of one.

"We had one of our guys step on a mine, wounding him and two others," remembered Sp4 William W. Karp, a platoon medic in Alpha Annihilator. The Steel Gimlet's helicopter diverted toward the platoon to conduct the medevac. The only clearing in the area was a waist-deep rice paddy. As the Huey hovered inches above the water, Karp tried to carry the soldier who had tripped the mine to the chopper. The man was the most seriously wounded of the three. "I carried him as far as I could. I thought I was going to pass out, but just then a sergeant took the man from me and struggled the rest of the way to the chopper. The wounded kid was white and the sergeant was black, but that didn't matter." The Huey banked off with the casualty. The man did not survive. As the patrol continued, they caught a Vietnamese male in a free-fire zone—a place where he should not have been. "The black sergeant—who was later killed himself—went into a rage and started beating the shit out of him, hollering that he was probably the dink that planted the mine the kid stepped on. We all got caught up in the rage and almost killed the bastard. We finally let him go, beat up but still alive."

"We all had borderline incidents," stated Capt. Hal Bell, who commanded A/3-21 after the Gimlets returned to FSB Center from the DMZ. "You never knew if the 'civilians' were friends, foes, or neutrals. It would depend on what kind of day or week we'd had as to how we would treat civilians. It really was awful, but that was the case."

The Gimlets' nomadic patrolling around FSB Center neither secured nor protected the villages of the Hiep Duc and Song Chang valleys, for that was not the stated mission. The Gimlets' only goal was to kill dinks. That was what the grunts called the enemy. It was also what they called most Vietnamese. The Gimlets killed a lot of dinks. The production of bodies was a demeaning mission and, given the virtually inexhaustible manpower available to the Communists, an unintelligent one. Success, as noted earlier, lay within the hearts and minds of the villagers, and their allegiance was won only through the protection offered by a permanent presence with an emphasis on civic action. As it was, one squad leader could observe only that it was "heart wrenching" to see the civilians killed and wounded by their arty preps of suspected enemy hamlets. "Terrible, terrible . . ."

The villagers had no reason to shift their allegiance away from the VC, who were that permanent presence (and who offered more than Saigon and the ARVN did). The Gimlets, with no connection to the people or the land, came to hate those they thought they had come to save. Charlie Tiger was approaching a lone hootch when a VC suddenly emerged from it. The VC cut loose with his AK-47 before turning to run away through the monsoon rain that was crashing down. Private First Class Gregory B. Harp recounted:

The point squad and the lieutenant hauled ass after him, and caught him and killed him. In their haste, however, they and everybody else had forgotten to check the hootch the dink had come out of. When our squad got up there, I and another guy immediately went in to check it out. There were two draft-age males, two women, and three or four children—another bunch of peace-loving

Vietnamese who just happened to be in a free-fire zone and liked
having people over for tea who carried AK-47s.

Harp lined up the Vietnamese and demanded to see their govern-
ment identification cards. As they produced them, Harp heard something move inside the family bunker under the hard-packed earthen
floor. He readied a fragmentation grenade while the GI with him trained
his M16 on the entrance. Harp continued:

> Any VC who was armed would have opened up by now for all
> the noise he was making, so I took a chance and yelled, "*Lai day,
> lai day, lai day,* you dumb motherfucker, or I'll blow your ass
> off!" At that point, one of the women screamed something in
> Vietnamese down the hole, and suddenly this old guy stuck his
> head out of the hole. I reached down and grabbed him by his pajama
> shirt and snatched him out of the hole. I said, "*Can cuoc,*
> motherfucker!" He babbled something in gook, but he had no I.D.
> There was so much adrenaline flowing I had to do something,
> so I made them all go squat in the mud outside where it was raining
> like hell. The fifteen year old pointed to a shirt in the hootch he
> wanted because he was cold, so I threw it in the mud and hit him
> in the face with it. Stupid thing to do, but I was pissed, scared,
> and relieved all at the same time. I just lost it for a minute, but
> the lieutenant grabbed my arm and said, "That's enough, Harp."

Another day, Charlie Tiger was moving down a trail when Private
Harp saw movement to the right of their column. A Vietnamese was
sliding down an embankment, and he saw Harp at the same time Harp
saw him. The Vietnamese took off like a jackrabbit down another trail,
and Harp, concerned that the man was a VC scout, tapped his team leader
on the shoulder and pointed. The two moved out in hot pursuit. Harp,
well in the lead, caught up with the Vietnamese as he crawled away
through a tapioca field, and stopped him with his M16. Harp ran up
and rolled the body over. The dead man had no weapon and no military gear. Harp rejoined his team leader "and when we made it back,
the company called in one VC body count. Of course, he could also
have been an enemy deserter, or a civilian, or your great Aunt Sally."

The Gimlets' first major encounter with enemy regulars occurred when Alpha and Delta Companies were placed opcon to the 4-31st Infantry in response to an offensive by the 2d NVA Division. The battle took place in the misty, monsoon-soaked Hiep Duc Valley, and it was a real shock to the system. The action began during the night of 5–6 January 1968 when another attached company was partially overrun in its night defensive position. In the morning, Captain Belcher's Delta Company was airlifted into the valley, where it worked in tandem with B/4-31 during a battalionwide sweep of the battle area. The NVA had melted away and it was not until 8 January, when Delta was north of the stream that cut the valley, that B/4-31 regained contact on the south side. Captain Belcher, a reckless, superaggressive black company commander, immediately joined Delta's lead platoon with his forward observer, first sergeant, and two radiomen, and they started across the shallow stream. They were mortared when they reached the opposite bank. Then, as the platoon hastily advanced across an open paddy toward the cover of a wood line, it was ambushed. Captain Belcher was one of the first to be killed. He was shot in the back as he ran toward the stream to rejoin the main body of his company. The two platoons on the other side were unable to push forward and join the pinned-down platoon. Meanwhile, the NVA, who were camouflaged to resemble walking bushes, began maneuvering across the paddy toward that platoon. It was the company's first real firefight, and one grunt who had been with the outfit less than a week described the panic of the moment:

A soldier with an M79 grenade launcher was lying beside me. We knocked off an AK position. He and I yelled for the others to shoot back. No one was firing except us. They were crying and hollering. The VC started flanking us, moving around to our right. I could hear them yelling to each other. Me and the M79er were keeping our heads down, shooting back when we could. Suddenly three VC stood over us. Before we could fire they shot and killed my buddy—I never knew his name—and one of them jumped down on me. They tied me with commo wire, my hands bound behind my back to my feet. Then they tied some wire around my neck and started dragging. I said my last prayers. Blood spurted from my mouth—I was strangling to death. When we reached the woods they untied my feet and pushed me into a bunker.

Black Death suffered fourteen KIA in the debacle in the pouring rain, and had four men taken prisoner. Among the captured GIs was the company first sergeant, who had killed one NVA with his M79 before having his hand shattered by enemy fire. The first sergeant, who did not survive captivity, was trying to keep the grenade launcher in operation one-handed when the enemy overran his position.

The next afternoon, 9 January, Captain Yurchak and Alpha Company started across the same terraced, water-filled rice paddies. American bodies lay where they had fallen. The day was hot and muggy, and a misty rain was falling. The NVA were still in position, and they ambushed Alpha Annihilator. "A GI near me stood up and fired his M16 to cover men retreating from exposed positions," recounted a grunt who did not fire his own weapon. "I could see bullets kicking puffs of dust from his clothes as he was hit. He crumpled slowly to the ground, firing till he died. A general panic took over. We seemed to be without leadership. I didn't know whether to run or stay hidden behind the paddy dike."

This confused grunt was captured, as were two other Alpha Company GIs. Thirteen were killed. One of those who barely escaped was Private Karp, who sought cover behind a dike when the ambush began. One of his good friends, a machine gunner, was shot in the legs on the other side. Karp fired his M16, then crawled out to his buddy. He was lying beside him, trying to figure out what to do next, when the machine gunner tried to push himself up. He was instantly shot in the chest, and red bubbles came out of his mouth. Karp asked God to bless and keep his friend, then heaved the dead man's M60 to the ammo bearer behind the dike and shouted for covering fire.

The ammo bearer froze. He said the weapon was jammed. He would not raise up to fire. Feeling naked, Karp rolled back over the dike and flattened himself behind the ammo bearer. Karp heaved two grenades to cover their retreat, but as they crawled back, bullets smacked into the mud around them. When hit, the mud looked as if an invisible finger had been drawn through it. An M79 man silenced an NVA machine gun, and Karp and the ammo bearer made it to the cover of a muddy pool. The platoon leader was there, but instead of giving orders, the panic-stricken lieutenant simply blurted that they had to get out, grabbed his radioman's harness, and disappeared with him over the edge of the pool. Karp spotted an ememy soldier crawling toward them and flung his last grenade in that direction. It fell short because the medic's water-soaked flak jacket had sapped his energy. It was a lucky thing, because the man crawling toward them was actually a light-skinned black trooper. Unscathed by the friendly fire, he made it into the muddy pool.

They were also joined by their black platoon sergeant, Sfc. Alan Dickerson, who had become separated from his weapon, helmet, pack, and web gear. All he had left was a bayonet. In fact, most of the grunts abandoned weapons and equipment while crawling to cover, and Karp had already given his .45 to another unarmed man. Dickerson decided that their best chance was to crawl rearward in small groups down a snaky little drainage ditch that ran from their pool. Dickerson had just shoved off with a wounded man and several others when an NVA jumped into the ditch with his AK-47. He put a killing burst into one GI just as the M79 man beside Karp fired at him. The round missed, but Karp had shouldered his M16 in that instant and he dropped the NVA with a head shot. Convinced that they were about to be overrun, the dozen men still in the pool crawled through the chest-deep water in the ditch to the point where it emptied into the rice paddy they would have to cross to reach the tree line the company had retreated to.

One of their guys lay dead in the paddy. Sergeant First Class Dickerson hollered for covering fire as his group ran toward the trees. Another man went down, hit in the head. Karp aimed his M16 at two NVA moving on their right and squeezed the trigger. The weapon blew up in his hands. The barrel was clogged with mud. The dozen grunts in the ditch decided to wait until dusk before crossing that open, fire-swept paddy. It had just gotten dark when Karp heard voices. He looked up from the ditch and was astonished to see several NVA in position a stone's throw away. The battle was over and the NVA were talking amongst themselves. Karp silently watched one of them pull on a sweater to ward off the evening's misty chill. The NVA disappeared when U.S. artillery began landing, but after the barrage more Vietnamese appeared in the flare-illuminated night. Two with ponchos and conical hats walked along the edge of the ditch and right past the terrified, unmoving soldiers lying in it before disappearing back into the darkness.

The grunts in the ditch crawled back the way they had come to reach the cover of a closer tree line. There they decided to pair up to make it back any way they could. It was nerve-racking for Karp and his partner as they walked along the edge of the trees. It was raining, and the flares, swinging as they came down, made everything appear to move. They had reached the previous night's laager site when an M60 machine gun suddenly opened up from fifty meters away. They realized then that the company had pulled back to the same location. Karp wanted to wait until dawn before they crossed those last fifty meters, but his partner wanted to keep going and said he would go first. When they got moving again, Karp was glad that his partner was a head-bobbing, lanky-limbed country boy. No GI on watch, no matter how uptight, could mistake that distinctive lope.

The 196th Chargers lost 66 men but claimed 429 NVA kills in the Hiep Duc Valley. Three weeks after the battle, Steel Gimlet's reign ended at the stroke of six months, and Lieutenant Colonel Snyder rotated in for his shot of career-building command duty with the 3-21st Infantry.

Being a history professor, Bill Snyder selected the call sign Cedar Mountain 6. Cedar Mountain was the site of a Civil War battle that was the first in the regiment's lineage. Some of Snyder's officers, comparing him to his predecessor, nicknamed him the Gentle Gimlet.

Snyder lost his first four men when the battalion deployed to FSB Colt during the Tet Offensive. The next major action began on 4 March 1968 when Alpha Company, by then commanded by Captain Osborn (Yurchak having been promoted and assigned to serve as Snyder's S3), was attached to the division cavalry squadron and participated in the destruction of the 3d Regiment, 3d NVA Division, in the foothills near Tam Ky. It was a three-day action. Wounds from enemy mortars and rocket-propelled grenades were numerous, and the cav unit had men killed, but Alpha Annihilator survived the battle without a fatality. The enemy, subjected to maximum arty, gunships, and tac air, as well as the cannons and machine guns of the cav's tanks and armored personnel carriers, left behind more than four hundred bodies, according to the official after-action reports.

Two days later, Alpha Company lost a man in a minor skirmish. Two days after that, on 11 March, Lieutenant Colonel Snyder was involved in his first major contact when Bravo Company bumped into an NVA battalion in the Que Son Valley. Maximum use was again made of supporting arms, but, caught in the open, muddy paddies as they were, six Barracuda GIs were killed. It was Captain Corrigan's baptism of fire as a company commander. When Corrigan reported that he was running out of ammunition, Snyder had his command-and-control (C&C) ship divert to FSB Center to take aboard an emergency resupply. Barracuda was under fire from the east, so Snyder's plan was to have the chopper fly in from the west, kick out the ammo from a hover, and then spin around and zip out the way it had come.

The plan ran afoul of an NVA in a tree. The C&C Huey was just coming into its hover and was about twenty feet above the LZ when the undetected NVA emptied his AK-47 down the length of the helicopter from nose to tail boom. He put twenty holes in the chopper. The door gunner was shot in the foot, and Snyder was cut across the forehead by a piece of flying metal from one of the holes punched in the floor. The wound was minor but a terrific bleeder. A crate of ammunition had also been hit, and Snyder shoved the smoking time bomb out the side door along with the rest of the packaged ammo. The shot-up Huey made it back to Center, where it died just as the pilot was setting it down.[2] Meanwhile, Corrigan's company recovered all its casualties and withdrew to the hill where the mortar platoon had been left to provide support. The mortars were still there, but the crews were not. All but three of the crewmen eventually returned, explaining that an intense enemy mortar barrage had driven them from the position, and that they had become separated from one another while rushing down the jungle-covered slope. The three missing men were not recovered: They had been ambushed and captured.

The Gimlets' next big contact—their last major one before the DMZ mission—began on 9 April when Captain Osborn's Alpha Company killed four VC they caught running across a rice paddy in a little, horseshoe-shaped valley. The VC had been following them, sniping at the

2. In addition to the Silver Star and Purple Heart he got for this action, Lieutenant Colonel Snyder was awarded a Legion of Merit (LM), a BSM for meritorious service, and an Air Medal (AM) with oak leaf cluster for making more than fifty helicopter flights in a combat zone.

company ever since it had begun patrolling there. On the morning of 11 April, an Alpha GI tripped a booby trap, which blew off his hand and foot. During the day, the company killed three more VC who had been trailing it. To fully screen this active valley, the company spread out and established platoon patrol bases. Alpha One was joined in its position by Echo Recon, and they set up around a number of deserted hootches concealed in thick bamboo. Shortly before midnight on 13 April, the NVA assaulted this joint perimeter. Less than two hours earlier a ridgetop observation post from Delta Company had spotted NVA signaling each other with flashlights from one side of the valley to the other. The observation post had alerted the Alpha and Echo elements in the valley, but the joint perimeter was caught off guard nonetheless. In fact, neither the Echo Recon commander, who was seriously wounded, nor the Alpha One lieutenant, who was killed along with his platoon sergeant, had had their men dig in. Nor had they put out claymore mines or trip flares. Most of the grunts had gotten out of the elements by setting up inside the hootches. Away from the supervision of their company commanders, the platoons had basically taken a siesta from the war.

The NVA ran right through them. Their mortar crews and machine gunners opened up first to keep the grunts' heads down, then the NVA assault element let loose a shower of grenades before charging through one side of the perimeter and out the other. The attack was over in moments. Thirteen Gimlets were killed, and almost everyone else was wounded. Six of the dead were from Alpha One, seven from Echo Recon. The NVA left four bodies. The rest of Alpha conducted a night march to reinforce the position while illumination rounds flooded the valley with light, and gunships worked out with miniguns and rockets until dawn. The medevacs began at first light. One stunned grunt wrote home that "it sure was a sorry sight. Dead and wounded GIs lying all over the place. I had to help wrap 'em in ponchos for extraction. The whole inside of the perimeter was blown to shreds. Rifles, rucksacks, web gear, and everything else was blown to bits. Everything was full of blood. Most of the guys didn't even have time to fire a shot. Some men were sleeping inside huts when the NVA hit. We pulled what was left of them out of the ashes."

CHAPTER 13 THE END OF THE LINE

The artillery prep on Lam Xuan East and Lam Xuan West commenced at 0755 on 2 May 1968 as the 3-21st Infantry's rifle companies moved toward their lines of departure. Colonel Gelling, the 196th LIB commander, helicoptered to Lieutenant Colonel Snyder's Mai Xa Chanh East CP at the junction of Jones Creek and the Cua Viet River. Gelling, a hard, old-school commander, did not actually retain operational control of the Gimlets, but he was on the scene because he was concerned that the Marines might not adequately support their attached Army battalion. Gelling assured Snyder that the brigade would provide him with a command-and-control helicopter and a forward air controller "unless the brigade has contingency missions elsewhere that necessitate me pulling one or both back from you."

Colonel Gelling, a short, feisty, hawk-nosed man, was chewing a cigar as he told Snyder, "Anything you need—if you're not satisfied with the way things are going up here—call me."

Gelling climbed back into his Huey. His next stop was Camp Kistler for a meeting with Colonel Hull, who was responsible for providing most of the 3-21st Infantry's supplies and supporting fires. Gelling was, as Snyder put it, "openly lobbying to make sure that I got a fair shake in Marine resources. He was more concerned about it than I was, and I was concerned."

The prep fires lasted twenty minutes. Because the Gimlets' own artillery battery had yet to be slingloaded up by Chinook, the rounds were delivered by the Marines' 4.2-inch mortars at Mai Xa Chanh West, and four artillery batteries firing out of Camp Kistler and the

DHCB. Lieutenant Colonel Snyder's plan called for an attack on two axes, with Jones Creek serving as both a guide and dividing line. Captain Corrigan's B/3-21 was to advance north from Mai Xa Chanh West to a graveyard west of Jones Creek and immediately opposite Lam Xuan East. From the graveyard, Bravo could support by fire the attack on Lam Xuan East by Lieutenant Kohl and C/3-21, which was to move up the opposite side of Jones Creek from Mai Xa Chanh East. Following another artillery prep, Charlie would move on to seize Nhi Ha, with Captain Osborn's A/3-21 following behind. Keeping abreast, Bravo was to simultaneously secure Lam Xuan West, which was connected to Nhi Ha by a footbridge that spanned Jones Creek. Captain Humphries was to remain in reserve with D/3-21.

The first shot of what promised to be a long day was fired by Barracuda before moving out of its night laager for the line of departure. The first shot was an accidental discharge. Captain Corrigan heard the distinct thump of an M79 going off, then saw a grenadier who was kneeling with the butt of his weapon against the ground and the barrel pointed up. The grenadier, who'd been cleaning a loaded weapon, was staring straight up. "So the whole hundred of us just kind of looked straight up, too," Corrigan remembered. "And we looked at each other, because you really didn't know whether you were better off just standing where you were, or running around in circles, depending on where the shell was going to come down. About twenty seconds later, the thing came down in the company area. It exploded, but luckily it didn't hit anybody."

The attack kicked off at 0808 with Bravo and Charlie Companies simultaneously crossing their lines of departure. Snyder's C&C Huey dipped low to their front, reconning the flattened hamlets that were their objectives. The guerrilla-chasing Gimlets had never participated in an operation of this size before, and Lieutenant Smith of Alpha Company told his men that "this must be a battalion commander's dream to have his whole battalion down on the ground while he's up in a chopper maneuvering 'em."

Lieutenant Colonel Snyder encountered no fire and saw no enemy during his aerial reconnaissance. Thus advised, Captain Corrigan was able to move his company quickly into position. With Barracuda anchoring the left flank, Kohl's men assaulted Lam Xuan East, a collection of blasted hootches and hedgerows halfway between Mai Xa Chanh East and Nhi Ha. The assault was a walk-through for Charlie Tiger. The grunts reconned by fire and, drawing none in return, moved in and methodically grenaded the bunkers and spiderholes they found in the rubble.

At 1055, Lieutenant Kohl reported that Lam Xuan East had been swept and seized without contact, and the two companies resumed the attack. The prep fires were shifted onto Nhi Ha and Lam Xuan West as the assault companies covered the last two klicks in a two-up-and-one-back formation. Corrigan reached his objective at 1155 and reported it secured fifteen minutes later—again without contact. Barracuda's march had taken it over the same ground that G BLT 2/4 had crossed in the opposite direction two nights before during its under-fire withdrawal. Along the way, some GIs had picked up Marine-issue flak jackets. The Army troops did not normally wear flak jackets, but the threat of enemy artillery fire caused them to be more cautious. Barracuda also recovered a 3.5-inch rocket launcher that the Marines had abandoned. Corrigan kept the weapon, using it to mark targets with white phosphorus shells. There were so many abandoned Marine and NVA weapons along the way that Corrigan later observed, "Back where we'd been, hell, if you found two or three rifles, you'd had a real successful day—and here you were damn near tripping over stuff. It impressed my people. It gave them the idea that this was serious."

This place has about as much cover as a fucking parking lot, thought Private Harp of Charlie One, which was moving with twenty meters between each man. The flat terrain between Lam Xuan East and Nhi Ha was nothing like the jungle-busting, ridge-running Charlie Tiger troopers had ever operated in. The fields of fire seemed to go on forever, broken only by dunes and low-lying hedgerows and tree lines. Spent LAWs lay on the ground, along with expended M16 brass and the shell casings and links from M60 machine guns. There were also Marine steel pots lying around, along with Russian-issue helmets and NVA footgear. Harp didn't notice one boot until he'd stepped on it; flies exploded from it. Harp looked down as he passed by and saw a black, rotten, maggoty foot encased in the mangled canvas and leather.

Heat waves radiated off the ground as if off asphalt.

Charlie One, having gone into Lam Xuan East on point, was in the drag position on the way to Nhi Ha. Lieutenant Hieb, the platoon leader, had gotten the call from Lieutenant Kohl, the acting company commander, to hold up as they had begun to move out of Lam Xuan East so that Charlie Two, under 1st Lt. Edward F. Guthrie, could take their place up front. The platoons were always rotated on a share-the-risk principle. What was unusual was that when Charlie Two humped past, Lieutenant Guthrie was the lead man, helmet and pack on, his CAR15 Colt Commando slung around his neck and held ready at the waist. "Hey, Ed, what the hell are you doing walking point?" Hieb called to him. "You're not supposed to be walking point!"

"These guys are draggin' ass, and I'm going to show 'em how to do it," answered Lieutenant Guthrie with an Oklahoma twang.

The problem was not only the foreign, forbidding terrain, but the fact that Captain Leach, who was nearly a living legend in Charlie Tiger, had departed two days earlier on R and R. Lieutenant Kohl, the company exec, had taken command in his absence. Although Kohl had been awarded both the Silver Star and the Bronze Star Medal for Valor (BSMv) while a platoon leader in Black Death, the grunts still didn't think he had the savvy to replace Leach.

Jones Creek, on the company's left flank, was generally oriented from the southeast to the northwest, but it curved due west above Lam Xuan East so that Nhi Ha actually sat on the northern bank. Lam Xuan West was due south across the bend. Charlie Tiger, having approached from the southeast, had to swing around to assault the brushy island of Nhi Ha from the east. Again there was no enemy fire, and the two platoons up front did not waste ammunition reconning by fire.

The company stepped up about three feet from the paddies onto the slight high ground of Nhi Ha proper with Lieutenant Guthrie's Charlie Two on the right and Charlie Three, under the acting command of a sergeant first class, moving abreast on the left. Lieutenant Kohl followed with his command group. The assault line, with a point team forward of each platoon, closed up to about five meters between men as they pushed through the first thicket of bamboo and brush at the hamlet's edge. The terrain opened up on the other side, and by the time Lieutenant Hieb and Charlie One, bringing up the rear, were inside, the rest of Charlie Tiger had already swept nearly halfway through Nhi Ha. The hamlet, defined by an outer wall of vegetation, was narrow in width but long on its east-west axis. The sweep was from east to west. There were two-walled and three-walled hootches, which were checked as they were passed, and hootches so badly shot up that only the cement foundations remained. There were also old entrenchments, both friendly and enemy, but the village appeared to be deserted.

As the two platoons drew to within fifty meters of the brush line that cut the hamlet in half at its narrow waist, Sgt. Paul L. Yost and Sp4 William J. Morse, now on point, stopped to alert Lieutenant Guthrie that there was movement ahead. They could see at least one man wearing a helmet. Guthrie, concerned about an intramural firefight, shouted a warning down the assault line that there were still Marines in position. But the men they'd seen were not Marines. They were NVA regulars with helmets, fatigues, and web gear, and they opened fire at that moment from their entrenchments in the heavy brush, killing the entire point team before the GIs knew what hit them. Guthrie caught a round in the back of the head that blew open his forehead on the way out. Yost took at least three rounds through his chest, and Morse was shot above the bridge of the nose. The bullet mushroomed and splattered out the back of his skull.

Private Harp of Charlie One was a small, wiry GI. Jolted by the sudden firing, he fell into a low spot of sand, ending up like a turtle on its back because of his rucksack. The ruck weighed almost as much as he did. The fire seemed to be coming from everywhere at once, and when he moved, bullets chewed up the sand beside him. Harp finally slipped free of the rucksack and rolled it over to get the machine-gun ammo off, along with a couple of hand grenades and his spare bandolier of M16 ammunition. He noticed then that the two-quart water bladder that he kept secured on the ruck had taken a round through it and was deflated.

The ambush, which was initiated at 1250, included rocket-propelled grenades. As Sgt. Jimmie Lee "Red" Coulthard, a machine-gun team leader in Charlie Three, dropped toward the mound to his front, he was eye to eye with an RPG that seemed hell-bent on taking his head off. The projectile was slow enough to see, and it whooshed over him just as he slid prone behind the mound. It exploded somewhere behind him. The air above him seemed electrified with death.

Over the cacophony of explosions and automatic fire, the pinned-down grunts tried to make sense of what was happening.

"Get some return fire going!"

"Who's been hit?"

It turned out that while Charlie Two's point team was being shot to pieces on the right flank, the point man for Charlie Three on the left—a private named Adams, who was to pick up three superficial wounds during the battle—had been able to clamber to cover in a gully. Specialist Derryl D. Odom, the backup man, was cut down, but the third man in line, Sp4 Eugene J. McDonald, was also able to find safety behind a brushy mound. Odom lay facedown and unmoving nearby. McDonald thought he was dead, but Odom, out in the open with a bullet-shattered arm, was playing 'possum where he had fallen. He knew that the enemy still had him in their sights, even if he couldn't see them through the brush.

The fourth man in the point team was Sp4 Johnny Miller, who made a dash around McDonald's mound to reach Odom. Miller made it two or three steps before he was hit in the head. McDonald heard him moan, and could see him sprawled out just beyond the mound. McDonald saw a second bullet thump into his back.

Johnny Miller was dead. Private First Class George L. Cruse, who had gone for the same mound as Sergeant Coulthard, let out an anguished cry—"They got Johnny!"—then shrugged off his rucksack and, acting on impulse and without coordinating covering fire, leapt up to make a run for Miller. It was the bravest, most stupid thing Coulthard ever saw. Cruse was blown away as soon as he exposed himself. The twenty-year-old Cruse had been a shy, quiet, kind of clumsy country boy from Liberal, Kansas. He was white. The man he sought to save was black. Both of them had been drafted. Miller, older than most grunts at age twenty-five, had been appalled by the poverty in the villages they usually operated in, and had written to his mother in North Carolina, asking that her church group send clothes over for the children. "They were just good, simple guys," said Coulthard.

*   *   *

Charlie Tiger was spread across the open ground in scattered bunches wherever the men could find cover. Staff Sergeant James M. Goad, the acting platoon sergeant—and the most respected career NCO in Charlie Three—earned the Silver Star for taking control of the fight in the absence of their platoon sergeant and acting platoon leader, who they assumed had been killed. "When the going got really tough, Goad was a good man," recalled the company's artillery lieutenant. "He had innate leadership abilities. When he said something, he said it with such a positive attitude that the men were willing to do it."

Staff Sergeant Goad wormed his way up to Coulthard's mound, and they returned M16 fire over it on full automatic.

"Get the machine gun up here!" Goad shouted.

Sergeant Roger W. Starr, the platoon's machine-gun squad leader, was behind a berm about forty meters to the rear of Goad and Coulthard. He got a BSMv for his response to their shouts. Starr, an amiable, twenty-one-year-old draftee from a dairy farm outside Sand Lake, Michigan, gave his M16 to one of his gunners, and, taking the man's M60 machine gun in return, rushed forward and clattered in unscathed beside Goad and Coulthard. The mound was too narrow for all of them, so Coulthard slid back into the shallow depression behind it to make way for Starr and his M60. They had to come up to their knees to fire over the shallow slope of the mound, so they took turns, Goad with his M16 and Starr with the machine gun. Starr directed most of his quick, jack-in-the-box bursts at an NVA machine-gun position that he could hear but not see in the hedgerow. Trying to keep low, he ended up shooting the top of their own mound with each burst before getting the weapon all the way up in the enemy's direction. Return fire also kicked up dirt across the mound, and at one point Starr felt something strike hot and sharp across the upper part of his left arm. He immediately dropped back down and saw that his sleeve had been torn and was bloody. He didn't know if the graze had been caused by a bullet or a shard from a bullet-shattered rock.

Staff Sergeant Goad and Roger Starr were about the only men in the platoon seriously engaging the enemy. While Coulthard crawled back to Charlie One to get more ammo for them, Starr and his impromptu assistant gunner, Sp4 Ray Elsworth—having no time to wait—

yelled to Charlie Two on their right that they needed ammunition right away! In response, Sp4 Pierre L. Sullivan, a grunt from the other platoon, ran to their mound and began firing his M16 from a prone position several meters to their right. The position around the edge of the mound was so vulnerable that Coulthard had avoided it when he'd been up there. Sullivan had always been willing to take chances—a trait that earned the nineteen year old the nickname Tunnel Rat because he frequently climbed head first into enemy tunnels with only a .45 and a flashlight. One of his buddies suggested that Sullivan was always going first because he was self-conscious about his small stature. Sullivan was not a draftee; he had enlisted. He wanted to prove himself. He was, however, a short-timer, and some weeks earlier, during a mountain-climbing patrol in the highlands, he had tried to sham his way out of the field by claiming that his eyes were bad. Captain Leach, who was death on malingering, ordered Sullivan to walk point. When he successfully navigated the dangerous crevices of the jungled mountain, the captain, who had been behind him the whole time, grabbed him and barked, "Don't you ever pull that shit again!"

Specialist Sullivan had been acting like his old self when he made his dash to join Starr and Elsworth. When Sullivan's M16 jammed, he sat up with his back to the enemy, began disassembling the weapon—and was shot in the head within seconds. He slumped forward and shook for several minutes before he died.

Starr, unable to reach Sullivan because of the fire, muttered, "I'm going to get sick."

Elsworth swallowed hard and answered, "So am I."

Sergeant Coulthard snaked his way forward again, having gone from man to man back with Charlie One, imploring each for grenades and ammunition. Tall, chunky Red Coulthard—a hard-drinking but level-headed and likeable farm boy from Mount Ayr, Iowa—left the ammo he had gathered with Goad and Starr, then moved to the left with another NCO toward an NVA machine-gun position. Coulthard had been in the Army since enlisting six years earlier at age seventeen. Coulthard and his buddy slid into a gully about fifty meters away from the enemy gun. After heaving grenades at it without effect, Coulthard decided to use a LAW on the bunker, which they could just see at an angle through the vegetation. The other NCO covered him with his M16. On cue, they both popped up, but the instant Coulthard fired

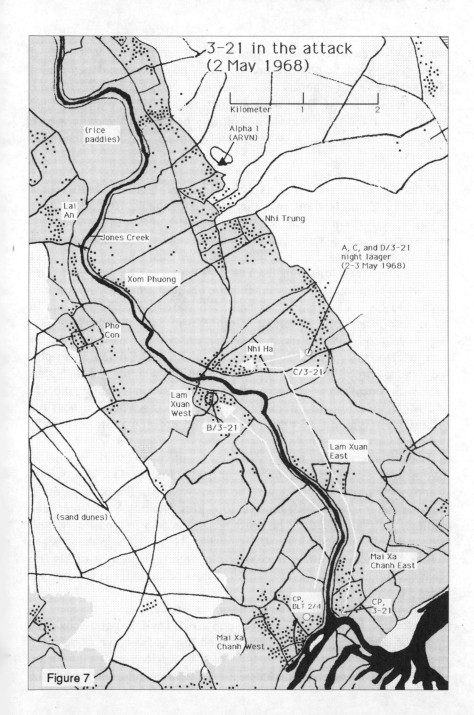

Figure 7

the LAW an enemy grenade exploded between them in a shower of debris. They knew that more grenades would be coming, and they almost climbed over each other as they hustled down the ditch. There were no more explosions. They realized then that the first explosion had actually been the LAW's backblast hitting the back of the gully, which was higher than the edge they were shooting over. They started laughing like crazy.

Pinned down on the left flank, Specialist McDonald of Charlie Three squeezed off single shots into the hedgerow ahead. He couldn't see anything, but the point man, Adams, was still down in his gully directing fire. Adams kept shouting for him to aim higher. Adams also hollered at McDonald to toss him some grenades since he was closer to the enemy. McDonald never had the chance. As he rose up to fire his M16 again, a round caught him in his left arm and flipped him over onto his back. His glasses and M16 were gone. Shocked and in pain, he did not look for either. A small bit of his thumb was missing, and blood bubbled up from where the round had lodged in his arm. McDonald yelled that he was hit, and a GI crawled up to pull the bandage from his medical pouch, wrap the wound, and then start back with him. They were eventually able to move in a running crouch, and McDonald joined a number of other walking wounded near the village well, where the company command group was in position.

The initial eruption of fire that killed Lieutenant Guthrie of Charlie Two also dropped his platoon sergeant, Sfc. Eugene Franklin, with a round in the thigh. Pinned down, the thirty-year-old Franklin—a black career soldier—bled to death. Nearby, Pfc. Thomas M. Walker, age eighteen, also lay dead in the brush. Another man in Charlie Two hit right off the bat was Sp4 Larry C. Schwebke. He was shot in the stomach just as he reached a little stucco-type hootch that the rest of his fire team had already passed, all of them moving upright in those last seconds before the ambush was sprung.

Schwebke cried out, "Oh, my guts!" as he fell.

Under fire, Pfc. John C. Fulcher spun around and dragged Schwebke up to the cover of the hootch, then pulled him as far down as he could into a small crater in the floor. Fulcher's best friend and fellow team member, Pfc. Douglas D. Fletcher, joined them inside. The roof of the little, twelve-by-twelve structure had long since been blown off, and the wall to the left was also missing. Fulcher and Fletcher, pressed against the inside of the hootch's front wall, slid to its left edge to return M16 fire—then ducked back as AK-47 rounds thudded into the stucco on the other side of the wall. Their buddy Schwebke held his bloody stomach, but apparently because of damage to his spine he moaned that it was his legs that hurt. Lying in an awkward position in the crater, he asked the other two to drag him back out and lay him in such a way that his legs would not hurt so much.

"Larry, they're shootin' at us," Fulcher answered. "They're goin' to shoot you again if I move ya."

Schwebke mumbled, "Okay, okay . . ."

Their squad leader, Sgt. Donald G. Pozil, made it to the rear wall of the hootch. A draftee, he had taken command of the platoon in the absence of Guthrie and Franklin—for which he would receive the Silver Star. His concern was to get his casualties to the rear. There was no door or window to pass Schwebke through, and moving him around the exposed edge of the wall seemed suicidal. Pozil had the GIs with him use their E-tools to chop a hole through the stucco. When the hole was big enough, Schwebke stretched out his arms so that the men on the other side could reach him and pull him through. He cried out in pain as he extended his arms. It seemed an eternity since he'd been shot.

Larry Schwebke, a farmer's son with a young wife in Iowa, died sometime between being dragged back by Sergeant Pozil's group and finally being lifted onto a medevac Huey. He was twenty-two years old and a draftee. Meanwhile, Fulcher and Fletcher, feeling very much alone, resumed their fire—until Fletcher's M16 jammed. Fletcher did not get shook. He simply sat back against the hootch wall and methodically disassembled the weapon, cleaned it, and slapped it back together. He thumped in another magazine, recharged the weapon, and rolled back into his firing position in the rubble.

Charlie Tiger received neither tac air nor gunship support—nor any direction from the company command group. Lieutenant Kohl, who was near the village well when the ambush began, stayed there for the duration of the fight. Crawling forward under heavy fire, Lieutenant Jaquez, the artillery spotter, found Kohl sitting up against the cement well on the side opposite the enemy. He had his helmet and flak jacket on, and both of his radios were on the ground beside him. No one else was there, and Jaquez realized that Lieutenant Kohl was physically shaking. Kohl was not giving orders on the radio. He was simply listening to the company net with a handset held to one ear, numbly relaying to battalion on his other radio that they were pinned down and needed help.

Lieutenant Kohl had seen a lot of action as a platoon leader, and had breathed a sigh of relief when his six months were up and he got a rear-echelon assignment. Now he was back in action and it was proving to be one firefight too many for him.

Jaquez screamed at Kohl to "get up and lead!"

Kohl yelled back incoherently, and Jaquez, with his radioman in tow, finally crawled forward and away from the immobilized company commander. Operating on his belly, Lieutenant Jaquez—a Mexican-American from Los Angeles—got Charlie Tiger some artillery support from three Marine artillery batteries. He worked their fires in as close as he dared in coordination with grunts up front who answered his radio calls, then he and his RTO crawled forward themselves to the point where they could hear enemy soldiers yelling back and forth in Vietnamese. Jaquez could see some of them hustling past several hootches on the left flank. After adjusting fire onto that area, he shouldered his own M16 in the excitement. Between radio transmissions, he used the ammo magazine already in the weapon and the six others in the bandolier hanging down from his shoulder.

Lieutenant Jaquez was awarded the BSMv. So was Charlie One's Lieutenant Hieb, a slim, bespectacled draftee commissioned from officer candidate school (OCS), and a twenty-four-year-old native of Twin Falls, Idaho. Hieb, holding open Nhi Ha's back door with his platoon, also moved from position to position under fire to organize individual and fire-team efforts to drag the casualties back from up front. His RTO was right behind him. When Hieb got up to run, his RTO got up to run. The RTO was such an obvious target that Hieb finally took the radio from him, slipped his arms through the shoulder straps, and told the GI to grab some cover. One of Hieb's better squad leaders, Sp4 John H. Burns, anchored their right flank with his troops behind an earthen berm that was some three feet high. Along with Burns, there was Brooks, Hobi, Harp, and a guy named Meister. When the NVA tried to move in on that side, their M16 fire was overwhelming. Their machine gunner, Pope, who had set up beside Burns, burned out his barrel with sustained fire. The NVA went to the ground. Burns's people kept pouring out rounds, and Harp ended up making three trips back to get ammo from the other squads. He got lost each time on his way back. The situation was that confusing.

The GIs in Charlie One could not fire to their front for fear of hitting Charlie Two and Three. Most of the survivors in Charlie Two had made it to a large crater and were pinned at the bottom of it. One soldier near the crater began digging a shallow trench toward it. When he got close enough, he heaved another E-tool to the men inside so they could dig from their direction, link up, and get out under cover. The digging seemed to take forever.

During the wait, Specialist Burns asked for a volunteer to help him drag back Sergeant Yost's body. Harp said he'd go. Their maneuver required them to crawl past a certain NVA position, and although high grass offered some concealment and the NVA appeared to be firing in a different direction, it was a risky prospect. The medic said to be careful, adding that he didn't want to lose anyone "trying to recover guys who are already dead."

"There's gotta be a better way to do this," Harp chimed in.

Burns exploded. "Harp, you chickenshit!"

Harp was always in trouble with Burns, mostly because he was so afraid he would screw up that he usually did. Burns tagged him as the squad dud, and in this instance he took Brooks with him to drag Yost's body back. There was a hole in Yost's chest and back that a fist could pass through, and he was blue around his lips and eyes and fingernails. It was a devastating, infuriating sight, and when an NVA on the right kicked up dirt around them with a sudden burst, Harp had to shoot back. He had seen the smoke rise from where the NVA had fired on full automatic, and he ran over to Pope, whose machine-gun position afforded a clear line of fire.

Harp jumped down beside Pope and shouldered his M16, exclaiming, "This little motherfucker is mine!"

Harp pumped two magazines into the spot—silencing the NVA, maybe temporarily, maybe for good—then rushed back to where Burns and the medic were getting Yost's body on a stretcher. Burns cranked up again, "Goddamnit, Harp, if I need you to shoot, I'll tell you to shoot.

Right now I need you to lift, so get on the goddamn stretcher and leave the shootin' to Pope!" A Marine Otter had moved up behind the village well to evacuate casualties. With Burns and Brooks up front and Harp and the medic in back, they moved out with Yost's stretcher in a running crouch, only to get hung up on a tree stump. By then they were all moving sluggishly, but in the heat of the moment Burns snapped around to scream at Harp again, "Harp, pick your fucking end up . . ."

At the same time that Charlie Tiger was ambushed, Captain Corrigan and Barracuda, across the stream in Lam Xuan West, also began taking AK-47 and M79 fire from Nhi Ha. Corrigan remained in position to provide suppressive fires into the left flank of Kohl's fight. It was Corrigan's second big action. The son of a West Pointer, twenty-six-year-old Corrigan was an ROTC Distinguished Military Graduate. He was a low-key, highly intelligent man and he ran a good company, although Snyder did not think he had the battlefield instincts of Leach or Humphries. Nevertheless, the battalion commander noted that Barracuda 6, however green, was a cool customer on the radio despite the bullets snapping over his head. Corrigan, lying prone, had called several of his lieutenants and platoon sergeants to his position beside the stream. There were no trees or bushes there, but the crown of the bank, which was three feet above the creek, provided some cover. The Barracuda GIs deployed along the southern bank could not see the NVA blasting away from the other side. The brush in Nhi Ha was too thick. Nor could they see Charlie Tiger. Until they determined who was where in the vegetation, Corrigan instructed them to return fire only with M16s, adding, "Don't use your machine guns, and no LAWs or M79s. We don't want to be killing our own people over there."

Barracuda began taking casualties at that point. The first to be hit was SSgt. William F. Ochs, a twenty-year-old career soldier assigned as the platoon sergeant of Bravo One. Ochs, who had been with the platoon for almost nine months and was a highly respected NCO, should have crawled when he returned from Corrigan's meeting and started passing the word. Instead, he ran along the bank in a crouch, shouting at his men not to fire their M60s and LAWs. Almost immediately he was blown off his feet by a round that caught him high up on his right leg. The bullet tore a four-inch-long gash where it went in, shattered the bone, and then exited just below his buttocks, taking a grapefruit-sized chunk of muscle and flesh with it. Ochs, in excruciating pain, screamed obscenities until a medic crawled over and thumped a morphine syrette into his leg. The whole leg went numb. Ochs was still shook up because his leg, which seemed held together by only a few strands of muscle, was bent crazily so that his foot was up by his ear. One of Ochs's squad leaders and good friends, Bob Waite, who had also crawled to him, placed a helmet under his head to make him comfortable and spoke encouragingly to him, doing for Ochs what Ochs had done previously for so many of their casualties. Hoping to distract Ochs, Waite got a can of beer out of Ochs's rucksack and opened it for him. Ochs managed a few sips. Meanwhile, Ochs could hear someone trying to organize a medevac on the radio: "The guy's bleedin' like a stuck pig. He's not going to last long. We can't stop the bleedin'!"

The helicopter pilot's response came in broken over the radio: "Get him . . . wood line behind you . . . we'll pick him up." As gently as he could, Waite straightened Ochs's leg so it would fit in the poncho they lifted him on, and then several other grunts carried Ochs toward the wood line. It was a hundred-meter trip. Under fire the whole way across, the litter team had to tug and drag Ochs along as they struggled on their hands and knees. They made it, though, and Ochs was medevacked within fifteen minutes of getting hit—quickly enough to save his leg.

At about the same time, approximately 1400, a rifleman in Bravo One, Pfc. Robert A. Romo, a twenty-year-old draftee from Rialto, California, caught another of the bullets snapping at them from across the creek. It hit him in the neck and killed him. Afterward, Romo's body was escorted home by his uncle, an OCS graduate serving as a platoon leader in the Americal Division. They were the same age and had been raised as brothers. Romo's death was a deciding factor in his uncle's decision to join the Vietnam Veterans Against the War and to throw away his Bronze Stars during the organization's 1971 protest on the Capitol steps. One of Romo's Barracuda buddies wrote home that he couldn't understand "why God would take his life. He never cussed, drinked, or smoked. The guy was twenty and never had sex with a girl . . . everyone else would seem like a devil compared to him."

At 1410, Captain Corrigan requested another dust-off for another wounded man, and the C&C Huey was dispatched without the colonel. Lieutenant Colonel Snyder, coordinating the action from Mai Xa Chanh East, intended not to carry the fight into the NVA entrenchments, but to have Charlie Tiger recover its casualties and break contact so that he could obliterate Nhi Ha with massed artillery and air strikes. As such, Snyder had immediately ordered Captain Osborn and Alpha Company to cover Charlie Tiger's exposed right flank. Leaving one platoon in Lam Xuan East, Osborn had his other two platoons rolling within ten minutes of the first shot. Knowing that any medevac attempt in Nhi Ha would result in a shot-down helicopter, Snyder also dispatched the USMC Otters attached from BLT 2/4 to resupply the engaged company with ammunition and evacuate its casualties. Each Otter had a .50-caliber machine gun manned by a Marine crewman, and Echo Recon GIs aboard to provide additional security. Captain Humphries and Delta Company, previously in reserve at the battalion command post, moved out some thirty minutes after the Otters departed Mai Xa Chanh East.

Overhead, a USAF forward air controller had arrived to help direct the Marine artillery pounding Nhi Ha. Meanwhile, at 1525, four artillery shells landed near Bravo Company in Lam Xuan West. The first one took Captain Corrigan by surprise. He was conducting a recon for a night defensive position with his FO team and one of his RTOs about a hundred meters from the main body of the company when the round exploded about thirty meters from them. They dropped down and stayed down as three more rounds slammed in. When they realized that no more were coming, they jumped up to rejoin the company. The Gimlets had never experienced NVA artillery fire. When Corrigan reported the incoming, a check was run to determine if it had been enemy or misplotted friendly fire. The NVA answered the question five minutes later by dropping several more salvos on Barracuda, thirty rounds total in a little less than thirty minutes. The incoming shells wounded four grunts, who were evacuated aboard the colonel's helicopter. The enemy then shifted their artillery fires onto Nhi Ha.

Alpha Annihilator's two reaction platoons moved cautiously toward Nhi Ha, taking individual enemy soldiers under fire along the way. Lieutenant Smith's Alpha Two was on the right flank and Alpha Three, led by 2d Lt. William B. Kimball, was abreast on the left. Radio communications with leaderless, shot-up Charlie Tiger were minimal, and the mood was tense. When the two platoons reached Nhi Ha's northeast corner, Smith dropped into a bomb crater and deployed his platoon to the right across the dry paddy. The men occupied old trenches or moved in behind hedgerows. The NVA were entrenched in a hedgerow in front of them.

Enemy fire became thick as more NVA ran up singly and in pairs to reinforce that position. Lieutenant Smith, very concerned about a possible counterattack, cut loose with his CAR15. The platoon's four-man machine-gun team also opened fire from the crater, and M79 men tried to lob rounds into the enemy trench.

While Alpha Two secured the right flank, Lieutenant Kimball and Alpha Three worked their way into Nhi Ha under stray fire from Charlie Tiger's fight to the front and from the occasional NVA artillery round that impacted amid the hootches and hedgerows. One shell slammed in beside Kimball and his platoon sergeant, SSgt. George L. Dale, but it failed to explode. The dud sat half-submerged in the sandy soil, and Kimball and Dale joked about their good luck. Moving on, the platoon halted in the cover of a tree line. There was heavy fire to the front. Kimball was lying in some bushes with Sgt. James L. Stone, the point squad leader, trying to figure out how to cross the next open area, when a GI from Charlie Tiger, the first they'd seen, made his way over to them. The trooper had a battle dressing wrapped around his head. "All of our guys are pinned down," he told the reinforcements as he pointed across the open area. "We got a bunch of dead and wounded across that paddy there, over 'round that blown-up house."

The wounded trooper wanted to lead them across, but Lieutenant Kimball said, "You've already been through it. Just stay here on this side."

Kimball then told Sergeant Stone to take his squad across the hundred-meter-wide clearing. American artillery fire was tearing up the left flank beyond the hootch. They could see dirt and trees flying in the air. Stone, who was getting increasingly upset, said, "My God, tell 'em to lift that fire—we can't go into that!" Kimball got the arty shifted, and Stone got his fire teams organized. He wanted Sp4 Ron Nahrstadt's team to go first, followed by Sp4 Terry H. Alderson's, but Alderson chose that moment to tell Stone that he had injured his knee during their up-and-down rush across the last clearing. Stone didn't believe him. Alderson was a good soldier and a good friend, but the fear in his eyes was obvious. Alderson's wife was expecting a baby any day, and he'd been anxiously awaiting each mail call.

Everyone in the squad was waiting to see if it would be a boy or a girl. Although angry, Stone didn't press the issue. He told Alderson to stay back with the other two squads in the tree line, then he put someone else in charge of the team.

Christ, we're all scared, Stone thought. There isn't a man among us who isn't scared as hell. Going first, Stone and Nahrstadt's team crossed the clearing at a run, then dropped behind a dike near the edge of the tree line. Stone and Nahrstadt were checking things out when three grunts from Charlie Tiger crawled up to them from the left. When Stone explained that they were from Alpha Company, one of them exclaimed, "Oh God, are we glad to see you guys! Man, the gooks are *everywhere!*"

Moving on to the demolished hootch, Sergeant Stone's squad linked up there with the only two GIs still on their feet. They looked scared. The wounded lay behind the shattered walls of the cement building. Stone got his fire teams fanned out to provide security, and Lieutenant Kimball came up with Doc Richards, the platoon medic. They worked fast. Anybody who could lend a hand helped get the wounded onto poncho litters, then they started back the way they had come. They took no enemy fire, but at one point some M79 rounds landed near the hootch courtesy of the Charlie Tiger GIs on the other side of the thick brush to the left. After some hollering back and forth the fire stopped.

Privates Fulcher and Fletcher of Charlie Two were best friends. They were redheaded country boys who could have passed for brothers. Fulcher was from Iowa, and Fletcher from Arkansas. They were both draftees, and both were awarded the BSMv for their actions at Nhi Ha. When the word was passed to pull back with their wounded, Fulcher looked at his buddy and said, "Doug, I'm not leaving Rich out there."

Private First Class Richard M. Gallery was dead, but Fletcher knew just what his buddy was feeling. "Let's go get him," he replied.

Rich Gallery was lying about twenty-five meters from the cover of their three-sided hootch. He had apparently been hit in the opening moments of the ambush. He was lying on his back, propped up by his rucksack. His helmet had been knocked off and his right arm was flung across his chest. Fulcher and Fletcher squatted down to cover themselves with a couple of M16 bursts, then they rushed to Gallery. Fletcher handed his M16 to Fulcher and knelt down to unstrap Gallery's pack so they wouldn't have to carry that, too. Gallery had been shot right below the hollow in his throat.

Just as Fletcher got the dead man's pack off, the NVA opened fire on them. Both of the M16s in Fulcher's hands were set on automatic and, firing them at the same time, he squeezed off both magazines. He then reached down to grab Gallery's right arm and help Fletcher hustle him back—and was shocked to realize how stiff the arm was. It was frozen in position across Gallery's chest. It was Fulcher's first experience with rigor mortis, and he thought with horrified wonderment that if he'd had the strength he could carry Gallery's body like a bucket, using the arm as a handle.

When the crater full of Charlie Two survivors finally made it to safety, it was time for everyone to pull out. The level of NVA fire had decreased, but Staff Sergeant Goad and Sergeant Starr of Charlie Three kept blasting away to cover the men around them who were moving back one at a time. Johnny Miller and George Cruse were sprawled in the open in front of the mound, and Sergeant Coulthard argued with Goad. "We can't go—John and George are still out there!" Coulthard felt like a coward for not trying to get them. Goad said they were dead, and when Coulthard asked if he was sure, Goad glared at him and snapped, "Goddamnit, they *are* dead—and we're pullin' out! Move out!"

In case everyone had not gotten the word, Goad, the de facto platoon leader, bellowed one more time that they were pulling back. The senior NCO who was the platoon leader on paper suddenly appeared, jumping over some bushes with several other grunts. They were lucky they did not get shot in the confusion. No one at the mound had heard any fire all afternoon from the position on the left where it turned out the sergeant had gone to ground. Goad had assumed he was dead. The platoon was unexcited about his resurrection, given that the sergeant was an overweight, disagreeable, passed-over lifer who was always talking about how much tougher Korea had been than this little war. The sergeant seemed to be just going through the motions until he could retire, and the grunts never forgot that during an earlier supply shortage in the bush he had refused to share his rations.

After taking cover in the depression behind the mound, the sergeant barked at Sp4 Thomas J. Bradford, one of the men who'd come back with him, "Where the hell's your rucksack?"

"I left it when we pulled back," said Bradford.

"Well, goddamnit, go back and get it!"

The NVA had ceased firing, but when Bradford got up, they cut loose, hitting him in the chest. Killed instantly, he fell backward almost atop the men in the depression. "It was so sad," recalled Coulthard. "It was so stupid, so stupid Bradford getting killed." Coulthard was dumbstruck and enraged that the sergeant had ordered the kid on such a fool's errand. "What the hell? He didn't give a shit about the ruck or anything else. He just said it to act like he was in charge again, like there was some semblance of something going on."

Private First Class Wayne Crist moved out with Bradford's body, and Goad shouldered Pierre Sullivan's body as they leapfrogged back toward Charlie One. Starr was the last to pull back from the mound after covering Goad with his M60. Starr got out of there at a run. Joining the tail end of the Charlie Tiger column, Lieutenant Jaquez requested max artillery fire on Nhi Ha when they cleared the ville. The FO was worried about an NVA counterattack as they straggled away. Enemy artillery was firing again, but no one was hit as they loaded the wounded and dead into the Otters that had come up behind them.

Alpha Two and Three pulled back on the right flank.

Charlie Tiger conducted a tense, under-fire retrograde through Delta One and Three, which had come up behind them, then the Otters rolled back to the battalion aid station in Mai Xa Chanh East. Medevacs landed there, their blades kicking up sandstorms. In addition to Barracuda's one dead and six wounded, Charlie Tiger had eleven dead and eight wounded. It had been a bad day, made no better by the official claim of only fifteen enemy kills. What really hurt was that the bodies of Guthrie, Cruse, and Miller had been left behind.

Meanwhile, Delta One had secured a laager site approximately six hundred meters east of Nhi Ha in what had once been a hamlet. The site was elevated two to three feet above the surrounding rice paddies, so the fields of fire were excellent. By 1800, Alpha Annihilator and the remnants of Charlie Tiger joined up there to form a joint perimeter with Black Death. Barracuda consolidated in the vicinity of Lam Xuan

West. Artillery continued to pound Nhi Ha, and Lieutenant Smith of Alpha Two commented that everyone dug deep holes because "they figured it was going to be a wild night. The guys were very much on their toes. They knew exactly where the next hole was, and they knew where their lines of fire were because we went over them three times. I strategically placed my M60 and interlocked our fires, and I paced off our positions. If I had to crawl somewhere in the pitch black I wanted to know exactly where it was."

"We couldn't believe what had happened," recalled Sergeant Coulthard. "We were worn out, just flat worn out. Scared to death. I wanted Captain Leach there bad. The feeling among us was that if he had been there, this wouldn't have happened."

Captain Leach, on his way to Australia on R and R, was back at the battalion rear in the main Americal Division base camp at Chu Lai. He was in a transient barracks when a trooper came from the orderly room to wake him. The trooper said that Charlie Tiger had been in heavy contact at a place called Nhi Ha.

"What the fuck are you talking about?" Leach exclaimed as he sprang up.

"Sir, they just got the shit kicked out of them."

Captain Leach found the battalion's acting sergeant major, who was his former first sergeant. "Jesus Christ, what happened?" he asked. When the former Charlie Tiger topkick told Leach about Lieutenant Guthrie, which was a real blow, the two of them went off and had four or five beers together. Then Leach got his gear organized and radioed ahead to inform the battalion commander that he was canceling his R and R and would come out on the first available helicopter in the morning.

PART FIVE MAGNIFICENT BASTARDS

Lieutenant Colonel Weise, CO, BLT 2/4: "At no time during the period 30 April through 2 May was the 320th NVA Division blocked from the north. BLT 2/4 was not reinforced during the battle, but the enemy continued to reinforce his units and to replace his casualties. Thus, the enemy became stronger while BLT 2/4 became weaker from casualties and exhaustion."

Less than ninety minutes after E and H BLT 2/4 had been forced back from Dinh To with heavy casualties on 2 May 1968, F and G BLT 2/4 were advancing from Dai Do for the next assault. The order had come from Colonel Hull, CO, 3d Marines, who was himself responding to instructions from division. BLT 2/4 was to seize Dinh To and then Thuong Do, which sat on the eastern bank of the tributary that drained into the Bo Dieu River. An ARVN mechanized infantry battalion in position near Dong Lai, opposite Dai Do, was to simultaneously advance up the western bank of the creek to seize Thuong Nghia, which was opposite Thuong Do. The tributary was to serve as the boundary between BLT 2/4 and the ARVN. It was a simple, straightforward plan, but an unrealistic one. The number of NVA on the battlefield was simply overwhelming.

Lieutenant Colonel Weise, CO, BLT 2/4: "We were in no condition for another assault, and I had so informed Colonel Hull. When the assault commenced, I moved close to the forward elements to let my exhausted Marines know I would be with them when the bullets started to fly. I tried to encourage them and talk to them. I told them I was very proud of what they were doing."

CHAPTER 14 DISASTER

At 1538 on 2 May 1968, an aerial observer in a lightweight, single-engine Birddog reported movement in the clearing between Dinh To and Thuong Do. The aerial observer spoke with Lieutenant Hilton, the forward air controller on the ground with BLT 2/4. Hilton confirmed that there were no Marine elements that far north (". . . anything running across that clearing is fair game"). As the aerial observer marked targets for air strikes with white phosphorus rockets, his adrenaline was up. "We got lots of 'em in there," the observer shouted excitedly. "There's a beaucoup bunch of people moving out of Dinh To. They're moving across to the north and northeast. There's maybe hundreds of 'em!"

The aerial observer also reported seeing litter teams with casualties. Lieutenant Hilton relayed the information to Weise. The battalion commander was excited, too: "Okay, okay, we got 'em on the run! We got 'em on the run!"

Colonel Weise smells blood, thought Hilton. Weise and his command group were at the forward edge of Dai Do with Golf Company. Weise, in fact, had just been briefing Captain Vargas, the company commander, about their upcoming assault when the aerial observer came up on the net. They too could see figures in the open fields, as well as the Phantoms and Skyhawks dropping napalm and bombs onto them. The aerial observer reported that those NVA not being chopped up in the open were cut off in the northwestern edge of Dinh To. Artillery blocked their escape routes. Some of the NVA coming out of Dinh To were within range of Golf Company in Dai Do. Weise later wrote that the most forward Marines "had the morale boosting experience of squeezing off carefully aimed shots and watching the enemy drop. I bet the reenlistment rate in the 320th NVA Division dropped after Dai Do."

Weise instructed Major Warren, his S3, to remain in Dai Do and take charge of the perimeter manned by the remnants of E and H Companies. Their other decimated company, B/1/3, was to remain in An Lac to secure the medevac and resupply points on the Bo Dieu River. The only elements still capable of mounting the assault were F and G Companies, and Weise planned to use both. Weise planned to accompany Golf Company. There were fifty-four Marines left in Golf, and as Weise saddled up with them he noted that, with the exception of grenadiers and machine gunners, almost all were carrying AK-47s. Weise saw only one M16; it was carried by Captain Vargas. The only other functioning M16 was carried by Weise himself. Nevertheless, Weise later wrote that this undermanned, badly equipped company went into the assault as "a viable, spirited fighting outfit despite its two-day ordeal. Captain Vargas knew his men well, and they knew and respected him for his outstanding competence as a combat leader and his compassion. I knew that I could depend on him and Golf Company."

Weise did not place the same trust in Captain Butler, whose Foxtrot Company, with about eighty men, was the most able-bodied in the battalion. Foxtrot had been rejoined about thirty minutes before the air strikes by its executive officer, weapons platoon, and one of its three rifle platoons. These elements had previously been outposted to My Loc on the Cua Viet River. Finally released from regimental control, they had been brought forward by amtracs to the company position in Dong Huan, at which time Foxtrot moved out for Dai Do. Upon reaching the hamlet, Foxtrot joined Golf for the assault on Dinh To.

The assault was a complete and bloody failure. Weise blamed both higher headquarters and Butler for the debacle. Golf Company, Weise explained, was to have led the attack and Foxtrot was to follow closely behind in reserve. When Golf ran up against the NVA who the aerial observer said were still in Dinh To, the stronger Foxtrot was to move forward, pass through Golf, and press the attack. Weise wrote that he chose to place his command group directly behind Vargas and ahead of Foxtrot "because I wanted to be in position to decide exactly when to commit Foxtrot, and because my presence up front seemed to boost the morale of my exhausted battalion."

In actuality, when the assault made contact with the NVA, Foxtrot was not behind Golf in Dinh To, but in the open fields east of the hamlet. A map that Weise later prepared to explain the situation shows Foxtrot straying out of Dinh To and into the open, and then bogging down there under fire while Golf continued forward unaware that it had no reserve and no rear security. The map shows Golf encountering the NVA far in advance of Foxtrot. But the map is inaccurate. Foxtrot never strayed out of position behind Golf because Foxtrot was never behind Golf to begin with. Golf and Foxtrot went into the assault on line, with Golf in the hamlet and Foxtrot in the open, and they were still side by side when the shooting started. Foxtrot was abreast of Golf and not in reserve, as Weise said it should have been, because that was what Foxtrot understood its mission to be. Lieutenant McAdams of Foxtrot One later wrote that before the attack:

> Captain Butler called the platoon commanders together to issue his order. Butler said that Foxtrot was to move parallel with Golf in a line formation. We were to keep just outside the village and when Golf made contact Foxtrot was to wheel in a counterclockwise motion just beyond Golf's point of contact and envelop the enemy. We did not move in trace of Golf and the orders I received did not hint of that maneuver being part of Foxtrot's role. After we were through Dai Do and somewhere along Dinh To or Thuong Do, and very much out in the open on Golf's right flank, the NVA opened up with very heavy fire. The ground seemed to be dancing with bullets and explosions.

Captain Butler, whose military career did not survive this incident, later contended (without visible bitterness) that he was following Weise's orders when he advanced with Foxtrot through the fields east of Dinh To. Such an explanation suggests that Weise wanted Foxtrot to prevent Golf from being outflanked in Dinh To (as E and H Companies had been in the previous attack), or that Weise had overestimated the damage done to the NVA in the preattack turkey shoot, and had spread his companies out so as to roll up as many of the supposedly disorganized foe as possible. As Hilton said, Weise was smelling blood.

Weise rejected Butler's explanation. The scheme of maneuver suggested by Butler's version of his orders would have left Weise no reserve and thus no flexibility. He said he would never have placed any Marines east of Dinh To because they had already learned the hard way that the area was under enemy observation and subject to preplanned machine-gun, mortar, and artillery fire. Weise explained instead that Butler had completely misunderstood his orders.[1] Furthermore, Weise wrote, "I had lost confidence in Butler's ability to control his company in a firefight because of his previous performance." After Dinh To, Weise said he concluded that no matter how intelligent and motivated Butler was, the amiable young captain ultimately lacked self-confidence and was "overawed by difficult assignments. Close combat is a terrible, shocking experience. No one knows how he will react until it happens, and I fully expected to have to command Butler's company myself when the shit hit the fan in Dinh To."

The attack kicked off at 1550. The hedgerows and surviving vegetation in Dinh To were thicker and more concealing than was thoroughly blown-away, wide-open Dai Do. As Golf Company started across the clearing between the two hamlets, the Marines reconned by fire with automatic weapons and M79s. Foxtrot did the same as it advanced on the burial mounds in the open fields on Golf's right flank. Both companies were moving fast, and Lieutenant Hilton commented that, to psyche themselves up, they went in "yelling and screaming, like, 'Go, go, go! Get 'em! Uh-rah!' I mean it sounded like a football stadium. It was massive. It rumbled. We knew we'd got 'em. We were going to finish 'em off. We were going to roll 'em up. But it was a trap. They set a trap and they let us get into it."

The grass that the Foxtrot Company Marines advanced through was above their knees, and dead NVA lay in it. One of the first to see the live NVA was HM2 Roger D. Pittman, a corpsman, who noticed them as they moved off a little elevated island in the fields about two hundred meters ahead on the right flank. There was a pagoda on the island, which was dense with vegetation and trees. For an instant Pittman thought that the figures were Marines, but he quickly realized that they wore neither helmets nor flak jackets. Their fatigues were khaki-

---

1. Questioned later, Captain Vargas said that he could not recall whether Foxtrot was supposed to be in reserve or on his flank.

colored. The seven or eight NVA were running east along a dike at the base of the island. Pittman stopped in his tracks and shouted, "What is that? Look at that, look at that! Get 'em, *get 'em!*"

The assault was moving fast, and no one paid attention to him. Doc Pittman, suited up in helmet and flak jacket, humped a lot of canteens and medical gear, but his only weapon was an M1 carbine, and he carried only a few straight clips and three or four more banana clips with tracers. The NVA were moving out of the carbine's range, so he backed up into the tree line at the edge of Dai Do and passed the word that a sniper team was needed. In a few moments a sniper came up and Pittman pointed out the NVA, who by then had reached an elevated trail and were running north on it, away from the Marines. They were totally exposed.

As the sniper took aim, they were shocked by a sudden and sustained blaze of NVA fire from the little island and the burial mounds in the grass. Doc Pittman scrambled into a bombed-out house that had no roof, no south wall, and only remnants of the other walls. There was a broken-up table on the floor with him. There was a doorway in the east wall, and a Marine charged through it, desperately looking for cover. "His eyes were as big as eggs," recalled Pittman. The Marine accidentally discharged his M16 as he ran in, and a long burst kicked up dirt across the floor. The last round impacted with a blur right in front of Pittman's face. The Marine threw himself down behind the south foundation of the house. Orders were being shouted to keep the assault going, and Pittman rose up just as five Marines rushed into the field from the tree line directly in front of him. His eyes stayed on those men. "There were five, then there were two—then there were none. They fell like rag dolls. I didn't want to believe what I'd seen. I was near panic. The cracking noise of AK-47s was constant and deafening, and dirt, stucco, and dust filled the air around me. I hugged the floor, holding my breath and waiting to die."

Moving forward with his M79 at the ready, Pfc. Doug "Digger" Light of Foxtrot Two also spotted NVA a moment before the shooting began. There were maybe fifteen of them standing in the tall grass, and in the instant that the assault line got close enough for the Marines and NVA to recognize each other, Light could have sworn that one of them smiled at them. He wondered if the NVA were shell-shocked or on opium. The enemy troops dropped down in the grass, and AK-47 fire seemed to erupt from every direction. The Marines fired back even as they sought cover, and Light got off his first grenade round before jumping behind a burial mound. The enemy were only forty meters away.

The firefight began at 1600, and in the initial shock wave what sounded like a round from a captured M79 landed directly to the right of Lieutenant McAdams of Foxtrot One. His platoon was forward on the left flank, with Foxtrot Two on the right. Foxtrot Three was in reserve. McAdams accidentally dropped his .45 as he ducked behind a burial mound on his left. The enemy soldier had him in his sights. There was another explosion almost on top of where McAdams had gone down, and when he rolled left to another spot of cover, he heard yet another explosion to his right. He moved left again. McAdams didn't realize it yet, but he'd been superficially wounded in his right shoulder, right shin, and left elbow.

Lieutenant McAdams's radioman, Mongoose Tyrell, was also wounded immediately by either RPG fragments or the same captured M79 that got the lieutenant. Tyrell never knew exactly what happened. He never heard the explosion that nailed him. One moment he'd been walking forward, and the next thing he knew he was drifting back from a warm, floating euphoria. He realized then that he was on the ground and that the whole world seemed to be firing at them. He was not in any pain, although he was wounded in his legs, arms, and face. He was simply numb. He couldn't open his right eye, and blood was rushing out as if from bad razor cuts. The corpsman who crawled up to bandage his worst wound, which was in his right calf, told him to get back to the medevac point. Tyrell unshouldered his radio and gave it to a Marine named Bingham with instructions to stick with the lieutenant. Tyrell started back without a weapon: A good-sized chunk of metal had hit the butt of his M16 and caused it to jam.

The acting platoon sergeant, LCpl. Ronald J. Dean—who had thumbed a ride to the front in an Otter the day before despite the jungle rot on his feet that had gotten him a light-duty vacation in the battalion rear— was also dropped in the opening volley. Dean was hit so hard that it felt as though he did a backward flip. It was as though a sledgehammer had been swung between his legs. He had, in fact, caught shell fragments in his testicles and across his stomach. When he caught his breath, Dean turned to the grunt lying beside him and said, "I got a little peter anyway—what's it look like now?" The Marine just shook his head, and Dean's stomach dropped.

Lance Corporal Dean, age twenty-two, was from Newnan, Georgia, where his father worked in a cotton mill. Having served with C/1/3 near Da Nang in 1965–66, he volunteered for a second tour because he was tinkering with the idea of a military career. He was a natural-born rifleman, but he was still only a lance corporal because of numerous reductions in rank. He drank too much in the rear, and was a hothead who loved to fight.

"We got into a big fistfight when he first got there," recalled Tyrell. "Dean was a wild man, but a wonderful guy."

Dean was bleeding badly, but there was no time to bandage his wounds. Adrenaline masked the pain. He got to his feet. The only way to survive was to close with the NVA and kill them. Dean began firing his M14 toward the burial mounds ahead of them and to their left. He grabbed Marines who were lying prone behind cover and shouted, "Let's go! If we sit out in the open, hell, everybody's going to die!"

Lance Corporal Dean was running forward when another explosion knocked him down, peppering his legs with fragments. Dean got back up and kept moving forward. Lieutenant McAdams was also back on his feet, directing the platoon's wheeling maneuver into the tree line running along the left flank. Golf Company was on the other side of the trees. McAdams and Dean reached the cover there with about fifteen other Marines, including a machine gunner and grenadier, and they took up firing positions that faced the open field they had just left. At a range of about a hundred meters, they could see NVA bobbing up from behind burial mounds to fire on Foxtrot Two on the far right flank. They opened up on those NVA, but when they fired a LAW the backblast marked them, and still more enemy soldiers blazed away at them from the left flank.

Golf Two advanced through Dinh To on the right and Golf One on the left. Golf Three was in reserve. By the time Foxtrot became engaged, Lieutenant Morgan of Golf Two had experienced four jams with his M16 as they reconned by fire through the thickly vegetated hamlet. He had discarded his fouled-up M16 and was going forward with .45 pistol in hand when Foxtrot One, on the other side of the trees to his right, began hollering for help with recovering casualties.

The momentum of Golf Company's assault died then and there as Lieutenant Morgan sent his machine-gun team and several riflemen to help Foxtrot. One of the riflemen was Lance Corporal Parkins, who had picked up an M16, a weapon he hated, to replace the M14 for which he had run out of ammo. Parkins was moving when several NVA with AK-47s popped into view in the brush in front of him. They were not looking in Parkins's direction, and he fired at them from the hip. The M16 jammed after the first shot. When Parkins looked down to pull back the bolt, he was knocked off his feet as at least one of the enemy soldiers turned toward him and returned the fire. It felt as though a red-hot poker had been rammed into his left shin. The bone was shattered. Parkins, lying prone, quickly pulled out the .45 he had scrounged up that morning along with two clips, and screamed for a corpsman.

The Marines in the machine-gun team were also wounded, and as the casualties were dragged rearward, things got chaotic. The NVA opened fire from the hedgerows to the front, and when Marines with AK-47s returned the fire, other Marines who couldn't see who was doing the shooting got pretty shook up. It sounded as though the enemy was right there in the bushes with them. Lieutenant Morgan ushered the ten survivors from his platoon into a crater on the left. It was a big crater, probably the result of a five-hundred-pound bomb. They were joined there by Staff Sergeant Wade and Golf One, which had pulled in from the left flank. The NVA fire got heavier, and the Marines expended a great volume of M60 and M79 ammunition in return, without visible effect, while those men who still had M16s kept their heads down and tried to clear jams.

When an enemy soldier stood up about fifteen meters in front of Captain Butler, it was his one and only look at the NVA who had his command group pinned down. The man had an RPG over his shoulder. He had totally disregarded cover, so focused was he on finding a target, but he was hit before he could fire. When the NVA fell backward, Butler's senior corpsman, who like Butler had his eyes a fraction of an inch higher than their paddy dike, managed a grin and said, "You know, Skipper, these guys are getting real personal."

Having found cover behind a burial mound, SSgt. Richard L. Bartlow, the commander of Foxtrot Two—which was pinned down in the high grass on the right flank of the battlefield—put his M79 into action. Bartlow was a cold, stern, and inflexible NCO, respected but disliked by his grunts. Bartlow was joined by Digger Light, who also carried a grenade launcher, and by a pair of tough Mexican-American Marines from California—Ernesto Tanabe and Tom Alvarado. Bartlow kept rising up to fire from the same spot, and while Light was down reloading, fell back with a neat little hole between his eyes. He died instantly. Alvarado was hit next. He was coming up to fire his M16 when a shot slammed into his helmet, dropping him like a stone. He was only unconscious, though. The bullet had gone in the front of his helmet and skidded around the inside of the steel pot to punch out the back without even scratching him. Alvarado picked his M16 back up as soon as he came around, but when he started shooting again a round hit the weapon's hand guard, knocking it from his grip. The M16 was rendered inoperable, so Light, who was steadily pumping out M79 rounds, handed Alvarado his .45-caliber pistol.

At that instant, Tanabe, rising up to fire, went down with a terrible backward snap of his head. It looked as though the whole front of his head had been blown away, but although his forehead was laid open and he was temporarily blinded by the concussion and the blood in his eyes, he was very much alive. Tanabe and Alvarado, in fact, got into an argument. Alvarado's M16 was damaged and he figured Tanabe didn't need his anymore, but Tanabe held tight. "You ain't getting my rifle," he shouted.

"You can't see anything to shoot!" exclaimed Alvarado.

"I'll shoot at the noise!"

An NVA jumped up and tried to get around their right flank. Alvarado shouted a warning to Light, but Light had already seen the soldier and in the same instant had squeezed the trigger on his M79 grenade launcher. The NVA was only twenty meters away, and the 40mm round took his head off. The body continued to run a few more steps before it fell into the tall grass.

Private First Class Light, who was nineteen, was awarded the Navy Achievement Medal for Dai Do. He was from Hurley, Virginia, a small town in the Appalachian Mountains, and he joined the Marines because he'd never seen anything or been anywhere. His people were coal miners, and he had himself worked in the mines during his summer vacations. Light was in Vietnam what he'd been back home: a hardworking, squared-away kid (although the marijuana they smoked in the rear was something new for him), who never reported any of the three superficial wounds he picked up. He was given a job in the company mail room near the end of his tour, but the "maybe-if-I'd-been-there" syndrome pulled him back to the bush. On his first mail run he'd brought all his combat gear along with the mail sacks. When the helicopter dropped him off he approached the company commander with his problem. "Captain, the first sergeant wanted me to be a mail clerk, but I don't want to be no mail clerk," he explained. The skipper asked if he'd go back to the rear if ordered, and Light said, "No, sir." The captain's solution was simple: "Well, Digger, then get back to your platoon."

The bag that Light had slung over his shoulder at Dai Do held about ninety rounds for his M79. He shot more than half of them during the fight, especially while firing cover for their wounded, who crawled toward the hasty position Foxtrot One had secured in Dinh To. The trees there provided good protection from the constant NVA fire. One of the casualties, a big guy named Johnny Corey, who'd been hit in the stomach, crawled to Light's burial mound from the right. Light's squad leader, Corporal Favourite, had gotten separated from them somewhere over on the right, so Light asked Johnny, "Where's Fave?"

"Fave's dead, and Devine's dead, and the new guy, Dick, he's dead, too."

"Are you *sure* Fave's dead?"

"He's dead, man. I *know*."

Corporal Favourite had been a much-beloved squad leader, and Alvarado impulsively got up to rush to him. Light had to grab Alvarado and hold him down as he tried to calm him. "Johnny said it wasn't no use, man. There's no use gettin' yourself killed."

Corporal Ronald L. Favourite, twenty-one, of Bryan, Ohio, had been a great guy in Digger's opinion—despite the fact that he was a Yankee. He was a stocky man with a sunken chest and a funny walk, but he had a big heart and a subtle sense of humor. He didn't let anyone get over on his squad. He was a pack mule on patrol, and if one of his guys was fading under the load, he'd help carry the man's gear without complaint. He would stand extra watches at night. He was a gourmet chef with C rations in an upturned helmet. When they finally recovered Favourite's body it didn't have a mark on it. He had apparently been killed by a concussion grenade.

*   *   *

Lieutenant McAdams of Foxtrot One, who'd already been wounded by shell fragments, was shot while in the cover of the wood line on the eastern edge of Dinh To. He was up on one knee trying to figure out where Golf Company and the NVA were in the vegetation when a bullet hit the ground beside him and ricocheted into his left leg near the groin. It ended up lodged in his buttocks. McAdams fell forward when he was hit. When he tried to stand he found that he could not. After a corpsman bandaged him, McAdams told his platoon sergeant, Lance Corporal Dean, to take command of the squad-sized group they had in the tree line while he went to round up some help from Golf. He had yet to find a weapon to replace the .45 he'd dropped, so McAdams was alone and unarmed as he snaked his way down a ditch in Golf's direction. Some forty meters later he bumped into Sergeant Major Malnar, who was in a trench with his pump-action shotgun, talking with another Marine in the command group. Enemy fire snapped overhead. McAdams was in pain and he excitedly told the sergeant major that he had a lot of wounded men, a lot of jammed weapons, and that they badly needed help on the right flank. Malnar told him that they were doing everything they could and that he should get to the rear. McAdams obliged him, although at his crawling pace it seemed he would never escape the roar of automatic weapons and explosions enveloping the hamlet.[2]

Meanwhile, McAdams's radioman, Corporal Tyrell—who'd been hit in the first volley—crawled out of the killing zone with bullets zinging over his head. When he didn't hear them anymore, he got up to run but stumbled hard and decided to stay down. He was heading toward a pagoda that was among the burial mounds in the field. When he got close to it, he saw an AK-47 trained on him from around one wall of the pagoda. Tyrell never found out what happened next. He was so scared that his brain turned off. He saw the rifle and the next thing

2. Lieutenant McAdams, in-country only eight days, was awarded a BSMv and Purple Heart. Upon recuperation, he was rotated back for a 1969–70 tour as a company commander with the 7th and 26th Marines, which resulted in an end-of-tour BSMv.

he knew he was on the other side of the pagoda lying beside the body of the NVA who had been holding it. He wondered if the man was already dead, or if he had killed him. He was not carrying his M16 because it had been damaged, but he still had fragmentation grenades clipped to his flak jacket. He kept moving even though he was completely lost. When Tyrell saw a Marine he recognized behind a burial mound he thanked God. The Marine was lying there shouting at him to come on over. Tyrell ran to his position, and the man explained that when he'd first seen the short, wiry Tyrell crawling through the tall grass he'd almost shot him.

"I thought you were a fuckin' gook!" the grunt said excitedly.

The man directed Tyrell toward the medevac point. When he got there, a corpsman exclaimed, "Your right shoulder's a mess!" Only then did Tyrell realize that he had not tripped when he'd gotten up to run—he'd been shot. The round had skimmed across the top of his shoulder, opening up a large gash. The doctor who checked the wound back aboard ship said, "Whoa, you were lucky—this sonofabitch must have been a twelve-point-seven!"

Other Foxtrot casualties were being treated on the spot by Doc Pittman, who had crawled along the tree line in which the reserve platoon was pinned down and established a hasty treatment area at the southeastern edge of Dinh To. The fire was so heavy that as Pittman had crawled through the shadows of the thick foliage, bullet-clipped banana leaves fell around him. He moved on through an old, overgrown garden on his belly, and was feeling more than a little lost when he finally saw the USMC-issue jungle boot of a man lying in the bushes. He looked around then and saw Marines he recognized from the company mortar section. They were in firing positions around a large bomb crater, and a very relieved Pittman crawled into it to set up shop. Most of the Marines returning fire from the crater's north lip were struggling with fouled M16s, and one who saw Pittman's hot little carbine called to him only half in jest, "Hey, Doc, how much you want for that?" Keeping his carbine slung and his pistol on his hip, Pittman replied, "No way!"

The mortarmen around the crater directed the wounded into it as they came back singly or in pairs. "They walked, crawled, and stumbled," Doc Pittman remembered. "Some didn't realize they were wounded and had only retreated because they had run out of ammunition, or a limb had stopped functioning, or both. All had that special look about them that said they had just been to hell." Teaming the badly wounded with the lesser wounded, Pittman sent all the casualties rearward as soon as he got a battle dressing on them, stopped the bleeding, and made sure they were well oriented enough to know which way was south. "Safety was relative, but sending them south seemed like the only thing to do," he explained. The fight was just north of their crater. Smoke and dust rose from the bushes there, and the able-bodied Marines at the crater's edge looked increasingly nervous. Many of the wounded were in shock, and none complained of pain, so Pittman administered no morphine. "The war wasn't over for those Marines," he said later. "They could still have had to fight for their lives, and being doped on morphine wouldn't help."

Almost all the M16s in Foxtrot were jammed, and Captain Butler saw that one of his Marines who'd picked up an AK-47 was having trouble with that weapon, too. The operating rod was bent, so it would fire only one round at a time. The Marine had to manually force the mechanism back each time to chamber the next round. Butler passed his still-working M16 to the Marine and took the AK in return. Behind the firing line, the wounded Tyrell, meanwhile, had reached an amtrac in Dai Do, which moved its load of casualties to the splash point on the Bo Dieu River in An Lac. There they boarded skimmers. When they reached the aid station on the beach at Mai Xa Chanh West, one of the casualties with Tyrell, a little machine gunner named Miller, became incensed at the sight of television crews filming the dead and wounded. "The bastards," he shouted. "We kick ass and they don't do nothin'—but when we're gettin' our asses whipped up here, they show up like a bunch of vultures. If they want blood, I'll show 'em blood!"

Miller tore away the battle dressing wrapped around his wrist to expose a hand that seemed to be hanging as though on a hinge. He thrust the red, wrist-shattered mess at the nearest lens and screamed at the cameraman, "You motherfuckers want some blood? Here's some blood!"

Medevacked to the hospital ship *Repose*, Corporal Tyrell, whose wounds were not critical compared to those of Marines being immediately prepared for surgery, was instead escorted to a ward where a female U.S. Navy nurse assigned him a bed and then said cheerfully, "You'd probably like to take a shower, huh?" Yes, yes, he would, he replied. Tyrell walked to the shower room. There was no one else there. He had stripped to his utility trousers, exposing the battle dressing over his right shoulder. Another dressing was wrapped around his right calf where the trouser leg was torn open. He spotted a mirror to his right as he came in "and when I saw my reflection I didn't recognize it as me at first. It was dirt and blood and everything but the person I knew."

CHAPTER 15 GOD, GET US OUT OF HERE

Captain Vargas, concerned that his forward platoons might be outflanked and cut off, instructed Lieutenant Morgan and Staff Sergeant Wade to abandon their crater in the middle of Dinh To. Vargas wanted them to move with the remnants of their platoons to the left flank and set up a perimeter there with their backs to the creek. This was accomplished without casualties. Morgan then radioed Vargas to report that because of thick vegetation the fields of fire around their new position weren't very good, and that he and Wade didn't have enough men to hold if the enemy attacked.

Captain Vargas was about fifty meters to their rear in a natural irrigation trench that his company headquarters shared with Lieutenant Colonel Weise and his command group. Vargas told Morgan and Wade to move back to that pos. When they arrived with their radiomen, Weise said to them, "Let's get our people together. We'll put up a three-sixty and hold what we've got. How many men do you have left?"

Captain Vargas had twenty men in his headquarters, to include the mortar section. Morgan and Wade, however, had only nine men apiece, and Sergeant Colasanti of the reserve platoon was down to eight. In the last two days, Golf Company had lost three-fourths of its Marines but none of its guts. After Morgan gave the colonel his single-digit head count, he added, "but we're all good under fire."

Two days before, Vargas had considered Morgan a typical greenhorn second lieutenant. Now he saw him as one of their stalwarts. The last two days had been a crucible for all of them. Vargas told Morgan and Wade to take the company mortarmen with them to reinforce their beleaguered two-platoon position. He said he would soon follow with the reserve platoon. As the meeting was breaking up, Morgan stood up in the trench just as the sharp report of a sniper's shot rang out; he saw dust smack off the trouser leg of the Marine in front of him. Blood jetted from that spot in the next instant. The wounded man was the colonel's regimental tac operator, and he was so flushed with excitement that it took a moment before he realized he'd been hit. He was quickly bandaged and directed rearward.

Lieutenant Morgan, meanwhile, started back for his platoon with the mortarmen-turned-riflemen in tow. As he approached the perimeter, he saw several Marines making a frantic run across the stream on their left flank. His immediate reaction was to shout at them to come back—but then he saw a dozen NVA coming out of the bushes in a frontal assault on their position.

It was 1645, and the NVA were counterattacking north to south down the length of Dinh To. Marines were screaming at Lieutenant Morgan to run because the NVA were right on top of them. Morgan and his radioman, who'd yet to be spotted by the enemy, quickly dropped into the cover of a ditch. Morgan got on the horn with Captain Vargas, who shouted that they should "pull back, pull back, pull back!" Morgan and Wade did just that. The two platoon commanders had completely lost contact with the Marines on the other side of the stream, but they were able to hastily organize those men still around them and get them back down a trench that paralleled the tributary.[1] That they made it out of there was due in large part to Lieutenant Deichman, their hard-charging exec, and Sergeant Colasanti of Golf Three, who had been moving the reserve platoon toward the blueline. Including the exec's radioman, there were eleven Marines in this line, which

---

1. Lieutenant Morgan was awarded a BSMv for Dai Do/Dinh To, and another during the 25 May 1968 engagement in Nhi Ha. He earned the Purple Heart on 4 June 1968 after the battalion had moved to Khe Sanh and after one of his patrols accidentally walked into a USMC minefield. Morgan was on his hands and knees, probing a path to one of his casualties with a bayonet, when the wounded man, thrashing wildly in his agony, detonated another mine. The explosion removed the thumb and fingers on Morgan's left hand, seriously wounded his right leg, and blew off his left leg at the hip.

was oriented in and along an abandoned enemy trench. Their orders were to provide a base of fire along with those in the command trench until all the forward elements had made it through and were well on the way back to Dai Do, where they would make their stand. The thin line produced a firestorm. "Grenades were being exchanged freely," wrote Deichman, who was wounded in the process. "I remember how fanatical the NVA appeared to be, openly and unhesitatingly charging us with reckless abandon."

Lieutenant Deichman was awarded the Silver Star. Sergeant Colasanti, who also won the Silver Star—and his fifth Purple Heart—during the holding action, wrote that "at one point we were involved in hand-to-hand combat. I got a couple with my K-Bar."

Lieutenant Morgan didn't know it then, but his platoon sergeant, Sgt. Richard F. Abshire, twenty-three, of Abbeville, Louisiana, had bought some of the time that the Marines splashing across the creek needed to escape. Morgan had left Abshire to honcho the men manning the perimeter when he'd moved back for the captain's meeting. Sergeant Abshire died on position and was posthumously awarded the Navy Cross. Abshire, a good, low-key NCO with a shock of dark hair and a ruddy, pockmarked face, had, according to his citation, thrown several grenades at the attacking NVA before ordering the retreat across the tributary. He remained behind and "resolutely provided covering fire, which enabled his men to reach positions of relative safety. After expending his ammunition, he was attempting to rejoin his unit when he was mortally wounded."

Corporal Yealock of Golf One was one of those who escaped across the chest-deep stream. He had been firing his M16 from a crater along with two machine gunners whose M60s were doing the most damage to the NVA, when he was hit in the left leg; one of the gunners was hit in the hand. Someone who seemed to be in charge told them to pull back across the tributary. It seemed the only way out. Yealock's wounded leg hurt so badly that it almost buckled under him as they rushed down the bank, but he made it to the water and started wading across with his M16 in one hand and a bayonet in the other. He could see rounds hitting the water. As they crawled up the opposite bank, the Marine to Yealock's right was hit in the arm. They crashed through a hedgerow and tried to figure out where they were. By that time Yealock had lost his rifle and had only two grenades left. They started down the stream to find the rest of the company.

The NVA seemed to be everywhere. They were—including on the left flank, where individual enemy soldiers and squad-sized groups moved into position to place RPG and AK-47 fire across the narrow creek. An ARVN mechanized battalion was supposed to have moved up on that side of the blueline in conjunction with BLT 2/4's attack through Dinh To. But the ARVN were not there. Coordinating and communicating with ARVN units was difficult at best, and it had been made worse in this instance because BLT 2/4 had neither the time nor the officers available to place a liaison team with the ARVN, as it normally did on joint operations. There had been no face-to-face meeting between the battalion commanders, only a series of quick radio conversations in which the U.S. Army adviser with the ARVN unit had said that his counterpart understood and agreed to the plan of attack.

Weise considered the ARVN vital to the operation's success. "Were it not for assurance from Colonel Hull of the ARVN support, I would not have agreed to another attack," Weise later wrote, although it remains unclear why Dixie Diner 6 would place the fate of his battered battalion in the hands of so untrustworthy an ally. "The assurance that I had was that if we got into something we couldn't handle, the ARVN, with their 90mm tank guns and .50-caliber machine guns, would move ahead of us on our left and blow the hell out of the enemy facing us."

The ARVN, however, were opcon to neither BLT 2/4 nor the 3d Marines, and when the joint maneuver encountered heavy resistance, the ARVN commander, either on his own initiative or on order from his superiors, withdrew his unit in the direction of Dong Ha. The U.S. Army adviser came up on the BLT 2/4 net to apologetically report that his battalion was peeling away from the Marines' flank, and with that the ARVN vanished from the battlefield. The Marines never forgave them.

There were dead Marines in the part of the trench that Lieutenant Acly, the Golf Company FO, reached with his radioman, Lance Corporal Prill, before the NVA counterattack. Acly moved up to the trench on his hands and knees, rushing from cover to cover. It was almost impossible to force himself forward through the hail of fire. He felt too heavy to move. He felt as though he was on a ladder that was too high, but on which he had to keep going up. The trench was sanctuary. There were four or five live Marines in his part of it. A thick, concealing hedgerow ran along its northern edge, and bamboo grew up along both sides.

Captain Vargas, who was down to the right, shouted at Acly to get some arty going, but Prill's radio malfunctioned. They couldn't raise anybody.

Panicked, one of the Marines in the trench bolted rearward—and immediately dropped with the loud, distinctive *smack* of a bullet hitting meat. The Marine had been shot in the upper thigh. Acly leaned out of the trench, grabbed the man's feet, and pulled him back in, then used his K-Bar to cut away the trouser leg so he could apply a battle dressing and get the bleeding stopped.

The NVA fire suddenly became more intense. Lieutenant Acly could see puffs of dust coming off a nearby hootch; the bamboo above their trench bucked back and forth from explosions and automatic weapons fire. Acly was cut up by splintered bamboo. The hedgerow along the forward edge of the trench kept grenades from bouncing in with them, but the explosions were so close that the concussion was like being punched in the stomach. The bamboo to the rear of the trench caught fire, and smoke filled the air around them. Prill, remaining in a crouch, lifted his M16 above the forward edge of the trench to spray anything that might be rushing them, but the hand guard was knocked off the weapon by enemy fire. When Acly shoved his M14 through the hedgerow to open fire, it too was hit almost immediately. He pulled the rifle back and was astonished to see that the barrel had been bent at a forty-five-degree angle behind the flash suppressor. He threw down the M14 and took up one of the abandoned M16s lying in the trench. A Marine was shot in the arm and began whimpering and raving. He tugged on Acly's arm as Acly tried to shoot, and mumbled that they were all going to die. The wound in the man's upper right arm barely bled, but it appeared as though the muscle had been turned inside out. It was bright red and jiggled—like Jell-O, Acly thought. Acly was becoming more and more unnerved by the man's keening. When the wounded Marine started to climb from the trench, Acly stopped him by barking, "Just stay down and keep your mouth shut and you'll be all right!"

After a terrible two to three minutes the enemy fire slackened. It seemed that they had survived. But then Prill suddenly started pounding Lieutenant Acly on the back. "Sir, everybody's takin' off!" he shouted. Acly could barely make out through the smoke the figures of Marines running to the rear. He and Prill grabbed the shell-shocked Marine, hauled him out of the trench, and pushed him ahead of them as they joined the retreat. Acly had lost his helmet, and his secondhand M16 was out of ammunition. They immediately hit some old barbed wire in the flaming, chest-high bamboo at the rear of the trench, and they tore their hands and arms as they forced their way through it at a run. Nobody cared. They didn't feel a thing. "It didn't look like a fighting withdrawal," Acly said. His group had caught up with other Marines as they crashed through a hedgerow. "There wasn't a lot of firing and maneuvering going on. People were just trying to get the hell outta there."

Lance Corporal Ron Dean, the acting commander of Foxtrot One at the right edge of the hamlet, had expended all his M14 ammunition on the NVA behind the burial mounds out in the fields. Now other NVA were charging out of the bushes and trees. Dean already had out his .45. He was at the prone, and the enemy soldier he saw most clearly was rushing right at him with his AK-47 held out in front of him. By the time Dean could aim his .45, the man was five feet away.

Dean shot him in the face.

Twice-wounded Lieutenant McAdams, late of Foxtrot One, had escaped the sudden crescendo of fire behind him by crawling down into the creek bed with another wounded Marine. They could see two Golf Marines trying to get back by swimming from the opposite shore. They were about twenty meters from McAdams when a burst of automatic fire splashed around the two heads. Only one head remained visible. That Marine made it to shore and disappeared into the brush. The NVA had not seen McAdams and his partner. They were in the shallows near the bank, where they could remain prone and keep their heads up as they crawled along the muddy bottom. The water gave them bouyancy, making crawling easier. McAdams was too numb to realize how narrow his escape had been.

Lieutenant Colonel Weise shouldered his M16 and Sergeant Major Malnar swung his twelve-gauge pump into action. Every man in the command trench was firing at the NVA who darted at them or rushed past in frenzied pursuit of Golf One and Two. They dropped several enemy soldiers within a few steps of their position. It was impossible to tell who was hitting whom. Everything was happening so fast as to be a blur of sound and motion. An NVA soldier on the right flank turned an automatic weapon down the length of the trench. The burst missed Vargas, who was firing his M16 to the front, but it killed his senior radioman and the 81mm mortar section spotter, who were on either side of Vargas. The mortar spotter lay in the trench, his mouth shot open.

Lance Corporal Pendelton, who was the captain's backup radioman, was hit by the same burst. While Sergeant Bollinger secured a battle dressing around Pendelton's wounded arm, Vargas used his K-Bar to cut the radio shoulder straps, then pushed Pendelton over the back of the trench and told him to crawl to the rear. Vargas then grabbed one of the radio handsets and began coordinating artillery support. Vargas shouted at everyone to get down in their four-foot trench just before the salvo slammed in some forty meters to their front. The concussion was stunning, and shell fragments ripped down tree limbs above their heads.

There was a definite pause in the enemy fire.

Moments later, several NVA who had gotten to a nearby hedgerow began flinging Chicoms. Some landed at the edge of the trench, and some rolled in. Some were duds and some were not. There were RPG explosions, and then a dozen NVA broke into the open on the left flank and rushed the trench. Captain Vargas stopped them with a full magazine of full automatic M16 fire. Most of the NVA went down dead or wounded; the rest disappeared into a hedgerow. There was another pause, and Weise shouted to Vargas that it was time to get out with their wounded. The dead they would leave. Malnar, who was to Weise's right on Vargas's other side, took up the call. "Start pullin' back the wounded—"

Big John Malnar was interrupted by the sudden, shattering detonation of an RPG against the forward edge of the trench. At that instant, Sergeant Major Malnar and Sergeant Bollinger, the colonel's radioman, were side by side and on their knees behind the earthen berm at the rear of the trench. Bollinger was firing his M14 and Malnar had lowered his shotgun as he turned his head to shout. The blast of the RPG flung them both backward, and Bollinger, suddenly on his back, saw blood burst from Malnar's mouth. A chunk of metal had hit the sergeant major in the chest and blown out the back of his flak jacket, killing him instantly.[2]

Sergeant Bollinger got back to his knees and reached for the M14 rifle that had been blown from his hands. He was in bad shape. His right humerus had been shattered and the artery cut. Feeling no pain, he glanced in numb shock at the bone sticking from the massive wound and at the blood pumping out of his upper arm.

Lieutenant Colonel Weise, who was still in the trench, resumed firing with his M16 after he saw Malnar go down. An instant later, an AK-47 round bounced Weise against the back wall of the trench. He felt the thud in his lower left side. It stung, but it didn't really hurt. The shock dulled the pain, and Weise fell forward across the front edge of the trench and squeezed off a few more shots. He tried to climb out of the trench but couldn't. His legs wouldn't work; there was no feeling in them. He had to grab onto the edge of the trench to keep from falling to the bottom of it. He was bleeding badly.

Lieutenant Colonel Weise's legs had gone out from under him because the bullet that punched through his flak jacket had lodged between his third and fourth vertebrae. Captain Vargas dropped his M16 and reached down to pull Weise out of the trench by his arms; then, with one hand locked around the collar of the colonel's flak jacket and his .45 in his other hand, Vargas started dragging Weise toward the rear. Weise, sitting upright with his legs dragging behind him, kept a grip on his M16. When Vargas would stop to catch his breath, the colonel blasted the bushes, where it sounded as though there were enemy soldiers. Vargas was pulling Weise along again when he suddenly saw an NVA coming over the bank of the creek on the left flank. The NVA saw them, too, but before he could swing his AK-47 up to fire, Vargas snapped off a shot with his pistol. The slug hit the dirt in front of the enemy soldier, then ricocheted up to catch the man in his cartridge belt and knock him back into the water. The NVA, dead, wounded, or just stunned, did not reappear, and Vargas was able to get Weise back

2. Sergeant Major Malnar, veteran of Saipan, Tinian, Okinawa, Inchon, Seoul, and most recently of Bastards' Bridge and the Cua Viet campaign, was posthumously awarded his second Silver Star and fourth Purple Heart for the Battle of Dai Do.

about fifty meters to the cover of a tree stump. Before Vargas headed back toward the command trench, he shouted at the Marines behind the stump to haul the colonel back to Dai Do.[3]

Meanwhile, Sergeant Bollinger, who was on his second combat tour with the Magnificent Bastards, had resumed firing his M14 despite his shattered right arm—only to be hit again as he blasted away on his knees. The first round caught him in the left bicep—missing the bone but cutting the nerve to his hand. As he dropped his rifle and spun around from the impact, another round hit him in the face. The bullet tore across his mouth from one side to the other, split his lips, blew out his front teeth, and tore away his mustache. He hit the deck with no rifle and a mouthful of blood and tattered flesh, and he knew he was in trouble. This time it hurt. It hurt beyond words.

The only Marine that Bollinger could see—the only man still in the trench—was Lance Corporal Kraus, the colonel's bodyguard, who was blasting away with his M16. Bollinger, in a panic because of the pain, screamed at him. "Kraus, I'm fuckin' bleedin' to death! Get this radio off of me!" Kraus smacked Bollinger in the face, which brought him to his senses, and then used his hunting knife to cut the shoulder straps on the sergeant's radio. Working fast, he secured a battle dressing around each of Bollinger's blood-streaming arms—the bandages didn't do much good—then got him up on his feet with an arm around his shoulder. The pair stumbled back to a position of relative safety, then Bollinger sank to the ground and passed out. He woke up when a black Marine tried to heft him onto his back. Bollinger mumbled that the man wasn't doing it right, and the exhausted grunt told him to shut up or he'd leave him. He got Bollinger back a little farther, then said he was going to find a stretcher and some help.

The Marine disappeared. Kraus was already gone. Bollinger was all alone. He passed out again. He opened his eyes as he was being lifted onto a stretcher, and he drifted in and out of consciousness as they hustled him back to where Major Warren, the operations officer,

3. Lieutenant Colonel Weise was awarded the Navy Cross and two of his three Purple Hearts for the Battle of Dai Do. He got the Silver Star for Vinh Quan Thuong, and a Legion of Merit with Combat V for his six months of command service with BLT 2/4.

was organizing a line of resistance in Dai Do. Bollinger didn't know where he was or what was going on. When a lance corporal he knew from the communications platoon went through his pockets to get the crypto sheets used to decode radio messages, he suddenly became alert and kicked out as violently as he could at what he thought was a gook. He got a whoa-hey-I'm-a-Marine response from the man, and then calmed down when a corpsman thumped a morphine syrette into one of his wounded arms. Major Warren appeared for a moment above his stretcher. Bollinger told Warren that the colonel was hit and the sergeant major was dead, but the morphine and shock fuzzied his thoughts. What he was really thinking about was how the major used to lead their morning exercises. When they lifted Bollinger's stretcher and carried him past Warren toward an amtrac that was taking aboard wounded, he shouted, "Hey, Major, no more PT!"

Lieutenant Colonel Weise was a big, strong man, and although the initial shock of the blow to his spine had rendered his legs numb, he was able to shake off the trauma and start walking back. The first Marine he ran into was Lieutenant Hilton, whose FAC team was about a hundred meters to the rear of the vacated command trench. Weise sat down. Hilton, who'd been so busy on the air net that he'd lost track of the details of the ground action, was surprised that the colonel was not in the company of his sergeant major and radiomen. Hilton was even more surprised when he realized that Weise was wounded. Weise was holding his side and there was a lot of blood. Hilton blurted, "Do you need any help?"

"No," Weise said. "Big John's been hit. I think he's dead. We've got to pull back. We've *got* to pull back."

Weise told Hilton, who was a big, bold, crazy young officer, to organize a delaying action to give the remnants of Golf and Foxtrot the breathing room they needed to reach the position that Major Warren had organized in Dai Do with Echo and Hotel Companies. To put Weise back in contact with Warren, Hilton stood behind one of his radiomen and changed the frequency on the radio from the air net to the battalion net. He told the radioman to stick with the colonel and help him back, then took the handset from his other radioman to speak with the aerial observer in the Birddog above them. "I want you to bring in everything you can. Fly as low and fast as you can—make as much noise as you can—but don't drop any bombs because they're in amongst us. I don't know where anybody is."

Packing an M79, Lieutenant Hilton—who was near the end of his tour after six months in helicopters and six months playing grunt—moved forward to organize the delaying action. Weise, who had previously considered Hilton a typically immature, smart-ass aviator, made sure he got the Silver Star. Hilton ran into Pace, the battalion interpreter, in the hedgerow in front of his original position. Pace had become separated from his two ARVN scouts. There were six Marines near Pace, and Hilton knelt beside them to explain the situation: "The colonel said delay. We've got to hold until we can get our people back."

Sergeant Pace was a career Marine from Lookout Mountain, Georgia. When Hilton told him what needed to be done, he answered, "Lieutenant, we're with ya, we gotta hold." Pace turned to the young Marines around them, shouting, "We're going to hold! How many you guys going to stay with the lieutenant?"

Holy shit, thought Hilton when all the Marines answered in the affirmative. I guess I'm here with 'em. They went forward to the next hedgerow and spread out behind it in a determined, nine-man line with about ten meters between each covered position. Those Marines they saw they waved back through their hedgerow. When one group went through and on across the open ground toward the next hedgerow, another group followed hard on its heels. The second group was made up of NVA. There were eight of them, and they were so focused on their chase that when they hustled through the breaks in the shrubbery, they did not see any of the grunts in the pickup squad at the base of the hedgerow.

"Those weren't our guys!" Hilton exclaimed to Pace.

Lieutenant Hilton quickly turned and aimed his M79 at the back of one of the running enemy soldiers. The NVA was literally blown apart by the 40mm shell. As Hilton reloaded, Pace rose up and blasted away with his M16. He was joined by several other Marines, and before the NVA realized what was happening, they were dead.

Lieutenant Hilton covered his men with the M79 as he directed them back to the hedgerow behind them. There were several wounded Marines there, and they stopped and made their next stand. Hilton saw Captain Vargas and several able-bodied grunts helping the wounded, so he slung his M79 across his back and joined them. Hilton tried to heft one of the wounded into a fireman's carry, but he was too tired, too drained. Instead, he grabbed a camouflage poncho liner and, along with three other Marines, rolled the man onto it and started back with him. They were all exhausted. They couldn't keep the poncho off the ground, and every time it bumped against the ground the Marine inside, grievously wounded in the buttocks, would let out a ferocious yell. He looked as though he was dying. A Marine ran up to take Hilton's place at one of the corners of the poncho, and behind that grunt came another with a stretcher.

Lieutenant Hilton rejoined his pickup squad in the hedgerow then, and they covered the casualty evacuation. Hilton was reloading his M79 when three more NVA caught him by surprise, busting out of their brushy cover and charging right at him. They had seen the broken-open, one-shot grenade launcher and had thought to take advantage of the Marine reaching into his demo bag for the next shell. Hilton quickly snapped the weapon closed and swung it up. His shot hit the nearest NVA squarely in the chest at such close range that the round had not traveled the fourteen meters required to arm its warhead. There was no explosion, but the impact of the shell was enough to kill the enemy soldier as it knocked him off his feet. The other two NVA dropped in the dirt in that same instant as Pace and his men opened fire. Hilton, quickly snapping his next round into the grenade launcher, thought he saw another NVA wheel around in midcharge and disappear into some bushes. That was where he fired next.

Lance Corporal O'Neill, the sniper, was behind a four-foot hedge with his partner when a Marine coming out of nowhere jumped over it. The Marine still had his helmet and flak jacket on, but he'd lost his rifle and other gear. All he had was a bayonet and a wild look in his eyes. The bayonet was bloody, as was the man's hand. "They're everywhere," he screamed. "God, get us out of here! They're everywhere, they're everywhere! Get outta here!"

The Marine took off in a frantic run, and O'Neill said to his partner, "What's he talkin' about? That's desertion if we run, isn't it?" O'Neill started to rise to look over the hedgerow so he could see what was going on, and there was Lieutenant Colonel Weise, bulling his way through the brush, pushing and limping. He fell when he got through, but there were other Marines with him, and they quickly got him moving again.

"Do you know who that was?" O'Neill gasped.

"No," said his partner.

"That was the battalion commander!"

"Damn, he looks hurt!"

"Well, I'm a firm believer in doing like they always say—follow your leaders. Let's get the hell outta here!"

The sniper team fell in with the colonel's group. O'Neill, hanging to the rear to provide some security, could see other Marines running back through the brush. He suddenly realized that there was an NVA about twenty feet to his right. The man was going in the same direction in the same cautious trot. They saw each other at about the same time. O'Neill veered to the left as the NVA veered to the right and disappeared. Neither combatant had fired a shot.

"It's amazing what the human body does when it's trapped," reflected Captain Vargas. "I actually believed I was not going to get killed. I was shooting as fast as I could because I knew it was my ass or theirs." After having dragged the colonel back, Vargas ran forward several more times with other Marines in the rear guard to personally haul back at least five more wounded men. He had picked up an AK-47 and secured several hand grenades from Marines in the rear, and he used them each time he rushed forward. "I had to go back. I couldn't leave them, not after what they had gone through." He was wounded when an RPG knocked him down and opened up his knee while he was hustling rearward with a one-armed Marine on his back. Later, Vargas was running forward again when he and an enemy soldier collided in the brush. "It was that crowded. There was so much confusion in there between the Marines and the NVA." The man fell down, then tried to swing his AK-47 around as he got up. Vargas had already drawn the knife that he kept strapped to the front of his flak jacket. "I got on him right away and just stuck the knife right in his throat. Other Marines had other NVA down on the ground, and they were fighting, too. Marines who were out of ammo were swinging their rifles or entrenching tools. It's amazing that any of us got out of there."[4]

---

4. Captain Vargas was awarded the Medal of Honor and three of his five Purple Hearts for the Battle of Dai Do. His Silver Star was from Vinh Quan Thuong.

Nearby, Private Kachmar and his buddy James Moffett, having lost track of the rest of Foxtrot Three during the retreat, had gotten mixed in with Golf Company. They ended up all the way down by the creek on the left flank. There were other survivors from Golf, most of whom had lost their weapons and gear, trying to climb up from the creek bed, and Kachmar reached down to help a sergeant. Kachmar had no more grabbed hold of the man's hand than the NVA opened fire again. Kachmar saw a bullet punch through the sergeant's chest as he struggled to get out of the water. The round thudded into the ground between Kachmar's feet on the bank. He quickly pulled up the sergeant and dragged him to cover. The man had a sucking chest wound, but Kachmar and Moffett sealed the hole with plastic and then started carrying him back toward the casualty collection point.

They were quickly pinned down. They could see NVA, whose uniforms were dark green from having just crossed the chest-deep stream, as they fired and rushed forward. Kachmar and Moffett fired like madmen, dropping some of the enemy soldiers. Kachmar, who'd taken cover behind a tree, fired until he was out of ammunition. He had never run out of ammo before. He was terrified. Spotting three NVA setting up a drum-fed RPD light machine gun in a dugout, Kachmar dropped his M16 and heaved a grenade at the position. The grenade exploded at the lip of the dugout, and without thinking Kachmar charged in right after the blast. The three NVA were all wounded and stunned. "One tried to get at his SKS rifle, which was maybe two feet from his hands, and I plunged my K-Bar into his chest," recalled Kachmar. He pulled out the knife and turned like a robot toward the next enemy soldier. "I stabbed him, too, but I twisted my knife. I couldn't get it out." The third NVA was sprawled against the back wall of the entrenchment, moaning in pain. "All these years later I want to say he was trying to get me, but I don't think he was. He was just moaning and I just choked him to death. I didn't even think about what I was doing. I just did it. It was like watching a movie. There wasn't any rage. I don't think I felt any conscious emotion whatsoever. I only thought consciously about what I did two or three days later, and I didn't feel like I actually did it. It all happened so fast."

Kachmar and Moffett ran back to their group, where Kachmar got ammo for his M16 from some of the walking wounded as they kept moving rearward. The sergeant with the sucking chest wound was a big man, and it took four Marines to carry him. Every time he started gasping for air they would put him down and Kachmar and another Marine took turns giving him mouth-to-mouth resuscitation. It seemed to help. The sergeant wanted water, but they adhered to their training and refused to give him any. Finally, the man started mumbling that he knew he was going to die. He did not sound scared, nor was he screaming in pain—the fire was simply going out in his eyes. "I really wanted that guy to live," said Kachmar. "I intensely wanted to see that man live." He screamed at the sergeant not to give up. He gave him mouth-to-mouth again. He kept talking to him. They got the sergeant all the way back to Dai Do, but when they set him on the ground where the corpsmen were working, he died. Kachmar, exhausted and overwrought, angrily pushed the sergeant's body with his foot and shouted, "You fuckin' gave up—I don't believe you fuckin' gave up!"

Cut off on the wrong side of the creek, Corporal Yealock's group from Golf One was buzzed by one of the Phantoms that had arrived to provide close air support. Luckily, the grunts, convinced they were about to be strafed, were able to wave off the low-flying jet. Moments later, a Navy Monitor appeared in the stream—the group had worked almost all the way back to the Bo Dieu River—and when the gunboat swung its machine guns toward the unidentified figures on the bank the Marines again began waving frantically. The Monitor pulled up close enough to let a ramp down on the bank for them to come aboard.

Lance Corporal Dean of Foxtrot One, wounded twice already, had just shot the charging NVA when an RPG explosion peppered his forehead with little fragments. Dazed, he realized that the Marine lying beside him was dead; the explosion had blown away half his shoulder. Dean couldn't find his pistol, so he was unarmed as he started crawling toward the rear, screaming at the handful of grunts who were still there to follow him.

Dean staggered into a nearby hootch, and saw a squad leader struggling to hold down a convulsing grunt named Walter Cleveland. Better known as Coffee, Cleveland was a big, happy-go-lucky black Marine who was popular even with the Johnny Rebs such as Dean and Digger. Coffee loved to wrestle and horse around with them. Dean helped the squad leader pin Coffee to the hootch floor, amazed that he was reacting so violently to what looked like a little ding in the arm.

"Goddamnit, we're all hurt," Dean yelled. "Just lie down!"

In moments, Coffee went limp under them. He was dead. Dean couldn't believe it until he rolled the body over and saw the massive exit wound in the big man's chest, near his heart.

Foxtrot Company Marines were moving back helter-skelter all over the place. Digger Light, along with Alvarado and Bob Young of Foxtrot Two, having worked their way into the tree line between the hamlet and their fire-swept field, got their wounded organized for the run to Dai Do. They had eleven casualties with them, all of whom were shook up but still listening and functioning, to include Tanabe, who was temporarily blind. They had all the wounded men hold hands or grab onto web belts—the stronger supported the weaker. With the most able-bodied casualties in the lead, their bleeding, stumbling daisy chain made its desperate run. It was a moment of wild confusion. They did not know the terrain. They ran through smoke, then made like a centipede over a dike, then ran on into more smoke and popping embers. They passed the bodies of Marines and NVA alike. Light and Alvarado brought up the rear, firing at anything that looked as though it might be following them. Huey gunships roared in directly over their heads, their machine guns blazing.

CHAPTER 16 WE TOOK A LOT OF 'EM WITH US

By the time Lieutenant Hilton got separated from his pickup squad, he had already expended all his M79 ammo—maybe a hundred rounds—and had handed the weapon to a Marine moving rearward. He had also dropped all his excess gear. He was traveling fast and light. All he had besides his .38 revolver, an aviator's weapon, was a LAW he had picked up. Hilton ended up along the creek on the left side of Dinh To, where he saw an exhausted, soaking-wet Marine crawling over the bank. He joined the man, and they spotted three NVA cautiously coming out of the trees a hundred feet ahead of them. The wet Marine showed Hilton how to prepare his LAW for firing, but when Hilton put it over his shoulder to shoot it, he said, "I better aim it up a little bit to loft it."

Bad move. Hilton watched aghast as the 66mm HE projectile shrieked over the heads of the three NVA he'd been aiming at. The enemy soldiers, who'd been looking around, dropped and then backed up into the tree line. Other NVA, however, were still running past in the brush.

Hey, we're surrounded! thought Lieutenant Hilton as he and the young Marine slid into the creek bed and crawled along in about three feet of water until they reached Dai Do. Hilton saw Sergeant Pace in the mob of Marines. Pace had just made it back with a wounded Marine he'd found staggering dazed and naked near an old barbed-wire fence. All the grunt had on were his jungle boots. When Pace grabbed the Marine's arm to help him back, he weakly jerked away and moaned not to touch him because it hurt too much. Pace then noticed that the man had been hit in several places. The Marine mumbled, "I'll make it, I'll make it," as Pace walked beside him. When they finally reached

Dai Do, the Marine sank to his knees and said, "I told you I'd make it." Then he died.

Lieutenant Hilton and Pace stared at each other and then hugged. "You got guts, Pace," Hilton said. "No," Pace answered. "You're the one with them." Given the casualties and the confusion, they wondered if they were the senior Marines on the spot, and Pace said half-jokingly, "Looks like you're in charge."

"Bullshit. I'm an air officer. *You're* in charge."

"Shit, I'm an interrogator. I don't know anything about this shit."

There were no coherent units left. "It was like a fire team here and a couple of stragglers there," recalled Lieutenant Acly of G Company, "and just about everybody had been hit or cut up or something was wrong with them. Everybody felt beat up." While running around along the forward edge of Dai Do getting Marines into defensive positions and organizing litter teams, Lieutenant Taylor of H Company saw Lieutenant Colonel Weise being helped back by Vargas on his shaky, semiparalyzed legs. Taylor, greatly concerned, asked him how he was doing. Weise, in much pain, answered through clenched teeth, "We took a lot of 'em with us."

Weise was led to Major Warren, and passed command to him with a simple, "It's all yours." A young corpsman helped remove Weise's torn-up flak jacket, slapped a battle dressing over the gunshot wound in his lower left side, and hooked up an IV of serum albumin to his left arm. Holding up the bottle, Weise was led to a stretcher on the floor of an amtrac alongside several of his young, badly wounded Marines. When the ramp went down in An Lac he was hustled to one of the skimmers. Moving down the river, Weise, who was on his back, could see Navy craft gliding by in both directions. The logistical lifeline had been reopened. They had accomplished their mission. A feeling of peace washed over him. He had given everything he had and done everything he possibly could. There wasn't anything else he could do. When he allowed himself to relax, Weise passed out on the floor of the skimmer. The shock and blood loss had finally caught up with him.

At 1740 on 2 May, Major Knapp, XO of BLT 2/4, heard the first report that Dixie Diner 6 was a casualty and that F and G Companies were withdrawing to the perimeter held by E and H Companies in Dai

Do. Knapp relayed the news to Fire Raider 6 and to the SLF commander aboard the *Iwo Jima,* adding that he was leaving Mai Xa Chanh West to get a handle on the situation. Within one minute, Knapp caught a skimmer at the boat landing near the medevac beach and proceeded at top speed for An Lac to take command of the battalion if necessary. Knapp had no information on how badly Weise had been wounded.

Meanwhile, Major Warren, the de facto, on-the-spot battalion commander, was running around bareheaded in Dai Do getting different people to do different things. Warren did not shout directions in the typical hey-Marine-get-your-ass-over-here fashion, but rather with an encouraging, "Hey, buddy, help us out with this," or "We need you over here, buddy." He never lost his cool. Warren had artillery and naval gunfire pounding into Dinh To in coordination with their suddenly available close air support. Huey gunships added to the racket, as did the Navy Monitor positioned where the westernmost tributary emptied into the Bo Dieu. Lieutenant Hilton was back on the air net and in contact with the Huey pilots, who indicated that they could see the bright air panels that Hilton had instructed the Marines at the front to put out once he'd determined that they had a front. When the Hueys began their strafing runs, a lieutenant on the ground net reported to Hilton that his men were taking friendly fire. Hilton immediately keyed the handset linking him to the pilots. "Hey, our guys say you're shooting at them!" he shouted. "You gotta go farther north! Do you see the air panels?"

The pilots answered in the affirmative. After the next strafing run, however, the lieutenant on the ground net screamed, "If they shoot at us one more time we're going to shoot 'em down!"

Lieutenant Hilton ran forward to ensure that confused Marines had not accidentally positioned the air panels to their south. They had not. It was the pilots who were confused, and Hilton was still up front when the next strafing run commenced. Hilton bellowed into his handset, "You're aiming right at me! My guys are going to shoot you down if you do that one more time!"

"Well, goddamnit—" the pilot began, but Hilton cut him off: "Do not shoot if you're not sure, because our guys *will* shoot you down!"

When corrected, the Huey's fire added to the devastating, overwhelming volume of ordnance that was churning Dinh To and preventing the NVA from continuing their assault into Dai Do. Meanwhile, the battalion moved into a small pocket in the eastern corner of Dai Do, still taking some fire as the Marines established vulnerable, barely concealed positions amid the skeletonized trees. "Tactically, it was a terrible place to be," Warren later commented. "If the NVA had had the numbers to keep coming, there was no way we could have stood our ground. We should have gone back to An Lac so as to have that open field in front of us. We didn't because to try to have people move and establish some other defensive perimeter would have been just a nightmare operation given that there was so little control and so few people left."

It was dusk when Major Knapp's skimmer landed in An Lac. Knapp contacted Warren and asked for a situation report before setting out across the paddies on foot to join Warren up in Dai Do and take command of BLT 2/4. As the perimeter was battened down in Dai Do, Knapp called his company commanders back to the hole that served as his CP. Using a piece of cardboard from a C-ration box, which he would take home as a souvenir, Knapp wrote the status of the personnel and equipment in each unit. The numbers did not reflect the total trauma of the battle because they included a lot of walking wounded.

Golf Company, still under the command of the thrice-wounded Captain Vargas, was incredibly weak, with only three lieutenants—Acly, Morgan, and Deichman—two Staff NCOs, three corpsmen, and twenty-nine enlisted men present for duty. The company had three radios and three machine guns, but no grenade launchers, no rocket launchers, and no tubes left in the mortar section.

Echo Company, commanded by its only remaining officer, Lieutenant Cecil, was not doing much better, with only two Staff NCOs, three corpsmen, and thirty-nine enlisted men. There were no machine guns and no rocket launchers, but they still had a grenade launcher, two mortar tubes, and six radios.

Hotel Company, led by lip-shot Lieutenant Taylor, had one other lieutenant left, Boyle, plus six corpsmen and fifty-six enlisted men. The Marines in the company had managed to hang on to six radios, two machine guns, three grenade launchers, and two mortar tubes.

Captain Butler's F Company was in the best overall shape, with two lieutenants, Basel and Wainwright, plus one Staff NCO, six corpsmen, and forty-two enlisted men. They had three machine guns and seven grenade launchers, plus two mortars and ten radios. Behind them in An Lac, Captain Murphy had one officer and thirty-two enlisted men with four tubes from the 81mm mortar platoon (which was presently firing into Dinh To), plus Lieutenant Muter and his eighteen-man recon platoon. In addition, three officers and sixty-eight enlisted men had just arrived at the splash point from Mai Xa Chanh West. Knapp had directed the headquarters commandant to round up all nonessential personnel at the BLT CP to reinforce the rifle companies, but, since it was already dark, Knapp elected to have them remain in An Lac. Also in An Lac was B/1/3, which had three officers and eighty-six enlisted men on hand. Knapp later told the division historical team, "We tightened in our defense, redistributed our people, and checked all radio nets to see that we had active FO teams, air teams, and so forth. We continued preparations by posting listening posts and firing close night defensive fires—we put them in very close. Requested illumination throughout the night from a flareship, and our request was approved and provided for."

During the madhouse retreat, Pfc. Otis E. Boss, who served as the radioman for the 81mm FO attached to Foxtrot, was left behind. Boss and his FO, a lance corporal, were at the tail end of the retreat when a squad of NVA suddenly appeared behind them. Boss shouted at the FO to make a run for it while he covered him. When Boss swung around to fire his M16, he was amazed to see the NVA turn tail for the protection of a tree line. By that time, though, the FO and everyone else was out of sight. Boss crawled to a pagoda among the burial mounds and lay exhausted in its cover while he searched the airwaves for an active frequency.

Lieutenant Hilton heard a terrified, whispering voice break in on the air net, repeating, "They're all around me, they're all around me."

"Where are you exactly?" asked Hilton.

"I don't know. They're all around . . ."

Hilton put Boss in contact with the aerial observer in the Birddog, and Boss said that he would identify his position by waving his helmet. The aerial observer saw the helmet immediately. So did the NVA. Huey gunships strafed the NVA soldiers firing at the pagoda, and Boss took advantage of the distraction by crawling away. He hadn't gone thirty meters toward what he thought was Dai Do—it had gotten totally dark—when the NVA saw or heard him again. They tossed Chicoms at him, but the Hueys rolled in again with machine guns blazing.

Boss made it to new cover. The decision was made to extract him by helicopter. The word was passed for everyone, including the mortar crews, to fire on signal into the western side of Dinh To so as to suppress NVA movement and allow Boss to crawl east to a clearing that would accommodate a Sea Horse. When the Marines opened fire, Boss immediately reported over the radio that they were shooting at him. The fire was shifted on his order. The aerial observer in the Birddog, meanwhile, had asked Boss to mark his position in the dark. The young radioman struck a match and held it inside his upturned helmet. The aerial observer spotted the brief flame and directed Boss toward the clearing. Boss got there on his hands and knees, but when the Sea Horse started to land the NVA opened fire from several directions and the helo had to break its hover and clear the area.

The suppressive fires cranked up again, and the Hueys strafed with rockets and machine guns. When they finished, the Sea Horse went back in while Boss, who was at the end of his tether emotionally and physically, guided the pilot by radio. "Come left, come left . . . no, no, come right, come *right* . . . ah, straight ahead, straight ahead . . . okay, stop, *stop* . . . back up, *back up* . . . come left—"

"How far am I from you?" the pilot interrupted.

"You're fifty feet."

"I'm settin' down—you run to me. Run to me!"

Private Boss clambered aboard the Sea Horse—the whole battalion cheered when the pilot reported that the rescue was a success—and returned to duty the next day. He was awarded the Silver Star for his actions during the three-hour ordeal.

At least one other Foxtrot grunt, LCpl. David R. Bingham, a skinny, scared-to-death young Marine, was left behind in Dinh To. Bingham, who was really nice but a little slow, was both the company screwup and the company pet. When the battle was over, his body was found in the rubble of a demolished, tile-roofed house three hundred meters farther north in Dinh To than the battalion had advanced. He was lying on his back with one hand on his stomach, and with NVA-type bandages around the wounds that had prevented him from keeping up with his comrades during the retreat. He had another NVA bandage tied around his head covering his eyes. The NVA who had taken him prisoner, and who had treated his injuries before deciding that he was too much of a burden to take with them, had blindfolded the eighteen-year-old Marine before shooting him in the head.

It was a long night in Dai Do. At 2045, there were exchanges of grenades and automatic-weapons fire between a platoon-sized group of NVA and Foxtrot Company, which covered the northeastern side of the perimeter. The NVA were probing, not attacking, and the Marines lobbed M79 rounds wherever they saw a shadow in the flarelight. The Marines could hear the NVA shouting to each other. The NVA also shrieked such things as, "You die tonight, Marine!"

One enemy soldier tried to get into the perimeter, although sniper O'Neill didn't believe it at first when the Marine beside him said he heard movement. The enemy had been lobbing in an occasional round with a captured M79, and O'Neill answered, "Nah, you probably hear the bloop gun firing."

"No, no, I hear *movement*—I really hear something!"

"Well, hey, you go wanderin' out there and somebody's going to shoot you."

"I hear something!"

Lance Corporal Cornwell of Echo Company, who was asleep in his nearby position, heard the same movement and snapped awake with a start. It took a moment before he realized that there was an NVA about ten meters ahead of them. The NVA was walking slowly and deliberately toward them, scanning the area ahead of him before each step. When Cornwell woke the two Marines with him, the NVA disappeared in the brush. They kept their eyes open; then the Marine on Cornwell's left suddenly tapped him on the arm. The NVA was crouched about six feet away. Cornwell fired his .45 at the same time his buddy did, then crawled toward the enemy soldier and found him lying perfectly still on his back, his brand-new AK-47 beside him. The man, a gurgling noise coming from his throat, was beyond using his weapon. Cornwell finished him with a bullet in the head.

At 2130, the NVA fired a recoilless rifle from a pagoda on the far side of the creek. The shells exploded near the rear of the Marine perimeter, where an amtrac had been parked to serve as an aid station. One shell landed in or near Hotel Company's mortar position. Eight Marines were seriously wounded. "You could hear 'em scream through the night," commented a sergeant when interviewed by the division historical section. Another said, "Our men on the Otter got up with a .50-caliber— they just totaled out the pagoda where the recoilless rifle was." A Navy patrol boat also poured .50-caliber tracers into the little cement structure, and Major Knapp shifted artillery fire onto the area. Knapp said that although "we had previously requested and received permission through Fire Raider, 3d Marines, to have blanket clearance to fire on the other side of the stream, because it was 2d ARVN Regiment territory, it took twenty minutes to get the fire mission cleared on this particular problem."

The wounded were treated in the amtrac, and a helicopter medevac was requested rather than running the risk of moving the wounded downriver in the dark. Major Warren guided the Sea Horse into the cemetery on the southeastern edge of Dai Do while standing on a grave mound with a flashlight. The pilot, flying blind, set down his helicopter right on the light. As Warren backed up, he tripped and fell in the dark. He had to roll to one side to avoid the Sea Horse's front tire as it settled down where he had been. There was no enemy fire.[1]

The next medevac was for Sergeant Pace, the battalion interpreter. He was lying on his back against a dike between two other Marines when he heard the crack of an RPG being fired. Hell, he thought, secure behind his cover, let 'em shoot—I'm going to sleep. He never heard the explosion, but he suddenly realized that something was wrong with his legs. They were numb; they wouldn't work. Pace reached down to squeeze them awake and came up with a handful of blood. Damn, they got me! he thought. The RPG had riddled his legs with seventy-two metal fragments. Pace tied off a battle dressing around one thigh as he hollered for a corpsman. Lieutenant Hilton recognized his voice and came to get him. Hilton helped Pace to the landing zone and assisted him aboard the Sea Horse, shouting over the roar of the blades, "I'll see you again someday, Sergeant!" It was a promise he kept.

Lieutenant Hilton spent most of the night in radio contact with the flareship that orbited above them, although he could not see the air-

---

1. Major Warren got the LMv for the Battle of Dai Do, as well as a BSMv for Lam Xuan East/Vinh Quan Thuong and a second BSMv as an end-of-tour award.

craft because of the slight overcast. The pilots could not see through the clouds either, so Hilton adjusted their flight path as they blindly jettisoned their parachute-borne flares. Hilton lay on his back with his radio and extra batteries and, without knowing it, slid into a quick, numb sleep. He jerked awake and grabbed the handset he had dropped. "Are you guys still there?" he asked.

"Yeah, you must've dozed off—we thought we'd lost you."

"No, no, I'm okay. I just fell asleep."

"Okay, hang in there. Get some coffee or something."

Hilton brought in several more flares—it was well after midnight—and the next thing he knew someone was shaking him. "Wake up, wake up—they're trying to get ahold of you!" Major Knapp had a radioman relieve Hilton. He managed to catch a few hours of sleep before waking up to help with the last hour of flares, which, like the nonstop artillery on Dinh To, carried them to daybreak.

Meanwhile, Colonel Hull decided to land the 1st Battalion, 3d Marines, in An Lac the next afternoon to continue the assault through Dinh To and Thuong Do. With an Army battalion in position along Jones Creek, Fire Raider 6 finally felt secure enough to commit his only remaining maneuver battalion. Fire Raider 3, Major Murphy, relayed this information to the BLT 2/4 CP in Mai Xa Chanh West via the secure net at approximately 2230, but it was not until 0100 that the combat situation had quieted down enough to allow this very welcome message to be radioed to Knapp and Warren in Dai Do. Assuming that the battalion net was being monitored by the enemy, the watch officer, Captain Mastrion (who had just flown back from the *Iwo Jima* despite his injured back), came up with a message that would frustrate NVA efforts to decipher it. Bearing in mind that 1/3's call sign was Candy Tuft, and that the fresh battalion would pass through BLT 2/4 in order to continue the northward attack, the message that Mastrion crafted read: "Sweetheart Boy will step on your back on his way to Santa Claus's home."

At first light on 3 May, the seventy-one H&S Company fillers who'd been shuttled to An Lac the evening before hiked up to Dai Do. They were distributed by grade to each of the skeletonized rifle companies. Other reinforcements had joined the support activities at An Lac and Mai Xa Chanh West, and these men were a mixed bag. A request had been sent to the *Iwo Jima* the evening before for "every able-bodied man on ARG shipping," and within forty-five minutes Sea Horses had brought to the BLT CP a platoon's worth of volunteers, which included two majors and three captains from the SLF staff. There were also a number of walking wounded from the ship's hospital. It was suspected that even a few gung-ho sailors had donned Marine gear, picked up weapons from the casualty receiving area, and gone ashore with or without permission. Lieutenant Hilton saw men in helmets and flak jackets who were wearing blue Navy work jeans. Corporal Schlesiona, aboard a skimmer, was convinced that some of the personnel at the splash point were sailors because "on at least two occasions when we landed with resupply materials, I ran across people who just didn't look right. Perhaps they were too clean or too raw looking, or just too generally uncomfortable in their attitude. They seemed not to know what to do, where to go, or even what questions to ask."

There was no enemy action in the morning. At 0815, Colonel Hull choppered into Dai Do. Major Knapp's report to Hull was reflected in his later conversation with the division historical section, in which he said that, "except for numbers, we had an efficient, effective fighting force." He added that "it was extremely gratifying" to observe how well organized the companies remained despite the loss of key personnel. "The number threes and fours stepped right up, took over, and did an excellent job with what they had. There was no loss of control. Command and control remained in effect. Communications were sustained throughout." Knapp's primary recommendation, at least for the historical branch, was "don't send bits and pieces. Send a whole battalion to do a battalion's job."

The Marines in BLT 2/4 were disgruntled with how Fire Raider 6 had piecemealed them into Dai Do. "If we could have had the entire battalion from the beginning," said Knapp, "it would have been an entirely different story." But they were angrier still with the ARVN, who had disappeared in the Marines' hour of need, and whose earlier negligence set the stage for the entire debacle. Prior to the engagement, the Dai Do complex had been in the TAOR of the two battalions from the 2d Regiment, 1st ARVN Division, withdrawn to defend Dong Ha. "It is inconceivable to me that the 320th NVA Division troops could have been so well dug in with mutually supporting bunkers, communications lines, and infrastructure without having done so over a period of days and probably weeks," wrote Major Warren. He was convinced that the ARVN had turned a blind eye to the buildup rather than tangle with an NVA force that would have eaten them alive. "It would have been nigh impossible for the ARVN not to have gotten wind of this activity, as these areas were occupied by ARVN family members and other camp followers."

At 1100, correspondents were finally allowed to visit the battlefield. The Marine casualties in Dai Do itself had already been evacuated, but dead NVA lay everywhere in the rubble, leaving the impression that the NVA had been butchered in a one-sided display of overwhelming firepower. One young correspondent, aghast at the human carnage, turned on Lieutenant Hilton, whom he'd been interviewing. "You guys are unmerciful! Why are you so cruel?" Hilton said he "grabbed the reporter by the seat of his trousers and the nape of his neck and escorted him headfirst into a bomb crater. I was going to beat the shit out of him, but somebody said, 'Get Hilton and get him outta here,' and three or four enlisted guys grabbed me and pulled me away."

At 1200, a light but hot meal was delivered to the field. Air strikes were being run the entire time on the north end of Dinh To and on Thuong Do. At 1445, two companies from the 1st Battalion, 3d Marines, began landing in An Lac aboard amtracs. They passed through Dai Do to continue the assault. The scene shocked them. The place looked like Tarawa in its own torn-down, churned-up way, and the stench of death was overwhelming in the hot, windless air of the wrecked hamlet. There were pith helmets and canteens, bloody battle dressings, and smashed weapons. There were dead NVA who had been killed when napalm sucked the oxygen from their lungs and who had not a mark on them, and there were dead NVA who'd been shot in the forehead, the backs of their heads blown away.

There were also dismembered bodies teeming with maggots strewn about the area. Lance Corporal Ross E. Osborn of A/1/3 paused to look at two NVA who still clutched their weapons in death, and whose "eyes were wide and staring at the sun, their faces contorted in horrid death grimaces. Their intestines protruded from their khaki shirts like purple balloons. You felt sorry for the bastards. You were glad they were dead, but they were soldiers, too. I remember everyone being very quiet."

After the battle it was estimated that BLT 2/4 had engaged more than 2,000 enemy troops, and that the battalion had "accounted for

537 known enemy dead as a result of ground action alone." The battalion had also taken four prisoners. An additional 268 NVA kills were credited to supporting arms ("For once," a correspondent wrote, "these estimates were probably not too far from reality."), which included twenty-seven air strikes during the three-day battle in addition to 1,147 81mm mortar, 2,383 naval gunfire, and 5,272 artillery rounds. This tabulation did not include counterbattery fire against NVA artillery in the DMZ, which had been massive in its expenditure of shells.

As 1/3 moved through Dai Do, BLT 2/4 was policing its immediate surroundings by dragging dead NVA to a central location and shoveling dirt atop them. Hospitalman Carmen J. Maiocco, a corpsman in D/1/3, wrote in his journal that the covering was "very shallow and you could see the shapes of the bodies just beneath the freshly turned dirt. I'll guess and say there were maybe 50 or 60 bodies. An image that stands vividly in my mind is of a human arm sticking up straight from the dirt. A few of our men walked by and shook the dead hand and even had their photograph taken in this grisly pose."

Battalion Landing Team 2/4 was awarded the Navy Unit Commendation (NUC). The opcon B/1/3 was included in a separate NUC given to the entire regiment for its successful defense of the supply routes on the Bo Dieu and Cua Viet rivers. However, 81 Marines had been killed during the three-day battle, and another 297 Marines in the five companies involved had been seriously wounded and medevacked. An additional 100 Marines had been wounded but treated in the field. Half the casualties occurred on the final day of the battle, and 41 dead Marines were left behind in Dinh To. While 1/3 passed through Dai Do and launched its assault on Dinh To, Major Knapp walked back to An Lac with Echo and Foxtrot Companies, where they loaded aboard Mike boats for the trip downriver to Mai Xa Chanh West. Knapp's orders to Major Warren, who remained in Dai Do, were to follow behind 1/3 with Golf and Hotel and recover the dead.

By 1730, the sweep through Dinh To was in full swing. The bags of rags that had been NVA soldiers were everywhere, too, and 1/3's Marines were stunned to see dead grunts lying with them amidst the battlefield debris. Marines did not leave bodies. Marines did not leave weapons and ammo and ammo boxes, nor packs, canteens, helmets, entrenching tools, or flak jackets. But they had. The impossible had happened here. "Dig this," said one numb Marine to another. "The NVA did some wounded grunts from Two-Four a job, man. Shot 'em skeleton dead in the back of the head."

"Wow," said his stunned companion.

"You want to go see 'em? They're over there by the river."

"No way, man."

"We found their empty rifles, man. It's for real. Five or six dudes lyin' facedown in a ditch. . . ."

Much of the ground was burned and black. When 1/3 reached the trench that had served as BLT 2/4's hasty command post, they found twenty dead Marines in it. Hospitalman Maiocco wrote in his journal that they were "piled in on top of each other, covered with flies, arms and legs all twisted. We couldn't speak. When we did speak it was in whispers."[2]

A haystack situated on the right flank of the trench was determined to have actually been a camouflaged gun position that afforded its occupants a straight line of fire down the trench. Thousands of spent cartridges were found inside the hollow haystack. The scene in the trench was all the more appalling to the recovery parties from BLT 2/4 coming up from the rear, because those who had been slaughtered were not only fellow Marines but friends. Lieutenant Acly of Golf Company looked down at Sergeant Snodgrass, whose intense blue eyes were still brilliant in his dead face, and he thought of how the noncom had shared his last cigaret with him the day before. Big John Malnar was also in the trench, along with the spotter from the mortar section, whose face was waxy and who had black ants crawling into his shot-open mouth. The senior company radioman's PRC-25 was still strapped on and functioning. Voices from the battalion net came out of the speaker on the dead man's back.

Lieutenant Morgan, also of Golf Company, stood beside the trench. Some of the dead Marines in it had been in his platoon. He had come

2. The 52d Regiment, 320th NVA Division, had retired from Dinh To and Thuong Do during the night to make for the DMZ. On 5 May, while in pursuit, 1/3 was ambushed by the NVA rear guard in Som Soi, one kilometer north of Thuong Do. Pinned down, 1/3 lost 15 KIA and 64 WIA (they claimed 151 NVA kills) before the enemy broke contact at dusk.

to Dai Do with thirty-eight men. Including his radiomen, he had only three left. He could not fathom the victory in that.

The dead Marines were pulled from the trench with difficulty. Several were stuck to the ground by dried blood. Rigor mortis had set in, so it was tough to straighten out the bodies so that they could be zipped into body bags. They were then carried to amtracs and skimmers, which had come up the creek to take them back. Discarded and inoperative weapons were thrown onto a pile aboard one skimmer, along with armfuls of web gear and other bloody equipment. The Marines left more than they recovered. It was dusk by the time the forty dead Marines in the area had been bagged like yesterday's garbage. While 1/3 began setting up for the night, to include positions in that bloody irrigation trench, the Marines of BLT 2/4 climbed aboard amtracs, skimmers, and Otters for the ride back to Mai Xa Chanh West. They were satisfied that they had recovered all their comrades. Actually, the last man would not be discovered until the next day when 1/3 pushed beyond the irrigation trench and found the body of David Bingham, the radioman who had been captured and executed.

It was 2100 when the last element off the Dai Do battlefield—the recon platoon at An Lac—secured inside the BLT CP. An amtrac near the medevac beach was pointed toward the DMZ so that when its back ramp was lowered the interior lights would not be visible to the enemy artillery spotters to the north. The battalion's KIAs were gathered outside the vehicle. Marines with flashlights unzipped the body bags and lined up the dead men by company.

"Sadness," recalled Doc Pittman, one of the fatigued corpsmen on the scene. "There was nothing but humble sadness. There was quiet. There was not a lot of talk."

The medical team in the amtrac worked on one body at a time. They started with G Company. Each body bag was unzipped on the vehicle's floor. Pittman was stationed to one side of the body, and another corpsman was on the other side. They filled out casualty tags, one to attach to the body bag and the other to the body itself. Up front were two majors from division, and another corpsman who had a log in which he recorded the name, rank, service number, unit, and cause of death of each KIA. A fourth corpsman was present to determine the cause of death. "Sometimes it was very apparent," said Pittman. "Sometimes we had to search and turn the bodies over. It was professionally done with no talking unless absolutely necessary."

Doc Pittman had seen worse—the enemy had not mutilated these dead, nor had the elements had time to. But he had never seen so many, and by the time they got through Golf and then Hotel Company he had reached his limit. Foxtrot, with which he had served, was next. "I could not do it. I could not stay there." When they stopped for a short break, Pittman, who was twenty-two years old, stepped out into the darkness. He found another corpsman to relieve him inside the vehicle. "I couldn't take any more. It was going to be real bad when it came to Fox Company. I didn't want the memories."

Pittman was exhausted, physically and emotionally, and he lay down on a stretcher near the amtrac. He realized just before he fell asleep that he was enraged. That bastard, he thought. That gung-ho, hard-charging bastard. He's after his bird at any cost.

Although Pittman at first blamed Weise, he later realized that the battalion commander, a remote figure, had been a convenient scapegoat for his anger and frustration. But even when he cooled down, Pittman would never understand the logic of frontal assaults or why, having paid the price, they then moved on as soon as the bodies had been counted. "It was absolutely—*absolutely*—ridiculous, and I always felt that somebody ought to have been hung. I lost so many friends. I was starting to grasp the picture of Vietnam by then, and I realized at that time that it was going to come down to just surviving. There was no purpose in that war, and there was no purpose in dying for those villages."

The bullet in Lieutenant Colonel Weise's back was removed aboard the *Iwo Jima*. The damage to his spine was not permanent, but he was still in a wheelchair when most of his officers came to the ship one or two at a time to say good-bye to the finest battalion commander any of them had ever served under. Weise also had a last farewell to make, and he asked Lieutenant Muter to push his wheelchair down to the ship's morgue. The morgue had been vacated for the colonel's visit. The body of Big John Malnar was lying on a cold steel table, around which was a curtain. Muter wheeled Weise into the partitioned area and left him there until called.

*   *   *

On 4 May 1968, the Marines at the BLT CP could see black smoke rising from the air strikes the Army battalion was calling in on Nhi Ha. The battle was three klicks away. It did not concern them. Because of the heavy casualties, the BLT 2/4 TAOR had been reduced to the two square kilometers around Mai Xa Chanh West to give the battalion the breathing room needed to reorganize. For the survivors, there was steak and potatoes and grape juice. Beer soon followed. "Division sent us 10 cans per man for our show at Dai Do," wrote Captain Murphy to a battalion veteran who had rotated out before the battle. "Judd Hilton B.S.'ed and we ended up with about 15 cases. The bunker is completely full of beer—there are 'priorities' you know."

Shedding helmets, flak jackets, and worn, torn utilities, Marines went swimming in the Cua Viet River along the southern edge of the perimeter. A lieutenant cracked a grin for a reporter and said, "Looks like a damn nudist colony."

"Despite losses, the battalion still had a strong nucleus of officers and senior sergeants," the reporter wrote. "And it still had confidence." The reporter had been a Marine in Korea. The spirit in the battered command had not been stamped out, and it made him proud. "According to both officers and men, the battalion's heavy losses at least did not result from tactical errors or plain carelessness." Trophies brought back from Dai Do were on display near the river. They included a Chinese-made mortar, a recoilless rifle, an antiaircraft gun, and a pair of 12.7mm machine guns, each on its own tripod. There were also two Chinese field telephones, plus piles of mortar rounds and other types of ammo, and some seventy AK-47s, SKSs, RPDs, and RPG launchers. A lot more enemy weapons had been captured, but the troops still had them.

One of the heroes of the battle was the tall, slender ex-VC who was Golf Company's Kit Carson scout. Corporal Schlesiona wrote afterward of "the admiration this man had gained for himself. Everyone I spoke to was quite aware that he could easily have deserted. It would not have been difficult for him to get into an NVA uniform and slip away." Schlesiona was in the river that morning when there was "an uproar about fifteen feet away. The Kit Carson was being attacked by a number of Marines misdirecting their desire for revenge. Before I could get to his aid, any number of other Marines had already pulled those guys off and were giving them quite an earful about how stupid they were. I have always believed that those Marines could not have known what a brave man they were attacking."

There was an uproar in Hotel Company, too, but only because Lieutenant Prescott—whom everyone thought had been shot in the spine the day before—suddenly appeared with nothing worse than a bruised back. Prescott was grinning from ear to ear as he walked into the company area. His men went nuts, and amid the laughter and welcome-back shouts, Prescott and Taylor joked about who was in command of the company. Major Knapp gathered everyone at the Buddhist temple that served as the CP to read them a note from Weise praising the men. There was also a minute of silent prayer for the dead. Then, wrote the reporter who had also worn the uniform, "the Marines looked up and one by one, in matter-of-fact tones, discussed the mechanics of getting ready for combat again—replacements, supply, equipment . . ."

PART SIX NHI HA

Sergeant Jimmie Lee Coulthard, C/3-21st Infantry, 196th LIB, American Division: "There sure wasn't any glory in being in Charlie Company other than it was a regular line company which would do what the hell they were told. We didn't do as good a job as we could have if we'd had better training and more experience, but they were a good bunch of guys and I was real proud to be in the company."

Opcon to the 3d Marines, the mission of Lieutenant Colonel Snyder's 3-21st Infantry was to seize and hold Nhi Ha and Lam Xuan West in order to check NVA infiltration down Jones Creek and prevent NVA action against logistical traffic on the Cua Viet River. Lam Xuan West had been easy to secure. Nhi Ha had not. Forced back with heavy casualties on 2 May 1968, the attack resumed the next day, although Lieutenant Colonel Snyder anticipated that the NVA had retired during the night. They had not. Elements of the 4th Battalion, 270th Independent NVA Regiment, had entrenched themselves in Nhi Ha and intended to fight it out. Lieutenant Colonel Snyder obliged them, though with a prudent, cautious approach that would have seemed heresy to the Marines and with a smothering abundance of firepower that had not been available in the first overtaxed days of the enemy offensive.

Private First Class Gregory B. Harp, C/3-21st Infantry, 196th LIB, American Division: "All my observations of the battle were through the peepsight of a rifle, and that is an extremely narrow view. I never saw a map. I was confused the whole time, and half-crazed from thirst and fatigue. My world consisted of a fire team, squad, platoon, and, once in a while, the whole company."

CHAPTER 17 BLACK DEATH AND CHARLIE TIGER

The NVA attempted to reinforce their positions in Nhi Ha. At 0028 on Friday, 3 May 1968, the personnel at Alpha 1 spotted the NVA through their night observation devices. Having marched south from the DMZ, the NVA were, when detected, in the vicinity of Nhi Trung—less than a kilometer south of Alpha 1 and two klicks above Nhi Ha. The firepower brought to bear on these NVA was locked, cocked, and ready to go in part because of an argument that 1st Lt. Travis P. Kirkland, an adviser with the ARVN battalion at Alpha 1, had had the night before with a major from the 40th Field Artillery at the DHCB. Kirkland had been calling in fire missions on smaller groups of NVA when the major, short of ammo from the afternoon battles, challenged the priority of these particular missions: "Lieutenant, you're lying—you don't have that many targets."

"Well, bounce your butt up here if you think I'm a liar, and I'll show you all the dinks you can handle," replied Kirkland.

The major arrived the following afternoon by helicopter, and Kirkland suggested he sack out because he probably wouldn't get any sleep that night. The NVA heading for Nhi Ha proved Kirkland right. A Marine with the naval gunfire liaison team at Alpha 1 was the first to alert Kirkland, who was in his own bunker. "Hey, LT, we've got people out here in the open." Kirkland asked how many there were. The answer was sixty-seven, but the doubting major grabbed the field phone and asked the Marine how he knew. "I counted the motherfuckers," the young Marine shot back.

At that point the major zipped up to the bunker line and looked through a night scope of his own. Suitably impressed, he told the FO lieutenant who was present from his own 40th Field Artillery to "get these people everything that's in range."

Additional artillery was fired into Nhi Ha itself. Lieutenant Colonel Snyder, located at Mai Xa Chanh East, planned to resume the attack with Captain Osborn's A/3-21 and Captain Humphries's D/3-21, which were in a night defensive position in the rice paddies six hundred meters east of Nhi Ha with Lieutenant Kohl's C/3-21. South of Nhi Ha on the other side of Jones Creek, Captain Corrigan's B/3-21 was dug in near Lam Xuan West, where it could support the attack by fire. The attack was to come in from the east and sweep west down the length of Nhi Ha, with Alpha Company on the north flank and Delta Company to the south. This was the same approach taken the day before by Charlie Company.

Lieutenant Colonel Snyder had available to him a forward air controller in an O-1E Birddog from the Air Force's 20th Tactical Air Support Squadron (call sign Helix). At 0815 on 3 May, Helix 1-5 came on station and established contact with Black Death 6—Captain Humphries of D/3-21—who was the most experienced company commander the Gimlets had on the ground. Humphries briefed the FAC, who had Marine and Air Force fighter-bombers plaster Nhi Ha at 0910, 0945, and 1040. There was a mishap during the second air strike, however. The FAC warned the company commanders to make sure that all their people were down each time he brought in a strike. Captain Corrigan and the Bravo Company FO, who were the closest to Nhi Ha in Lam Xuan West, could get only so far down as they helped adjust the strikes. The two were kneeling behind several banana trees at the edge of the hill that served as the company command post while watching an Air Force Phantom drop 250-pound high-drag bombs. "It was amazing," Corrigan recalled. "The bombs went off, and then right where the cloud of smoke was there was something small that got bigger and bigger and bigger—and then, wham, my forward observer got hit right beside me. It looked like it was coming in slow motion at us, but the whole thing couldn't have taken more than half a second. My brain couldn't have told my body to duck in time."

The white-hot chunk of metal was the size of a golf ball. It hit Pfc. Rod "Rocky" Bublitz, the Barracuda FO, in the shoulder with such force as to almost rip off his arm. While Captain Corrigan requested an emergency medevac for Bublitz and another injured GI, the FAC came up on the battalion net and shouted, "I *told* you guys to stay down!"

Lieutenant Colonel Snyder also had available to him a command-and-control UH-1D Huey from the 174th Assault Helicopter Company (the Dolphins) of the 14th Combat Aviation Battalion, 1st Aviation Brigade. Since Snyder commanded by radio from Mai Xa Chanh East, his C&C Huey was used for resupply and medevac missions. The wounded were quickly lifted out of Lam Xuan West, but within two hours the C&C bird had to conduct another medevac when Barracuda was again on the receiving end of friendly fire. This time three men were hit by the artillery prepping Nhi Ha as the assault companies began moving in. One soldier's kneecap was shattered. He sat upright on the floor of the Huey and smoked a cigaret that one of the crewmen had given him. He stared at his mangled leg in numb, painless shock—the morphine was hitting him—and although he appeared to realize that his leg would have to be amputated, he had a relieved, I'm-on-the-helicopter-I'm-outta-here expression. He didn't say a word during the entire flight back to the DHCB. When they landed, a Navy corpsman who didn't realize the severity of the man's wounds grabbed him to put him on a stretcher. "Hold on, goddamnit—take it easy," the GI shouted. "I want to keep my goddamn leg as long as I can!"

The assault got rolling at 1100. Captain Osborn had Lieutenant Smith's Alpha Two on the right flank, and Alpha One, under 2d Lt. James Simpson, abreast on the left flank alongside D/3-21. Lieutenant Kimball and Alpha Three followed in reserve. The assault line was closing on the first hedgerow at the eastern edge of Nhi Ha when Sgt. Bernard J. Bulte, a squad leader in Alpha Two, saw three NVA pop up to his front and dash toward that wall of brush. Two of them were carrying AK-47s, and the third had an SKS. The hedgerow slowed them down, and they bunched up as they pushed through it, almost scrambling over each other's backs. Bulte put his entire M16 magazine into them. All three enemy soldiers went down as other troopers to his left and right began blasting away into the brush. They moved cautiously to the hedgerow then, and Bulte saw that he'd hit one of the NVA in the head. The man had pitched forward and the top of his head lay inside his pith helmet like a chunk of melon.

The squad deployed along the hedgerow and the bodies were checked.

One of the dead soldiers carried medical gear, and one had what appeared to be the insignia of an NVA lieutenant pinned to his gray fatigue shirt. One of the new men was unsettled by the scene, so to toughen him up, a team leader told him to search the body with the head blown open. As the replacement removed the pistol belt and then turned out the dead soldier's pockets as instructed, he kept his face half-turned from the body.

"They got scared and they panicked," Sergeant Bulte later said, explaining why the three NVA had been such easy targets in his rifle sights. Bulte had been in Vietnam for more than five months, but this was the first time he'd had a clear target. As he realized that he had just killed the three, he was numb for a moment, then he had a sense of absolute power. It felt good—but it lasted only a few moments. Bulte did not hate the enemy. He could not. He had seen them suffer too much. He had seen Kit Carson scouts, who seemed to be the most brutal soldiers on either side, use their boots on the faces of prisoners who had already talked, as well as place an M16 muzzle in the mouth of a man whose arms were tied. Once, while their Kit Carson worked over another prisoner, Bulte had searched the NVA's wallet and found a photograph of the soldier back home with his children. "You know, that guy was just like the rest of us," Bulte said. "We were all there because we had to be. It's one thing to fight a faceless enemy, but to see them as individuals—to see their faces and the fear in their eyes— that's a different thing. Killing them was part of the game, and you really had to detach yourself to remain effective and do your job."

The assault continued. Captain Humphries moved forward with Delta Two, under 2d Lt. Erich J. Weidner, on the right flank, and Lieutenant Skrzysowski's Delta One on the left. Delta Three, whose lieutenant had been killed four days before, was being led by its platoon sergeant, SSgt. Robert E. Gruber, and brought up the rear of the company's two-up-one-back formation. The assault platoons, operating slowly and cautiously in the blown-away, wide-open hamlet, used hand grenades on the entrenchments they passed over—all were empty—as they worked their way through Nhi Ha hedgerow by hedgerow. The NVA—in the tree line that divided the village—waited until the assault line was within fifty meters before their mortar crews began pumping out rounds. On hearing that signal, the foot soldiers in the spiderholes commenced firing with automatic weapons, light machine guns, and rocket-propelled grenades.

The first casualty was Pfc. Paul L. Barker, an ammo bearer with the machine-gun squad in Delta Three, who fell in the blast of a mortar explosion before he had time to take cover.

Barker, hit badly in the chest, had been in-country just three weeks. He was a twenty-year-old draftee, and he hated the Army. A funny, well-built farm boy, he had run with some small-town toughs before dropping out of high school in South Paris, Maine. He became a father at sixteen, and finally married the mother of his daughter three years later between Basic and AIT. Barker had been befriended by an M79 man in another squad during his short time in Vietnam, and his buddy crawled to him to give him mouth-to-mouth, while shouting at the top of his lungs for a medic. The platoon medic got to them, but Barker was already dead. His buddy, crying freely and nearly hysterical, refused to listen and kept trying to breathe life into Barker as fire snapped overhead.

The contact began at 1222. The NVA were entrenched across the narrow waist of Nhi Ha, in the tree line along the western edge of the rice paddies in the middle of the hamlet. Lieutenants Skrzysowski and Weidner deployed their platoons in the irrigation ditch that ran behind the hedgerow on the eastern side, and—earning Silver Stars in the process—they moved along the ditch firing themselves as they made sure their men kept their heads up and fired in the right direction. The NVA were impossible to see. Whenever smoke or dust rose from one of their positions, though, the target was engaged by M60s and M79s, as well as with LAWs.

Artillery worked the enemy side of the clearing and, between fire missions, the FAC in the Birddog rolled in to punch off WP marking rockets. The FAC brought the jets in one at a time. The Phantoms and Crusaders came in low and slow with wings tilting left, right, left, right, as each pilot lined up on the target in turn. The jets came in from behind the grunts, and the pilots released their 250-pound high drags just as they flashed over the row of upturned faces in the irrigation ditch. Fins popped from each bomb to retard the rate of descent as it dove toward the target, giving the pilot time to escape the blast radius. It was an incredible show. The bombs seemed to float as they went over the heads of the grunts in the same instant that the pilot hit the afterburners and pulled straight up. The multiple explosions were thunderous, with smoke mushrooming up thick and charcoal black above the flames. Smoking hot bomb fragments thudded down on both sides of the battlefield.

The napalm canisters burst like fireballs in the tree line. The NVA kept firing. Captain Humphries, a small-statured Texan who packed a CAR15 and a 9mm Browning in a shoulder holster, had his trademark corncob pipe clenched sideways in his mouth as he lay behind a berm with his FO and RTOs and helped adjust the air and arty. He was a former enlisted man—an OCS graduate—and he was Airborne and Ranger qualified. He was also a natural leader and a veteran of more than six months with the Gimlets. Black Death 6, as he was best known, used his reserve platoon, Delta Three, to establish an LZ in the eastern end of Nhi Ha—into which the C&C Huey landed to kick out ammo resupply and take aboard the four men wounded in the opening moments of the engagement. Humphries's company suffered few additional casualties during the prolonged fight. He was an aggressive commander, but he never took reckless chances with the lives of his troops. He loved them too much. Humphries, exacting and hard-nosed, was also a personable, gregarious man who ruled with an informal hand. He knew his troops by name and would talk with each man as a patrol moved out. He joked easily with them, but he made it clear that each was an important part of the team. He told them that they were his family and that he was going to write a book about them when he got home.

Delta Company was knocked for a serious loop when Black Death 6 was hit the following month after a tough, two-day action to secure an NVA hill in the FSB Center TAOR. Humphries was not wounded by enemy fire but by a "dud" U.S. hand grenade that sat unnoticed in the battle litter until a new man accidentally stepped on it. The explosion killed the GI. Humphries's shoulder was torn up, and he lost his right eye. With a black eye patch in place, he soldiered through the rest of his career—including a 1970–71 Vietnam tour as operations officer of his old 3-21st Infantry.

Captain Humphries got his second Silver Star for Nhi Ha. His effect on morale was such that the recon sergeant with his FO team, Sp4 Terrance Farrand, who did not have to be in the battle, made sure he got there. Farrand, fresh from a Bangkok R and R, had rejoined the artillery liaison officer at the Mai Xa Chanh East CP only after the battle had been joined. When he asked about getting back to his company, the liaison officer said, "Listen, the situation's hot. The only thing we've got going in is ammunition and radio batteries. We can try and get you in tomorrow."

Farrand wouldn't take no for an answer. The idea of giving Captain Humphries less than 100 percent was unfathomable, and he pressed the liaison officer. "Well, I've got to get there, that's all there is to it."

Specialist Farrand went in with the next ammo drop. The C&C Huey landed in Delta Three's LZ, and, after helping unload the ammo under fire, Farrand ran, crawled, and ducked his way forward. He slid in beside a prone and very busy Captain Humphries, who said, "What in the hell are you doing here?" Farrand replied, "I heard you people got yourself in a mess, and I thought I'd better show up." As he began working with the FO lieutenant, Farrand cracked one last grin and said, "Hey, Cap, can you believe that two short days ago I was lying up in a bed with sheets? And I had lobster!"

On Black Death's right flank, Lieutenant Smith of Alpha Two radioed his platoon sergeant, Sfc. Alan Dickerson, who was in another crater. Smith had told Doc Fennewald to stick with Dickerson, and he asked to speak with the medic. "He's dead," Dickerson said.

"*What?* He can't be!" exclaimed Smith.

"He's dead."

"I never did see his body," recalled Lieutenant Smith, who thought the world of Doc Fennewald. "I probably wouldn't have looked at it anyway." Fennewald had been shot in the forehead while moving in a fast crouch toward a soldier shouting for a medic. "It was a senseless death," added Smith. "Whoever was wounded wasn't badly hurt, but Fennewald probably perceived that he was."

Specialist Four Daniel F. Fennewald, twenty-four, of Spanish Lake, Missouri, was awarded a posthumous BSMv and Purple Heart (as were all KIAs in the Gimlets, regardless of the circumstances of their death). Fennewald was the kind of genuine, sincere guy whom anyone would want to have as a friend for life. He was stocky and sandy-haired, with an articulate, quiet, and gentle manner. He never cursed. He never complained. He also never carried a weapon. He was a conscientious objector, and although he would hump a ton of medical gear and water for the casualties, reserving only one canteen for himself, he would not join in the killing.

Lieutenant Smith commented that Fennewald was "a wonderful doc and a prince of a fella. He knew about every sore on every man in that platoon. He was that conscientious and helpful."

The volume of fire rose and fell as the battle dragged on. During one of the lulls, Sp4 Neil E. Hannan of Alpha Two crawled out of his squad's big bomb crater and worked his way back to the LZ to get more ammo. Hannan, a wiry, brown-haired kid, was an intelligent, intense, and typically insecure nineteen year old from blue-collar Versailles, Ohio. He was determined to be a good soldier, and he was. He had been in Vietnam for two months. Hannan was dragging a crate of grenades in one hand and a crate of small-arms ammunition in the other on his way back to the crater when a mortar fragment caught him in the right thigh. It went through his trouser leg and left a red slash up near his groin. Hannan clambered back into the crater. The rope-handled ammo crates were cracked open. Everyone was firing like crazy. Hannan himself went through thirty magazines, and had to repeatedly use his squeeze bottle of gun oil on his smoking M16. The squad grenadier lobbed so many M79 rounds across the clearing while sitting cross-legged at the edge of the crater that he finally said in a bored voice, "Hell, give me that .45 for a while." They fired everything they had, including LAWs, and they heaved grenades when they saw NVA advancing among the trees on their right flank. "You know, it's not easy to stick your head up and fire at those bastards when they have machine guns firing back at you," Hannan wrote in a letter home the next day. "Hell, I was throwing grenades like a maniac too. I was in a bomb crater digging with my damned hands and I was scared as hell. I was just hoping that a mortar wouldn't land in my hole. And to think that I used to pity the Marines."

In position near the LZ, Sergeant See, who ran the machine-gun squad in Delta Three, was to the rear of an earthen berm. He had unshouldered his ruck—which had fragments in it from the shell that killed his ammo bearer, Barker—and he was on his knees, alert, with his M16 in his hands. He expected the NVA to try to flank them. There was a lull in the fire up front, and See was able to hear a mortar round leaving its tube. He started shouting, "Incoming!" but he was still on his knees when the first round exploded before his eyes on the other side of the berm and knocked him down. It felt as though someone had hit him in the right shoulder with a baseball bat. He was afraid to look at his arm for fear that it had been ripped off. It felt that way. When he finally did look, he saw a chunk of metal the size of a silver dollar sticking from the shoulder. He pulled it out and flipped it away.

The grenadier attached to See's machine-gun team, Pfc. Ronald L. Edwards, had been hit in the same explosion. He'd been leaning against his ruck on the forward side of the berm. Sprawled out now, he emitted the low moan of the seriously wounded as he called for help: "Uh-uhhh-uh-uh . . . Seeee . . . Seeee . . ."

Mortars were still exploding around the LZ, and no one was moving.

Edwards kept calling for help. Oh God, I can't leave him out there, thought See, a rich kid from Beverly Hills, California, who'd gotten his draft notice immediately after earning a degree in business administration. He had instant sergeant stripes from the NCO Academy at Fort Benning. See crawled over the berm to reach Edwards, who had thick blood coming out of one ear, in addition to multiple fragment wounds in his head and legs. Man, this guy's in bad shape, See thought, but what he said was, "Edwards, you're okay, you're okay. What hurts worst?"

"My legs . . . my legs," Edwards mumbled.

See wrapped battle dressings around the wounds. The mortaring had ceased. See helped Edwards to his feet with one arm over his shoulder so he could get him back over the berm, where a medic took over. The medic also tied a battle dressing around See's shoulder. As See put the bloody, ripped shirt back on, the medic asked him if he wanted to be medevacked. See declined. It was no time to leave.

The action in Nhi Ha lasted six hours. A and D/3-21 lost two KIA and had twenty-two WIA. Officially, sixty-seven NVA were killed, but Lieutenant Colonel Snyder, unable to crack the enemy line with firepower, finally ordered his assault elements to disengage and retire to their night laager east of the hamlet. All of their seriously wounded had already been medevacked on the spot by the C&C Huey on loan from the 174th AHC Dolphins. The aircraft commander was WO1 Kenneth W. Johnson, a tough former Airborne sergeant. Johnson and his copilot, WO1 Martin H. Wifholm, were plugged into the fire control nets so they could get the trajectories of the arty, tac air, and naval guns firing counterbattery missions against the NVA artillery in the DMZ, and thus work up the safest flight path into the LZ in eastern Nhi Ha. It was real hairy stuff. Since the tac air got most of the enemy's attention, they went in repeatedly right under the high-drag bombs that the Phantoms had just released.

During one low, fast approach, the door gunner spotted NVA in a bunker about seventy-five meters out on the flank. He could see one NVA's face through the aperture, and he exclaimed, "Jesus Christ, there they are! I'm going to take 'em under fire!"

"Don't shoot!" Johnson shouted back on the intercom. "For some reason they ain't shootin' at us, so we don't shoot at them. Let's just do our job, get the wounded, and get out of here!"

Five more air strikes hit the western side of Nhi Ha to cover the withdrawal of the two companies. The strikes were conducted in the face of heavy ground fire. Although the NVA had not brought anti-aircraft weapons to the village, they did use their AK-47s in mass, producing a screen of fire that the jets had to fly through. It was an effective tactic. During the final strike, a Marine Crusader making its third pass took hits and never pulled up. It went in about twenty-five hundred meters northwest of Nhi Ha on the other side of Jones Creek. The Crusader bounced when it hit, then turned into a ball of fire as it pitched nose first into the ground. The explosion was clearly visible to a lot of grunts, who were stunned and horrified—and incredulous at the bravery of those NVA foot soldiers who had blasted a jet out of the sky.

"Did you see a chute, did you see a chute?" battalion asked urgently on the radio.

"Shit, no, I didn't see a chute," answered one dumbstruck officer. "We lost that guy."

Maybe not. Almost an hour later, the U.S. personnel at Alpha 1, who had binoculars and a commanding view of the battlefield, spotted a lone figure east of the crash site on their side of Jones Creek. They reported on the radio that "he appears to be dazed, he's kind of wandering around." There was hope that the pilot had managed a low-altitude ejection. When the FAC diverted to the scene and confirmed the sighting, the C&C Huey immediately contacted the FAC. "We're comin' in low and hot, so direct us up." Using the orbiting Birddog as a beacon, the Huey headed north ten to fifteen feet off the deck. The chopper rose up only to hop over tree lines. Johnson, the pilot, spotted the olive-drab figure in a rice paddy, and he could see that the man was bareheaded and wore no web gear. He did not appear to have a weapon. The figure stopped and looked at the approaching helicopter, and Johnson said on the radio, "We've got the pilot in sight. We're going in to pick him up."

Approaching, Warrant Officer Johnson had his Huey in a hard deceleration with the nose high before he was close enough to see the man's black hair and the baggy cut of his fatigues. "That's a dink, that's a goddamned dink!" Johnson exclaimed as he pulled up and around. "It's not the pilot, it's an NVA. It's a hard-core NVA and we're going to engage him."

The 3d Marines' headquarters, monitoring the 3-21st Infantry's command net, broke in, "Don't shoot him. We're going to want to take him prisoner."

"Just what in the hell do you guys expect us to do out here? We've got our butts hanging out. We're going to kill him."

The Marines responded with a direct order not to shoot the NVA on the grounds that he could have intelligence value. They planned to mount a patrol from Alpha 1 to capture the man. Johnson brought his Huey into a low, tight, clockwise orbit that put the enemy soldier on the door gunner's side of the ship. The door gunner, Sp4 Wallace H. Nunn, sat behind a mounted M60D equipped with twin, D-handled grips and a butterfly trigger. Nunn, who thought that the NVA was probably a lure to an ambush, spoke to Johnson on the intercom, "They've got to be fucking crazy. I can have an accident here, you know."

"Hold your fire," replied Johnson.

The ARVN patrol was visible as dots about a klick away as it moved out from Alpha 1. Johnson, also concerned that the NVA was bait, did not want to wait the twenty to thirty minutes it would take the ARVN to reach the scene. That was all the time an NVA unit would need to set up in the hedgerows around the paddy. "Look him over real goddamn close for weapons," Johnson finally said on the intercom. "We're gonna go in and get him."

"This is fuckin' nuts!" shouted Nunn.

"No shit."

Specialist Nunn kept his M60 on the NVA until they landed behind the man, at which point he popped the radio cord on his flight helmet and jumped out with the M16 he usually kept behind his seat. The soldier turned to face them with his hands up, and Nunn screamed, "Get the fuck on!" He intended to kill the guy at the first sign of resistance, but the NVA, who looked terrified, obediently trotted toward him and clambered aboard the Huey.

Meanwhile, the search for the pilot of the Crusader had been aborted. Captain Stephen W. Clark of Marine All-Weather Fighter Squadron 235 had been killed in the crash, and was posthumously awarded the Silver Star and Purple Heart. The man whom Johnson and his crew picked up was an NVA medic, a deserter who had simply walked south from his unit in the DMZ to find somebody to surrender to. He was in his early thirties and, when questioned in the rear, said that he had been a schoolteacher before being conscripted. He could identify his unit only as the "fourth battalion," and he was officially passed off as having "no information of tactical value."

Nunn held a .38 against the prisoner's head during the flight back, but it was an unnecessary precaution. The enemy soldier, squatting on the helicopter floor, was so scared to be airborne that all he could do was stare at the terrain sweeping under them. When the Huey shut down at the 3-21st Infantry CP, the NVA, who was still holding on for dear life, was jerked out roughly and led to Captain Householder, the intelligence officer, who waited beside a dwelling. The NVA pulled North Vietnamese currency from his wallet and tried to press it on Householder. To further prove his sincerity, he reached into a baggy thigh pocket and produced a stick-handled grenade. "I just held that thing up, looked at the helicopter pilot, and smiled," Householder said later. "He had his dark visor down, so I couldn't see his eyes, but his mouth dropped open when he realized that the prisoner had been in his chopper with a grenade."

Captain Leach arrived at Lieutenant Colonel Snyder's CP in Mai Xa Chanh East during the Nhi Ha engagement. Leach, who had been with Charlie Tiger for more than five months, had managed to miss his company's first nose-to-nose encounter with the NVA because of the timing of his R and R. In his absence, Charlie Tiger had been shot to pieces. Furious and anxious to rejoin his command, Leach, who was a fiery individual, spoke urgently with Snyder. "Those are *my* guys.

We're gettin' in trouble here. This is what it's all about, and I want to be with 'em. I trained 'em. They know me, they work well for me, and I'm responsible for 'em!"

Lieutenant Colonel Snyder, who had greeted Leach with, "My God, am I glad to see you!" briefed him then from his map. Snyder wanted Leach, who was his most experienced company commander, not only to resume command of Charlie Tiger, but also to act as a task force commander with authority over A and D/3-21 until Nhi Ha had been taken. Snyder, meanwhile, would remain at Mai Xa Chanh East to organize its defenses and ensure that no kinks developed in their lifeline with the 3d Marines. "Okay, Leach, you run that show up there. I've got enough problems back here," he concluded.

Major Yurchak, the operations officer, joked with Leach as he got ready to move out. "I'm going to get out of your way 'cause you love this stuff. This is going to be fun for you!"

Captain Leach, age twenty-nine, had dark hair and intense green eyes and was muscular and animal-like. He was, in fact, the closest thing the battalion had to a war lover. Tattooed on his right shoulder was a Ranger tab over Airborne wings. He walked point on patrols, and carried death cards that congratulated enemy soldiers for having been dispatched by Charlie Tiger.

When the C&C Huey took Leach from Mai Xa Chanh East up to the laager east of Nhi Ha, it landed amid 152mm artillery fire that had begun crashing in from the DMZ. The Huey barely touched its skids to the dirt when Leach clambered out fast and flung himself prone. Everyone was relieved to see him, especially Lieutenant Jaquez, the company FO. Leach joined Jaquez after the shelling ceased and asked to be brought up to date. Jaquez, depressed by the raw brutality of the previous day's action, was especially disenchanted with Kohl, the acting company commander, although he tried to be circumspect when he told Leach that indecision during the fight may have contributed to the disaster.

Leach got the idea. He found Lieutenant Kohl hunkered down in a bomb crater, and asked him what had happened. "We really got the shit kicked out of us," Kohl answered.

"Hey, Gerry, listen—we've got to get you out of here. You've had enough. C'mon, we're going to get you on a helicopter."

"Yeah, sir, I think you're right."

Leach had not been sure of Kohl's condition until he gave his defeated answer. "If Kohl had said, 'Hey, sir, you can't do that, I gotta stay here,' I would have said, 'Fine.'" Leach did not normally reward burnout cases with a chopper ride to the rear, but he knew of Kohl's decorated service as a platoon leader. "That kid had been shot at and shot at and shot at, and demonstrated his bravery over and over—and when somebody like that looks at you like a whipped dog and doesn't know what to say, then you get him the hell outta there."

They didn't do it smart, Captain Leach thought as he went over the lessons of the ambush with his remaining lieutenants. They should have reconned by fire. They should have had tac air available. The men of Charlie Tiger, who believed themselves to be in the best company in the best battalion in the best brigade (in what was generally acknowledged, however, to be the worst division in Vietnam), were convinced that Nhi Ha would not have been such a black eye had Leach been there. They had absolute faith in him. Leach was from little Fairmont, Minnesota, the son of a laborer. With no immediate interest in college, he went from high school to the U.S. Navy, where he was a boxer and earned appointments to both Annapolis and West Point. He chose the latter and graduated with the USMA Class of 1963. Following jump school and Ranger training, he served as a platoon leader at Fort Lewis before volunteering for Vietnamese language school and a combat assignment. His 1965–66 tour was split between duty as an assistant adviser to the 37th ARVN Ranger Battalion in Quang Ngai Province, and the staff of the ARVN corps headquarters in Da Nang. Assigned next as a company commander at Fort Benning, he immediately volunteered for a second Vietnam tour so he could command a rifle company in combat, which he considered the ultimate experience of any infantry officer.

Captain Leach returned to Vietnam in October 1967 as the assistant S3 of the 3-21st Infantry and took command of Charlie Tiger the following month, after the battalion moved from Chu Lai to FSB Center. He earned his reputation with the troops on one of his first patrols when Sergeant Skinner, the point squad leader, was shot in the head while crossing a footbridge in pursuit of a fleeing VC. The lone VC had been a lure. The trap was a VC squad dug in across the footbridge. Their fire pinned down the lead squad, and Skinner, who was either unconscious or dead, lay out of reach in a pool of blood. Leach's solution, after deploying the company to provide a base of fire, was to personally run to Skinner across an open paddy, heft the man into a fireman's carry, and sprint back with bullets kicking up all around him. Skinner was not dead. The round had hit near one ear, followed the curve of the back of his skull, and exited near his other ear. He recovered with nothing worse than hearing damage in one ear.

"From that time on, Captain Leach could do no wrong by me," said Sergeant Coulthard. Such confidence in his abilities was more valuable to Leach than the BSMv he got for rescuing Skinner, because he intended to reshape Charlie Tiger. The grunts were mostly draftees and the product of soft, unrealistic training. Leach told them that he would be proud to lead NVA soldiers; in comparison to the average GI, they were masters of jungle fighting. "Captain Leach made you do what the dinks did as far as camouflage, stealth, things like that," recalled Coulthard. "He liked to operate at night. We had to hump, too, and if you were moving in daytime you had to have fresh camouflage on your helmet, your pack, all over. After a couple of hours you'd put on new camouflage made of the vegetation you were in. If you didn't, he got hot." The grunts responded. They did not want to be in Vietnam, but they wanted to survive—and superaggressive, superprofessional Captain Leach seemed to be one of the few officers around who knew how to react in tight situations. Leach was personable enough, but he was too hard, intense, and businesslike to have been loved. He was, however, admired. "If Captain Leach told you to march to hell, you would," said Private Harp. "First, because if he said you could, you knew you could. Secondly, he would be on point, and, finally, if you did not obey his orders he would kick your ass so hard it would make hell look like a cakewalk."

By 1830 on 3 May, A and D/3-21 had begun to withdraw from Nhi Ha. Specialist Hannan of Alpha Two was moving back beside a machine gunner who carried his M60 across his shoulders in an exhausted pose, when the NVA said good-bye with a burst of AK-47 fire. Exasperated, the machine gunner shouted, "You sonsofbitches!" as he turned on his heel to fire back into the hamlet.

In the night laager, Charlie deployed along the perimeter from twelve to four o'clock, Delta took four to seven, and Alpha occupied seven to twelve. At 1922 and 2035, the NVA shelled the laager—again without producing casualties—with 152mm field guns located in the DMZ. Between shellings, the grunts, occupying the same holes as the night before, ate C rations, reloaded their magazines, removed the safety tape from grenades they had ready in their positions, rearranged trip flares, and wired in claymore antipersonnel mines.

Just before dark, Specialist Hannan watched a silhouette walk into their lines, kneel beside the GIs three holes down—and begin speaking in Vietnamese. The thoroughly disoriented NVA, who was wearing green fatigues and carrying an AK-47, immediately realized his mistake and made a run for it. Though stunned himself, Hannan quickly shouldered his M16 and pulled the trigger on the man at thirty paces. There was a flash of sparks as his shot hit the magazine or metal parts of the man's weapon, but Hannan lost sight of the figure in the dark. The NVA got away.

At 2120, before the flareship arrived to give the Gimlets some illuminated security, another NVA came out of the dark where B/3-21 was positioned near Lam Xuan West. He was a deserter unconnected with the fight in Nhi Ha. Captain Corrigan, who described the NVA soldier as "young, skinny, and scared," had the prisoner blindfolded and tied with his arms behind his back until a helicopter came to get him in the morning. He was sent on to the 3d Marines, where it was determined that he "belonged to the 126th Independent Regt, whose mission was to send elements south from the DMZ to mine the Cua Viet River. Intelligence gained from the rallier included infiltration routes, unit base areas, and mining tactics."

"Our morale was at its lowest and not one man wanted to go back in there," wrote nineteen-year-old Pfc. Charles C. Cox of D/3-21 in a letter home regarding the third attack on Nhi Ha. The attack commenced at 0936, Saturday, 4 May 1968, after two air strikes and the usual arty prep. "Dad, I was scared to death. . . ."

Captains Leach and Humphries, who were great friends, had worked up the attack plan during the night, placing Delta on the left flank and Charlie Company on the right. Moving through Nhi Ha, Black Death 6 again had Lieutenant Skrzysowski on the left with Delta One, and Lieutenant Weidner's Delta Two on the right. Delta Three was in reserve. Something is not right, thought Skrzysowski, surprised that they had received comparatively little fire during their cautious approach

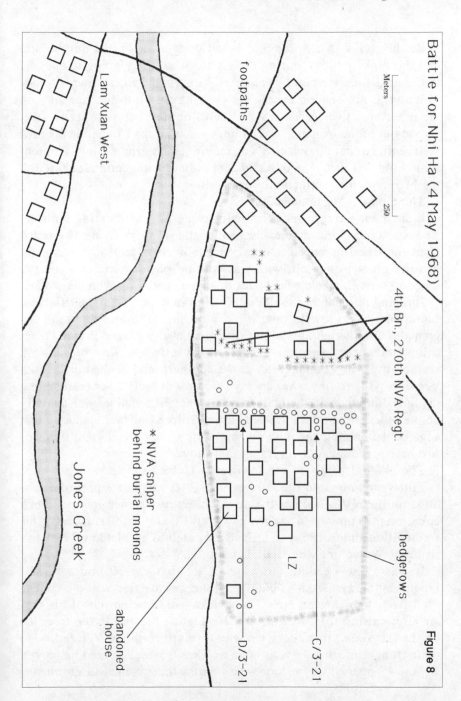

Battle for Nhi Ha (4 May 1968)

footpaths

Lam Xuan West

Meters

250

4th Bn., 270th NVA Regt.

* NVA sniper
behind burial mounds

Jones Creek

hedgerows

LZ

abandoned
house

C/3-21

D/3-21

Figure 8

to the hedgerow where the attack had bogged down the day before. Did the dinks pull out during the night, or are they going to suck us in the next time we move? Humphries instructed Skrzysowski to advance with his platoon across the clearing and into the tree line on the other side that the enemy had held the day before. Skrzysowski started out of the irrigation ditch running behind the battered hedgerow, then realized that no one else was moving. The grunts could feel that something was wrong, too, but when the lieutenant continued through the hedgerow they reluctantly came along.

The ambush began at 1020.

Lieutenant Skrzysowski was halfway across the clearing with the lead squad in a skirmish line when automatic weapons suddenly erupted from the tree line ahead. One of Skrzysowski's sergeants was shot, and the grunt to his left, who was coming out of a crater when the shooting started, was knocked back in with a shattering shoulder wound.

Jumping into another shell crater with his radioman and a rifleman, Lieutenant Skrzysowski opened up with his M16 and threw all his grenades. To his right, his M60 gunner had also managed to find cover, and he too opened fire at targets heard but not seen. Most of the NVA seemed to be in a bomb crater at the southern end of the north-south tree line. At least one other enemy soldier was well ensconced among the burial mounds on the platoon's left flank. The sniper was actually on the other side of the shredded east-west tree line that ran along that edge of the hamlet, and with an automatic weapon and great fields of fire he banged away at anything that moved.

The NVA also lobbed mortar fire on Delta Company.

Thirty minutes into the contact, the FAC ran in a flight of Phantoms on the NVA. Neither the air nor the arty seemed to have much effect on the entrenched enemy, however. Lieutenant Skrzysowski, his ammunition almost exhausted, finally shouted to his platoon, "We can't sit here! We've got wounded! Let's move!"

It was 1120. Leading the way, an act that earned him a BSMv, Lieutenant Skrzysowski—a blunt, patriotic, twenty-five-year-old college grad from Manchester, New Hampshire—clambered out of his crater after calling for covering fire. He planned to run to the tree line on the left flank, then work his way forward to the NVA tree line to their front. Unfortunately, as soon as Skrzysowski cleared his cover, an AK-47 opened up on him with a burst that seemed to go on forever and blew him into another bomb crater, shredding his rucksack in the process. He was by himself and in excruciating pain. He had taken a round through his upper right thigh and buttocks, and the sight of the meat hanging from his leg made him think he had lost his testicles. His other leg, although not bloody, was paralyzed and numb, and he thought he had also been shot in the spine. He felt as though he'd been hit in the chest with a sledgehammer, but that was actually the least of his injuries: A bullet had hit one of the last magazines left in his bandolier and peppered his chest with metal fragments.

Lieutenant Skrzysowski's M16 had been hit and rendered inoperable, but he thanked God that he still had his .45-caliber pistol. Groggy with shock, he suddenly realized that his medic was in the crater with him, administering morphine and wrapping his wounds with battle dressings. "Shit, we gotta get you out of here," the medic said urgently.

"How in the hell did *you* get out here?" asked Skrzysowski.

"Let's go," the medic answered, taking charge.

Crawling out of the crater with rounds cracking over their heads, the medic led the way. Skrzysowski was right behind him, barely able to use his legs to push but able to pull himself along with his hands. Exhausted, he made it back through the hedgerow and into the cover of his platoon's trench, where he checked his wounds. They were bad, but not as bad as he'd first thought. His testicles were still there, and his back was not hit: The pain in his unwounded left leg was actually from a spinal disc damaged by the weight of his pack when he'd bounced into the crater.

Several men were still pinned down in the killing zone. To get them back, Lieutenant Skrzysowski, immobile in the trench, worked his radio to keep the arty on target while Sergeant First Class Mathis moved among their positions to organize suppressive fires. Under this cover, the men in the killing zone made it back one at a time. Sometime later, after Delta One's casualties had been moved rearward to Delta Three's LZ, several GIs from the reserve platoon dropped into the forward trench and told Skrzysowski that they had orders from Black Death 6 to get him on a medevac, too. They carried him back in a poncho, and then hefted him aboard the C&C Huey—which landed despite the latest mortar attack. Skrzysowski was the only casualty on board. It had been two hours since he'd been hit.

Smoke hung in the air from the mortar explosions, as did the smell of gunpowder. The day was scorching hot, the noise of gunfire constant. Sergeant First Class Mathis was in constant motion, checking the platoon positions with his radioman, Cox, crawling behind him on his hands and raw knees. The NVA fire over their heads sounded to Cox like angry hornets, and he made sure to keep his radio antenna pulled down. Mathis and Cox discovered three troopers who had found sanctuary in a bomb crater two or three hedgerows back. They refused to budge. Everyone else was doing his job, to include scared, sweat-soaked Cox, who at one point ended up feeding ammo belts into an M60 whose gunner blazed away like mad. When dirt started popping up behind them, Cox thought a trooper to their rear was firing wild. He suddenly realized that the NVA sniper on the left flank had zeroed in on the M60, and he and the gunner scrambled to a new position along their hedgerow. They resumed firing.

Fifteen minutes after Black Death ran into trouble on the left flank, Captain Leach and Charlie Tiger were engaged on the right by three NVA in an observation post on the near side of the contested clearing. Charlie Tiger GIs killed the NVA with grenades, then Leach's popular first sergeant, forty-two-year-old Sfc. William R. Brooks, of Morriltown, Arkansas, pulled an AK-47 from the enemy trench and held it up to show the captain. At that moment, Brooks was nailed in the forehead and killed instantly as heavy fire erupted from the NVA positions on the other side of the clearing. Charlie Tiger was at the last hedgerow with Lieutenant Hieb and Charlie One on the right flank, and Staff Sergeant Goad, the acting commander of Charlie Two, on the left. Charlie Three, led by 1st Lt. Dale W. Musser, who had been on an administrative run to the rear when the battle began two days earlier, brought up the rear. Musser was an excellent platoon leader, but Leach had him in reserve for the same reason he'd earlier sent him to the rear: Musser was furious about the booby-trap death of Lieutenant Dunlap of Delta Company. Leach explained that he'd "yanked Musser's ass out of there to give him time to cool down, but he was still smarting. He was so mad that I was afraid he'd pull a John Wayne. I didn't want him to get killed, so I put him back in reserve."

In the first moments of the engagement, Captain Leach, who wore a helmet and flak jacket and was swinging a CAR15, had to kick a couple of GIs in the ass for having hunkered down out of harm's way.

"Start firing your goddamn weapons!" he shouted. "And don't fire on automatic—fire on semi or you'll just eat up all your ammo, and we don't know what the fuck's in there!"

"When a firefight starts, it's pandemonium," recalled Captain Leach. "If you can get your guys just to return fire, you're doing well. We had guys who never fired their weapons. When a soldier takes fire, the first thing he does is take cover. If you can get that kid to get his goddamn weapon up there and just fire in the right direction, you got it made."

Having crawled forward to a mound, Captain Leach started pumping away with his CAR15—until it jammed. He was enraged. He was also receiving plunging fire from an NVA whose location he could not figure out. Lieutenant Hieb spotted the NVA in one of the surviving hootches and shouted, "Hey, they're shootin' down at you from the rafters!"

"Shoot that sonofabitch because he's going to kill me!" screamed Leach.

The position was silenced with a LAW, but the fire continued from other entrenched, invisible enemy positions.

Charlie Tiger responded in kind. "We pounded the shit out of 'em," said Leach. Helix 1-5 ordered several more Skyhawk strikes, which utilized napalm and five-hundred-pound high-drag bombs. Each pass was made from a different direction so as to give the NVA less opportunity to organize the effective antiaircraft fire they had the day before. When the FAC departed to refuel and rearm with marking rockets, the arty was turned back on. "With all that shit rolling in, the sound level must have been a hundred-and-fifty decibels," said Private Harp of Charlie One. "I mean your ears hurt." Like every other man, Harp had found a piece of cover—in his case beside Pope, their machine gunner—and he poured fire across that clearing. They had no specific targets. Harp probably went through seventy-five magazines with his M16. "The receiver group on my rifle got so hot I could hardly hold the damn thing. The whole palm of my hand was blistered. The barrel was pouring off white smoke, and I used three bottles of LSA to keep the bolt from freezing up." Pope's M60 consumed ammo with equal vigor, and Harp ran back several times during the fight to get M16 bandoliers for himself and extra machine-gun ammo for Pope. "Pope's gun literally glowed red from time to time. He burned out the barrel and had to start using his spare." Harp was scared, hungry, and thirsty. He had run out of water the day before, and he was wobbly in the unrelenting, lip-cracking heat of the day. "All that kept me going was on one of my trips to the CP for ammo I fell in a shell hole with a little green water. I stuck my canteen down in the sandy mud and got about one-third of a canteen of something that was mostly water. Put six iodine tablets in it, shook it up, and tried to chug-a-lug the shit as fast as I could in the hopes that I wouldn't taste it too much."

At 1325, Lieutenant Colonel Snyder went airborne over the battle in his C&C Huey. Thirty-five minutes later, Helix 1-7 arrived on station to control the seventh air strike of the day. It lasted twenty-five minutes. Under the cover of the snake 'n' nape and automatic cannons, Captain Leach sent Lieutenant Hieb and two squads low-crawling across the right side of the clearing, where enemy fire was minimal. If they could blast out a foothold on the other side, they might break the stalemate.

Captain Leach, meanwhile, got on the horn with Black Death 6, whose fires seemed to be straying toward Hieb's assault. "You gotta watch your fire to your right flank. You got to keep it in front of you because we got those guys up there." The fire was not adequately shifted. Leach, who had already secured an M16 from a medic, shrugged into the harness of one of his RTOs' radios—he wanted to move fast without his command group in tow—and started toward Black Death 6 on his hands and knees. His pucker factor was up, but he made it into Humphries's crater and began pointing out exactly where Delta's troops should not fire. Leach and Humphries were still talking when a rocket-propelled grenade crashed into the crater some thirty meters to their right, wounding several noncoms who were firing from that position.

In the continuing cacophony, one of Humphries's medics, Sp4 Rollin D. Davis, twenty, of Grand Junction, Iowa, was killed. Captain Leach radioed ahead before crawling back to the berm where he had left his command group. Lieutenant Hieb called on the company net: He had reached the enemy side of the clearing but was under a massive amount of fire and could make no headway. Leach ordered Hieb to pull back, then asked Helix 1-7 to bring in the tac air to help the two squads break contact. Hieb popped smoke as instructed. Leach, after giving the FAC an azimuth, direction of fire, et cetera, said to him, "Okay, you're going to be dropping it twenty meters right in front of 'em, so you *got* to do it right."

It was 1604. Lieutenant Hieb, wanting to cover the withdrawal with his CAR15, sprinted by himself toward the next hedgerow. He stepped in a hole on his way across and fell heavily with his pack, knocking the wind out of himself. He jumped into a thicket of bamboo. The first Phantom made its strafing run a safe distance away, but then Hieb, whose ruck was hopelessly tangled in the bamboo, looked up to see the next jet lining up for a run right at his forward location. He couldn't pull his ruck loose, so he frantically shrugged out of it and left it suspended in the bamboo as he sprinted away. The Phantom released its napalm canisters. Expertly applied, they sucked the oxygen from the air as they drove the NVA to the bottom of their holes, allowing Hieb's platoon to crawl back without casualties. All that was later found of the lieutenant's rucksack were a few little melted bits of the aluminum frame.

At 1617, the ninth air strike plastered Nhi Ha. Meanwhile, the C&C Huey, without the colonel, conducted medevacs and ammo drops in Delta Three's LZ. The Huey came in low and hot each time, with cover fire courtesy of the wounded Sergeant See, who still had two men left in his machine-gun squad, plus a half-dozen anonymous GIs who'd also been detailed to work the landing zone. They fired in the general direction of that invisible, dug-in sniper in the burial mounds on the left flank. The NVA was about a hundred meters away. Every time somebody moved, he fired. After one ammo drop, See, who'd run out to haul the stuff off the open LZ, ended up pinned down behind six cases of machine-gun bullets.

"Goddamnit!" he screamed at his pickup squad, which was not returning fire. "Give me some cover fire, I gotta get out of here!"

The GIs did not raise their heads from their holes. The sniper ceased fire on his own accord. Sergeant See, who was furious, got only apathetic looks from the anonymous GIs as he shouted at them about their inaction. They weren't fools. They didn't intend to die in this stupid war.

These GIs were not alone in their attitude. Two men were medevacked during the day with combat fatigue, including a grunt who was so hysterical that it took several men to load him yelling and screaming onto the Huey. The other man crawled back to the LZ quietly and on his own, still wearing his helmet and web gear and dragging his M16. He was crying, "I can't take it. . . . I can't take it. . . ." The man was a Regular Army sergeant first class. See was shocked, and then angry. "He was the type of guy who was supposed to be hard-core," See said later. "After all the crap we'd been given by E-7s during our training about how to be a role model—here's this guy who just became a coward. Everyone wanted to climb on a helo and say the hell with it, but we had a job to do and that's the way it was."

At 1830, the C&C Huey was hit by the NVA sniper while it lifted up from the LZ. The pilot lost control of the tail boom, which swung wildly from side to side as the Huey smacked back down on the ground. Sergeant See, who had rolled away from the descending chopper, was joined in a flash behind the cover of his earthen berm by the chopper crew. They were understandably shook up. The first thing they wanted to know was whether the grunts had any extra steel helmets for them. "No, we don't," See said with an inward smile at how uptight the airmen were. Within ten minutes, another Huey bounced in and out of the LZ to take aboard the downed crew while the grunts fired away at the burial mounds.

Although few NVA had been seen, fifty-seven were reported killed. Lieutenant Colonel Snyder had several conversations with Captain Leach about what the NVA had in Nhi Ha. Leach kept telling him that they were up against at least a full-strength company, but Snyder replied that it was "not nearly that many," and that they seemed large in number only "because they're so well dug in they can move back and forth." On that they could agree. Their arty and tac air weren't doing any good against the enemy entrenchments. Finally, at dusk, after nearly nine hours of stalemate, Leach said to Snyder, "Hey, listen, I don't know how to attack this goddamn thing any way but going right up the center. Now, we'll go again if you want us to go."

Two Gimlets had already been killed that day, and thirteen more wounded. Lieutenant Colonel Snyder did not believe that a frontal assault could be successful "at any reasonable cost of casualties." He told Leach to "pull back to the laager position. We're going to pound it some more with artillery and air."

A tenth and final air strike was brought in at 1920 by Helix 1-5 to help Charlie and Delta break contact. But as the two companies leapfrogged back through Nhi Ha by fire teams, the NVA pursued them to the edge of the ville. Red and green tracers crisscrossed in the smoky dusk as troops fired and ran, then fired and ran again. Pandemonium reigned. When they reached the laager, Private Cox was approached by a buddy who exclaimed, "Jesus Christ, Cox, I almost shot you! As we were giving cover fire, you ran right into my sights. Why I stopped pulling the trigger at that time I'll never know—but you came that close to getting shot!"

It was another long night in the three-company laager. At 0352, shortly after the enemy probed the perimeter with AK-47 fire and grenades, a Charlie Tiger listening post lobbed a few grenades of their own at two NVA who were visible in the paddy around the laager. The NVA went down as if dead, and the LP pulled back on order. At 0405, two more enemy soldiers walked right into Charlie's line. Specifically, they walked up to Sp4 Bill Dixon of Charlie Two, who was in a three-man position with Privates Fulcher and Fletcher, who were half-asleep behind a paddy dike. Dixon, awake and on watch, was sitting with his M79 when the two NVA, who must have been lost, appeared before him as silhouettes. One knelt down to start speaking to him in Vietnamese. Dixon, who had a shotgun load in his grenade launcher, shot the man in the head at point-blank range. While the other NVA spun away to run, Dixon slapped his hand on Fulcher who, startled awake, had instantly and automatically put his hand on his M16 rifle. "Stay down—there's another gook out there yet!" shouted Dixon.

The NVA fired his AK-47 as he escaped. When Fulcher exclaimed, "What the hell's going on?" Dixon answered urgently, "I shot one!"

"Where?" asked Fulcher.

"Right there."

"Right *where?*"

"Right *there!*"

The first illumination round went up then, and Fulcher was shocked to see a nearly decapitated NVA soldier lying within an arm's length of them. Brains were splattered all over Fulcher's rucksack, and he barked, "What the hell'dja let him get that close for?"

Specialist Dixon had not been taken completely by surprise. He had heard the NVA speaking in muffled, definitely non-English tones as they'd approached, but he had assumed that it was the two Puerto Rican GIs in the position to their right who usually conversed in Spanish.

The dead man wore black shorts and a gray fatigue shirt. Because he carried binoculars and a brand-new AK-47 with white parachute silk over the barrel, it was conjectured that the man had been an artillery spotter, probably a lieutenant.

Captain Leach, who had some hard words about the one that got away, took the AK-47 to replace his jammed-up CAR15 and used it during the remainder of the DMZ operation. Afterward it was presented to the Helix FACs as a thank-you and ended up on a plaque in their Chu Lai club. Meanwhile, artillery illum was being fired. The troops could hear the ascent of each round and then the pop, and they watched each flare sway on its parachute in its slow, smoke-trailing descent. The flares were timed so that as one hit the ground and went out, another would burst above them. If the timing was off, the plunge into darkness was instant and total. Private Fulcher, for one, would shudder at the thought of NVA rushing toward them. "But then another flare would pop and it'd still be blank out across the paddies. It was great having the lights on, as we used to say."

CHAPTER 18 ALPHA ANNIHILATED

At 0655 on Sunday, 5 May 1968, two USAF FACs arrived on station to coordinate the preparatory air strikes for the 3-21st Infantry's fourth assault on Nhi Ha. This time, two-thousand-pound bombs were to be used. The suggestion to employ such heavy ordnance had come the previous evening when Lieutenant Colonel Snyder had spoken by radio with a frustrated FAC who said, "Let me lay on a couple of sorties tomorrow with two-thousand-pound fuse-delays. They'll penetrate the ground before they explode. The ground shock is tremendous. If there's anybody left in those dugouts then, it'll do 'em in."

Lieutenant Colonel Snyder had been enthusiastic about the idea. He had not suggested it himself because he had been unaware that such munitions were available. The FAC went on to advise him that if they used the two-thousand-pounders the men closest to the enemy positions would have to pull back as a safety precaution.

By 0715, Captain Corrigan's B/3-21, the company closest to Nhi Ha, had withdrawn approximately five hundred meters south of Lam Xuan West. Captain Leach and his three-company task force remained in their well-entrenched laager six hundred meters east of Nhi Ha. Snyder went airborne in his C&C Huey. When the two-thousand-pounders plunged into the hamlet, he had a ringside view of the spectacular subsurface explosions that erupted mushroomlike with much smoke and dirt. The effect was most dramatic at ground level. Even at a safe distance, it was like being in an earthquake. Foxholes seemed to sway and move as the shock wave rolled through, and metal fragments rained down to bounce off a helmet or two. The last bomb fell at 0930, and the ground assault commenced ten minutes later with Captain Leach and Charlie Company advancing toward Nhi Ha behind the artillery prep. Captain Osborn and Alpha moved out behind Charlie Tiger. It took twenty minutes to reach Nhi Ha, then ten more minutes to cautiously cross the first hundred meters inside the ville. At that point, Charlie halted and Alpha leapfrogged past to continue the assault up to the clearing that was the hamlet's no-man's-land. Despite the obvious destruction caused by the blockbusters, one lieutenant said later that "no one was optimistic that this was going to be a picnic."

By 1040, two of Alpha's platoons, expending ammunition freely as they reconned by fire, had low-crawled across the clearing without contact. Joined shortly by Charlie, both companies proceeded to sweep the western half of Nhi Ha. The troops were alert and cautious as they walked through the rubble. When an NVA soldier in a spiderhole tried to raise his AK-47 through his overhead cover, a sergeant in Charlie Tiger reached down and jerked the weapon out of the man's hands before dispatching him with a burst from his M16. There were no other live NVA visible. At 1132, after a lot of grenades had been wasted on a lot of empty entrenchments, Leach reported to Snyder that Nhi Ha had been secured. Along the way, the three bodies that Charlie Tiger had left behind three days earlier were recovered. "They were totally destroyed," recalled Lieutenant Smith of Alpha Annihilator. "It was one of those times that you swallow real hard because if you don't you're going to throw up. Some people did." The bodies had swollen and turned black, and the stench was terrible. Their bloated faces were unrecognizable. Their mouths were frozen open in death. Flies covered them, and their wounds were alive with maggots. "God, I hate fucking maggots," said Private Harp, who helped to gingerly place the torn-up remains into body bags. "Somebody grabbed one by his pistol belt, and the body broke in half. The bones in his rib cage popped out. I didn't know whether to puke, cry, or hide, so instead I just went back to work. You just kind of disconnect and do what you have to do. It wasn't really me picking up that mangled mess, it was me watching me. I was just an observer to someone else's nightmare."

Thanks to tac air and the blockbusters, Nhi Ha looked like Hiroshima. Lieutenant Colonel Snyder instructed Captain Leach to hold the village with Charlie Tiger and Captain Osborn's Alpha Annihilator, which would remain in his task force and under his command. Captain

Humphries's Delta Company was detached and ordered to occupy Lam Xuan East as the battalion reserve. Captain Corrigan's Bravo Company, never part of the task force, reoccupied Lam Xuan West. Sections of 81mm mortars from HHC/3-21 were attached to both Leach and Corrigan, and resupply was carried out during the afternoon. Water, always in short supply, was obtained from bomb craters. Nhi Ha smelled of death, and there were plenty of small, stiff enemy corpses to be seen as the troops began selecting their positions and digging in. There were NVA who'd been burned black by napalm, and NVA whose heads had been removed standing up in caved-in, chest-deep trenches. A grunt described one of the more memorable corpses, which was found "down in a bomb crater about thirty feet deep. He was floating in the water and had turned the same putrid green color as the water. The body was swollen to about twice normal size. Looked like something from a Hollywood horror movie—I mean the guy did not look real."

The official body count was forty-four. To celebrate the victory, Major Yurchak, the S3, had the bell removed from the village's Catholic church in the western half of Nhi Ha. "That'll be our war booty—whenever the Third of the Twenty-first has a reunion, we'll ring the bell!"

The bell, which bore the raised inscription NHI-HA-1925, made it back to FSB Center but was subsequently donated to an orphanage in Tam Ky. Meanwhile, Captain Leach christened his patrol base in Nhi Ha "Force Tiger." Leach set Charlie Company in along the northern half of the perimeter and gave Alpha the southern half. As the men dug in they were subjected to sniper fire, which slowed the process as GIs knelt to use their E-tools instead of standing up to dig. Although many of the NVA entrenchments were still intact, the GIs did not use them because, as one grunt put it, "the little man would have known exactly where to put his incoming." Because of the threat of enemy artillery fire, timber and masonry from the hamlet's blown-down buildings were used to reinforce foxholes and provide overhead cover. One trooper joked to the new guys in his platoon, who were taking turns digging in, "No shift for me—give me that shovel! I've been here longer than some of you guys, and I know enough that I like my hole in the ground real well. One of my favorite things when I'm getting shot at is a hole!"

The NVA did not shell Nhi Ha during Force Tiger's first night there, but it was a long, hairy night nonetheless—especially for the fire-team–sized listening posts that the two companies established after dark for early warning. The LPs were set up in bomb craters. Each had a star-light scope, as well as a sack of hand grenades and an M79 to cover their withdrawal if detected by the NVA. At 2205 on 5 May, the first sighting was made east of Nhi Ha: seventeen NVA moving south across the paddies and sand dunes two klicks away. Artillery fire was worked along their route. Thirty minutes later, a company of NVA, two hundred strong, was spotted two klicks to the west on the other side of Jones Creek, and another fire mission was initiated.

Artillery fire echoed through the pitch-black night.

At 0050 on 6 May, a Charlie Tiger LP spotted five NVA moving toward Force Tiger in a slow, cautious fashion. An hour later, two more NVA with AK-47s were seen walking right at the LP. The GI with the M79 waited until they were within fifteen feet before he fired them up with a canister round. One NVA was blown away, and the grunts in the LP returned to the perimeter. There was an uneasy lull punctuated by an enemy soldier with a captured M79 who fired on Charlie Tiger.

At 0425, contact was made where Sergeant Stone, a squad leader in Alpha Three, had established an LP in a big crater in the dark, unfamiliar lunarscape. The LP was within a hundred meters of their line. Stone had been instructed to go out farther, but as he told his grunts, "No way, you know, we'll never make it back." Stone, awakened by Private King, whom he was to replace on watch, had just edged up to the lip of their crater when he saw two NVA with AK-47s and khaki fatigues coming in their direction. One had halted, and the other was catching up with him. They were only twenty meters away. Stone could see them clearly in the eerie white light of the latest illumination round, but he had not asked King where the detonators were for the two claymore mines they had set up in front of the crater.

Sergeant Stone woke his four men one at a time, whispering to each as he began to stir, "Be quiet—don't move—we got gooks right in front of us." He bent over King and asked, "Where're the detonators?" King said they were by the tree limb lying in front of their crater. Stone, feeling around with one hand while he kept his head down, could not find them. Jesus, they're gonna be in the hole with us pretty quick, Stone thought as he broke squelch on his radio handset to indicate that they were in trouble. He tried to whisper in response to the CP's questions about how many NVA there were, how far away they were, et cetera, but he finally signed off with a hushed, "They're too close, I can't talk," and placed the handset aside as he went back up with a fragmentation grenade. He lobbed the grenade toward the two NVA he had seen—he could sense others out there—then opened fire with his M16 on automatic. He slid back down, ejected the empty magazine, and fumbled for a fresh one in his bandolier. He was so scared that he put the magazine in upside down. He finally thumped it in correctly, then realized that his four charges—all new replacements—were still lying where he had awakened them, doing nothing more than looking up at him. He had told them not to move, and they were following orders. Stone screamed at them, "Get up and shoot, get up and shoot!"

Specialist Four Allan G. Barnes did most of the shooting as he lobbed M79 rounds toward a muzzle flash behind a tree stump. Reloading, Barnes turned to Stone, "How's that?"

"Closer, Barnes, *closer!*" Stone answered.

Each time Stone rose up to fire his M16, the NVA behind the stump would also pop up with his AK-47 on full auto. They were firing right at each other, but they kept missing. Barnes found the claymore detonators and blew one of the mines, but it had no visible effect. Stone decided they'd better pull back before it was too late. Wasting no time with a radio call to the CP to request permission to withdraw, Stone simply shouted at his team, "Okay, you guys take off. Go for the perimeter. Me and Barnes will cover for you, then we're comin'!"

Sergeant Stone squeezed off another M16 magazine and Barnes another M79 round as the three replacements clambered over the back side of the crater, then they dropped, reloaded, and started after them. They were scared and moving fast, and they left their radio and grenades. Clearing the crater, they were stunned to see the three greenseeds lying prone on the other side. Stone shouted at them to get moving. Running for the perimeter, they hollered their catchall password—"ALPHA GIMLETS!"—and screamed at the men on the line not to open fire. This was a real concern as RPGs had begun flashing past them. No one was hurt, though, and no one fired. As soon as the men from the LP were safely inside the perimeter, their platoon leader, Lieutenant Kimball, hustled over to Stone and asked, "What's out there, what's out there?"

"There's gooks *all over* out there!"

Referring to Captain Osborn by his call sign, Lieutenant Kimball said, "Cherokee says he might send you back out, so keep your squad together."

"Shit, we ain't going *back out*," exclaimed Stone. "There is gooks *all over* out there!"

"Oh, no problem, no problem—"

"Well, don't tell me to go back out. We ain't going back out. We're a *listening post,* and I already toldja: They're out there!"

The LP was not reestablished. Later, when it was light, a patrol sent out to retrieve the radio from the LP's crater discovered a slit trench behind the tree stump. The three badly wounded, barely moving NVA in the trench were finished off at point-blank range, and two AK-47s and an RPG launcher were recovered, along with a blood-spattered machine gun found in the open paddy behind the trench.

Meanwhile, at about 0500 on Charlie Tiger's side of the perimeter, Private Harp of Charlie One, occupying the center of the line, spotted several NVA on the left flank directly ahead of Charlie Two, which at that moment was reporting movement somewhere to the front. The NVA were close, and Harp could see their silhouettes—they were wearing Russian steel helmets—as they started to set up a machine gun at the lip of a crater. Harp's squad leader, Specialist Burns, was in position with him but could make out nothing where Harp pointed. Burns whispered to Harp that he was "full of shit, as usual," but Harp pressed his squad leader to let him "fire a '79 round on their position to pinpoint them for the other platoon."

Burns considered Harp a punk and a screwup, and his response was, "You stupid shit, if you fire the '79 it'll give our position away."

"They're pointing a machine gun at us, Burns—they have some idea where we are. Besides, a '79 gives away a lot less than a '16 would, and I can't reach them with a frag." Somebody in the dugout suggested that Burns call the CP to advise them of the situation and let them decide. When Burns did, Captain Leach told him to recon by fire with an M79. Before letting Harp shoot the grenade launcher, Burns barked in a low, angry whisper, "If the captain wants to use a '79, it's smart. If you do, it's stupid. Fuck you, Harp."

The M79 round exploded within ten meters of the NVA machine gun, which opened fire in response. Charlie Two actually had about twenty-five NVA to its front, as did Charlie Three on the right flank. As illum and HE were delivered by artillery—the NVA could be heard

Sfc. Buford Mathis (left) and his RTO, Pfc. Charles C. Cox, of D/3-21, about two hours before the 4 May 1968 assault on Nhi Ha. *Courtesy C. C. Cox.*

Sgt. Larry See (wearing glasses), D/3-21. *Courtesy L. H. See.*

Capt. Dennis A. Leach, CO of C/3-21. Leach commanded the task force that seized Nhi Ha and held it despite repeated NVA counterattacks. *Courtesy J. S. Hildebrand.*

The Gimlets took this church bell as a souvenir when they took Nhi Ha on 5 May 1968. It was eventually donated to an orphanage in Tam Ky. *Courtesy J. S. Hildebrand.*

Lt. Col. Snyder sits in the ruins of the church at Nhi Ha after the operation. *Courtesy J. S. Hildebrand.*

Sgt. Starr awaits medical evacuation after being blinded in his right eye during the attack on the night of 5–6 May 1968. *Courtesy R. W. Starr.*

Sgt. James L. Stone, A/3-21. *Courtesy J. L. Stone.*

Capt. Robert E. Corrigan, CO of B/3-21 (at far left), after receiving the Silver Star. *Courtesy W. P. Snyder.*

2d Lt. Terry D. Smith, a platoon leader in A/3-21, was shot and also hit by mortar fragments during an ambush near Nhi Ha on 6 May 1968. *Courtesy T. D. Smith.*

Sgt. Larry Haddock, A/3-21. *Courtesy N. E. Hannan.*

Sp4 Neil E. Hannan, A/3-21. *Courtesy N. E. Hannan.*

Sp4 Thomas E. Hemphill, a grenadier in A/3-21, in front of his position on the Nhi Ha perimeter. *Courtesy T. E. Hemphill.*

Sp4 William W. Karp (center), senior medic in A/3-21. *Courtesy W. W. Karp.*

Sp4 Bill A. Baird (center), A/3-21, was wounded and captured on 6 May 1968. He remained a prisoner in North Vietnam until 1973. *Courtesy N. E. Hannan.*

Another patrol saddles up in Nhi Ha. *Courtesy J. L. Stone.*

Lt. Col. William P. Snyder (right) receives a commemorative plaque before leaving U.S. Army Vietnam headquarters to assume command of the 3-21st Infantry. *Courtesy W. P. Snyder.*

screaming as the shells exploded—individual GIs engaged individual NVA with M16s, M60s, and M79s. Hey, we can finally see the sons of bitches, thought Sgt. Roger Starr of Charlie Three, who was too excited to be scared as he pumped M16 bursts at NVA maneuvering forward from burial mound to burial mound. They were fully exposed in the flarelight. Starr saw several bareheaded NVA, who were swinging AK-47s and wearing shorts, go down in his rifle sights, and when he couldn't make out any live ones, he shot the dead ones again. Some were less than fifty meters away. There were, however, a lot of muzzle flashes and RPG sparks in return. Sergeant Starr's shooting gallery ended abruptly when a small, buckshot-sized piece of metal from an explosion he wasn't even aware of pierced his right eye like a hot needle. The pain was sudden and intense, and it immediately rendered him completely blind as his uninjured left eye watered up, too. Starr, clutching his face, dropped to the bottom of his machine-gun team's dugout and screamed for a medic. There was little bleeding as the medic taped pads over both of Starr's eyes. Starr, who had been in the company for ten months, figured that his right eye would heal up fine—he was wrong, the eye was permanently blind—and as he was led back to the company CP all he could think was, This is the trip back home![1]

The NVA, crawling in the shadows, pulled back at 0530 but, apparently reinforced, they came back for more thirty minutes later. The final cost was two Americans and one Kit Carson scout wounded; the NVA lost thirty-four soldiers and sixteen weapons. Trapped behind burial mounds, the last NVA were killed after the sun came up. "It was a goddamn turkey shoot," said Captain Leach, who moved elements of Charlie Two out into the paddies on the flanks to keep the NVA pinned down while Charlie One and Three picked them off from the front. "We were just killin' 'em—we were shootin' the shit out of 'em—but they fought to the last man. That took a lot of guts." The fight finally boiled down to one NVA behind a burial mound, and two more in a bomb crater. At that point, Specialist Burns earned the Silver Star

---

1. Sergeant Starr was awarded the Silver Star, BSMv, and two Purple Hearts for Nhi Ha, in addition to an end-of-tour BSM.

when he muttered something to the effect of "Fuck this shit," and launched an impatient charge on the NVA in the crater. "Burns ran straight at them," said Private Harp. "He caught the first NVA with a single shot from his M16. Apparently he thought the other one was already dead, because he just started walking toward their crater." A Chicom came flying out of the hole and Burns backpedaled a few steps before falling backward into another crater. "Now Burns was really pissed. He jumped in the hole with the dink and shot him or stuck him, or both. I'm not sure. Burns was so pissed off by then he was liable to have ate him."

Captain Leach shouted at everyone to cease firing on the sole survivor behind the burial mound, and he had his Kit Carson scout attempt to talk the man into surrendering. Meanwhile, Sergeant Coulthard of Charlie Three was joined in his position by Specialist Green, a machine gunner. Green borrowed his M16 and sighted in on the last-stand position. Green was a tough, stocky GI from Alabama described by Coulthard as "a good old boy who enjoyed gettin' it on with the NVA." When the enemy soldier answered the calls to surrender by rearing up with his arm back to fling another Chicom, Green squeezed off a single round. The NVA had a rag of a bandage around his head. The bandage went flying as Green's shot blew off the top of his head. "Who the hell shot him?" Leach exploded. Green theatrically blew smoke away from the rifle barrel, and answered, "I did. I'm not going to fuck around and get somebody killed up here."

On Monday, 6 May, Lieutenant Colonel Snyder instructed Captain Osborn to conduct a reconnaissance in force along the enemy's route of withdrawal. The immediate target of the sweep was Xom Phuong, twelve hundred meters northwest of Nhi Ha on the eastern bank of Jones Creek. A raised footpath connected Nhi Ha with the southern tip of Xom Phuong. The terrain in between was wide open, and Captain Leach, who was to remain in position at Force Tiger, was convinced that the order to cross such vulnerable terrain was "very poorly conceived." Noting that he "didn't want to bad-mouth Snyder," whom he respected, Leach added that "we never had the combat support wired before Osborn went out. We had no tac air on call, and we didn't even have a good target list for our artillery fire support plan. I talked with Snyder about this, saying, 'Our mission is to defend, so let's do our reconnaissance, let's start patrolling at night and setting up ambushes along the hedgerows and along the creek bed because we know that's the way they're coming down.' Instead, Osborn was going right across the open, and my question was, 'Why in the hell are we doing this?'"

The mood in Alpha Annihilator was extremely uptight as the men saddled up. The squad leaders in Alpha Two had a heated debate about whose turn it was to be on point. Specialist Four Sydney W. Klemmer, who was in the squad that lost the argument, told his good friend Sergeant Bulte, who was in a different squad, "I don't like this. I don't like this at all. We *know* they're out there."

Bulte was angry. He was also very concerned for Klemmer. "Just keep your head down," he replied.

The sweep commenced at 1330 with Lieutenant Smith's Alpha Two on the left flank and Lieutenant Kimball's Alpha Three on the right. Captain Osborn moved in their trace, keeping his newest platoon leader, Lieutenant Simpson, in reserve with Alpha One. The well-spoken Osborn was a handsome Texan who had been awarded a Silver Star for the body count his company had run up when attached to the division cavalry squadron in the Que Son Valley. Despite such accolades from above, there were grave doubts about the captain in the rank and file. "Osborn blundered into stuff," was how the battalion operations officer put it. Osborn was, in fact, a quartermaster officer involuntarily detailed to the infantry. He had not asked to command a grunt company in combat, and young, inexperienced, and unsure of himself, his command style was harried and overbearing. He never listened, and he never seemed to learn from his mistakes. His troops hated him. His lieutenants resisted him. Lieutenant Smith had frequent shouting matches with Osborn over the radio and would "wind up doing the normal tricks," such as pretending that transmissions were garbled or giving short answers that failed to provide a clear picture of what was happening. In a letter to his wife, Smith wrote that Osborn "is not too swift. He gives me a case of the ass just about every day. It's bad enough fighting the elements without putting up with an Old Man that doesn't really know what he's doing."

"Alpha Company had a reputation in the battalion for always being on its ass, which was a goddamn shame because Osborn's soldiers were good kids," said Captain Leach. "They were just under bad leadership."

As the sweep kicked off across the paddies between Nhi Ha and

Xom Phuong, Lieutenant Smith shared a grimace with Lieutenant Kimball. "This is going to be fun," Smith said disgustedly. "This is going to be *crazy.*" The day was hot and bright, and their assault line was well spaced because of the openness of the terrain. Smith's left flank was bounded by Jones Creek and was relatively secure (Barracuda had moved a platoon up on the other side), but Kimball was extremely concerned about the tree line that paralleled their line of advance on the right. Both lieutenants were concerned about the tree line that ran across the far end of the paddy, shielding Xom Phuong, which lay some two hundred meters on the other side. The village cemetery was on the near side of the tree line. The paddies were dry and hard, full of golden, thigh-high rice that was ready for harvest.

Alpha Annihilator was still more than a hundred meters from the cemetery when someone spotted an NVA sprinting rearward from an individual burial mound ahead of the rest. The GIs blazed away at the man as Smith and Kimball, convinced that an ambush force was waiting in the tree line, quickened their pace toward the cover of the mounds. The running soldier had been a lure, however. As the assault line approached the mounds, an enemy machine gun opened fire on Alpha Three from an inconspicuous hole dug in the forward slope of one of them. The enemy gun crew was inside the earthen hump. Sergeant Stone's squad, deployed across Alpha Three's front, dropped along a paddy dike while the other two squads in column behind it found cover of their own. The platoon sergeant, Staff Sergeant Dale, was lying behind the dike to Stone's right. Dale shouted instructions to Specialist Henry, their machine gunner, who engaged the NVA bunker with his M60 while his assistant gunner, Private Melindez, fired two LAWs at the mound. Each time Melindez rose up to fire, Stone and his squad increased the volume of their covering fire.

Melindez put both LAWs right into the hole. The enemy fire ceased, then an NVA appeared, staggering toward the tree line behind the burial mounds. Everyone blasted away at him as Staff Sergeant Dale, just off the radio, shouted at Stone to assault the bunker with his squad. "Jesus Christ, this is looking right into the gun," Stone yelled back. He was very concerned that the bunker might still be occupied. "Call Cherokee back and tell him to send a squad from Second Platoon up to the bunker on the left flank! They're already over to that side!"

* * *

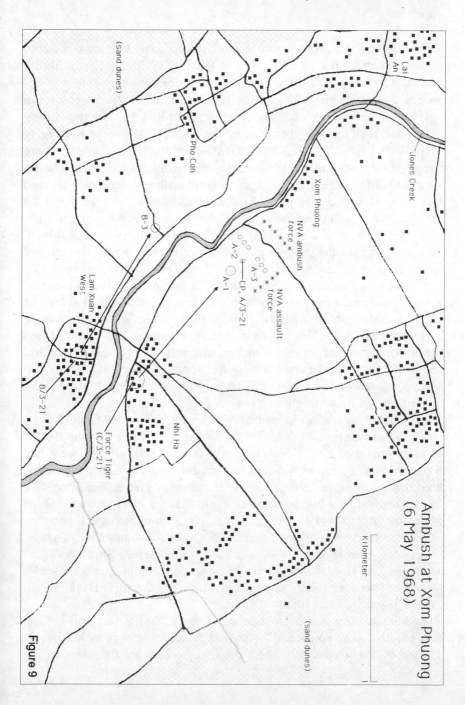

(sand dunes)

Lai
An

Jones Creek

Pho Con

Xom Phuong

NVA ambush
force

B-3

A-2
A-3
A-1
CP, A/3-21

NVA assault
force

Lam Xuan
West

B/3-21

Nhi Ha

Force Tiger
(C/3-21)

(sand dunes)

Kilometer

Ambush at Xom Phuong
(6 May 1968)

Figure 9

Surprisingly, Captain Osborn agreed. He instructed Lieutenant Smith to conduct the flanking maneuver in support of Alpha Three. Smith, who had halted Alpha Two when Alpha Three was engaged, was behind a dike with his RTO and the left flank squad. He moved up to Sgt. Thomas F. Crews's squad, which was deployed across their front, to lead the rush into the cluster of mounds ahead. At twenty-five, Terry Smith was known for such up-front leadership. He was a big, strong country boy from Galena, Illinois, who had grown up toting hay bales. He enlisted for OCS after graduating from college because he figured that the draft was bound to get him. He had been in Vietnam for three months. "As Smith would say, he'd rather be back home with his wife, seeing his baby son for the first time," a fellow lieutenant observed. "But he also said that he was paying his debt back to the country, and when the shit hit the wall he was right up there, front and center."

It was about a hundred feet to the next burial mound, and Lieutenant Smith sprinted toward it by himself. He wanted to see what kind of position and view the mounds would offer to their flanking maneuver.

Smith was shot before he could reach the mound. The round, which came from the right, caught Smith in the right thigh about two inches above the knee, and exited with a hot, painless flash that spun him around and knocked him down. The bullet hole was small, but the exit wound on his inner thigh was massive.

Lieutenant Smith lost his helmet but kept a grip on his CAR15 as he crawled past the mound to his left and sought cover behind the mound directly ahead of him. Smith was still trying to figure out what had happened to him when an NVA gun crew in the mound to his left, undetected until that moment, opened fire across his platoon's front. The firing hole was concealed by a big, battered rice pan that lay halfway up the slope of the mound. The NVA were firing right through the thatch pan.

Lieutenant Smith, stunned that the NVA would so desecrate a grave, was twenty feet from the bunker's blind side. Before Smith could do anything, Sp5 Terrance W. Allen, the gung-ho machine-gun team leader in Alpha Three, suddenly ran toward him from the right flank, shouting, "I'll get it, Lieutenant—I'll get it!"

Specialist Allen had a grenade in his hand. Smith, screaming, "Get down, get down, you idiot!" watched Allen, who was either overly excited or confused about where the firing hole was. He jumped right in front of the rice pan and was immediately blown backward by a burst across his stomach.

"No, no, *no!*" Smith roared.

Allen was moaning terribly as Lieutenant Smith, enraged, pulled a fragmentation grenade from his web gear, crawled to the side of the burial mound, reached around, and threw it in. He quickly rolled away. The grenade went off with a muffled boom. Smith always carried four grenades—two frags and two smokes—and he pulled the pin on his second frag, rolled over to the mound again, and tossed it inside. The bunker fell silent. Smith wanted Sergeant Crews's squad to take advantage of the situation and move up to his position so they could start their flanking maneuver. Smith urgently motioned to Crews.

"I wanted him to crawl, but damnit—damnit—they got up and did an assault, which totally blew my mind," recalled Smith. "Crews came across that damn killing zone with his squad, and they were firing every time their left foot hit the ground—just like they were taught in basic training. I couldn't believe they did that." Short, stocky Sergeant Crews, age twenty-five, who spoke with a slow Alabama drawl, was one of the platoon's old-timers and a good squad leader. "He misunderstood what I wanted him to do. I didn't have my radioman at that moment, and Crews didn't have a radio. It was mostly hand signals and shouting, and shouting was useless because of the noise."

Sergeant Crews was mortally wounded in the sudden eruption of fire from the other camouflaged, previously silent positions among the burial mounds. The rest of the squad members rushing forward with him over the cover of their dike were also dropped by the sudden wall of fire. Most were wounded, but Bulte's worried buddy Klemmer, along with Sp4s John A. Johnson and Richard F. Turpin, were either killed outright or mortally wounded. They went down right before Smith's eyes, even as he frantically screamed at them to get down and crawl. "If they had crawled forward we could have gotten in among the burial mounds and beaten those goddamn dinks," Smith recalled. "It was terrible. It was defeat. I felt like a failure. Before, I had really felt that I could go through the whole damn war and not get hurt. I was gung-ho and confident. I didn't take unusual chances. I used my head, I thought. I can't believe I let my men get in that position. I got them killed in a way that should never have happened."

*   *   *

Although Lieutenant Smith was awarded a BSMv for his bravery, he would never forgive himself for his perceived failure. Smith was alone among the enemy positions, except for the gut-shot, mortally wounded Allen, who was screaming, "Put a bandage on me, put a bandage on me!"

"Shut up, we'll get one on you," Smith answered. "Just shut up."

The NVA fire had grown in intensity from the right flank—Smith had no idea what was going on over there—and, in response, he could see one of his GIs behind a dike prepare to fire a LAW. The LAW malfunctioned. It would not fire. "Shit, this is useless," Smith muttered. He grabbed hold of the dying Allen and, pushing with his good leg, started back across the clearing on his belly. "We were in that field of fire. If you stuck your head up, you were dead." The NVA were lobbing in mortar rounds, 82mm stuff, and Smith took a fragment in his left leg. It was red-hot. He could feel it. His bladder was bursting, and he pissed in his pants. He didn't care. Someone crawled up to him, grabbed Allen by the shoulder straps of his web gear, and said he would take over. Smith kept crawling rearward by himself. "I absolutely went into shock. I thought I was stronger than that. I muttered to myself what a bad soldier I was—ineffective—I got too many people killed. I muttered all kinds of things. I totally lost control."

Staff Sergeant Dale of Alpha Three, a stunned witness to the massacre of Alpha Two on the left, kept Sergeant Stone and his men firing forward from the prone positions they had assumed along their paddy dike. Dale, a stocky, confident, twenty-six-year-old career NCO, was on his second tour, but he had been with Alpha Annihilator for only about two weeks. Dale's RTO, Specialist Woodward, kept shouting at him about the tree line that ran down the length of their exposed right flank. "Don't you think we need to put out some security? We need to put out some security. . . . You better put out some security!"

Specialist Woodward suddenly began shouting, "They're comin' up on the right! They're comin' up on the right!"

It was 1444. The figures coming out of the trees wore web gear and green fatigues, and some had steel helmets. They advanced at a trot in a loose, well-spaced skirmish line.

"Are those ARVN?" someone shouted.

The distinctive cracking of AK-47s was heard above the general roar. "Those are goddamn NVA!" someone else bellowed.

The result was pandemonium. Staff Sergeant Dale, given his orders by radio from Osborn—who was retreating with his command group at that moment—shouted for everyone to pull back and jumped up to run with most of the troopers along the dike. Sergeant Stone was not one of them. Half his squad had taken off with Dale, but Stone and one of his team leaders, Sp4 Ron Nahrstadt, ended up scurrying over a dike to their left that offered some protection from the overwhelming fire on the right. Moving low to the ground, they had yet to see any enemy soldiers. There was a lull in the fire. Stone rose up slightly to look back over the dike—and there was an NVA standing less than ten meters in front of him. The enemy soldier, who had an AK-47, wore a bush hat that sported a red star. He was looking down at one of Stone's men, Sp4 Allen A. Straus, who lay facedown and unmoving in one of the furrows of what had been a garden. Stone hadn't even known that Straus had been hit. He appeared to be dead. He was. His body was later recovered from that spot.

Lying prone behind the dike, Sergeant Stone quickly sighted his M16 on the NVA's chest and dropped him with a single shot.

Sergeant Stone, twenty-one, was a farmer's son from Kearney, Nebraska, who had been in Vietnam for more than seven months. He was an excellent squad leader. As soon as the first NVA went down, Stone saw a bareheaded NVA rise up from a position about twenty meters away and to the right of the first one. The enemy soldier was trying to spot him, but after Stone squeezed off another carefully aimed shot, the head went down and stayed down. A third NVA suddenly stood up. He was farther away, perhaps forty meters, and was in the open, looking around with his AK at the ready. Stone dropped him with a body shot. The NVA were too close for him to miss.

Specialist Nahrstadt's rifle jammed, and he shouted urgently, "Should I throw a grenade? Should I throw a grenade?"

"Yeah, throw a grenade, throw a grenade!"

Nahrstadt pitched one over the dike—and was spotted by two NVA who launched a running, shouting charge right at Stone and Nahrstadt. Dirt sprayed across Stone's face from rounds striking the dike, but he stayed calm, remained prone, and increased his rate of fire. One of the NVA went down. The other disappeared in the furrows that ran up to the dike in neat rows. Stone couldn't see any other GIs around them, and he shouted to Nahrstadt, "We gotta get outta here!"

"What about Alderson?" Nahrstadt asked.

"Where is he?" asked Stone, looking around anxiously.

Stone spotted Alderson—the twenty-five-year-old team leader in his squad who'd frozen up the first day in Nhi Ha because he was so uptight about his pregnant wife back in Texas. He was lying along their dike, just on the other side of Nahrstadt. Alderson, seriously wounded and unconscious, was barely breathing. Stone told Nahrstadt to take his M16. Nahrstadt answered, "It's jammed, too!"

"We gotta get outta here," Stone said again to Nahrstadt, indicating that they had no choice but to leave Alderson.

Alderson died there amid the rice stalks.

"You go—I'll cover ya!" Stone shouted, and Nahrstadt took off, the NVA firing at him as if in a shooting gallery. Nahrstadt hit the dirt, then it was Stone's turn. He made it the twenty or so meters to Nahrstadt before he too dropped down, losing his helmet in the process. Nahrstadt took off again. Stone retrieved his steel pot and ran up to where Nahrstadt had flung himself down. He lost his helmet again. He scooped it back up—he wasn't going to let go of it. This might just be the time it saves me, he thought. He was so shook, though, that he never thought to buckle the chin strap. Continuing to leapfrog toward the rear, Stone was firing cover for Nahrstadt's next move when he glimpsed his greenseed grenadier, Specialist Barnes, running in the same direction as they were. Barnes was closer to the NVA on the right, and he was yelling like crazy as he ran. Barnes suddenly went down as though he'd been hit. Stone, not seeing him reemerge from the rice, ran to where he thought Nahrstadt had ducked. Nahrstadt was not there. God, where's he at? Stone wondered. Well, I'm on my own now.

Nahrstadt made it to safety.

Barnes, unseen in the rice, was dying or already dead. Sergeant Stone, meanwhile, could see a machine gun atop a burial mound toward the rear, but not the face of the gunner. "Who are you?" he bellowed. "Who are you?" If there was an answer, he could not hear it over the roar of fire. All he could see was the gunner waving at him to come on in. Fearing that it was a trap, Stone cautiously worked his way closer. When he saw that the soldier behind the M60 was black, he let out a sigh. Well, that ain't no NVA, he thought. Moving past the M60 gunner, who was from Alpha Two, Stone found the CP group flattened behind the raised footpath on the left flank. Captain Osborn immediately asked him, "Where's Lieutenant Kimball—where is everybody?"

"I don't know," answered Sergeant Stone. "For all I know, they're all dead. They give the word to pull back, and when they said pull back, Sergeant Dale and them up and took off!"[2]

Captain Osborn was finally able to get Lieutenant Kimball on the radio. Kimball was still up on the right flank. He was trying to call for artillery when his transmission was cut off. Lieutenant Kimball and his RTO, Sp4 Curtis E. Bandy, had just been killed. Bill Kimball, a tall, handsome blond, had been in Vietnam for three months and had been wounded in the Que Son action. He was another OCS citizen-soldier—he had a wife waiting for him back in New Jersey—and a fun-loving extrovert who had been well thought of in his platoon. He had learned fast. He always listened to his grunts. Posthumous awards, especially for officers, seem to take on a life of their own, so Kimball's Silver Star citation may or may not be an accurate reconstruction of his last moments: ". . . Lieutenant Kimball courageously charged an enemy bunker, killing five enemy soldiers. He then proceeded to another position when he became wounded in the right arm. . . . While his men were maneuvering back, he courageously remained in an exposed position, placing accurate devastating fire on the enemy. . . . While performing this unselfish act, Lieutenant Kimball was mortally wounded . . ."

Alpha Three, completely disorganized, still had men pinned down on the right flank, including Sp4 Bill Eakins, who, although wounded in the back, had tackled a panicked soldier and calmed him down in a crater. Also stranded was Sp4 Thomas E. Hemphill, a grenadier who had jumped in another crater with one of the replacements. The enemy fire was ringing right over their heads. The new man, who was petrified, kept asking what he should do. Hemphill, a country boy with a Georgia accent, told him to keep his head down, adding, "but if anybody comes over that hole, you shoot the sorry thang!" Hemphill, keeping

2. Sergeant Stone received the BSMv for Nhi Ha. He also got an Army Commendation Medal for Valor (ARCOMv) for Hiep Duc (January 1968), and another BSMv and the Purple Heart for the Que Sons (March 1968).

his own head down, lobbed about fifteen M79 rounds toward the tree line on the right. There was a lull then, and he heard movement in the next crater over. He hollered to ask who it was. Luckily, it was some of his buddies, so Hemphill and his greenseed scrambled into the position with them. One of Hemphill's best friends, David Betebenner, was among those in the crater. His steel pot had a hole in it. He'd been shot in the head and was unconscious and barely breathing. Betebenner, a soft-spoken, deeply religious man, had been up firing his M16 when he'd been hit. "It upset me real bad," Hemphill remembered. "I cried for a minute—I did. He was a good friend of mine. He was a good old fella. He had a little girl. . . ."

No one knew what had happened to the rest of the platoon. They decided they had to pull back to the left. After throwing a smoke grenade in that direction, they ran through the colored smoke as cover and made it back to the black machine gunner on the mound. David Betebenner was dead when they moved out. They left his body in the crater. "I closed myself out to any new people that come in then," said Hemphill. "You were friendly to 'em and helped 'em out, but I never got close to 'em. You didn't want to get close to somebody who could get killed. It was like losing a brother."

Staff Sergeant Dale was shot in the back during the retreat. He went down with a gaping exit wound in his chest, and two grunts dragged him to safety. The NVA swarming through Alpha Three came on toward Sergeant Bulte and his squad on Alpha Two's right flank. The enemy soldiers screamed and popped up to fire AK-47 bursts to cover one another as they advanced from crater to crater. Bulte's squad was not returning fire. The grunts were as low as they could get behind their own paddy dike. The air was electric with enemy fire. They didn't know what to do. Bulte shouted at his men to pull back to the raised footpath on the left flank, and by the time he himself made it to the safer side of the footpath he had lost touch with everyone in his squad except his radioman and one of his riflemen.

"My guys were absolutely scared to death," Bulte recalled. "They were just running for their lives. It was complete havoc. It was out of control."

Clambering over the footpath, Sergeant Bulte swung his M16 back the way he had come—and was horrified to see Doc Richards of Alpha Three lying out there near a group of enemy soldiers. One leg was almost completely blown off below the knee, and he was waving an arm and shrieking, "Please, please help me . . . save me . . . help me . . ." Sergeant Bulte, a quiet, intelligent twenty-three year old, dropped all his gear except his M16 and a bandolier of ammunition and, when there was a lull in the fire, he rushed back over the footpath, weaving his way toward Doc Richards in a low crouch. Bulte dropped beside Richards just as the NVA began firing at him. When the roar eased off, he grabbed the medic by the back of his pistol belt and carried him like a suitcase. He'd made it only ten to fifteen meters before they started taking more fire. Bulte was too tired to move Richards any farther. He needed help. He told the medic that he was going to run back and get some of the men who were covering them.

Sergeant Bulte didn't believe he could make it back again. Doc Richards saw the doubt in his eyes. "Don't leave me!" he pleaded. "Don't leave me! Will you come back for me?" Bulte felt guilty as he promised Richards that, yes, he would come back. Bulte ran to the raised footpath. He didn't know most of the GIs there—they weren't in his squad—but when he argued, "C'mon, we can get this guy out of there," two of them—Sp4 W. R. May and Pfc. J. W. Bell—agreed to give it a try. When there was another lull in the NVA fire, they made their move. On the way back, Bell brought up the rear, providing covering fire while Bulte and May dragged Richards by his arms and legs. They were moving fast and as the medic's mangled leg bounced on the ground he screamed in agony. "Oh my God, it was a bloodcurdling scream," recalled Bulte. "It was horrible."

Doc Richards survived the ordeal.

Piling back over the footpath, Sergeant Bulte—who got the Silver Star for his part in the rescue—made radio contact with Lieutenant Stull in the command group. Stull couldn't see the NVA from where he was, but Bulte could. He relayed adjustments so the FO could call for smoke rounds on Alpha Three's former pos to cover their withdrawal, and HE rounds on almost the same ground to slow down the NVA. The enemy troops were forced to seek cover, but Stull and Bulte would always wonder if their fires might have hit some of their comrades stranded out there. The NVA, meanwhile, were working the area over with 82mm fire. Lieutenant Stull—who was also awarded a Silver Star for his actions that day—happened to look up and see two shells descending on the small crater his team occupied. He dropped down, and seconds later one shell hit the near edge of the crater and the other the far edge. Stull had his helmet and flak jacket on, but some metal fragments the size of shotgun pellets dinged him in the groin and under one arm. A bigger piece slashed across an ankle, ripping the canvas jungle boot and drawing blood. It felt like a sprain.

At 1540, the NVA attempted to envelop the pinned-down company on its left, where Sgt. Larry Haddock of Alpha Two had his squad deployed along Jones Creek. Haddock, a stocky, blond-haired twenty-three year old, was one of sixteen children to an Oklahoma oil-field worker. He was a taciturn, fieldwise soldier. Haddock had directed his men into the streambed, and they were returning fire over the shallow embankment when he noticed movement to their rear. Turning, Haddock saw a line of hunched-over figures approaching through the tall brush on the other side of Jones Creek. For a split second he thought they were friendlies. The point man of the column was tentatively waving to him—apparently the NVA were also confused as to who was where—when Haddock recognized the NVA-issue camouflage nets on the pith helmets the soldiers wore. Haddock shouted a warning, and his grenadier and good friend Sp4 Larry R. McFaddin—a Kentuckian who took everything in stride—wheeled around and fired his M79. The round scored a direct hit on the pith helmet of one of the enemy soldiers, blowing him away. The rest of the squad, which actually had no cover to the rear in the sandy creek bed, desperately mowed the grass across the stream with automatic-weapons fire.

The NVA disappeared.

Other enemy soldiers, meanwhile, gave a wide berth to Sergeant Haddock's squad as they worked their way down Jones Creek to a position opposite Captain Osborn's command group. Specialist Bill Karp, the senior medic, was sitting with his back against the raised footpath when he saw two figures coming their way across the stream. The figures, in a low-to-the-ground crouch, were moving with some purpose. Karp shouldered his M16, sighted in, and pumped off half a magazine.

The two figures fell, either hit or seeking cover.

Thinking that the Barracuda platoon securing the flank on the other side of Jones Creek was farther north than it actually was, Captain

Osborn shouted at Karp, "Stop, don't fire over there—B Company is over there!"

Awww shit, Karp thought, I just got two of our guys. He had not. As Alpha Company's wounded straggled back, Karp, who was half-deaf and had a ringing headache from his own close encounter with a mortar shell—as well as a superficial fragment wound in his right arm—treated them with battle dressings and words of encouragement. Karp, a quiet twenty-three-year-old college dropout and draftee, was from Alice, Texas. One of the grunts he treated had lost an ear—presumably to a tracer round, because the wound was cauterized and barely bled. Karp secured a big bandage around the man's head, and would have left it at that had the man's buddy not said, "Doc, you think you ought to check him for anything else?" Karp had not because he had seen neither blood nor tears on the man's fatigues. He felt pretty stupid when he lifted up the back of the casualty's shirt and saw that the round that had removed his ear had traveled down his back just under the skin. There was a bullet hole in the muscle at the top of his shoulder, and the exit wound was down at his waist. As Karp tied more bandages and tried to maintain a conversation that would not betray to the man how badly injured he was, the one-eared, semishocked grunt kept trying to get up to see what was going on. Karp, working from his hands and knees, kept pushing the man back down and saying gently, "Just hold still now."

While a Helix FAC helped adjust artillery to cover their move, a completely traumatized Captain Osborn—who was, ironically, awarded another Silver Star for his supposed leadership during this fiasco—instructed Alpha Annihilator to withdraw to Force Tiger. The word was passed by radio and by shouts. With exceptions such as Specialist Karp, who moved his casualties back as a group,[3] the withdrawal was a strung-out, every-man-for-himself affair. Some GIs dropped their weapons and gear to run faster, and were crying hysterically by the time they made it back. Sergeant Haddock was another exception. His squad along the streambed was the last to pull back, and Haddock sent his men

---

3. Specialist Karp was awarded a BSMv for the Hiep Duc ambush, another BSMv and the Purple Heart for Nhi Ha, and an end-of-tour ARCOM.

rearward one, two, or three at a time while the rest provided covering fire. Haddock went with the last group, his M16 in one hand and a radio in the other. They had to jump up and down as the mortars kept crashing in, and Haddock, exhausted, finally let go of the twenty-five pound radio. One of the shells exploded within a half-dozen meters of Specialist Hannan, and although it did not even scratch him, it did bowl him over. When Hannan regained his senses, he saw Haddock kneeling beside him and firing his M16 at the burial mounds. Haddock looked at him. "You okay, kid?" he asked.

"I think so," Hannan answered as he sat up and shook off the shock.

"Okay," Haddock said. "Let's get outta here. . . ."

The NVA, bursting with victorious enthusiasm, were on top of their bunkers, shouting and shooting and not caring who saw them. Officially, fifty NVA had been killed, but no grunt bought that. Alpha Annihilator had twelve KIA. "I can't believe those great guys are dead," Specialist Hannan wrote in a letter home. "Somehow I'm still alive. I'll never know how in God's name I made it out. Men were left on the battlefield wounded and crying. . . ."[4]

At 1650, two fighters finally began running air strikes on the enemy positions. Meanwhile, the C&C Huey was bouncing in and out of Force Tiger to evacuate the wounded—nineteen altogether—to the 3d Medical Battalion, 3d Marine Division, at the Dong Ha Combat Base. One of the casualties was mortally wounded Staff Sergeant Dale of Alpha Three, who had a piece of plastic secured over his sucking chest wound. Lieutenant Smith and another wounded GI, loaded aboard on either side of Dale, took turns administering mouth-to-mouth during the flight. Carried off the chopper pad on stretchers, Smith and Dale ended up side by side in the triage facility, and Smith screamed

---

4. Several of Alpha's KIAs were not killed instantly. They died alone after dark, abandoned in the rice paddies with immobilizing wounds. "It was really a spooky, sad, terrible moment," said Sergeant Bulte. "There were guys willing to go back out there that night to look for our missing. We had guys actually volunteer, but somebody at the company or battalion level decided it was too dangerous. Why get any more men killed to try and get maybe one or two men back? They had a point, but if that was me out there and I was begging for help and no one would come out and get me—how would I feel?"

frantically at the corpsmen, "Give him mouth-to-mouth, give him mouth-to-mouth!" A Navy doctor bent over Dale with his stethoscope, then quickly moved to the next casualty. Smith, in shock, thought the doctor was abandoning Dale as hopeless. He screamed bloody murder as he tried to get up from his stretcher. Corpsmen held Smith down as they used long, blunt-tipped scissors to cut off his bloody fatigues and jungle boots. "I was mad as hell," said Smith. "I don't know if they gave me anything to quiet me down. They probably did. Your mind is going in a million different directions at a million miles an hour. Everything's coming to a head—it's like a fuse blowing."

Pinned down in a crater, Sgt. Charles F. Desmond and Sp4 Bill A. Baird of Alpha Two were among those left behind. Both were greenseeds. Baird had been wounded in the opening moments of the engagement, presumably by an enemy-issue claymore set up at the edge of the burial mounds. The explosion had shattered his tailbone—he could neither move nor feel his legs—and shredded his jungle boots, blowing off four of his toes. Both legs were bloody and mangled. Not understanding what had happened to him, Baird, who had lost his helmet, kept firing his M16 even as he faded in and out of consciousness. He expended almost all of his ammo. When his weapon finally jammed, he started pitching hand grenades, determined to survive.

Meanwhile, Sergeant Desmond was beginning to understand that the company had pulled back without them. He shouted at two GIs with steel pots and green fatigues who were half-concealed in the tall rice to his left—but when they turned toward him, he realized that they were actually NVA.

Terrified, Desmond dropped them both with his M16.

It was dusk by then, and no one else was firing. When it got completely dark, Desmond could see the silhouettes of NVA moving across the paddies, checking bodies and recovering weapons. Desmond removed all of his gear, keeping only his M16 and two magazines. He whispered to the semidelirious Baird that he was going to try to get some help. With that, Desmond, a black NCO, climbed out of the crater and, presumably hoping that his dark skin would cause him to be mistaken for another NVA, he started walking toward the stream he knew was on the left flank. The NVA were so close he could hear them talking, but he made it to the stream without being noticed despite the illumination rounds going up. Desmond slid into the concealing water and hugged the bank. He was so scared that he was shaking all over, rippling the water around him. He thought the shimmering movement would give him away, so he kept telling himself, "If you want to live, stop shaking."

Sergeant Desmond had been in Vietnam all of two weeks.

Specialist Baird never forgave Desmond for leaving him, which was understandable but unfair. If Desmond had tried to carry Baird, they would have been an obvious target. The eighteen-year-old Baird was an unschooled country boy from Holmsville, Ohio, best known for his good humor and unmotivated approach to soldiering during his two months in the 'Nam. Immobilized and alone, Baird groggily hoped that the shadows moving and stopping around him were friendlies looking for survivors. Then he heard their singsong Vietnamese voices, and four or five NVA almost tripped over him in the dark. The closest one let out a surprised shout as he swung his AK-47 around and squeezed off a quick shot. The round hit Baird's left ear and exited cleanly through his neck just below the hairline. His head was ringing as he desperately screamed, "*Chieu hoi!*"

The NVA rushed up to Baird. When they saw that he was grievously wounded and posed no threat, one of them secured a bandage around his head while explaining in English that the reason they had shot him was because "you Americans are tricky, and we thought you might get away." The NVA took his dog tags, web gear, and jammed M16, then lifted him onto a poncho. They worked with speed and urgency. They wanted to get out of the flarelight and back to their positions. The NVA litter team stopped in a hamlet—probably Xom Phuong—where other enemy soldiers crowded around Baird. "Jesus Christ," he muttered to himself. "You mean all these sons of bitches was out there?" The NVA gave him a few puffs on a cigaret, a sip of hot water, and a mouthful or two of rice. He started to black out again, but they poked and prodded him, all the while jabbering, "*My, my, my*"—which he was later told was Vietnamese for American. A fresh team of NVA picked up his poncho litter and moved off toward the DMZ. As the NVA carried him through the night, Baird—who was destined to spend the next five years in prison camps known as the Plantation, the Portholes, and the Hanoi Hilton—found himself thinking back to his first week at the Americal Division base camp in Chu Lai. Everything had seemed so secure then. He had lain on an air mattress feeling a mellow buzz from a combination of warm beer and his first joint, and had looked at the beautiful beach and thought, Shit, there ain't no goddamn war. . . .

During the night, between enemy mortar and artillery attacks, the LPs deployed by C/3-21 in Nhi Ha and D/3-21 in Lam Xuan East made at least seven sightings of squad- and platoon-sized groups of NVA. One enemy soldier wearing a gas mask darted close enough to Charlie Tiger's perimeter to heave in a tear-gas grenade. Captain Leach called his LPs on an hourly basis, and at 0518 on Tuesday, 7 May 1968, the LP leader on the right flank rendered his sitrep in what began as a fatigued monotone, "Well, we've been observing maybe fifteen, twenty gooks for the past half-hour, runnin' around in the paddies—hey, wait a minute—there's a motherfuckin' tank!"

"A what? A what? A what?" Leach shot back.

"A motherfuckin' tank!" the LP leader answered with awe in his voice. He reported that the tank was headed southwest at a range of about two hundred meters before it disappeared behind a tree line. Then he said, "Can we come in? We want to come in. We want to come in." Captain Leach denied permission—"Keep observing, see where he goes and what he does"—then contacted battalion, which contacted the 3d Marines to determine if any USMC tanks or amtracs were in the area. None were. Leach knew that the NVA had used Soviet PT-76 light amphibious tanks with 76mm main guns near Khe Sanh during the Tet Offensive. He was persuaded that an NVA tank really was out there, especially when the ARVN advisers at Alpha 1 reported shortly thereafter that they too could hear what might be a tank. Artillery and air strikes were called in, although the USAF flareship and USMC aerial observer overhead never could see a definite target. Regardless, it was an unnerving episode. "We could hear the tread going *clank-clank-clank*," said Sergeant Coulthard, "and everybody was panicking because we'd already fired all our LAWs." Coulthard, however, could not hear a tank engine, and when he investigated with his M16-mounted night scope he, for one, concluded that the whole incident was the result of strained nerves and overactive imaginations. "With the starlight, we could see that the wind had come up and was dragging flare canisters across the dry paddies by their attached parachutes," he explained. "You could hear them going *clank-clank-clank*. The sound really carried at night. We laughed about it—we was just kind of relieved—but other guys said, 'No, it sure the hell ain't flares, there's some tanks out there,' so who knows. But I never could see it."

Informed of the disaster that Alpha Annihilator had walked into, the company exec, 1st Lt. Robert V. Gibbs, helicoptered up from Chu Lai in the morning. Gibbs, a blunt, no-nonsense character, questioned Sergeant Stone, whom he knew to be one of the company's best squad leaders. Gibbs wanted to know the status of their missing. When Stone said that the men were still out there, Gibbs shouted, "Whaddya mean they're still out there? What the fuck are you talking about, you sonofabitch?" Stone was in tears. Gibbs stomped over to Captain Osborn's position and barked, "How the fuck could you leave our guys out there?"

Osborn shouted back, "Look, I'm the company commander—and we had to!"

"Christ," replied Gibbs. "Well, when the hell are we going back out to get 'em? They could still be alive out there."

Inexplicably, no recovery mission was launched that day. Instead, the Gimlets improved their positions at Force Tiger and prepped Xom Phuong with artillery. Two missing men who were able to stumble back did so on their own, including Sergeant Desmond of Alpha Two, who came across the rice paddies waving his arms and hollering, "Alpha Gimlets!" Grunts crowded happily around him, and Desmond, relieved beyond words, could not suppress an ear-to-ear grin. Desmond was awarded the Silver Star. The greenseed sergeant also got out of the field after his traumatic experience. The battalion surgeon said that he had combat fatigue—"He did well until he got back, then he kind of fell apart."

The enemy shelled them during the day, then in the late afternoon an NVA column of approximately two hundred soldiers was spotted moving south along Jones Creek at a point some sixteen hundred meters northwest of Force Tiger. "The dumbshits were coming down in the open in broad daylight," said Captain Leach, who instructed the 106mm recoilless rifles and the three USMC tanks attached to his task force to open fire. The tanks cut loose with .50-caliber machine guns and 90mm main guns, and the NVA disappeared into the tree lines along Jones Creek. Four artillery batteries fired into the area while Leach made contact with one of the cruisers offshore, which then provided eight-inch fire. "Naval gunfire was blowing the shit out of that area," remarked Leach. "They just put it right on top of 'em, so I'm talking to the ship and I'm really gettin' 'em fired up. I'm saying, 'Jesus Christ, you're *killin'* 'em! Keep going, keep going!' and they're going crazy out there on the ship. This was right down their alley. They loved it."

Seventy NVA were reported killed in the turkey shoot.

During the night, four more enemy tanks were reported in the area. At about 1300 on Wednesday, 8 May, following another prep by air and arty, Alpha Annihilator, reinforced by a platoon from Charlie Tiger, finally advanced on Xom Phuong to recover the casualties left behind two days before. The three Marine tanks accompanied the assault line to neutralize the tree line on the right flank, while a Barracuda platoon advanced on the other side of Jones Creek screening the left. The arty was lifted at the last possible moment, then the lead platoon, on line between the tanks, reconned by fire when they were halfway to the burial mounds.

"Still got AK-47 fire with all the firepower we dished out," an incredulous grunt wrote in his diary.

Lieutenant Gibbs, seeing that some of the company's uptight survivors were ready to bolt, screamed at them to hold their ground. While the rest of Alpha Annihilator provided covering fire, Alpha Two carried out the sorry task of loading the dead aboard the two USMC Otters that had come forward with them. The grunts in the platoon were nervous because they could not hear over the engine noise, and everyone worked fast so the NVA would have little time to get their range and shell them. They found their dead where they had left them, although the bodies were barely recognizable after two days in the baking sun—with the exception of one body, which was still white, indicating that the man had only recently died of his wounds. All the rest of the corpses were bloated, black, and maggot-filled. The bodies with the worst wounds were literally falling apart. The fluid under their skin made them look watery. The stench was gagging. It was unbearable work. When GIs pulled at the bodies, the skin came away in their hands like blistering paint. Sergeant Bulte found his buddy, Sydney Klemmer, lying face-down. He recognized Klemmer's strawberry blond hair. Bulte felt that he had to be the one who brought his friend back, but he was afraid to turn him over. When he did he saw Klemmer's distorted face—half of it was swollen and purple—and the multiple wounds. "Those casualties were so unnecessary," Bulte said. "It was such a waste." For Bulte, the good soldier, the war that he had always kept at an emotional distance suddenly became very personal. He lost his enthusiasm. He was just going to get through this and go home. "It was pointless—stupid—what we did. It was such a dumb move. There was a bad undercurrent in the whole company."

When they returned to Force Tiger, Sergeant Bulte, traumatized and distraught, walked past Lieutenant Colonel Snyder, who seemed to him to be blank-faced with shock. Not because Bulte held Snyder solely to blame—he didn't—but because he was so angry and he felt he owed it to Klemmer, Bulte looked the colonel in the eye and shouted, "We were fucking guinea pigs out there! What was the point of sending us out there? A lot of good people died for nothing!"

Lieutenant Colonel Snyder offered no response. The Otters parked outside Alpha's side of the Force Tiger perimeter and dropped their ramps. The hot stench inside the vehicles was thick for those men who climbed in to pull out the bodies so that they could be identified and medevac tags tied to them. Two gas masks were made available. Men had to be ordered to handle the bodies. "We just flopped 'em out," said Specialist Hannan. He grabbed ahold of one corpse by the hair and the seat of the pants, but the maggot-eaten scalp pulled off as he lifted up. "I almost cracked," said Hannan. Captain Leach, furious at whoever had ordered the dead to be unloaded where all the shaken survivors could see them, instructed the detail to load the bodies back aboard and told the Otter drivers to get back to battalion with their cargo. "I looked in the Otters and blood was dripping out of them, and here are these dead American kids just stacked up inside," sighed Leach. "It was just terrible. You talk about morale going down. . . ."

CHAPTER 19 TURNING THE TABLES

When the NVA worked over Nhi Ha with 152mm fire, as they did several times a day in nine-gun salvos, Alpha 1 provided early warning by radio to the 3-21st Infantry. From Alpha 1, the muzzle flashes could be seen along the the ridgelines on the North Vietnamese side of the DMZ. In addition, radar able to lock onto the enemy firing positions ensured that counterbattery bombardments, usually from the cruisers offshore, were almost immediate. The NVA, although too well entrenched to be put out of action by anything less than a direct hit, refused to pinpoint themselves further with a second salvo, so the counterbattery fires bought time for the men on the ground. Friendly casualties were few. One of the wounded, however, was no less than Captain Leach, commander of the two-company task force in the village. Leach was up doing something when one of his RTOs began yelling that Alpha 1 had reported incoming. As Leach ran for cover, one of the rounds exploded behind him. The concussion picked Leach up and sent him headfirst into the rubble of a demolished house. Because the shell had sunk perhaps a foot into the soft soil before detonating, Leach's only injuries were cuts on the top of his head.

The shellings, which jangled nerves and kept everybody with one ear cocked to the north, also produced some memorable near misses. Lieutenant Hieb of Charlie One had to chew out his RTO because the man didn't want to wear his flak jacket. When he did wear it, he left it hanging open because it was so hot. "I want it on and I want it zipped," Hieb finally told him. After some moaning and groaning, the radioman did as he was told. Shortly thereafter, during another barrage, Hieb and his RTO jumped into the same foxhole. As they talked, Hieb noticed a big shell fragment lodged in the zipper of the GI's zipped-up flak jacket. When Hieb pointed it out, the RTO managed a weak grin. Hieb later remarked that "after that I never had to tell him to put his flak vest on. It was the only thing that saved him."

With Force Tiger situated astride the NVA infiltration routes along Jones Creek, Captain Leach said, "I knew goddamn well we were going to be hit. It was just a matter of time." Because Lieutenant Colonel Snyder felt that the situation "was perfectly within Leach's capabilities as a very able and tough-minded infantryman," he did not move his battalion command post forward to Nhi Ha. The decision to remain back at Mai Xa Chanh East was, Snyder said, "a matter of personal debate for me," but such a rearward location gave him the freest access to the 3d Marines, upon whom they depended for support. In this instance, Snyder needed bunker material, extra ammunition, and firepower. He got what he needed, thanks to Colonel Hull. As Snyder put it, Hull "raised holy hell" whenever his attached Army battalion did not get what it requested through the Marines' support system. "Colonel Hull was a rough cob in some ways, but he was a gentleman of the old school. Since I was now his guy, he was determined that I was going to get my fair share of what resources they had," said Snyder.

The 3d Marines provided the three tanks, as well as four 3.5-inch rocket-launcher teams from BLT 2/4, which would be lethal in the event of an enemy armor attack. The rocket launchers were also effective against ground troops. One team went to Alpha Company and two to Charlie; the fourth was attached to Bravo in Lam Xuan West. The Marines were stunned by how well equipped their Army counterparts were. Each soldier had at least thirty loaded magazines in his defensive position. One Marine joked with the GIs that "a good Marine doesn't need more than seven magazines, at least that's what they say." After the Army grunts shared what they had, the Marine offered to buy some of their claymore mines. Specialist Hannan answered, "I'm not going to sell a Marine a claymore. I'll give it to you. How many do you want?" The Marine grinned and said, "You guys do things *right*. If I ever get out of here, I'm going to talk to my congressman!"

The Marines and GIs went into action together after dark on Thursday, 9 May 1968, when elements of the 76th Regiment, 304th NVA Division, crossed the DMZ with the mission of overrunning Force Tiger. The NVA, moving south along Jones Creek, first had to run the gauntlet of firepower brought to bear by Alpha 1. This was the tenth night in a row that the NVA had attempted to slip past Alpha 1, and one of the ARVN advisers at the outpost, 1st Lt. Travis Kirkland, wrote in his diary, "No sleep is the order of the day." By then, the personnel at Alpha 1 had developed a routine with which they orchestrated the massive amount of firepower available to them. They used a new type of artillery ammunition that the GIs called Popcorn to start the show, usually with a six-gun salvo. Each round contained approximately 150 golfball-sized bomblets that showered down when a charge split the shell casing in midair. The bomblets, equipped with stabilizer fins to ensure that each landed on its detonator, would bounce up several feet before exploding. The night observation devices at Alpha 1 provided a clear enough view for spotters to see which NVA had packs on. When the first Popcorn shell popped overhead and released its bomblets, the spotters could see the NVA pause in midstep at what must have sounded to them like an illumination round. Instead of a burst of light, however, the enemy was in for a lethal surprise. The nine hundred bomblets in a six-gun salvo, exploding a few at a time at first, quickly reached a shattering crescendo. The screams of the wounded and dying NVA could be heard on Alpha 1.

When the NVA sought cover in the tree lines along Jones Creek, the artillery fire ceased and a USAF AC-47 Spooky gunship lit up the area with multiple flares, then hosed down the woods with six-thousand-round-a-minute miniguns that drove the NVA back into the open paddies where the artillery could harvest them. Killing in such ways and at such distances turned the NVA into dehumanized targets. Once, after a particularly effective pass by Spooky, Lieutenant Kirkland shouted into his radio, "Do it again, do it again! I can hear 'em yellin'!" and got in response, "Do it again—that's what my wife told me when I went to Honolulu on R and R."

Lieutenant Colonel Snyder, incredulous that the NVA commanders would subject their units to this firepower night after night, remarked that the result was "absolute slaughter." Once the NVA had been forced out of the tree lines, Spooky would orbit over the ocean to allow the artillery a free hand. The artillery shot as if without counting, although it sometimes had to cease fire because in the hot, humid night air the smoke from parachute flares and white phosphorus shells became so dense that it concealed the enemy. Lieutenant Kirkland commented that the awesome volume of firepower "would literally light up the sky. I'm told that during this period we controlled more artillery from Alpha 1 than was being fired in the rest of South Vietnam."

The courage of the NVA running this gauntlet was stunning. Most of them made it somehow on 9 May, and at 2108 a Charlie Company LP reported seeing ten to fifteen NVA coming across the paddies toward Force Tiger. The uptight GIs on LP duty were little more than a stone's throw beyond the perimeter. The NVA were two hundred meters away to the northeast. Other NVA appeared to the north. Artillery was fired and the enemy ran northwest. At 2156, another Charlie Tiger LP engaged a squad of NVA with M79 fire as it moved in from the northwest. Two NVA were seen to fall. The enemy had yet to open fire. Their movements appeared to cease as Charlie Company continued placing M79 fire on them, along with the arty. Flares popped overhead, one after the other, to reveal in harsh, black-and-white relief an empty, cratered landscape of burial mounds and fallow rice paddies.

The sightings began again at 2337. This time there were a hundred NVA in view as they maneuvered in from the north, northeast, and northwest, darting from burial mound to burial mound with artillery blasting them.

The movement, whether a probe or the preparation for a major attack, ceased at this point. It began again at 0016 on Friday, 10 May, when another hundred NVA were spotted within 150 meters of Force Tiger. This is it, Captain Leach thought. She's going down tonight. The NVA began lobbing RPGs toward the perimeter. Leach requested gunships and flareships, and instructed his LPs to return as the rate of artillery-delivered HE and illum increased. By then, Captain Osborn's Alpha Company GIs, deployed along the southern half of the perimeter, could see more NVA crossing the footbridge that spanned Jones Creek and connected Lam Xuan West and Nhi Ha. Leach had not expected an attack from that direction because of Bravo's presence in Lam Xuan West. Because he had no faith in Osborn, Leach positioned him to the south where he would be out of the way. The NVA, however, were coming from both directions. Osborn's LPs soon reported the movement of fire-team–sized groups of NVA, then requested to pull back to the perimeter. When Osborn denied them permission to withdraw, the whispered radio messages from the listening posts grew desperate. "There's gooks all over out here in front of us. . . . They're right in front of us. . . . They're *beside* us—they're going to get us! Request permission to return to the perimeter!"

"Permission denied. Stay out and observe."

"We need to pull back!"

"You stay out there," Captain Osborn said in his best unthinking, I'm-the-boss voice. "If you come in, I'll shoot you myself."

Lieutenant Gibbs, who was the most experienced officer in the company—he had taken charge of Alpha Two—came up on the net and shouted, "What the fuck? You think the LPs should all get killed? This is *it,* they're comin'! Let 'em come back! What the fuck's the difference—the NVA are here!"

Shouting himself, Captain Osborn said they could not be sure that it was not merely a probe. Gibbs moved from his bunker to confront Osborn. After a heated, face-to-face exchange, Osborn finally relented. Lieutenant Stull, the company's forward observer, who had been working arty on the NVA at the direction of the terrified LPs, came up with a plan to help them slip back. Stull passed the word that on the signal of a star-cluster flare, an eight-inch WP artillery round fused to detonate at two hundred meters above the ground would be fired. Everyone on the perimeter was to close their eyes, duck their heads, and count to fifteen when the flare went up. The idea was that the blazing white phosphorus airburst that was to follow the flare would momentarily rob the NVA of their night vision and allow the LPs to run back in. The plan mostly worked. Except for the men from two LPs, who were shot at when they made their move, the rest were able to sprint to safety. One of the LPs that drew fire, under Specialist Hannan of Alpha Two, scrambled into a crater and, undetected, sweated out the night there as fire from both sides crisscrossed in the darkness right above their heads.

The other unlucky LP was from Alpha One. Its leader, Sp4 Carl F. Green, twenty, of Shady, New York, was killed by an RPG while up and moving. Two of his men, wounded by fragments, were able to crawl in.

Meanwhile, two GIs with the LP from Charlie Two were wounded as they came in, while the leader of another LP reported to Captain Leach that they could not move because there were NVA between themselves and their lines. Leach responded, "Well, okay, then get yourself in a fucking hole." When radio communications with the LP were lost shortly thereafter, Leach suspected that either the NVA had stumbled across their hiding place or friendly fire had taken them out. At 0103, Spooky 1-2 came on station to add the ripping roar of its miniguns to the cacophony of mortar and artillery fire. The amount of illumination over the battlefield was massive. The NVA, who were mostly behind burial mounds, got bogged down, although they continued to fire RPGs and throw Chicoms. The enemy did not expose themselves by firing their AK-47s. Leach had his troops hold off with M16s and M60s and return fire with only mortars, LAWs, and M79s. The lull in visible enemy movement lasted four hours. Presumably, the NVA were using the time to bring additional units into preattack positions as each cleared the Alpha 1 gauntlet. Leach, dug in behind his central platoon, Charlie One, was on the horn without pause, placing arty on enemy avenues of approach while maintaining fire on the troops already hunkered down in front of them. "We don't know where the main attack's going to come, so don't give your positions away," Leach told his platoon leaders. "Don't fire from your bunkers. Move out in the trenches. Fire your M79s and LAWs and then move to a new position."

The noisy lull ended at 0535 when the NVA initiated an intense mortar and artillery bombardment of Force Tiger. Lam Xuan West and Mai Xa Chanh East were also shelled. Captain Leach was still awake. Except for two hours of sleep each day before sundown, he had been on his feet for almost four days. Leach was kept going not only by adrenaline, but by a bottle of military-issue amphetamines delivered by Snyder and the battalion surgeon, Captain Hildebrand, when they helicoptered forward for a visit soon after Nhi Ha had been secured. The amphetamines were for Leach and his platoon leaders. They gave Leach's voice a quick, irritable edge as, in response to the enemy barrage, he keyed his handset to speak with Cedar Mountain 6. "As soon as this shit lifts, you know what's going to happen," Leach said. "You better get Delta Company moving right now. You better get 'em up here because we've got a battalion of dinks out there who are getting ready to hit us."

Lieutenant Colonel Snyder told Delta, his reserve company in Lam Xuan East, to be prepared to move north to Force Tiger on order. Meanwhile, Leach's artillery spotter, Lieutenant Jaquez, realized that

their 81mm mortar section was not returning fire. During the afternoon, Jaquez had preregistered their fires on a brushy little island in
the paddies that seemed a natural rallying point for the enemy should
they try to organize a ground attack. Dodging shell fire, Jaquez ran
to the mortar pit and, yelling and screaming, physically dragged the
crewmen from their bunker. He had them start firing on that registration point—where, after the battle, an NVA flamethrower was found,
its operator killed before he could put the weapon to use.

The enemy shelling lasted twenty minutes. When it lifted, there was
a sudden eruption of muzzle flashes and green tracers as the NVA fired
their AK-47s for the first time. A 12.7mm machine gun, positioned to
the northeast, also opened up. The NVA foot soldiers started darting
forward. "The NVA were not reckless," said Lieutenant Hieb of Charlie
One, whose platoon manned the center of the line and was under the
most fire. "Those guys were good, and they were cunning, and they
stayed low. You had a very difficult time picking up their movement."
Hieb watched as an RPG scored a direct and disabling hit on the Marine
tank assigned to his sector. The tank had not had a chance to fire a
single round. Amid all the flashes and shadows, Hieb finally saw the
head and shoulder movements of an NVA lying prone while attempting to slide a bangalore torpedo under the perimeter wire. Hieb and
his RTO were in a small dugout behind the main line, and the enemy
soldier was directly to their front. Hieb did not have any positions in
front of him, so he opened up on the man with his CAR15. Others
blazed away at the sapper, and at some point in the confusion Hieb
realized that the NVA was lying quite still. He was dead. There were
plenty of others to go around, and Hieb's M60 team, positioned to his
left front, fired like madmen at the movements. "The barrel got so hot
that I could see it glowing red in the night," Hieb remembered. "Somebody
burned his hands pretty severely trying to get that barrel off and replace it with a new one. The volume of fire was very, very intense.
We just kept firing and firing and firing to keep them away from the
wire."

The bunkers at Force Tiger, most of which were large enough for
a fire team, were half-submerged and moundlike in appearance. Each
had a firing port to the front and an exit to the rear leading into the
slit trench that connected each position. Private Harp of Charlie One
was asleep in his team's bunker when the ground attack began. He

had not meant to go to sleep. Exhausted, he had simply leaned up against the back wall to rest, but had drifted off as soon as the weight was off his feet. Harp never heard the RPG that hit the top of his bunker explode; he simply found himself sprawled on the bunker floor with an egg-sized knot on the back of his head. The pain was throbbing. Dirt fell on his face from the broken sandbags of the overhead cover. No one else was in the bunker. "I could not get my eyes to focus. I was coughing up sand and trying to get sand out of my eyes. I thought we were being overrun." Totally disoriented, Harp climbed out into the slit trench and headed toward where he thought his squad leader, Burns, was firing from. "Shit was going off all around, ours and theirs." Harp had yet to reach Burns when he saw two NVA coming in fast. They were about fifty feet away. One was carrying a satchel charge, the other an AK-47. "I think I saw light reflecting off a bayonet at the end of it." It was too dark to aim through the peep sight, so Harp looked over the front sight the way one would with a shotgun. "I put the 16 on 'crowd'— automatic—and fired a magazine at them in six-round bursts. Caught the guy with the satchel charge in the chest. He fell back in a hole, and about three seconds later one hell of a firecracker went off. The other guy fell just in front of the crater. I think I got him, but I'm not sure. At any rate, he was not coming my way anymore."

Two Marine gunships arrived an hour into the attack and made strafing runs in front of Charlie One and Charlie Three, which was under fire on the right flank. At about the same time, the NVA launched a supporting attack on the left flank. Staff Sergeant Goad, the acting platoon leader in Charlie Two, juggled radios as he tried to shift their fires where needed when not personally handling an M79 grenade launcher. He also fired several LAWs, and mashed down the detonator hooked up to his claymore mines. Goad had prepared his defenses well. He had used an E-tool during the afternoon to dig the claymores into the forward slopes of the burial mounds, then arranged vegetation over the holes as camouflage. When he ran out of claymores, he scooped out additional holes the size of large coffee cans, placed C-4 explosive at the bottom of each with a blasting cap wired to a claymore detonator embedded in the plastique, and then packed the holes with captured enemy munitions and handfuls of metal links and casings from their own expended machine-gun ammunition.

Enemy soldiers were shredded by the explosions.

The NVA set up a recoilless rifle to blast Charlie Two, but the amount of fire it drew prevented its crew from punching off a single shell.

Private Fulcher, in position with two new men, fired his M16 through his bunker aperture—and saw an RPG screaming toward him trailing a rooster tail of sparks that made him think of a giant bottle rocket. Luckily, the RPG hit the sandbags just three inches below the aperture. Meanwhile, the Marine tank with Charlie Two rolled into a firing position that put its 90mm main gun directly over Fulcher's bunker. When the tank fired its first earsplitting, earthshaking round, Fulcher and the two replacements thought they'd been hit by enemy artillery.

They dropped to their guts so fast that their helmets bounced off. Shaking off the shock, Fulcher realized what had happened and stuck his head out of the dugout. "Back up," he screamed at the tank commander. "You're going to blow us up before you blow up the gooks!" Fulcher grabbed the detonator for his own half-dozen camouflaged mines. He had memorized which cord ran to which claymore, but when he squeezed the detonator he got no response. Furious that he had a dud, he plugged in the next wire and mashed down the detonator again. Nothing. Fulcher frantically tried every wire, but not a single claymore detonated. He couldn't figure out what was wrong. After the battle, he discovered that the tank's first shot, a canister round, had chewed up all his claymore wires.

On Charlie Three's side, where there were the fewest enemy, Sergeant Coulthard spotted an NVA about twenty meters away. The man just barely broke the natural outline of things, and he moved forward only when each flare died as it hit the ground. Lieutenant Musser couldn't see what Coulthard was pointing at, so Coulthard finally took aim in the flarelight with his M16, and started squeezing off shots at the man. Musser told him he was giving away their position, and to throw hand grenades instead. Coulthard, throwing frags, didn't know it yet, but he'd already killed the NVA with a round through the top of his collarbone. The body lay in the shadows, wearing an ammo vest, its grip loosened on its folding-stock AK-47.

Captain Leach had requested a backhoe with which to construct tank emplacements, but no engineer support had been made available. Without parapets, the tanks were sitting ducks. The tank parked beside Leach's CP had already been disabled by a rocket-propelled grenade. Leach was talking with his other tank commander, the one supporting Charlie Two, when the Marine suddenly exclaimed, "I'm starting to take fire—"

The tank was hit by an RPG at that instant.

The bruised and concussed crews of both knocked-out tanks popped their hatches and jumped down in the slit trench between the bunkers. Leach was certain that a lone NVA was going to sprint through their lines to reach the abandoned tank beside his CP, so while he kept busy with a radio in each hand he told his RTOs, "Some sonofabitch is going to climb up on that tank and start hosin' us down with the .50-cal. Don't you let anybody get up there!"

Captain Leach was also concerned about the fireworks to his rear where Alpha was dug in, but he could not raise Captain Osborn on the radio. "Not once did Osborn get on the radio, so I had no idea what was going on over there," recalled Leach. What was happening along Alpha's side of the perimeter was the same as on Charlie Tiger's, only with fewer NVA involved. One of the guys in Sergeant Stone's bunker fired his M16 on automatic at the bobbing figures before them, only to have an RPG explode nearby. Stone shouted at the rifleman, "Jesus, don't shoot on automatic—they think we're a machine-gun position!" Everyone had ducked down in anticipation of the next RPG, except for Pfc. Jesse Alston, who kept raising his head to look out the firing aperture. "Jesse, stay down, stay down!" Stone shouted. But the man put his head up again just as the next RPG exploded directly in front of the bunker. Alston cried out as he fell back. Stone hunted around in the darkened bunker for a battle dressing, and as he bandaged the wound on the side of Alston's head he realized that it was not too serious. It was bad enough, though, that the shook-up Alston volunteered to stay down and reload ammo magazines for the rest of the fight.

Surprisingly, the NVA continued pressing their attack even after the sun rose. At 0700, a Helix FAC came on station, followed in about twenty minutes by two A-4 Skyhawks from Marine Attack Squadron 121. Captain Leach told the FAC to bring in the air strikes immediately. When the FAC asked, "Well, how close do you want 'em?" Leach answered, "I want 'em about thirty meters from the perimeter. Do you see this tank here? I want you to use this tank as a reference point. . . ."

One of the Skyhawks executed a nonfiring pass over the target area and took AK-47 fire and one hit.

"That was perfect," Leach told the FAC.

The next low-level pass was to deliver the five-hundred-pound snake-eye bombs. "Get everyone down in their holes," Leach said when he got his platoon leaders on the horn. "Get under the overhead cover. Don't worry about what's on the goddamned perimeter—we got it comin' in!" Leach stunned his command group when he said with deadly seriousness, "Guys, I'm going to say a little prayer right now," and then dropped to his knees on the bunker floor. "It's time to ask for help from above."

The first Skyhawk, taking hits, pulled out of its pass in a skyward roar as the high-drag bombs seemed to float toward the NVA behind the burial mounds. The strike was bunker-shaking perfection. "They put 'em right on the bastards," Leach said. "It was beautiful. It was just death. The shit was flying right over us!" There was a definite lull in the NVA fire as the two Skyhawks continued to place their ordnance on target. Then, at 0740, some of the enemy began to pull back to the north. The medic in Leach's bunker suddenly shouted, "Jesus Christ, look at 'em run!" Private Harp was able to sight his M16 on three NVA who had their backs to where he stood in the slit trench. "The first one was running about a hundred meters from me. I fired once. He fell and never got up." The other two realized they'd been spotted and started zigzagging as they ran on. "I dropped the second one with two shots. I fired five times at the third guy. He fell, holding his arm, but got up again and threw or dropped his weapon as he got behind a grave. He got away."

Captain Leach was so excited that he put down his radio for the first time since the attack started and raised his captured AK-47. He got off only a few bursts before some shook-up troops, who thought at first that an NVA had gotten inside the lines, shouted at him to knock it off.

On Alpha's side, Sergeant Stone joined a grenadier who was lobbing shells at the retreating NVA from the slit trench. Stone opened up with his M16, but he was so tired that he kept nodding off between bursts. Meanwhile, Lieutenant Gibbs, the de facto company commander, instructed Specialist Hannan to bring his stranded LP in from the crater where they had been cut off during the battle. Hannan caught a bullet in the radio on his back while running in.

The LP from Charlie Tiger with which contact had been lost and that Leach feared had been overrun also made it back at about the same time. "I was awestruck," remembered Leach. "I don't know how those kids survived, but I was never so goddamned happy in my life as I was when I saw those three come marching back in." The LP leader still had a grip around the hand grenade he had intended to throw when he'd first heard the NVA coming eight hours before. He had pulled the pin at the sound of movement, but when he saw how many NVA were out there he'd realized it would be suicide to give away his position by lobbing the frag. Unfortunately, he had dropped the pin and could not find it. "He had to hold the spoon down on the frag all fucking night," one trooper explained. "That morning, when they finally came back in, his hand had locked around the frag so he could not let go. It took two men to pry his fingers loose and throw the damn thing."

Lieutenant Colonel Snyder considered the NVA attack to be "poorly planned," an appraisal confirmed at 0742 when, in the middle of the retreat from Nhi Ha, the NVA launched a two-platoon effort against Captain Corrigan's Bravo Company in Lam Xuan West. Barracuda destroyed the attack at a range of thirty meters with automatic rifles, machine guns, grenade launchers, rockets, claymores, a recoilless rifle, mortars, artillery, and a helicopter gunship. Attacking an entrenched and fully alerted position after sunrise was madness. Snyder believed that the NVA units had been committed behind schedule because of the delay in getting past Alpha 1. The enemy depended on well-rehearsed battle plans. Because they lacked a sophisticated communications system, Snyder said, "Once anything went wrong, there was no way they could control what was happening, other than shouting at one another. So people would come in and charge, and once you disrupted the attack they didn't know what to do. They would just lay there right around the perimeter and we'd flush them out in the morning."

The NVA completed their retreat under the cover of mortar fire. At 1055, the medevacs began landing for the Gimlets' one KIA and thirty WIA. Captain Leach saw a black grunt heading for the dust-off with a big bandage on the side of his face. Before Leach could give the man a few words of encouragement, the GI approached him and asked, "Are you okay, sir?" Leach, feeling humble and almost overwhelmed with emotion, grabbed the man's arm and said, "We're going to get you out of here right away."[1]

Amid shell fire, Captain Humphries and Delta Company humped into Force Tiger before noon, policing up two NVA from spiderholes along the way. Apparently relieved to be alive, the two enemy soldiers were laughing as they were led into the perimeter. Leach made sure that they were helicoptered out quickly because he knew there were troops who would have summarily executed them. That was the angry mood of the moment. Leach had ice water in his veins when it came to the bush-whacking guerrillas they chased down south, but he put his foot down when it came to mistreating NVA regulars who had fought the way these had. "These guys are soldiers, and they're going to be treated like soldiers," he told his men. "They're goddamn good soldiers."

While the perimeter sweep was being organized, Leach stormed over to Captain Osborn's command post. "I was taking Benzedrine," Leach remembered. "That shit works on you. I was a little crazy by then." Leach confronted Osborn in a low, angry whisper. "Why weren't you on the fuckin' radio?" Then he exploded in a booming rage. "What the fuck, you sonofabitch—you weren't on the radio all night! What the fuck's the matter with you?"

Osborn just gave Leach a blank stare.

The perimeter sweep commenced at 1300. Killing NVA stragglers along the way, the grunts had pushed out two hundred meters in two hours when the NVA rear guard opened fire from the tree lines to the northwest along Jones Creek. Air strikes were called in. Enemy shelling began at dusk, resulting in three injuries and the last medevacs of the day.

During the night, Lieutenant Stull, the Alpha Company FO, over-heard some angry conversations about the trooper killed the night before on LP. "That was the ball-buster," said Stull. "That was the one that made everybody crazy." The grunts could not fathom why the LP had not been immediately pulled back when it had NVA crawling all over

1. Captain Leach was awarded the Silver Star and his second Purple Heart for Nhi Ha. He also received two BSMv's and an AM during his two combat tours.

it. Stull, who enjoyed a pretty good rapport with the men, interrupted one group to ask, "What's the problem?" The answer: "Well, we got somebody that needs to be taken out."

"Whaddya mean 'taken out'?" Stull asked.

"Well, you know . . ."

Lieutenant Stull immediately approached Sergeant Dickerson of Alpha Two. "What the hell's going on? They're talking about fragging somebody! Is it me?"

"Nah, nah, nah, you're okay. You're cool," said Dickerson.

"Hell, if it's me, I'll start walking home right now. You guys don't have to frag my ass!"

Sergeant Dickerson repeated that Stull was not the target. It was Captain Osborn. Dickerson, a career man with seven years in uniform, was as angry and burned out as his grunts, and he told Stull that the company headquarters and each platoon were going to provide a GI armed with a grenade. One of the four grenades was going to be defused and the pile jumbled so that the men would not know which one was inactive when they picked the frags back up. All four were to roll their grenades into the company commander's bunker. If one of them had pangs of guilt afterward, he could rationalize that he had tossed the defused grenade.

"Hey, that's not where it's at," Stull protested. "Being stupid like the captain is one thing. Being vindictive is another. Maybe we should try to cool the guys down."

Sergeant Dickerson disagreed. "Well, how many motherfuckers is he going to kill before his number comes up?"

The idea of using a captured AK-47 on Captain Osborn was also discussed. Some of the grunts went directly to Lieutenant Gibbs, who was the most respected officer in the company. Gibbs, who had no doubt that they meant what they said, told them to cool it, that he would handle it. Gibbs called Lieutenant Colonel Snyder and reported that Osborn was "not going to live very long," and added that "if his men don't kill him, I think I will." Snyder cut him off. "Lieutenant, stop talking that way," he snapped.

The battle with the NVA was not over yet. Artillery had been fired all night long as enemy platoons, throwing grenades, had moved around the perimeter to recover casualties from the night before. On the morning of Sunday, 11 May 1968, the sweep around Force Tiger commenced again. Staff Sergeant Goad of Charlie Two bent over to pull an AK-47 from a hole in which he had found several apparently dead enemy soldiers. The weapon discharged when he pulled on it. Goad had been holding the barrel with his right hand. His arm jerked violently away as the shot tore through it, but he was still on his feet. Before he could think, he swung up the M79 in his left hand and unloaded a canister round into the hole. If one of the NVA was still alive, that finished him. It also destroyed the evidence of what had happened. Goad would never know if he had been shot by a diehard NVA at the other end of the AK-47 barrel he'd been tugging on, or by a dead man whose fingers were stiff around the trigger.

"It would be a hell of a deal," he said later, "to make it through all that bullshit—and then have a dead man shoot me."

Staff Sergeant Goad's arm hung uselessly. The bullet had entered his forearm and exited six inches farther up through the elbow, shattering it. He was in shock. When a medic tried to administer morphine, he declined, saying, "Hell, it ain't hurtin'." Captain Leach ran over to find Goad cradling his elbow with his good hand. Goad, stud that he was, was embarrassed. "Sir, I'm really sorry. I'm really sorry for screwing up."

The C&C Huey immediately medevacked Staff Sergeant Goad to the 18th Surgical Hospital in Quang Tri City. While he was sitting on a gurney in the triage area, the pain suddenly came down on him—as did the emotions of the moment. Colonel Gelling, the brigade commander, helicoptered up to see him as he was being prepared for surgery. Gelling later wrote that despite the pain, Goad's only concern was for "what was happening to the men in his squad. He was not overly emotional, but actually cried when talking about the men in his squad and wondering who was going to take care of them. He specifically asked me to carefully select a squad leader to replace him because the men in his squad were so outstanding that they deserved special consideration." Gelling added that Goad's action reflected "the deepest concern I've ever seen by one man for those who fought with him."[2]

The NVA rear guard was still in position. Several GIs were wounded by enemy fire from the northwest. Four air strikes later, the sweep began

2. Sergeant Goad received the Silver Star, BSMv, ARCOMv, and Purple Heart, but his wound canceled his plans for OCS and resulted in his involuntary separation from the service because of physical disability.

anew. The single Marine tank that had survived the night attack—it had been positioned with Alpha Company—fired its 90mm gun into likely enemy hiding places, as did the M79 grenadiers advancing across the parched brown lunarscape. Troops used their M16s liberally, and grenaded all the craters and spiderholes as they systematically progressed with the tank.

Sergeant See of Delta Company checked out a brush-camouflaged dugout that the tank had just blasted. The two NVA inside the dugout had been reduced to hamburger. One of the GIs picked up a pith helmet with a red star on it and discovered that it was full of brains. See spotted another NVA with ants crawling out of his mouth and maggots squirming in his eye sockets. When is it going to end? thought See, trying not to gag at the sight and the smell. Some troopers wrapped olive-drab sweat towels around their mouths and noses to filter out the stench. The bodies were everywhere, as were the big green flies and the human debris caused by heavy ordnance. "You'd see something weird-looking on the ground," remembered Sergeant Coulthard of Charlie Three, "and all of a sudden you'd realize, Jesus Christ, it was part of a hand or part of a head." Private Harp encountered a dead NVA who lay atop his AK-47 in a small gully. The man had been hit by napalm. "He looked like some kind of obscene burned rubber doll," said Harp. "He was kind of melted. He had no features at all, just the general outline of a man burned into black rubber. His uniform had been completely burned off. All that was left were his boots. They were completely intact. Strange shit, napalm."

There were so many dead NVA that the tank could not avoid running over bodies. Leaving broken weapons where they lay, the troops slung working AK-47s over their shoulders as the sweep progressed. They also checked the bodies for intel material. Private Harp removed the helmet, web gear, grenades, and an intact AK-47 from one NVA with a blown-open head. As he did so, the man's shredded body began to pull apart. The soldier's papers included a couple of hundred piasters, a military document, a letter written in Vietnamese, and a photograph of the dead man with a young woman and two children. "For a minute I thought I was going to cry for that guy," Harp recalled. "But then I remembered Yost and Morse and Sullivan, and all those guys from Alpha Company, and those guys from Second Platoon that we scraped into a poncho, and my attack of humanity passed as I went on to the next corpse to police up his gear. An awful lot of very brave people on both sides died extremely violent, miserable deaths at Nhi Ha. I'd had a bellyful."

The Gimlets' DMZ adventure, which was essentially over at that point, cost the 3-21st Infantry a total of 29 KIA, 1 MIA, and 130 WIA—71 of whom required medical evacuation. The battalion was credited with 358 NVA kills and 4 prisoners. An additional 91 kills were claimed by air, and 130 by artillery. The Gimlets' reward was to be included in the Navy Unit Commendation awarded to the 3d Marines. It was a proud moment for the battalion. "Even the Marines admit that we're really kicking ass," Specialist Hannan wrote home from the DMZ. Specialist Farrand of D Company commented that no one was scared anymore "because everyone was too into what they had to do. You didn't sense fear. You sensed fatigue, seriousness, anger at the enemy, and a lot of backslaps and forced levity. Everybody was a brother to everybody. The NVA were up against a force that wasn't going to move."

The exception was Alpha Annihilator. Captain Osborn was, in the words of his replacement, "a broken man who couldn't wait to get out of the bush" and the company was "listless and hurting."

Nine days after the battalion pulled off the DMZ, Alpha was attacked in its night defensive position in the Que Son Valley. In their haste and confusion, the GIs in Alpha Two's LP left behind their starlight scope when they pulled back to the perimeter. Captain Osborn ordered the three-man team to retrieve it. The NVA were waiting, however, and fired an RPG. Sergeant Patterson and Specialist McFaddin—the grenadier who had saved the day in the creek at Xom Phuong—were killed instantly. McFaddin's arm was torn from his body and sent flying. The third man, seriously wounded, was able to crawl back under covering fire from the perimeter. Snyder relieved Osborn the next morning.

In turn, demoralized Alpha Company went to 1st Lt. Hal Bell, who had recently taken over Alpha Two and was soon to be promoted to captain. Snyder commented that "within six or eight weeks, Bell had pretty much turned the company around. Bell turned them into a bunch of tigers." Commissioned from OCS after college, Bell, who had a winning personality and got along well with his men, also had the advantage of having attended the sixty-day British Jungle Warfare School in Malaya. He spent ten months commanding the American Division's Combat Tracker Platoon, which employed tracker dogs—specially trained black labrador retrievers—and helped units find the enemy when contact was lost. Bell, thinking of making a career in the Army, had extended his tour to get a rifle company. He would eventually quit, disgusted at the no-win policy of Vietnamization that got a lot of GIs killed even as it lost the war.

In the meantime, however, Bell brought enthusiasm, aggressiveness, intelligence, and experience to Alpha Annihilator. In addition to enforcing the basics, he emphasized squad-sized night operations as the best way to catch the VC and NVA in the Que Sons and the Hiep Duc Valley. Despite a lot of initial resistance from edgy, gun-shy troops, he remarked that "once you get used to it, your confidence level goes up." The patrols killed a lot of surprised enemy soldiers who were moving at night in small groups or bedding down in remote hootches. "Once those guys started to get some successes, it became their idea of fun," said Bell. "They would tell you the most ghoulish stories of what people were doing when they got 'em." Bell added that although the troops had demonstrated that "they would not put up with bullshit from incompetent leaders, the GIs' recuperative powers are absolutely marvelous. It just amazes me some of the things they did. And they were not Regular Army—they were just draftees, and the lieutenants were just college kids. But if you've got some captains, lieutenants, and sergeants that don't screw up too bad and keep track of the fundamentals of the foot soldier, then those soldiers do very, very well."

The Gimlets' last recorded casualty on the DMZ occurred on 12 May 1968 when a soldier was hit in the back by fragments from the intermittent shelling on Force Tiger. The Gimlets killed a few more NVA as the operation wound down. Small groups of NVA were spotted after dark on 11, 12, 13, and 14 May as they crawled through the grass around Force Tiger to harass the perimeter and listening posts with grenades. The closest NVA were engaged with M79s, and the ones farthest away, visible under the near constant illumination, became targets for the artillery.

On 15 May, the 3-21st Infantry was relieved in place by elements of BLT 2/4, which marched up from Mai Xa Chanh West. The Army grunts got down in their bunkers when the Marines started filing along the paths through their claymores, trip flares, and concertina, as they expected all the movement to draw enemy artillery fire. Alpha Company was scheduled to turn over its positions first. A Marine lieutenant walked up to Sergeant Stone of Alpha Three and said, "We're here to relieve your position. Have your men get out."

"We dug these goddamn holes—we ain't gettin' out till they give the order to move," Sergeant Stone answered. "They got this place zeroed with rockets. You know, your men are welcome to get in with us, but I'm not telling my men to get out of here."

Staying under cover until it was finally time to leave, Alpha Company formed up into platoon columns and started south. A trash fire was burning inside a crater just outside the bunker line. Enemy munitions had been piled nearby—they were to be destroyed in the crater—and, somehow, what was later thought to be a satchel charge ended up in the blaze. The explosion set off the rest of the NVA ammunition in a huge fireball, which tipped over the Marine Otter parked nearby and sent the GIs standing on it flying. The explosion shook everyone up. They thought at first that the NVA were shelling them. Sergeant Stone, heading back across the paddy in his file, noted that he "turned around and looked back, and here's all this smoke and stuff going up. That was my last look at Nhi Ha. We kept right on going."

Charlie and Delta Companies pulled out of Force Tiger by 1500 on 15 May, and all four of the 3-21st Infantry's rifle companies spent the night dug in near the battalion CP with a flareship overhead. One NVA was spotted as he reconnoitered their perimeter. At 0700 on the sixteenth, USMC Sea Knights and Sea Stallions began lifting the battalion from the vicinity of Mai Xa Chanh East to the airfield at Quang Tri City. The move took eleven hours and forty lifts.

From Quang Tri, C-123s airlifted the Gimlets to FSB Baldy. Chinooks then moved the platoons from Baldy to FSB Colt, and on the morning of 17 May 1968 the Gimlets were back in the bush under 196th LIB control.

"What struck me the strongest was going back out in the Que Son Valley and starting to hump all over again," said Sergeant Coulthard. "I think that's when my discouragement with the war began. Not that I turned against the war, but I thought, My God, we're going to have to do this for a long, long time. It's when I really realized the magnitude of what the hell we were trying to do—and the enemy's willingness to pay the price."

EPILOGUE

Officially, the Battle of Dong Ha, as the 3d Marine Division labeled the series of actions above the Bo Dieu and Cua Viet rivers, lasted from 29 April until 15 May 1968. The brunt of the NVA offensive was borne by BLT 2/4 and the 3-21st Infantry in the Operation Napoleon/ Saline TAOR, under the opcon of the 3d Marines. Considerable combat was also experienced by 1/3 in this sector, and by 3/3, 1/9, 3/9, and 1/26 near Cam Lo and Thon Cam Vu in the Operation Kentucky TAOR, as well as by the 1st ARVN Division above Dong Ha. Another highlight was the deployment of the 1st and 2d Battalions, 5th Cavalry, 1st Cavalry Division (Airmobile), which operated under the 3d Marines from 6 to 17 May. The Cav called its participation Operation Concordia Square, and its units ranged from northeast of Nhi Ha to north of Dong Ha.

The campaign was marked by heavy shellings of allied positions. More than a hundred tons of ammunition in the supply depot at the DHCB was blown up on 14 May. Total casualties in units under the operational control of the 3d Marine Division during this period were 233 killed, 821 wounded, and 1 missing in action. The Navy's TF Clearwater lost 15 killed and 22 wounded. ARVN casualties, haphazardly reported, were 42 killed and 124 wounded. The NVA reportedly lost 2,366 dead and 43 prisoners.

The carnage bought only a week of relative peace for 3d Marine Division units along the DMZ before the next NVA offensive began.

HEADQUARTERS, BLT 2/4

Lieutenant Colonel Weise retired as a brigadier general, and is a self-employed consultant. He is the father of three, the grandfather of eight, and lives with his wife in Alexandria, Virginia. Major Knapp retired as a colonel to Fallbrook, California. Major Warren retired as a lieutenant colonel and is now in the advertising/marketing department of a color printing company. The father of four, he lives with his wife in Springfield, Virginia. Captain Forehand is now in the import/export business, and lives with his second wife in Escondido, California. Lieutenant Hilton retired as a lieutenant colonel and is a pilot with Continental Airlines. Married and the father of two, he lives in Jupiter, Florida. Lieutenant Muter is an insurance agent. Married with five children, he lives in Portland, Oregon, and San Diego, California. Lieutenant Dawson retired as a captain and is now retired from a post-military career in mechanical engineering. He is the father of six, a grandfather fourteen times over, and lives with his wife in Yucca Valley, California. Lieutenant Lillis lives with his wife and three children, and is a general practitioner in Leesburg, Virginia. Sergeant Bollinger was medically discharged with a 100 percent disability. A bartender, he lives with his second wife and their daughter in Marmara, New Jersey. Sergeant Pace retired as a gunnery sergeant. The divorced father of two sons lives in Lookout Mountain, Georgia.

E BLT 2/4

Captain Livingston is married and the father of two daughters. He is presently a major general on active duty. Lieutenant Jones is assistant superintendent for the Caroline County (Maryland) Public Schools, and lives with his wife and two daughters in Denton, Maryland. Gunnery Sergeant Eggleston has been a postal employee since his retirement. He lives in Los Angeles. Sergeant Rogers retired as a master gunnery sergeant. Married and divorced after the war (he has one son), he is now a logistics manager with an international security company and lives in Alexandria, Virginia. Corporal Cardona was discharged as a sergeant. The married father of two is an elementary schoolteacher in Carrizo Springs, Texas. Lance Corporal Cornwell went through a whirlwind marriage and divorce after the war (he has one child), then hit the road for three years on a Harley-Davidson chopper during which time he sold guns and drugs and never went anywhere without a sawed-off shotgun. He was suffering from what was later termed posttraumatic stress disorder (PTSD). He finally settled down in another marriage (which lasted eight years), and is presently a police detective in Bridgeton, New Jersey. Lance Corporal Hahner was discharged as a sergeant. He got a vocational degree in welding and now works in a sawmill. Married with three children, he lives in Rio Dell, California. Private First Class Serna was court-martialed twice on Okinawa for fighting, disobedience, and sleeping on guard, and left the service a slick-sleeve private. He was eventually awarded a 20 percent disability for wounds and 80 percent for PTSD. He has never since held down a steady job, and has been in and out of jail on drug-related charges. He has two daughters from his first marriage and three stepchildren from his second. He is presently in recovery and lives with his wife in Sacramento, California.

F BLT 2/4

Captain Butler is a regional parts and service manager for Isuzu. He lives with his wife and three children in Grapevine, Texas. Lieutenant McAdams is a tax lawyer in Portland, Oregon. He married and has two children. Staff Sergeant Balignasay retired as a gunnery sergeant. The father of eight and grandfather of six, he lives with his wife in Oceanside, California. Corporal Tyrell spent eleven years in the service and was discharged as a staff sergeant. Following counseling for PTSD, he now works for the postal service and lives with his wife and stepdaughter in Springfield, Massachusetts. Lance Corporal Dean is the supervisor for a building grounds and maintenance crew. He is married with one son, and lives in Quinton, Virginia. Lance Corporal Gregg is a chief warrant officer in the USMCR, and he and his brothers are partners in a trucking business. The father of two, he lives with his wife in Cresson, Pennsylvania. Private First Class Kachmar is a sergeant in the Army National Guard. The divorced father of two is a county administrator in Allentown, Pennsylvania. Private First Class Light was discharged as a sergeant. He now manages an engineering business. He has two children and one grandchild and lives with his wife in Pounding Mill, Virginia. Hospital Corpsman Pittman is a physician's assistant, a senior partner in a group practice, and lives with his second wife (he has two children by his first) in Denver, Colorado.

G BLT 2/4

Captain Mastrion is a colonel planning to retire with his wife to Fredericksburg, West Virginia. Captain Vargas is a colonel with a wife and three daughters. He plans to retire to San Diego. Lieutenant Acly left the service as a captain and now owns a public relations consulting business. He lives with his second wife in Milwaukee, Wisconsin. Lieutenant Ferland was married before the war and divorced eleven years and three children after his return. Presently a colonel in the USMCR and a quality assurance supervisor with the missile systems section of Raytheon, he lives in North Hampton, New Hampshire. Lieutenant Morgan is still a water- and snow skier and he races his sailboat despite his missing leg and hand. Divorced after having two daughters, he is a stockbroker in Charleston, West Virginia. Staff Sergeant Del Rio retired as a first sergeant and now works for the water department in El Toro, California. He and his wife have four children. Corporal Schlesiona was discharged as a sergeant and is a manager with IBM Corporation. He has three children from his first marriage, and now lives with his second wife in Oxford, Connecticut. Lance Corporal Lashley left the service as a corporal and subsequently joined the Vietnam Veterans Against the War. Now a psychiatric social worker, he lives with his wife and two daughters in Salinas, California. Lance Corporal Parkins is in his third marriage and is the father of four. He is employed by the state psychiatric hospital and is studying to be a registered nurse in Oxford, North Carolina.

H BLT 2/4

Captain Williams retired as a colonel. A businessman, he lives with his wife and four children in Oceanside, California. Lieutenant Prescott is an executive in a packaging supply company. He has two children from his first marriage, and now lives with his second wife in Winston-Salem, North Carolina. Lieutenant Taylor retired as a lieutenant colonel. Twice married, he has a son and owns a ranch and a business as an outfitter of big-game hunts and wilderness pack trips near Steamboat Springs, Colorado. Staff Sergeant Taylor retired as a first sergeant and is now a golf course superintendent. The father of two lives with his wife in Holly Ridge, North Carolina. Staff Sergeant Ward retired to go into business with his wife as an independent insurance agent. Now a widower and disabled from an auto accident, he lives in Homestead, Florida. Lance Corporal Barnes was medically retired on a 100 percent disability as a corporal due to combat wounds. Now married and the father of two, he is a graduate of college and theological seminary and is a minister with the Community Church in Gloucester, Massachusetts. Lance Corporal Donaghy was discharged as a sergeant. A phone company technician, he lives in White Plains, New York. Lance Corporal O'Neill was commissioned after college and went on to retire as a major. Married with three children, he is a construction inspector with the state transportation department and lives in Oceanside, California.

B/1/3

Gunnery Sergeant Doucette was divorced after eighteen years of marriage and two children, then married and divorced four more times. He now lives with his girlfriend and works for the city park district in Bangor, Maine. Staff Sergeant Robinson retired as a master sergeant. The married father of two lives in Newburn, North Carolina. Private First Class Roughan has been afflicted with PTSD since the war. Now married, with four children and two stepchildren, he manages a self-storage company and lives in Shrewsbury, Massachusetts.

HEADQUARTERS, 3/21ST INFANTRY

Lieutenant Colonel Snyder retired as a colonel and is now an instructor at the Air War College. He and his wife live in Montgomery, Alabama. Major Yurchak retired as a lieutenant colonel and changed his name to York. He is a resource manager with the Department of the Army and lives with his wife in Gettysburg, Pennsylvania. Captain Hildebrand is a general surgeon living with his wife in Canon City, Colorado. Captain Householder left the service as a major. The father of three and a grandfather twice, he is an insurance executive living with his wife in Waco, Texas.

A/3-21

Captain Bell is married and the father of two. He is a commercial real estate broker in Oakland, California. Lieutenant Gibbs owns a company in the merchant banking business. He lives with his wife and son in Rumson, New Jersey. Lieutenant Smith was divorced after the war (he has two children), and now is a partner in an accounting firm in Charlotte, North Carolina. Lieutenant Stull is a major in the National Guard and an ROTC instructor. Married and divorced after the war (he has two sons), he lives with his second wife in Lexington, Kentucky. Sergeant Bulte was discharged as a staff sergeant. Married and divorced twice after the war (he has a daughter), he is a route salesman for Eagle Snacks and lives in Manchester, Missouri. Sergeant Haddock was divorced shortly after the war. Now remarried and the father of three, he is a master scheduling specialist for an oil-pump equipment manufacturer in Claremore, Oklahoma. Sergeant Stone was discharged as a staff sergeant. He runs a Phillips 66 gas station with his brother, and lives with his wife and three daughters in Lexington, Nebraska. Specialist Karp is a salesman living with his wife and three children in Houston, Texas. Specialist Baird was left in a wheelchair by his injuries (he was medically discharged as a staff sergeant), but he faced his five years in NVA prison camps well and is relatively well adjusted after the ordeal. He has a 100 percent disability rating, and lives with his wife and two sons in Fredericksburg, Ohio. Specialist Hannan is the director of purchasing and traffic for a paper mill. He lives with his second wife (he has two children) in a two-hundred-year-old log cabin that he rebuilt in the deep woods near Bangor, Michigan. Specialist Hemphill was discharged as a sergeant. A machine operator, he is the father of one girl and grandfather of two boys. He lives with his wife in Austell, Georgia.

B/3-21

Captain Corrigan retired as a colonel, and lives with his wife and two children in Pope Valley, California. Staff Sergeant Ochs left the service after thirteen years at the urging of his first wife. The father of three, he now lives with his second wife in Monson, Massachusetts.

C/3-21

Captain Leach married after the war and both of his sons joined the Army Airborne as enlisted men. He retired as a brigadier general, and is now living with his wife in Brainerd, Minnesota. Lieutenant Hieb was divorced after the war (he has three children from that marriage). Now remarried, he retired as a lieutenant colonel to Tacoma, Washington. Lieutenant Jaquez married after the war (he has two children) and worked as an information systems supervisor with the University of Southern California. Forced to retire because of a liver disease, he now lives in Long Beach, California. Staff Sergeant Goad went through severe PTSD after the war. He lives with his wife in Las Vegas, Nevada. Sergeant Coulthard went through a lot of alcohol and three marriages (he is the father of four) after the war while working as a deckhand and then a riverboat pilot on the Ohio and Mississippi rivers. He has since worked through his PTSD problems and is an alcoholism counselor in River Falls, Wisconsin. Sergeant Starr is a bank senior vice president, and lives with his wife in Louisville, Kentucky. Specialist McDonald is presently a supervisor with an insurance company, and lives in Jackson Heights, New York. Private Fulcher is the father of four, the owner of a Mexican restaurant, and lives with his family in Geneseo, Illinois. Private Harp was discharged as a sergeant after a second combat tour, and stumbled through bouts with PTSD, relying on alcohol, marijuana, and acid. Clean and sober for more than twenty years, he is an electronics technician living with his widowed mother and his sister in Oldsmar, Florida.

D/3-21

Captain Humphries retired as a colonel. Now employed by the Department of the Army, he lives with his wife in Bad Tolz, Germany. Lieutenant Skrzysowski left the Army as a captain, and retired from the Reserves as a lieutenant colonel. He now works for the Department of Defense and lives with his wife and two children in Bowie, Maryland. Sergeant See is semiretired and lives with his second wife (he has two children) in Malibu, California. Specialist Farrand was discharged as a sergeant. A gunsmith, he lives with his wife and six sons in LeClaire, Iowa. Private Cox was married and divorced after the war. Now an outside plant technician for Ohio Bell, he lives in Salineville, Ohio.

OTHER UNITS

Lieutenant Kirkland (1st ARVN Inf. Div.) retired as a lieutenant colonel. He went on to earn a doctorate and is now a professor at Northwest Iowa Community College. He lives with his wife and daughter in West Union, Iowa. Warrant Officer Johnson (174th AHC) retired as a major. Today, after two marriages, five children, and six grandchildren, he is a marketing vice president with DynCorps Aerospace Operations in Fort Worth, Texas. Specialist Nunn is a managing director with the Smith Barney investment firm and lives with his wife and daughter in Drexel Hill, Pennsylvania.

APPENDIX A

Key Personnel of BLT 2/4, 9th MAB (opcon to the 3d Marines, 3d Marine Division), during Operation Night Owl and the Battle of Dai Do (27 April–3 May 1968):

CO: Lt. Col. William Weise (until WIA on 2 May); then Maj. Charles W. Knapp (acting until relieved by Lt. Col. Louis A. Rann on 6 May)
XO: Maj. Charles W. Knapp
Sgt. Maj.: Sgt. Maj. John M. Malnar (until KIA on 2 May)
S1 (Personnel): 1st Lt. R. L. Jones
S2 (Intelligence): Capt. Richard J. Murphy
S3 (Operations): Maj. George F. Warren
S4 (Logistics): Capt. L. L. Forehand
Medical Officer: Lt. Frederick P. Lillis, USN; with Lt. Runas Powers, USN, and HM1 Walter R. Gorsage, USN
CO, H&S Company: 1st Lt. Edward S. Dawson

ECHO COMPANY

CO: Capt. James E. Livingston (until WIA on 2 May); then 2d Lt. Michael L. Cecil (acting)
XO: 1st Lt. David R. Jones (until WIA on 2 May)
FO: GySgt. James Eggleston (WIA on 2 May)
1st Sgt.: not available
GySgt.: GySgt. Roscoe Chandler
1st Plt. Comdr.: 2d Lt. Michael L. Cecil
1st Plt. Sgt.: not available
2d Plt. Comdr.: 1st Lt. James Sims (until WIA on 2 May)
2d Plt. Sgt.: not available

3d Plt. Comdr.: 1st Lt. David R. Jones (acting until WIA on 2 May); then Sgt. James W. Rogers (acting)

3d Plt. Sgt.: not available

FOXTROT COMPANY

CO: Capt. James H. Butler

XO: 1st Lt. James Wainwright

FO: 2d Lt. J. M. Basel (WIA on 30 April)

1st Sgt.: 1st Sgt. Theodore D. Duchateau

GySgt.: SSgt. Pedro P. Balignasay (acting until WIA on 1 May); then the assigned company gunnery sergeant, GySgt. P. E. Brandon, who had been in the battalion rear on an administrative run when the battle began

1st Plt. Comdr.: 2d Lt. David K. McAdams (until WIA on 2 May)

1st Plt. Sgt.: LCpl. Ronald J. Dean (acting until WIA on 2 May)

2d Plt. Comdr.: SSgt. Richard L. Bartlow (until KIA on 2 May)

2d Plt. Sgt.: Sgt. Albert Archaleta (until WIA on 2 May)

3d Plt. Comdr.: 2d Lt. Robert Lanham (until WIA on 1 May)

3d Plt. Sgt.: SSgt. Chateau

GOLF COMPANY

CO: Capt. Robert J. Mastrion (until medevacked on 28 April); then Capt. "J. R." Vargas (acting until medevacked on 3 May)

XO: 1st Lt. Jack E. Deichman (WIA on 2 May)

FO: 2d Lt. Peter A. Acly (WIA on 2 May)

1st Sgt.: not available

GySgt.: GySgt. Billy R. Armer (until WIA on 27 and 28 April); then SSgt. Reymundo Del Rio (until medevacked on 2 May)

1st Plt. Comdr.: SSgt. Reymundo Del Rio (until he became company gunnery sergeant on 28 April); then SSgt. Wade (acting)

1st Plt. Sgt.: SSgt. Wade

2d Plt. Comdr.: 2d Lt. Frederick H. Morgan

2d Plt. Sgt.: Sgt. Richard F. Abshire (until KIA on 2 May); then Cpl. Pless (acting)

3d Plt. Comdr.: 1st Lt. James T. Ferland (until WIA on 2 May); then 1st Lt. Jack E. Deichman (acting)

3d Plt. Sgt.: Sgt. Robert J. Colasanti (WIA on 30 April and 1 May)

HOTEL COMPANY

CO: Capt. James L. Williams (until WIA on 30 April); then 1st Lt. Alexander F. Prescott IV (acting until WIA on 2 May); then 2d Lt. Bayard V. Taylor (acting until WIA on 2 May); then 1st Lt. Alexander F. Prescott IV (acting after returning to duty on 3 May)

XO: 1st Lt. Alexander F. Prescott IV (in field), and 2d Lt. Bayard V. Taylor (in battalion rear until battle began)

FO: 2d Lt. Carl R. Gibson (until KIA on 30 April); then the FO team radioman, LCpl. Carl M. Spaethe (acting)

1st Sgt.: 1st Sgt. Clifford Martin

GySgt.: GySgt. Bobby B. Wagner

1st Plt. Comdr.: 2d Lt. Boyle (WIA on 30 April)

1st Plt. Sgt.: SSgt. Richard A. Kelleher (until WIA on 30 April)

2d Plt. Comdr.: SSgt. Robert J. Ward (until medevacked on 1 May); then Sgt. Bruce Woodruff (acting)

2d Plt. Sgt.: not available

3d Plt. Comdr.: SSgt. Ronald W. Taylor (until WIA on 30 April); then Sgt. Joe N. Jones (acting); then 1st Lt. William B. Zimmerman (acting until returned to the battalion headquarters on 1 May); then 2d Lt. Bayard V. Taylor (acting until he assumed command of the company on 2 May); then Sgt. Joe N. Jones (acting)

3d Plt. Sgt.: Sgt. Joe N. Jones

APPENDIX B

Key Personnel of the 3-21st Infantry, 196th Light Infantry Brigade, Americal Division (opcon to the 3d Marines, 3d Marine Division), during the Battle of Nhi Ha (1–15 May 1968):

CO: Lt. Col. William P. Snyder
XO: Maj. Walter D. Burchfield
Sgt. Maj.: 1st Sgt. George M. Titko (acting)
S1 (Personnel): not available
S2 (Intelligence): Capt. John M. Householder
S3 (Operations): Maj. Paul N. Yurchak
S4 (Logistics): not available
Medical Officer: Capt. Jan S. Hildebrand
CO, HHC: Capt. Stephen F. Russell
CO, E Company: 1st Lt. Jerry D. Perkins

ALPHA COMPANY (ALPHA ANNIHILATOR)

CO: Capt. Cecil H. Osborn (pseudonym)
XO: 1st Lt. Robert V. Gibbs
FO: 2d Lt. William A. Stull (WIA on 6 May)
1st Sgt.: not available
1st Plt. Ldr.: 2d Lt. James Simpson
1st Plt. Sgt.: not available
2d Plt. Ldr.: 2d Lt. Terry D. Smith (until WIA on 6 May); then 1st Lt. Robert V. Gibbs (acting)
2d Plt. Sgt.: Sfc. Alan Dickerson
3d Plt. Ldr.: 2d Lt. William B. Kimball (until KIA on 6 May)
3d Plt. Sgt.: SSgt. George L. Dale (until KIA on 6 May)

BRAVO COMPANY (BARRACUDA)

CO: Capt. Robert E. Corrigan
XO: not available
FO: Pfc. Rod Bublitz (until WIA on 3 May)
1st Sgt.: Sfc. Charles A. Cunningham
1st Plt. Ldr.: not available
1st Plt. Sgt.: not available
2d Plt. Ldr.: not available
2d Plt. Sgt.: not available
3d Plt. Ldr.: not available
3d Plt. Sgt.: SSgt. William F. Ochs (until WIA on 2 May)

CHARLIE COMPANY (CHARLIE TIGER)

CO: 1st Lt. Gerald R. Kohl (acting) until relieved on 3 May by the assigned company commander, Capt. Dennis A. Leach, who had been in the battalion rear preparing for an R and R that was canceled by the battle
XO: 1st Lt. Gerald R. Kohl (until relieved on 3 May)
FO: 2d Lt. John R. Jaquez
1st Sgt.: Sfc. William R. Brooks (until KIA on 4 May)
1st Plt. Ldr.: 1st Lt. Roger D. Hieb
1st Plt. Sgt.: SSgt. Isadore Davis
2d Plt. Ldr.: 1st Lt. Edward F. Guthrie (until KIA on 2 May); then Sgt. Donald G. Pozil (acting); then SSgt. James M. Goad (acting until WIA on 10 May); then Sgt. Donald G. Pozil (acting)
2d Plt. Sgt.: Sfc. Eugene Franklin (until KIA on 2 May); then Sgt. Donald G. Pozil (acting)
3d Plt. Ldr.: Sfc. Henry A. Lane (acting) until relieved on 3 May by the assigned platoon leader, 1st Lt. Dale W. Musser, who had been in the battalion rear on an administrative run when the battle began
3d Plt. Sgt.: SSgt. James M. Goad (acting) until relieved by the assigned platoon sergeant, Sfc. Henry A. Lane, who had been the acting platoon leader when the battle began

DELTA COMPANY (BLACK DEATH)

CO: Capt. James F. Humphries
XO: not available
FO: 2d Lt. Robert Bybee
1st Sgt.: not available
1st Plt. Ldr.: 2d Lt. Richard J. Skrzysowski (until WIA on 4 May); then Sfc. Buford Mathis (acting)
1st Plt. Sgt.: Sfc. Buford Mathis
2d Plt. Ldr.: 2d Lt. Erich J. Weidner
2d Plt. Sgt.: Sfc. Floyd W. Buell
3d Plt. Ldr.: SSgt. Robert E. Gruber (acting); then 2d Lt. Richard A. Holt
3d Plt. Sgt.: SSgt. Robert E. Gruber

GLOSSARY

AIT Advanced Individual Training
AK-47 standard Communist 7.62mm automatic rifle
Amtrac LVTP5 amphibious tractor
AO Area of Operations
Arty artillery
ARVN Army of the Republic of Vietnam
Birddog O-1E observation plane
BLT Battalion Landing Team
Blueline a stream or river
C&C Command-and-control helicopter used by commanders to supervise field activities
CAR15 shortened, all-metal version of the M16 5.56mm automatic rifle
CAS Close Air Support
C-4 plastic explosive
Chicom Chinese Communist (usually refers to enemy hand grenade)
Chinook CH-47 transport helicopter
Claymore aboveground antipersonnel mine
CO Commanding Officer
CP Command Post
Crusader Navy A-7 jet fighter-bomber
DHCB Dong Ha Combat Base
DMZ Demilitarized Zone, dividing line between North and South Vietnam on the 17th parallel
E-tool Entrenching tool, military term for a collapsible shovel
FAC Forward Air Controller
FO Forward Observer
FSB Fire Support Base
H&S Headquarters & Service Company
HE High Explosive
HHC Headquarters and Headquarters Company
HST Helicopter Support Team

Huey   nickname for the UH-1 series of helicopter
Illum   illumination round or rounds
KIA   Killed In Action
Kit Carson scout   Communist soldier who defected to the allies and
   volunteered to serve with U.S. units as a scout/interpreter
Laager   nickname for a unit's night defensive position
LAW   66mm Light Antitank Weapon
LCU   Landing Craft, Utility
LD   Line of Departure
LIB   Light Infantry Brigade
LP   Listening Post
LZ   Landing Zone
M14   nonstandard U.S. 7.62mm automatic rifle
M16   standard U.S. 5.56mm automatic rifle
M60   standard U.S. 7.62mm machine gun
M79   standard U.S. 40mm grenade launcher
MAB   Marine Amphibious Brigade
MAF   Marine Amphibious Force
MAW   Marine Aircraft Wing
MIA   Missing In Action
Monitor   LCM-6 gunboat with revolving turret
NCO   Noncommissioned Officer
NVA   North Vietnamese Army
OCS   Officer Candidate School
OP   Observation Post
Opcon   Operational Control
Otter   M76 amphibious tracked vehicle
Phantom   F-4 jet fighter-bomber
RPD   standard Communist 7.62mm light machine gun
RPG   Rocket-Propelled Grenade
RTO   Radiotelephone Operator
S1   personnel officer
S2   intelligence officer
S3   operations officer
S4   logistics officer
Sea Horse   CH-34 helicopter (Korean War vintage)
Sea Knight   CH-46 transport helicopter
Sea Stallion   CH-53 transport helicopter

Sitrep   Situation report

Skimmer   nickname for the fourteen-foot assault boats used by the Marines (they were made of fiberglass and had 35-horsepower Mercury outboard motors)

SKS   Communist rifle

Skyhawk   A-4 jet attack bomber

SLF   Special Landing Force

Spooky   AC-47 gunship

TacAir   Tactical Air Support

TAOR   Tactical Area of Responsibility

TF   Task Force

TOT   Time On Target (method of artillery fire involving several batteries firing on the same target at the same time)

VC   Viet Cong

Ville   village

WIA   Wounded In Action

WP   White Phosphorus ("Willie Pete")

XO   executive officer

SELECTED BIBLIOGRAPHY

BOOKS

Berry, Lt. Col. F. Clifton. *Chargers*. New York: Bantam, 1988.

Crum, James E. *Pigman, Vietnam 1968–69*. Canal Fulton, Ohio: J. E. Crum, 1988.

Cutler, Lt. Comdr. Thomas J. *Brown Water, Black Berets: Coastal and Riverine Warfare in Vietnam*. Annapolis, Md.: Naval Institute, 1988.

Grant, Zalin B. *Survivors*. New York: Norton, 1975.

Helms, E. Michael. *The Proud Bastards*. New York: Zebra, 1990.

Krulak, Lt. Gen. Victor H. *First to Fight: An Inside View of the U.S. Marine Corps*. Annapolis, Md.: Naval Institute, 1984.

Lowry, Timothy S. *Valor*. New York: Berkley, 1988.

Telfer, Maj. Gary; Lt. Col. Lane Rogers; and Keith Fleming. *U.S. Marines in Vietnam: Fighting the North Vietnamese, 1967*. Washington, D.C.: History and Museums Division, Headquarters, U.S. Marine Corps, 1984.

PERIODICALS

Braestrup, Peter. "'Magnificent' Is the Word for Marine Fighters." *Pacific Stars & Stripes*, 29 May 1968, 11.

Hammond, Lt. Col. J. W. "Combat Journal, Part I." *Marine Corps Gazette*, July 1968, 20–29.

———. "Combat Journal, Conclusion." *Marine Corps Gazette*, August 1968, 46–51.

May, Tony. "With the 196th Light Infantry Brigade: Letters from the DMZ." *Vietnam Combat*, 1989, 46–57.

"Soldier Slips Past Enemy Night Perimeter." *Southern Cross* (Newspaper of the Americal Division), June 1968, 8.

Weise, Brig. Gen. William. "Memories of Dai Do." *Marine Corps Gazette*, September 1987, 42–55.

———. "They Called Him Big John Malnar." *Leatherneck*, July 1991, 47–49.

DOCUMENTS

All USMC documents cited are in the USMC Historical Center at the Washington Navy Yard; all U.S. Army documents cited can be found in the National Archives's Suitland, Md., branch.

"The Battle of Dong Ha" (Capt. W. H. Dabney, G3A, 3d Marine Division).

"Combat After Action Report (Operation NAPOLEON-SALINE), Headquarters, 3d Battalion, 21st Infantry, 196th Infantry Brigade, Americal Division."

"Command Chronology, 3d Marines, April 1968."

"———, May 1968."

"Command Chronology, 1st Battalion, 3d Marines, May 1968."

"Command Chronology, 2d Battalion, 4th Marines, October 1967."

"———, November 1967."

"Command Chronology, Battalion Landing Team 2/4, December 1967."

"———, January 1968."

"———, February 1968."

"———, March 1968."

"———, April 1968."

"———, May 1968."

"———, June 1968."

"Duty Officer's Log, S2/S3 Section, 3d Battalion, 21st Infantry, 196th Infantry Brigade, Americal Division, 19 April–17 May 1968."

"Operations of U.S. Marine Forces, Vietnam, May 1968."

3d Marine Division Historical Section The tape-recorded interviews conducted at the BLT 2/4 CP at Mai Xa Chanh West on 21 and 22 May 1968. The reel-to-reel tapes are stored at the National Archives in Suitland, Md.

Acly, 2d Lt. Peter A. (G BLT 2/4)

Allen, Cpl. Terry L. (H BLT 2/4)

Barela, LCpl. James L. (H BLT 2/4)
Bennett, Pfc. Thomas J. (H BLT 2/4)
Burgos, LCpl. Joel S. (H BLT 2/4)
Devoe, Sgt. Donald F. (H BLT 2/4)
Emery, Cpl. Kenneth L. (G BLT 2/4)
Ferland, 1st Lt. James T. (G BLT 2/4)
Jones, Sgt. Joe N. (H BLT 2/4)
Knapp, Maj. Charles W. (XO, BLT 2/4)
Kraus, LCpl. Greg R. (CP, BLT 2/4)
Lawson, 1st Lt. Luther L. (CP, BLT 2/4)
Lawyer, Pfc. Gary W. (H BLT 2/4)
Martin, HM3 Larry G. (G BLT 2/4)
McCarter, HM2 Terrell E. (G BLT 2/4)
Morgan, 2d Lt. Frederick H. (G BLT 2/4)
Murphy, Capt. Richard J. (S2, BLT 2/4)
Osborn, LCpl. (H BLT 2/4)
Patton, Cpl. William A. (H BLT 2/4)
Pierce, Cpl. Wendell M. (H BLT 2/4)
Richardson, Pfc. Gary R. (H BLT 2/4)
Stallworth, Pfc. Sylvester (H BLT 2/4)
Summey, Cpl. James A. (H BLT 2/4)
Ward, SSgt. Robert J. (H BLT 2/4)
Warren, Maj. George F. (S3, BLT 2/4)
Whitefield, Pfc. (H BLT 2/4)
Woodruff, Sgt. Bruce (H BLT 2/4)
Zayemopoulas, Cpl. Evangelos E. (H BLT 2/4)
Zimmerman, 1st Lt. William B. (CP, BLT 2/4)

INDEX